THE CRISIS OF CONNECTION

D1599342

The Crisis of Connection

Roots, Consequences, and Solutions

Edited by
Niobe Way, Alisha Ali,
Carol Gilligan, *and*
Pedro Noguera

NEW YORK UNIVERSITY PRESS
New York

BRESCIA UNIVERSITY
COLLEGE LIBRARY

NEW YORK UNIVERSITY PRESS
New York
www.nyupress.org

© 2018 by New York University
All rights reserved

References to Internet websites (URLs) were accurate at the time of writing. Neither the author nor New York University Press is responsible for URLs that may have expired or changed since the manuscript was prepared.

Library of Congress Cataloging-in-Publication Data
Names: Way, Niobe, 1963– editor. | Ali, Alisha, 1970– editor. | Gilligan, Carol, 1936– editor. | Noguera, Pedro, editor. | Kirkland, David E., author of afterword.
Title: The crisis of connection : roots, consequences, and solutions / edited by Niobe Way, Alisha Ali, Carol Gilligan, and Pedro Noguera.
Description: New York : New York University, [2018] |
Includes bibliographical references and index.
Identifiers: LCCN 2017044872 | ISBN 9781479802784 (cl : alk. paper) |
ISBN 9781479819294 (pb : alk. paper)
Subjects: LCSH: Interpersonal relations—Sociological aspects. | Interpersonal relations—Psychological aspects. | Interpersonal relations—Moral and ethical aspects.
Classification: LCC HM1106 .C75 2018 | DDC 302—dc23
LC record available at https://lccn.loc.gov/2017044872

New York University Press books are printed on acid-free paper, and their binding materials are chosen for strength and durability. We strive to use environmentally responsible suppliers and materials to the greatest extent possible in publishing our books.

Manufactured in the United States of America

10 9 8 7 6 5 4 3 2 1

Also available as an ebook

To our children

TABLE OF CONTENTS

Introduction

The Crisis of Connection

NIOBE WAY, CAROL GILLIGAN, PEDRO NOGUERA,
AND ALISHA ALI

At the beginning of the twenty-first century, we are beset by a crisis of connection. People are increasingly disconnected from themselves and each other, with a state of alienation, isolation, and fragmentation characterizing much of the modern world. The quintessential "we," as in "We the people" or "We hold these truths to be self-evident," which once served as a reference to a collective consciousness and state of communion, if not community, has lost all meaning. In the place of the "we," we have been left with the "me," the solitary individual, whose needs, wants, and desires take precedence over the collective.[1] Human society has evolved to a stage where the rights of the individual, particularly those with wealth, power, and status, supersede all other rights and responsibilities.

Though the concept of a crisis of connection is not yet widely utilized, signs of its existence are everywhere. The decreasing levels of empathy and trust, and the rising indices of depression, anxiety, loneliness, and social isolation indicate a loss of connection at the individual and community levels. The impact of such a crisis is evident in the rising rates of suicide, drug addiction, and mass violence, and the high rates of incarceration, hate crimes, domestic violence, and sexual assault on college campuses, as well as astronomical inequality in income, education, health care, and housing. The crisis is, furthermore, reflected in our competition for basic human needs—safety, good schools, housing, nutrition, clean water, and health care—and in our tendency to treat social problems as individual or group-specific rather than collective concerns. We have conditioned ourselves to accept a variety of social maladies, such as the presence of homeless people living on the streets, as unfortunate but inevitable features of modern society and thus not a reflection of any type of crisis. In this book, we provide evidence that we are indeed in the midst of a crisis because as the bonds of solidarity and cohesion weaken, our ability to address our societal problems and pursue our common interests is severely damaged. Lamenting the current state of affairs, an opinion editorial in the *New York Times* recently concluded: "When there is no 'we' anymore . . . then there is no legitimate authority and no unifying basis for our continued association."[2]

While a failure to recognize an inclusive "we" or a common humanity has been evident throughout human history, it is the disconnection within, as well as across, communities that appears to have increased throughout the nineteenth and twentieth centuries and now accelerates as we push further into the twenty-first. Jane Jacobs, the activist, urban planner, and visionary author of *The Death and Life of Great American Cities*,[3] documented how cities during the twentieth century were being transformed into inhospitable and impersonal environments by planners such as Robert Moses, who placed greater value on highways than neighborhood parks. He failed to recognize how the erection of high-rise apartments was undermining the "stoop culture" that had long been present in neighborhoods and had contributed to safety and a high quality of life. In his now seminal work *Bowling Alone*, political scientist Robert Putnam drew attention to what he described as a decline in social capital—the benefits and privileges derived from an individual's participation in social networks.[4] Putnam showed that civic organizations (e.g., bowling teams) and social institutions (e.g., the family, the workplace, schools, and religious organizations) that once provided the bonds to hold society together have weakened, and as they have lost their influence, alienation and individualism have grown.[5] Yet, despite widespread agreement about the fraying of human connection across *and* within communities, there is a lack of consensus as to the root of this crisis or what might be done about it.

Over the past four decades, however, the basis for such a consensus has emerged from discoveries within a wide range of disciplines, from neuroscience, developmental psychology, and sociology to evolutionary anthropology, health sciences, and primatology. The collective insights from these fields, coalescing in the newly emerging field of the science of human connection,[6] compose a five-part story about the roots and consequences of the crisis of connection and the potential solutions. Although each part of the story—based on findings from different scientific disciplines—has been known for decades, we have failed to see the entire picture due to our tendency to segregate scientific disciplines and methods (see Ali and Sichel, this volume). Like the Indian parable in which the blind men are unable to "see" the elephant because they feel only the tail, the ear, the trunk, the side, or the tusk,[7] each scientific discipline has remained largely isolated, focused on one component of the human experience and using one type of method, and rarely, if ever, communicating with other disciplines or methods. This "blind men" approach to science has resulted in an inability to hear or see the full story of human experience in culture and context or what lies at the root of our crisis of connection and how we can effectively address it.

The aim of this edited book is to tell the five-part story evident in the science of human connection that explains: (1) who we are as humans, with a focus on our capacity and need for connection; (2) what has led to our crisis of connection; (3) the evidence of the crisis; (4) the consequences of the crisis; and (5) the potential solutions.

The five-part story from the natural and social sciences begins with studies from developmental psychology, evolutionary anthropology, primatology, and neuroscience. We learn from the research, including the narrative based research with girls and boys, that humans are inherently responsive and relational beings, born with a voice, with the ability to communicate and engage with others, and with the desire to live in relationships.[8] We are not simply the rugged, aggressive, and competitive individuals that we are often made out to be.[9] In fact, our tendency toward altruism and cooperation is now recognized as a key factor in our survival as a species.[10] Over the past half century, researchers of infants, children, and adolescents have repeatedly found that we are, by nature, empathic, caring, cooperative, and interdependent and that connection is integral to human development.[11] Primatologist Frans de Waal has called for "a complete reassessment of our assumptions about human nature" to account for this new and not so new research.[12]

However, according to the second part of the story evident in the sciences, there is a conflict between human nature and the modern culture we have constructed. We want to connect within and across communities, but we live in a society that is rooted in ideologies, beliefs, and values that prevent us from finding what we want and need most to thrive. Patriarchal ideologies, for example, lead us to privilege stereotypically masculine qualities and characteristics over those deemed feminine. Thus, we value self over relationships, individual success over the common good, the mind over the body, and thinking over feeling. Such priorities and preferences explicitly devalue core elements of our humanity and contribute to a decline in familial and communal bonds and a disconnection from oneself and others.[13] Not only is contemporary society organized around patriarchal ideologies, it is also aligned with those of capitalism and White supremacy, in which the needs of some (e.g., the employers, the rich, and White people) are considered more important than the needs of others (e.g., workers, the poor, and people of color).[14] Such "hierarchies of humanness" are perpetuated and reproduced through widely shared stereotypes that justify the hierarchy, denigrate groups of people, and legitimize neglect and violence.[15] Such stereotypes circulate in homes, schools, neighborhoods, workplaces, and the media, and compromise our ability to listen to ourselves and each other, create inclusive communities, or recognize our common humanity. Our ideologies and their corresponding stereotypes and values, in other words, lead to a crisis of connection.

In the third part of the story, the science of human connection provides evidence of the crisis itself. Research in developmental and social psychology, social neuroscience, sociology, and the health sciences shows three broad patterns of increasing disconnection from ourselves and each other. One is a decline in levels of trust and empathy, the second is rising indices of depression and anxiety, and the third is increasing levels of loneliness and social isolation around the world.[16] As the barriers to human connection calcify, our ability to see beyond them becomes ever more limited and our awareness that we are part of one human family becomes ever more faint.

The fourth part of the story then draws on evidence in the social and health sciences that reveals the dire consequences of losing our connection to ourselves and to others.[17] With declining rates of trust and empathy come, according to the data, increasing rates of income and educational inequality, hate crimes, and mass incarceration.[18] With rising rates of depression, anxiety, loneliness, and isolation, we have increasing rates of suicide, drug addiction, mass violence, health problems, and a decline in life expectancy among the most alienated groups, including a growing number of White working-class males.[19] Epidemiologists Richard Wilkinson and Kate Pickett conclude that the two most important factors determining the health and well-being of people living in industrialized countries are social status and friendships. Those who lack friendships or who have low social status are at greatest risk for health problems, substance abuse, and premature death.[20]

In his book *Descartes' Error*, neuroscientist Antonio Damasio reveals that the separation of reason from emotion is a manifestation not of rationality but of brain injury or trauma, suggesting that the culture of the Enlightenment, in splitting thought from emotion, has traumatic effects.[21] Similarly, French sociologist Émile Durkheim, writing over a hundred years earlier, described the anomie and alienation that result when there is a mismatch between the needs of the people and the values of the society in which they live.[22] Psychologist Sigmund Freud, writing in *Civilization and Its Discontents*, describes a collective neurosis manifest in aggression and a "death wish" as the price of civilization.[23] For all three—Damasio, Durkheim, and Freud—a crisis endemic to modern society and rooted in a particular set of ideologies threatens our existence.

In the fifth and final part of the story, we draw from the sciences to suggest potential solutions. In the developmental psychology research that began in the early 1980s with studies of girls and young women,[24] and then continued in the 1990s with studies of boys and young men,[25] we find the human potential to resist disconnection. Girls and boys remind us that we have the capacity, as humans, to reject ideologies that hurt and, in some cases, kill us. The story thus comes full circle and illuminates a solution that is not ideologically driven, but rather based in what we know from the social and natural sciences about our human capacity and desire to live in connection with each other. From the gospels of Jesus to Pope Francis's call for a "revolution of tenderness," from the work of Albert Einstein to the Dalai Lama, we hear the message that love is the solution. Not the "selfless love" that Virginia Woolf warned against in writing about the Angel in the House or the "anemic love" that Martin Luther King Jr. spoke of in his 1965 speech at Oberlin College, but a love that includes the self and is rooted in justice and a sense of a common humanity.

In this chapter, we first tell the five-part story as it emerged starkly in the 1980s and 1990s from narrative-based, developmental research with girls and boys. Such research not only revealed a crisis of connection occurring during development as children are initiated into a set of cultural ideologies premised on a "hierarchy of humanness." It also indicated the root of the problem (i.e., the clash between nature and culture), the consequences of the crisis (i.e., drug and alcohol use, suicide, eating disorders, cutting, violence), as well as the solutions to the crisis rooted in resistance. Following the description of what we learned from listening to girls and boys, we repeat the same five-part story in the sciences but this time as told from a wide array of scientific disciplines and not simply from the narrative-based studies of girls and boys. The same story that the girls and boys told us about a crisis of connection, its roots, consequences, and solutions, is revealed in the larger body of science that includes social neuroscience, evolutionary anthropology, primatology, sociology, social and developmental psychology, and the health sciences. The research in these disciplines indicates that the crisis of connection is occurring not only during child development but also in society more broadly. We close our chapter with a brief description of the applied work that tells the fifth part of the story. If we act on the knowledge we now have from the science of human connection, we can become, as Brazilian educator Paulo Freire urged, "more fully human" by connecting the "me" to a "we," but a "we" that includes rather than rules out a "me" so that no one is silenced or pushed to the margins.[26] A "we," in other words, that truly encompasses all of humanity.

The Crisis of Connection in Human Development

The paradigm shift in the sciences leading to the recognition that humans are inherently relational and responsive beings began, ironically, with the inclusion of women in studies of human development in the 1970s. The "different voice" that developmental psychologist Carol Gilligan wrote about in her groundbreaking book, *In a Different Voice*, was one that had been ignored because it joined reason with emotion and spoke of the self as living in rather than apart from relationships. It was, in fact, a human voice.[27] With this recognition, the question for developmental psychologists turned from how we gain the capacity to love to how our desire and ability to love come to be muted or stunted as we grow older. Here the research with girls proved crucial (see Gilligan, Rogers, and Noel, this volume).

Moving from girlhood to womanhood, girls in the research led by Gilligan and conducted by the Harvard Project on Women's Psychology and Girls' Development in the 1980s and 1990s were narrating a crisis of connection: a turning point or crossroads in development where what had seemed ordinary—having a voice and living in relationship—suddenly became extraordinary. Paradoxically, girls on the cusp of adolescence were being pressured to forgo genuine relationship in which they could openly express their thoughts and feelings in order to have fake relationships in which they could not.[28]

Over a period of ten years, Harvard Project researchers listened to hundreds of girls, diverse in ethnicity and social class, from ages seven to seventeen, in a range of public and private schools and after-school programs in the United States. Their goal was to learn from girls about their experiences of coming of age. With the focus on coming of age and with girls as the narrators, the researchers illuminated an intersection where psychological development came into conflict with social adaptation. Listening to girls, they heard what artists have observed and recorded across time and cultures: prior to adolescence, girls will speak with striking honesty and openness about their thoughts and feelings and raise astute questions about the world around them. They reveal their human capacity for empathy, mutual understanding, and self-reflection and see the human world in a remarkably clear-eyed manner. In a discussion of whether it is ever good to tell a lie, Elise, an eleven-year-old sixth grader in an urban public school, and a participant in the Harvard Project's after-school program on strengthening healthy resistance and courage in girls, said: "My house is wallpapered with lies." This candid scrutiny of the human world was a stark and common finding of the research with girls. Tessie, also eleven, explained why it is important to speak about conflicts in relationships rather than "just keep it inside":

> When you are having an argument with your mother or brother and you just keep it inside and don't tell anyone, you never hear the person's point of view. And if you are telling someone about it, you are telling it from

both sides and so you hear what my mother said, or what my brother said. And the other person can say, well, you might be mad, but your mom was right, and you say, yeah, I know. So when you say it out loud, you have to listen.[29]

During middle and late childhood, girls will say what they see and know about themselves and others from watching and listening to what goes on around them.

Yet as girls become young women and enter secondary education, they are initiated into the gendered splits and hierarchies of a patriarchal order. It is at this point that the researchers heard their open and honest voices waver. Girls who had been lively and outspoken at eight and nine, ten and eleven, came under pressure to be a certain kind of girl—the kind of girl other people want to be with. Someone who will be included rather than excluded; someone who doesn't say what she "really" thinks and feels, who is not "too loud" or too honest; a girl who is less likely to interrupt the social order or disrupt the surface flow of events with her questions and comments; a girl who feels pressure to adopt a public story of girlhood that ironically ensures that her voice is not heard or taken seriously.

"I never utter my real feelings about anything," Anne Frank wrote in her diary at age fifteen. Her confession is echoed by countless girls during early and middle adolescence. Neeti, sixteen, an outstanding student and school leader, explained, "The voice that stands up for what I believe in has been buried deep inside me." Iris, seventeen, said, "If I were to say what I was feeling and thinking, no one would want to be with me. My voice would be too loud." Sheila, sixteen, described how she looks out for herself by never saying what she is actually feeling and thinking. In this way, she can dismiss what others may say about her since they don't really know who she is. "Brilliant isn't it," she asked her interviewer, who agreed. It is, in its own way, a brilliant strategy. But, as the interviewer then reflected, it is one by which Sheila protects herself at the expense of what she had said that she wanted: "honesty in relationships."

The rising incidence of the phrase "I don't know" among girls as they approach and enter adolescence led the researchers to the realization that this disclaimer of knowing served for the most part not as an admission of ignorance but as a cover for knowledge. An injunction, "don't," had come to stand between "I" and "know."[30] Raising the tone of their voices at the end of their responses, suggesting that they were asking rather than answering a question, adolescent girls also began to show signs of psychological distress, manifest in the sudden high incidence among adolescent girls of depression, eating disorders, cutting, suicidal acts, and other forms of destructive behavior.[31]

Coming of age, girls articulated a crisis of connection: if they said what they were feeling and thinking, no one would want to be with them, and if they didn't say what they were feeling and thinking, no one would be with them, they would be all alone. Either way they would lose connection. Either way, the loss of connection was imminent. What's more, the choice they faced between having a voice and having relationships is psychologically incoherent, in that without a voice, there is no one present, there is no relationship, and without relationship or resonance, voices recedes into silence. It was the incoherence of a move that girls recognized to be socially and culturally adaptive and enforced by the educational system that created for many girls, at the edge of adolescence, an experience of crisis. Either way, by speaking or not speaking, they would lose their connection with others. To add to the confusion, they were facing a loss of connection that was said, in the name of maturity and being a good woman, to be not a loss but a gain. Many girls were doing well, some exceptionally well according to standard measures of accomplishment and success. And yet they registered the loss and felt the sadness.[32]

Yet, listening to girls speak about their worlds also highlighted a potential to resist the loss. By not splitting their minds from their bodies, their thoughts from their emotions, and their honest voices from their relationships, girls retained their ability to think inductively—to reason from experience—as well as their capacity for empathy, cooperation, and mutual understanding. These fundamental human capacities rely on the integration of mind and body, thought and emotion, self and relationships. The research with girls thus elucidated both the mechanisms of disconnection by which our desire and ability to live in connection become compromised or disabled and the ways in which the loss of connection can be averted.

With the disruption of connection, with the crisis that renders human connection seemingly quixotic, it becomes possible to establish and maintain the hierarchies of oppression, the splitting of humans into superior and inferior on the basis of race, class, caste, gender, religion, nationality, and sexuality. But in a variety of ways, some more effective than others, girls will resist losing their connection with their bodies, their emotions, and their relationships. They resist the structures of patriarchy that divide human qualities into "masculine" and "feminine," and privilege those considered masculine (mind, self, and thought) while devaluing those gendered feminine (body, relationships, and emotions). When Neeti, eleven, was told by the camp director that her homesick cousin could not call his parents because it was against the rules, she spoke up for her cousin and challenged the director's prioritizing of rules over relationships: "Sorry," she said, "he's only seven . . . people are more important than rules."

The patriarchal bind that renders women captive to a morality that would silence them in the name of goodness is countered by a resistance grounded in a recognition that without a voice, without a self, there can be no relationship, only the chimera of relationship. It was the refusal of some girls to give up their desire for relationship in order to have fake relationships that drew attention to a potential for transformation. Crisis in its medical meaning signifies a turning point that holds both danger and opportunity. The crisis of connection signals the risk of losing connection and all that implies, but it also creates an opportunity to resist the loss and thus to break what has become a vicious cycle.

The research with girls also contributed to our understanding of the crisis of connection by showing how a healthy resistance to losing connection becomes a political resistance to the structures that divide us from one another, and how this political resistance then comes under pressures to become a psychological resistance or a reluctance to know what we know. By joining girls' healthy resistance, by educating and developing their honest voices and their ability to be present with others and with themselves, women tapped into their own desire to live in connection and their resistance to silencing themselves. Supporting girls' healthy development and encouraging their resilience thus challenged the structures of patriarchy that had placed girls in a bind. Mothers and fathers, teachers and counselors committed to fostering girls' well-being found themselves working to disassemble the structures that would force girls to choose between having a voice and having relationships.

By highlighting the tension between the more valued "masculine" traits (reason, the self, independence) and the requisites for being a good woman (being caring, empathic, responsive to others, and selfless), the research with girls made it clear why women's and girls' voices remain key both to understanding and to solving the crisis of connection.

The work with girls and women initiated by members of the Harvard Project included the Women Teaching Girls/Girls Teaching Women retreats (see Dorney, this volume), the Strengthening Healthy Resistance and Courage in Girls Project (see Gilligan, Rogers, and Noel, this volume), the Women and Race Retreats,[33] and the Company of Women/Company of Girls Theater Project.[34] The voices of preadolescent girls and their articulation of the crisis of connection prompt women to recall what for many had been a lost time. But such projects with women and girls also make it clear that strengthening healthy resistance and courage in girls ultimately implies a political transformation. It means freeing democracy from patriarchy.[35]

The research with girls was pathbreaking and radical in its implications. It revealed how the human voice—emotional and relational as well as thoughtful and self-assertive—leads to a crisis of connection and also how this crisis is met with a healthy resistance: a reluctance to lose connection with oneself and with others, a refusal to remain silent about what one sees or to lose touch with one's experience and come not to know what one knows. In this way, the research of the Harvard Project and more particularly its studies with girls and women elucidated a potential to break rather than repeat a destructive pattern, to end a destructive cycle, to free love and create a more caring and humane society.[36]

Other researchers have also noted patterns of resistance among girls and women. Developmental psychologist Janie Ward's research (see Ward, this volume) reveals patterns of resistance among Black girls and their mothers and distinguishes between resistance for survival and resistance for liberation.[37] Resistance for survival includes strategies that provide short-term solutions such as dropping out of dehumanizing schools that are not educating students. Resistance for liberation encompasses strategies that offer long-term solutions such as challenging the quality of education in public schools. Ward finds that Black mothers of girls socialize their children to resist for liberation by communicating to them the nature of their challenges and ways of addressing them.

Similarly, the research of developmental psychologist Deborah Tolman documents the ways in which girls and young women resist a culture of misogyny that disconnects girls from their bodies and leads to slut shaming. She offers concrete solutions that nourish the humanity of girls and women (see Tolman, this volume).

Drawing from hundreds of interviews conducted throughout adolescence with boys from a wide range of ethnicities, races, and social classes, developmental psychologist Niobe Way and her research team reveal a story similar to the one found in the research with girls.[38] Like girls, boys openly express their desire for genuine connections with others, including with boys. They reveal the human capacity for mutual understanding, care, and empathy and demonstrate remarkably astute abilities to read the human world. Yet as they reach middle to late adolescence and as expectations of manhood intensify,[39] they begin to experience a crisis of connection in which they speak about losing trust and closeness in their male friendships and, for some, no longer believe it's possible to have intimate relationships with other boys even though they continue to yearn for them. Rather than "I don't know" evident in the girls' research, the boys begin to say "I don't care" in response to questions about whether they want close male friendships. Only a few years earlier, however, their desire for such friendships was clear. While girls say "I don't know," boys say "I don't care," reflecting a gender binary essential to patriarchy—where women don't think and men don't feel.

When Justin, at 15 years old in one of Way's studies,[40] was asked to describe his friendships, he responded:

> [My best friend and I] love each other . . . that's it . . . you have this thing that is deep, so deep, it's within you, you can't explain it. It's just a thing that you know that that person is that person . . . and that is all that should be important in our friendship. . . . I guess in life, sometimes two people can really, really understand each other and really have a trust, respect, and love for each other. It just happens, it's human nature.[41]

During early and middle adolescence, boys often speak about having or wanting male friendships with whom "you have this thing that is deep, so deep it's within you, you can't explain it." Set against an American culture where boys and men are perceived to be "activity-oriented," "emotionally illiterate," and interested only in independence, these findings are surprising. Although norms of masculinity suggest that what boys want and need most are opportunities for competition and autonomy, approximately 85 percent of the hundreds of boys in Way's studies indicate that boys' closest friendships share the plot of *Love Story* more than *Lord of the Flies*. Black, Latino, Asian American, and White boys from working- to middle-class families in the United States spoke of valuing their close male friendships not because their friends were worthy opponents in the competition for manhood but because they were able to share their thoughts and feelings—their deepest secrets—with these friends.[42]

Hector said at the age of fourteen: "I've got two best friends—Willy and Brian. Like sometimes when me and Willy argue, me and Brian are real close. Then when me and Brian are not doing so good, me and Willy are real close. It's like circles of love. Sometimes, we're all close." Jason said at fifteen: "My ideal best friend is a close, close friend who I could say anything to . . . 'cause sometimes you need to spill your heart out to somebody and if there's nobody there, then you gonna keep it inside, then you will have anger. So you need somebody to talk to always." When asked to explain why he feels close to his best friend, Marcus said: "If I'm having problems at home, they'll like counsel me, I just trust them with anything, like deep secrets, anything." While boys spoke about enjoying sports or videogames with their friends, the emphasis was almost always on talking together and sharing secrets with their *best friends*.[43]

The boys in Way's studies also believed that the intimacy in their male friendships was essential for their health and well-being. Stephen said in his freshman year:

> You need friends to talk to sometimes, you know like you have nobody to talk to, you don't have a friend, it's hard. You got to keep things bottled up inside, you might just start . . . crying or whatever. Like if a family member is beating on you or something and you can't tell a friend, you might just go out, just you know do drugs, sell drugs whatever.[44]

Chen at 15 years old said that he needed "someone to talk to, like you have problems with something, you go talk to him. You know, if you keep it all to yourself, you go crazy. Try to take it out on someone else." Another boy concurred, saying that "without friends you will go crazy or mad or you'll be lonely all of the time, be depressed. . . . You would go wacko." Kai said bluntly at the age of fourteen: "My friendships are important 'cause you need a friend or else, you would be depressed, you won't be happy, you would try to kill yourself, 'cause then you'll be all alone and no one to talk to."[45]

Like the girls in the research conducted by the Harvard Project, the boys resist cultural expectations that lead them to silence vital parts of themselves. For boys, this means resisting codes of masculinity that would turn a core human desire and need for close friendship into a "girly and gay" thing, which, in a homophobic and misogynist culture, is equivalent to being lame, and no one wants to be lame.

As these boys reached late adolescence, however, they began to describe the loss of close friendships and trust with other boys. Justin said in his senior year:

> I don't know, maybe, not a lot, but I guess that best friends become close friends. So that's basically the only thing that changed. It's like best friends become close friends, close friends become general friends and then general friends become acquaintances. So they just . . . if there's distance whether it's, I don't know, natural or whatever. You can say that but it just happens that way.

Michael said in his senior year:

> Like my friendship with my best friend is fading, but I'm saying it's still there but. . . . It's sad 'cause he lives only one block away from me. . . . It's like a DJ used his cross fader and started fading it slowly and slowly and now I'm like halfway through the cross fade.[46]

When asked about whether he still had a best friend in his junior year, Guillermo replied:

> Not really. I think myself. The friend I had, I lost it. . . . That was the only person that I could trust and we talked about everything. When I was

down, he used to help me feel better. The same I did to him. So I feel pretty lonely and sometimes depressed . . . because I don't have no one to go out with, no one to speak on the phone, no one to tell my secrets, or to help me solve my problems. [Why don't you think you have someone?] Because I think that it will never be the same, you know, I think that when you have a real friend and you lost it, I don't think you find another one like him. That's the point of view I have . . . I tried to look for a person, you know but it's not that easy.[47]

Rather than simply being a period of progress, adolescence for the boys in Way's studies appears to also be a period of loss. As their bodies were almost fully grown and their minds increasingly attuned to cultural messages about manhood and maturity, they began to distance themselves from the very relationships that they relied on previously so that they wouldn't go "crazy or mad or be lonely all the time." While some boys, such as Guillermo, explicitly indicated their feelings of sadness over the loss, other boys expressed not caring about the loss. Yet like the little boy in Maurice Sendak's story who claimed not to care until he was swallowed up by a lion,[48] their repeated responses of not caring as well as the increase in suicide rates nationally among boys at the exact same age as their reported losses suggest that they do, in fact, care deeply.

In response to a cultural context that links the need for emotional intimacy with an age (babyish), a sex (female), and a sexuality (gay), these boys "mature" into men who are autonomous, emotionally stoic, and isolated. The ages of sixteen to nineteen, however, are not only a time of disconnection for the boys in Way's studies, but also an age in which disconnection is common for boys across the United States, as suggested by the rising rates of self- and other-directed violence during this period.[49] Just as the boys during early and middle adolescence predicted, not having friends to share their deepest secrets makes them go "wacko."[50]

The reasons for boys' crisis of connection in their friendships during adolescence can be divided into thin and thick culture explanations. Thin culture explanations repeat narratives that are familiar to many but only skim the surface. When boys were asked directly about the loss of trust and close male friendships, they repeated well-worn narratives about why such friendships disappeared. Having girlfriends, busy work and school schedules, and changes in schools and neighborhoods were risk-free and frequently stated reasons for the loss of friendships and trust. The boys invoked these explanations freely but not without expressing frustration, sadness, and anger at their losses and a wish to regain what they had earlier in their development.[51]

Thick culture explanations focus on the norms of masculinity and maturity in American culture that make such friendships a gay, girly, or childish thing rather than a human capacity, desire, and need. When Jason, a ninth grader who had a close male friend with whom he shared all his secrets, was asked if and why male friendships are important, he explained that with them "you are not lonely . . . you need someone to turn to when things are bad." Three years later, he said in response to the same question about his friendships that while he had nothing against gay people, he himself was not gay. He also told his interviewer that he no longer had any close male friends, although he "wouldn't mind" having such friendships like the ones he had when he was younger. Other boys during late adolescence responded similarly. When boys didn't directly discuss this link between sexuality and friendships, they did indirectly with the phrase "no homo," a verbal tick that was repeated after every intimate phrase. "We're close, no homo." "We talk, no homo." Questions about close male friendships became questions about sexuality only during late adolescence.

The boys revealed the ways in which American norms of masculinity, or the pressure to "man up," split the mind from the body, boys from girls, straight boys from gay boys, and thinking from feeling. When asked what it would be like to be a girl, Andy at the age of sixteen said: "It might be nice to be a girl because then you wouldn't have to be emotionless." The assumption here is that boys and men are supposed to think and not feel and girls and women are supposed to feel and not think (lest they sound like men). In such a culture, boys struggle to hold on to their friendships and girls, as suggested by the Harvard Project research, struggle to hold on to what they know.

Constructions of maturity are also to blame for the crisis of connection among adolescent boys. Despite decades of work on the importance of connectedness in human development,[52] the essential components of maturity in the United States continue to be independence and stoicism—qualities that are privileged in a patriarchal society. Mohammed said in his junior year: "But I don't know. Recently, . . . you know I kind of changed something. Not that much, but you know, I feel like there's no need to—I could keep [my feelings] to myself. You know, I'm mature enough." Interpreting a desire to share feelings as a sign of *immaturity*, Mohammed shuts down. He understood implicitly that there are consequences to becoming "mature." Other boys were also aware of these consequences as they explicitly linked maturity and manhood with self-sufficiency, saying things such as "Now I'm a man, I need to take care of myself and not rely on others." One only needs to ask the question of what it would mean for us to define manhood *and* maturity as the ability to have mutually supportive relationships to underscore how far modern society is from valuing them.

Developmental psychologist Judy Chu finds that young boys also face pressures to disconnect from their relational presence and emotional openness. She shows how in the transition from preschool to first grade, boys will replace relational presence (their attentiveness, articulateness, authenticity, and directness in relationships) with relational pretense and posturing. But she also documents boys' resistance, their struggle to maintain their openly expressive voices (see Chu, this volume).[53] In her two-year longitudinal study of four- and five-year-old boys, she finds that the boys start off reading the emotional and relational world with remarkable acuity and are able to articulate their need and desire for one another. They implicitly reject the autonomy associated with masculinity by seeking out the support of other boys in the classroom and defending their peers when others are bullying them. They display, in other words, a healthy resistance to debilitating norms of masculinity that manifest in their school and peer group cultures. Over the school year, however, Chu notes that the boys begin to behave in more stereotypic ways by creating, for example, a "mean team" that explicitly excludes girls. Although some of the boys privately admitted to liking girls, on the "mean team" girls are the enemy. Chu's research indicates that the crisis of connection occurs at different moments in development and not simply during adolescence. When children and adolescents are pressured to adhere to patriarchal dictates in and out of the classroom, they begin to disconnect from themselves and each other in the name of being "normal."

Developmental psychologist Onnie Rogers finds that boys accommodate and resist not only gender stereotypes but also racial stereotypes (see Rogers, this volume). In her study of Black adolescent boys attending an all-boys school in Chicago that serves boys of color, she finds three patterns in their construction of their identities. The first entails Black boys adhering to the gender and racial stereotypes that are projected onto them by society. The second pattern is Black boys claiming to be "the exception" to the racial stereotypes but adhering to gender stereotypes. The third pattern involves Black boys resisting both racial and gender stereotypes and noting that the negative messages projected onto them about being Black as well as male are, indeed, stereotypes and thus not accurate representations of boys, men, or Black people. Rogers concludes that while her findings may be distinct to the school context in which she collected her data, it is critical for researchers to investigate the processes of resistance and accommodation to stereotypes across intersecting social identities.

The research with girls and boys in developmental psychology tells us a five-part story that sheds light on both how the crisis of connection emerges and how it might be countered. They underscore, first of all, our human capacity to feel another person's feelings, to observe the human world, to voice what we see and hear and know, to be curious about each other, to notice cultural contradictions, and to want and fight for authentic relationships in which we are heard, seen, and supported. They reveal, in other words, our human capacity and need for connection and our ability to resist cultural norms that hurt us. Second, girls and boys reveal the patriarchal ideologies and their corresponding stereotypes that privilege the stereotypically masculine over the stereotypically feminine and split boys from girls, the mind from the body, thinking from feeling, and the self from relationships. They remind us that our definitions of maturation and manhood, with their emphasis on autonomy and independence, make it hard for us to find what we want and need most to thrive. Third, we learn from boys and girls about the crisis of connection as they grow older and learn not to say what they know and feel as it is deemed too risky. They imply what a teenage character explicitly says in a John Hughes coming-of-age film: "When you grow up, your heart dies."[54] The fourth part of the five-part story that we learn from girls and boys is the consequences of the crisis that appear right at the moment during development when boys become "boys" (or how boys are often said to be), and girls begin to disconnect from what they know.[55]

The girls and boys in the developmental research also reveal the fifth and final part of the story—the potential solutions. By demonstrating their human capacity to resist cultural pressures to disconnect from what they know about themselves and others in the name of being a "perfect girl" or "a real man," they show us a way out of the crisis of connection. This body of developmental research indicates that the story of human development is not simply one of accommodation to oppressive cultural forces. It is also a story of resistance to dehumanization.[56] It is this story of resistance that allows us to recognize our common humanity in the face of forces that divides us from ourselves and from one another and to see that in resisting the loss of connection to ourselves and others, we have an opportunity to create a more just and humane society.

The Crisis of Connection in Society

When we listen to the larger body of research in primatology, evolutionary anthropology, child development, neuroscience, social psychology, sociology, education, and the health sciences, we hear, once again, the same five-part story as we heard in the narrative-based developmental research with girls and boys: (1) the human desire for connection, (2) the ideologies and their corresponding stereotypes that disconnect us from ourselves and each other and lead to a crisis of connection, (3) evidence of a crisis of connection, (4) the consequences of the crisis, and (5) the potential solutions.[57]

Part 1: The Nature of Humans

Whereas once humans were described by scientists and philosophers as primarily aggressive and competitive and in need of social and political institutions to control our violent impulses, new and old research across a wide range of disciplines underscores our capacity for empathy, cooperation, and altruism, and our desire for relationship.[58] In his book *The Age of Empathy*, primatologist Frans de Waal observed:

> Empathy is part of our evolution, and not just a recent part, but an innate, age-old capacity. . . . We involuntarily enter the bodies of those around us so that their movements and emotions echo within us as if they're our own [from the beginning of life].[59]

In *Mothers and Others*, evolutionary anthropologist Sarah Blaffer Hrdy states:

> From a tender age and without special training, modern humans identify with the plights of others and without being asked, volunteer to help and share, even with strangers. In these respects, our line of apes is a class by itself. . . . This ability to identify with others and vicariously experience their suffering is not simply learned: it is part of us.[60]

Our evolutionary past reveals our capacity and need for relationships and the ways in which "mothers and others" have nurtured our social and emotional needs over the ages.[61] Like Charles Darwin, Hrdy maintains that our social capacities lie at the root of our survival as a species. Furthermore, she asserts that our stories of ourselves have overlooked a central aspect of our evolutionary history, namely our child-rearing capacities and patterns. Without mothers, fathers, uncles, aunts, siblings, cousins, grandparents, and others who serve as "alloparents" in raising the children, we would not have had the opportunity to hunt or gather or, more broadly, survive as a species. The necessity for the *collective* raising of children early in our histories led evolution to select for the very social and emotional skills that were and are necessary for humans to thrive.

The groundbreaking work on attachment and loss by the British psychiatrist and psychoanalyst John Bowlby countered what had been accepted wisdom about human development by observing young children who were separated from their caregivers, whether due to the exigencies of war or by having to go to the hospital. Witnessing the children's distress at the loss of connection, Bowlby identified a trajectory of responses to loss that began with protest and, when protest proved ineffective, led to despair and ultimately to detachment.[62] More recently, Carol Gilligan and Naomi Snider observed how the trajectory of children's protest to loss observed by Bowlby parallels the resistance to loss that the Harvard Project researchers detected in their studies with girls. Such resistance, however, can turn into despair and detachment if it doesn't prove effective at repairing the loss. Gilligan and Snider further note that patriarchal ideals of masculinity and femininity correspond to what Bowlby identifies as pathological responses to loss, namely compulsive self-reliance and compulsive caregiving.[63] These responses to loss are problematic in that they become barriers to regaining or restoring connection.

In addition to the work on loss, Bowlby and developmental psychologist Mary Ainsworth provide compelling evidence of attachment, revealing the ways in which infants and young children seek the proximity of their caretakers during times of fear or stress.[64] Such behavior increases the likelihood of protection and survival from predators and is thus, they argue, evolutionarily adaptive. One sees evidence of the attachment system in the ways in which babies signal to their caretakers through smiling or vocalizing when they are seeking interaction or through crying when they want to be soothed. Secure attachment, in which children know that their caretakers will respond to them when they are in need, has been linked to positive adjustment over the life span. In contrast, insecure or anxious attachment, in which children lack confidence in their caretaker's responsiveness, has been associated with maladjustment.[65] The different ways that children attach and the impact of such attachment styles on developmental outcomes have been examined for over half a century. Researchers have consistently found that children's early attachment styles have a lifelong impact on human development.[66]

Other developmental psychologists have also documented the social and emotional nature of human beings. Michael Tomasello counters previous assumptions about what motivates behavior by showing that young children have strong desires to help, inform, and share, without expecting any reward.[67] Children display naturally altruistic and selfless tendencies, independent of influences from their caregivers or socialization. His research also reveals that as children grow, their altruism and empathy become more selective but do not diminish. Even in the first years of life, infants can discern the underlying goals and intentions of others and show empathy toward them, crying when they hear other infants cry.[68] Tomasello's research indicates that those children who cooperate with each other are more likely to share the rewards of their work together. This latter finding has significant implications for strategies to address the crisis of connection.

In his "still face" experiment, developmental psychologist Edward Tronick provides a searing demonstration of the relational nature of human beings. In a two-minute video of a mother and her one-year-old baby, we initially see the pair engaged in a responsive relationship, smiling and cooing with delight. The mother is then instructed by the experimenter to become still-faced and stop responding to her infant's gestures and smiles. Instantly the baby picks up the break in connection. When the baby's repeated efforts to reengage her or his mother are ignored by the mother, the baby becomes visibly distressed.[69] The experiment shows that even in the first year of life, humans are social creatures who register the loss of connection, who move to repair ruptures in relationship, and who become visibly distressed when their efforts at repair are met with no response.[70]

Underscoring the importance of close relationships throughout the lifespan, social psychologists at the University of Virginia find that perceptions of task difficulty are shaped by the proximity of a close friend.[71] In an experimental design, the researchers asked college students to stand at the base of a hill while carrying a weighted backpack and to estimate the steepness of the hill. Some participants stood next to close friends whom they had known a long time, some stood next to friends they had not known for long, some stood next to strangers, and the rest stood alone. The students who stood with close friends gave significantly lower estimates of the steepness of the hill than those who stood alone, next to strangers, or to new friends. The longer the close friends had known each other, the less steep the hill appeared. In a similar study, college students were asked to recall a positive social relationship, a neutral one, and a negative one immediately before estimating the steepness of a hill. Researchers found that those who recalled a positive social relationship estimated the hill to be less steep than those who recalled a neutral or negative one. In addition, the closer the participants felt to the person they were recalling, the less steep the hill appeared to be.[72] The world sounds and looks less stressful when standing next to, or even thinking about, a person to whom one feels close.

Further evidence for the social and emotional nature of humans comes from social neuroscientist Matthew Lieberman in his book *Social: Why Our Brains Are Wired to Connect*: "[We] are wired to be social. We are driven by deep motivations to stay connected to friends and family. We are naturally curious about what is going on in the minds of other people. . . . We will spend our entire lives motivated by social connection."[73]

Social psychologist Ethan Kross and his colleagues find that social rejection lights up the same region of the brain as physical pain, indicating that biologically we are as wired to maintain a sense of belonging as we are to remain physically safe.[74] Furthermore, Lieberman notes when our brains are not engaged in anything specific, we think about other people like a reflex, suggesting that our brains are actively promoting cooperation, empathy, and understanding even during "down time."

Like the voices of girls and boys in the narrative-based developmental studies, the research from primatology, evolutionary anthropology, developmental psychology, and social neuroscience underscores our natural capacity and need for empathy, mutual understanding, cooperation, and care and shows us what happens in their absence.

Part 2: The Roots of the Crisis of Connection

The second part of the five-part story highlights a tension between human nature and culture. While the research underscores our human capacity and desire to live in relationships, contemporary society rests on a set of ideologies, values, and beliefs that divide us from ourselves and each other. We devalue our friendships and emphasize our individual achievements. We privilege stereotypically masculine qualities over feminine ones and insist on a set of stereotypes that perpetuate a hierarchy of humanness with wealthy, White, Christian, and straight men being on top and all others being on the bottom.[75] Success is measured, furthermore, only in economic terms and not in indicators of social and emotional wellbeing.[76]

Empirical evidence of the growing tendency to privilege the masculinized "me" over the femininized "we" is found in a set of studies that examine how our language has changed over time.[77] A search of texts between 1960 and 2008 in a Google database conducted by psychologist Jean Twenge and her colleagues found that words and phrases such as "self," "I come first," and "I can do it myself" were used more frequently over time, while words and phrases like "community," "collective," "tribe," "share," "united," and "common good" declined.[78] Using the Google database but expanding their search to texts throughout the twentieth century, psychologists Pelin Kesebir and Selin Kesebir found that the usage of words such as "thankfulness," "appreciation," "kindness," and "helpfulness" dropped by up to 56 percent by the end of the twentieth century.[79] In her search of the same database, psychologist Patricia Greenfield also found that individual oriented words increased while communal words decreased throughout the twentieth century.[80] Psychologists Nathan De Wall and Richard Pond gathered the lyrics of the *Billboard* top 10 hit songs from 1980 to 2007 and found that the use of "we" and "us" as well as "love" decreased while the use of "I" and "me" and words such as "kill" and "hate" increased.[81] A study of 49,818 American college students who completed the Narcissistic Personality Inventory (e.g., "I can live my life any way I want to"; "If I ruled the world, it would be a better place") found that the average college student in 2009 scored higher in narcissism than 65 percent of students in 1982.[82] These trends of self-focus and aggrandizement fit with what we hear in popular culture, with pop artists, for example, singing lyrics such as "I am the greatest man that ever lived" or "I am god."[83]

Stereotypes about gender, race, class, sexuality, nationality, and religion, furthermore, pervade our daily conversations and justify our ideologies that we share in modern society. They communicate a set of incoherent beliefs about ourselves and each other, such as that only some of us think (e.g., White and Asian males) while others feel (e.g., females, Latinos, Black people, gay males, and poor people), with the implication being that none of us think *and* feel. We, in other words, have gendered, raced, sexualized, and classed core human capacities and put them in ideological hierarchies so that certain capacities (e.g., thinking) are privileged over others (e.g., feeling). The science of human connection reveals not only that all humans think and feel but that thinking and feeling often go together.[84] Thus, when we stereotype ourselves and each other, we disconnect from what we know about ourselves and about our common humanity.

Stereotypes, furthermore, intersect so that those about Asians, for example, are not the same as those about Asian women nor are those about Asian women the same as those for White women.[85] While some stereotypes appear "positive" (e.g., Asian people are smart, boys are good at math), they position one group in opposition to another (girls vs. boys, Asians vs. non-Asians) and serve to reify what are perceived to be innate differences.[86] The stereotype that Black people are good athletes suggests that Black people who do not possess this competency are not "true" representations of their race.[87] In this way, the Black male scientist who lacks athletic prowess is deemed "not Black enough," the Asian teen who struggles in math is not really Asian, and the boy who is emotionally sensitive is not really a boy.[88] Regardless of the specificity, stereotypes have a dehumanizing effect by suggesting that a particular group of people is competent in only one dimension—if that—of what makes them human.[89] By dividing ourselves into hierarchical binaries that reduce ourselves and each other to being either competent or incompetent in fundamental parts of who we are as humans, we further our disconnection with ourselves and with each other and abet the crisis of connection.

Stereotypes, and the ideologies they serve, justify inequity and inhumane treatment. If Black and poor families are stereotyped as not valuing education, it's easier to rationalize the lack of investment in the public schools that serve such children. If Asian families are stereotyped as valuing only academic achievement, schools are justified in not providing social and emotional support for those students. If undocumented immigrants are stereotyped as having fewer basic needs than others, it is not necessary to provide them with safe working conditions and access to good housing, health care, and schooling. If "girls don't like math," schools can ignore gender disparities in math performance. If "women talk too much," it is okay for men to "shut them down." If "men are from Mars and women are from Venus," then misunderstanding and miscommunication are inevitable.[90]

Studies over the past four decades have concluded that stereotypes have devastating consequences on health and well-being and lead to a disconnection with the self and with others.[91] Sociologist Michael Kimmel (this volume), for example, reveals the damage to boys and men caused by a code of masculinity that emphasizes stoicism and aggression, as well as dominance of men over women.[92] Sociologist Pedro Noguera (this volume) finds that African American and Latino boys are doubly trapped by gender and racial stereotypes that undermine their relationships and limit their academic achievements and their future possibilities.[93] Describing the ingrained nature of stereotypes for boys of color, Noguera claims that the images we hold toward them are powerful in influencing what people see and expect of them. Our assumptions related to race and gender and all other social categories are so deeply entrenched that it is virtually impossible for us not to hold them unless we take conscious and deliberate action.[94]

In *Pink Brain, Blue Brain*, Neuroscientist Lise Eliot concludes:

> Infant brains are so malleable that what begins as small differences at birth become amplified over time, as parents and teachers—and the culture at large—unwittingly reinforce gender stereotypes. The good news is that appreciating how sex differences emerge—rather than assuming them to be fixed biological facts—we can help all children reach their fullest potential.[95]

Evidence for Eliot's point includes the findings that gender differences in math and science are found only in some cultures (e.g., the United States, the United Kingdom, and Australia) and not in others (e.g., many Eastern European, Middle Eastern, and Asian countries).[96] If such stereotypes reflected nature, one would find gender differences around the world. We have made what is culture into what is nature.[97]

Contemporary society, with its technological innovations, has made it even easier to perpetuate harmful and inaccurate stereotypes; thus challenging them is ever more pressing. Writing about Twitter, columnist Bret Stephens contends:

> We have created a virtual world where people feel free to let their racial prejudices [and stereotypes of all kinds] and fantasies run wild. . . . Bigotry flourishes on Twitter, since it offers the bigot the benefits of anonymity along with instantaneous, uncensored, self-publications. It's the place where their political minds can be as foul as they want to be—without the expense or reputational risk of showing their face at a Richard Spencer rally.[98]

One only needs to look at any form of social media to see the ways that stereotypes of all kinds get spread around the world at mind-boggling speeds. Opinion writer Lindy West points out that "unfortunately, as any scientist can tell you . . . more often than not, sunlight makes things grow."[99] And as stereotypes grow like weeds, the crisis of connection within *and* across communities grows as well.

Part 3: The Crisis of Connection

The crisis of connection itself, or the third part of the five-part story, is found in the declining levels of trust and empathy and the increasing rates of depression, anxiety, loneliness, and isolation over the past century. A recent Pew Research Center report found that only 19 percent of young people in the millennial generation in the United States (born between 1980 and 2000) think that "most people can be trusted," whereas 31 percent of generation X (born between 1961 and 1980) and 40 percent of baby boomers (born between 1941 and 1961) believed that when they were the age of the millennials.[100] Similarly, in a nationally representative sample, 46 percent of American high school students in 1976 and adults in 1972 held the opinion that "most people can be trusted," whereas only 16 percent of high school students in 2012 and 31 percent of adults in 2014 said the same thing.[101] Among high school students in 2012, 47 percent said that most people are "just looking out for themselves rather than trying to be helpful" and 49 percent said that most people "would try to take advantage of you if they got a chance."[102] The researchers concluded that their findings suggest "a culture growing ever more toward disconnection and away from close communities. Trusting no one and relying on yourself is a self-fulfilling prophecy in an individualist world where the prevailing sentiment is 'do unto others before they do it to you.'"[103] Other signs of a decline in trust since the 1970s include the shift in automobile drivers' willingness to pick up hitchhikers, the rise in gated communities, and the increase in "home security" services.[104]

Not only interpersonal trust but also trust in public institutions has declined in the United States. According to the Pew Research Center, 78 percent of people reported trusting their government in 1958, whereas only 19 percent did in 2015.[105] Interpersonal trust and public trust have also been declining in other countries around the world. According to the World Values Survey, 30 percent of the public in the United Kingdom in 2014 believed "most people can be trusted," while 40 percent believed that in the 1980s. In addition, nearly 70 percent stated you "need to be very careful" when dealing with strangers, whereas 60 percent of the public believed that strangers could be trusted in 1959.[106] In a national survey of Australians, the Scanlon Foundation found that 52 percent of the public reported that they *can* trust others in 2012, but only 45 percent reported that just a year later.[107] According to the Gallup World Poll, public trust in governments has also been declining across the Organisation for Economic Co-operation and Development (OECD) countries over just the past decade,[108] with an average of 44 percent of the population reporting trust in their government in 2006 and an average of 37 percent reporting such trust in 2014.[109]

In addition to trust, there has also been a decline in empathy. In a cross-temporal meta-analysis conducted of 13,737 US college students who filled out an empathy questionnaire between 1979 and 2009, researchers report that there has been a 40 percent decline in empathy or in the amount of time that college students spend "thinking about other people's feelings," with the steepest decline occurring after 2000. Among college students in 2009, 75 percent scored lower in empathy than the average 1979 student.[110] In another study in the United States, 75 percent of 2006 college students scored higher in beliefs that people "deserve what they get" (e.g., "people who meet with misfortune have often brought it on themselves") than the average 1970s student.[111]

Sociologist David Ramey finds that the same minor classroom transgressions between White and Black students in the United States are perceived differently, with White students viewed as struggling with mental health or behavioral challenges, while Black students are perceived as being "unruly" and "unwilling to learn."[112] Problems in school among Black students are also more likely than those same problems among White students to be perceived as a product of poor parenting, poor character, and cultural deficiencies, and as permanent to their character.[113] Social scientists have also found that White Americans are more likely to subject Black juveniles to harsher punishments than White juveniles and more likely to perceive Black juveniles as similar to adults in their blameworthiness than White juveniles.[114] Similarly, police have been found to be more likely to perceive Black youth as guilty and deserving of punishment than White youth.[115]

A decline in empathy is seen in countries throughout world. Anger spread across the European Union when Angela Merkel, the chancellor of Germany, agreed to accept one million refugees into her country and asked the other EU nations to follow suit. Despite the fact that many of these same countries have produced refugees themselves at various points in history, the call for accommodation not only evoked a fierce reaction of opposition, but also gave rise to nationalist parties, some of which were elected to office (e.g., Hungary), and prompted Britain's "Brexit." Similar reactions to the global refugee crisis are evident in other regions. A national survey in Australia by the Scanlon Foundation finds that empathy has been rapidly declining over the past decade, with 23 percent of people in 2011 reporting that they thought refugees arriving in boats should be sent back and that number increasing to 33 percent in 2014.[116] Similar examples of hostility include mobs of South Africans attacking Somalis and burning their shops, Mexicans preying upon Central Americans and others seeking passage to the United States, and Dominicans ordering a mass expulsion of Haitians even as undocumented Dominican immigrants seek refuge in the United States and across the Caribbean.[117]

In addition to a decline in trust and empathy, there has been an increase in depression and anxiety. While the decline in trust and empathy underscores the disconnection to others, the latter underscores our growing disconnection from ourselves. One out of six Americans took an antidepressant or other psychiatric drug in 2013, three times as many as in 1996.[118] According to the World Health Organization, depressive disorders were ranked as the third leading cause of disability in 2004 and will move into the first place by 2030. Lifetime prevalence rates of depressive disorders range from 3 percent in Japan to 16.9 percent in the United States, with most countries falling between 8 and 12 percent.[119]

Anxiety disorders are also increasing around the world. A survey of 40,192 college students and 12,056 children aged nine to seventeen in the United States who completed measures of anxiety between the 1950s and the 1990s found that the average college student in the 1990s was more anxious than 85 percent of the students in the 1950s and 71 percent of the students in the 1970s. Children as young as nine years old were found to be more anxious than children in the 1950s, with the researcher reporting that "the change was so large that normal school children in the 1980s reported higher levels of anxiety than child psychiatric patients in the 1950s."[120] Globally, approximately one person in thirteen currently suffers from anxiety disorders.[121] Such disorders are more commonly reported in Western than in non-Western societies, with a review of eighty-seven studies across forty-four countries indicating that the prevalence of anxiety ranged from 5.3 percent (3.5–8.1 percent) in African cultures to 10.4 percent (7.0–15.5 percent) in European/Anglo cultures.[122] These findings, as well as the lifetime prevalence rates of depressive disorders in the United States compared to other nations, suggest, once again, that societies that privilege individualism over relationships are more at risk for a crisis of connection.

The data on friendships, loneliness, and social isolation also suggest a crisis of connection. Sociologists report that the percentage of adults who report having no close friends has increased from 36 percent in 1985 to 53.4 percent by 2004. Furthermore, in 1985 the modal number of close friendship that adults had was three, while in 2004 it was zero, "with almost half of the population now reporting that they discuss important matters with either no one or with only one other person."[123] The number of socially isolated Americans has more than doubled since 1984, increasing from 20 percent to 40 percent of all Americans.[124] More than four times as many Americans describe themselves as lonely now than in 1957.[125] A 2010 national survey in the United States, furthermore, indicates that one out of every three adults in the United States over the age of forty-five now reports feeling lonely, whereas only one out of every five adults reported feeling lonely ten years previously.[126] Currently, more than 50 percent of adults in the United States live alone, and each year thousands of people die with no one to claim their belongings or to take responsibility for their funerals.[127] A 2010 report by the Mental Health Foundation found that the eighteen- to thirty-four-year-olds surveyed were more likely than those over fifty-five to feel lonely and depressed because of loneliness.[128]

Such patterns of increasing isolation are found throughout Europe and Asia as well. According to national surveys, half a million people in the United Kingdom over the age of sixty spend each day alone with no social interaction,[129] and in two-thirds of European countries, more than 10 percent of persons aged sixty-five or over either have no friends or never meet up with them.[130] In addition, a recent survey found that almost three-quarters of older people in the United Kingdom are lonely.[131] A 2017 poll by Age UK found that half a million people over the age of sixty usually spend each day alone, with no social interaction, while half a million more do not typically see or speak to anyone for six days a week.[132] Strikingly these increasing rates of self-reported loneliness and social isolation are most common in countries where autonomy and independence are privileged over relationships and community or in countries that are increasingly moving toward such value systems.[133] The "empty-nest elderly family" in China accounts for almost 25 percent of the households headed by older adults, and this number is expected to increase to 90 percent by 2030.[134] Using national samples, a study of older adults in China showed that although about 16 percent felt lonely in 1992, the number had increased to 30 percent by 2000 and is likely much higher at this point.[135]

As evident in the declining rates of trust and empathy and increasing rates of depression, anxiety, loneliness, and social isolation, the crisis of connection is hitting epidemic proportions.

Part 4: The Consequences of the Crisis of Connection

The consequences of the crisis of connection, or the fourth part of the story evident in the science of human connection, are made up of two components.[136] One explicitly links the declining rates of empathy and trust with increasing or high levels of income inequality, educational inequity, violence (e.g., police violence, sexual assault), and hate crime. The other links the increasing rates of depressive symptoms, anxiety, loneliness, and social isolation with suicide, drug addiction, domestic and mass violence, and physical health problems, including death. In a study of thirty industrialized countries, epidemiologists Richard Wilkinson and Kate Pickett found that those societies that value independence over friendships have higher rates of depression, addiction, and violent crime. Their research suggests, furthermore, that it is not the valuing of independence and individual rights that causes problems, but the privileging of independence over friendships.[137]

Research also finds that countries that are the highest in levels of social distrust and the lowest in empathy are also the highest in income inequality.[138] Those countries that report dramatic increases in income inequality since the late 1970s also report dramatic decreases in trust and empathy over the same period. While income inequality around the world is the highest it has been for the past half century,[139] levels of interpersonal and political trust are at all-time lows.[140] Income inequality has also been linked to a lack of friendships, with those countries reporting the highest levels of income inequality also reporting the lowest levels of friendship support among both the rich and the poor.[141] The findings suggest the effects are circular, with a decline in trust and empathy leading to lower levels of social support, which then lead to less trust and empathy. Wilkinson and Pickett state:

> In the course of our research [studying income inequality in twenty industrialized countries] we became aware that almost all problems which are more common at the bottom of the social ladder are [also] more common in more unequal societies. . . . Modern societies are, despite their affluence, social failures.[142]

By prioritizing the rights of the individual over those of the collective, by ignoring the need to build and reinforce bonds of community and solidarity, we undermine our need for collective trust and action. Wilkinson and Pickett conclude that "greater material equality can help to create a cohesive, co-operative community, to the benefit of all."[143] The data suggest, as well, that with more cohesive and connected communities, greater material equality will also emerge.[144]

The effects of a decline trust and empathy are visible not only in our economic system but also in our educational and criminal justice institutions.[145] Black students in the United States are more than three times as likely as their Whites peers to be suspended or expelled, and Black students are more likely to receive harsher punishment for the same transgressions.[146] Black girls are also more than two times more likely to be disciplined for minor infractions like dress code violations or loitering, two and a half times more likely to be punished for disobedience, and three times more likely to be cited for being disruptive.[147] Furthermore, the simple fact that dropout rates can be as high as 70 percent in some urban public schools,[148] as well as that racial and economic disparities in educational resources and attainment continue to be dramatic even in such a wealthy country as the United States, are testaments to a complete and utter lack of empathy for people of color and for the poor and working class in the United States.[149]

Similarly, low levels of empathy are also reflected in our system of criminal justice. Since 2010, over two million people have been incarcerated in the US penal system, a dramatic increase that began in the 1970s and has accelerated ever since. Nearly 50 percent of the incarcerated are Black, even though Black people constitute merely 12 percent of the US population. Today, one-third of Black males will be arrested and sent to prison during their lifetime, and between the ages of twenty and thirty-four, one out of nine Black people will be in prison.[150] Black youth are more likely to be sentenced to adult prison than are White offenders, and once convicted, Black offenders receive longer sentences compared to White offenders for the same crime.[151]

While it is difficult to determine if police violence against Black people is increasing in frequency, the ubiquity of camera phones and body cameras has made the issue more visible and public than ever before. Research suggests that such violence is linked to stereotypes and a general lack of empathy. A study by social psychologist Phillip Goff and his colleagues found not only that Black faces were more associated with apes than White faces but that when people were primed with ape-related stimuli, they were more likely to endorse violence by police officers toward a Black suspect than a White suspect.[152] This deeply disturbing finding provides empirical evidence for the links among stereotypes, a lack of empathy, and violence.[153]

A lack of empathy and stereotypes have also been linked to the high rates of violence against girls and women, with reports of sexual assault on college campuses on the rise.[154] Thirty-five percent of women worldwide have experienced either physical or sexual intimate partner violence or nonpartner sexual violence in their lifetime.[155] The recent uptick of reports of sexual harassment and assault, as part of the Me Too movement, has underscored a shocking lack of empathy toward girls and women.[156]

Stereotypes and a lack of empathy are also likely to be at the root of the high or increasing levels of hate crimes.[157] Hate crimes are now being reported in the media on a daily basis. As with police violence, sexual assault, and many other acts of violence, it is unclear whether the rates are increasing or whether they are simply receiving more media attention.

However, we now regularly read about people being shot, stabbed, and attacked because they identify with a particular race, religion, nation, sexual orientation, gender, or non-gender binary.[158] Hate crimes against Muslims have increased dramatically in Christian-dominated countries since 9/11.[159] According to a report by the Southern Poverty Law Center, the number of hate groups in the United States hit an all-time high in 2011 and remained at near-historic levels in 2016.[160] The Ku Klux Klan is now holding rallies in public places.[161] Australia had its highest levels of reported racial discrimination in 2014, with 40 percent of people born in Asian countries reporting such discrimination over the past twelve months.[162] Italy is also experiencing a dramatic increase in hate crimes directed at immigrants.[163] Hate crimes directed against lesbian, gay, bisexual, and transgendered people and communities have also risen since 2011.[164]

Not only are there devastating consequences of a decline in trust and empathy and the perpetuation of stereotypes; there are also negative effects of increases in depression, anxiety, loneliness, and isolation that include suicide, drug addiction, domestic and mass violence, and physical health problems, including premature death. Depression and social isolation have been consistently linked to suicide, and all three problems have significantly increased over the past half century.[165] According to the Centers for Disease Control and Prevention in the United States, the US suicide rate has increased every year from 1999 to 2014 among both women and men and in every age group except those seventy-five and older. Now, entire schools and communities have been identified as "suicide hot zones" because of sustained increases that appear to operate like a contagious disease.[166] Between 1999 and 2010, the suicide rate among Americans between thirty-five and sixty-five years of age rose by 28 percent, with the rates increasing 30 percent for men between the ages of thirty-five and fifty, 50 percent for men in their fifties, and 60 percent for women in their sixties. The suicide rate for children under age fourteen has doubled just since 1980.[167] More people in the United States now die of suicide than car accidents. The problem is not limited to the United States. Across the United Kingdom, the most recent statistics show that suicide is now the leading cause of death for men between the ages of twenty and forty-nine.[168] Globally, suicide rates have increased 50 percent of the past half century.[169]

Research has also linked depression, anxiety, and social isolation to drug addiction, with increasing rates of all three problems corresponding with an unparalleled growth in opiate addiction and overdose.[170] Deaths from a heroin overdose in the United States increased by 286 percent from 2002 to 2013.[171] Police officers and emergency service personnel in several cities are now asked to carry naxolone, an anti-overdose medication, with them so that they can respond quickly to heroin overdoses. Owners of fast-food restaurants report finding over-dosed customers in their restrooms on a regular basis.[172] While opiate addiction is a problem in many countries, the United States is disproportionately represented in the opiate statistics, with two million of the eight million heroin users from all the countries around world being from the United States.[173] This latter pattern provides additional evidence that it is those individualistic modern cultures that are most at risk for a crisis of connection.

In addition, social isolation has been linked to domestic and mass violence.[174] According to the Centers for Disease Control and Prevention, people who are socially isolated and lack social support are more likely to perpetrate intimate partner violence as well as child maltreatment and elder abuse.[175] While homicide rates across the nation have declined in recent years,[176] incidents of mass violence, defined as violence that kills at least four people, occurred in the United States in 2015 at the rate of approximately one per day.[177] The significance of this dramatic increase in mass violence can be truly appreciated when one considers that prior to 2005 such incidents occurred only a few times a decade. Since the 2012 shooting at an elementary school in Newtown, Connecticut, there have been approximately 239 school shootings in the United States.[178] Those under the age of eighteen are now called "children of the mass shooting generation."[179] Evidence that such violence is linked to a crisis of connection is found in the data that show that perpetrators of these crimes are almost always described as lonely and isolated.[180] They are also typically White, male, and young, individuals who would seem to have the most opportunity in American society. Yet due to alienation and isolation, they lash out against others.[181] One of the brothers who maimed and killed people participating in the Boston Marathon openly discussed on social media that he was feeling lonely and longing for a close friend.[182] Christian Toro, who was arrested with his brother for building bombs in their Bronx apartment, was reportedly "lonely" and looking for a close friend.[183] In a YouTube video made just before he killed six people and injured fourteen near the campus of UC Santa Barbara in 2014, Elliot Rodger said to the video camera, "Tomorrow is the day of retribution, the day in which I will have my revenge against humanity. Against all of you. For the last eight years of my life . . . I've been forced to endure an existence of loneliness . . . I've had to rot in loneliness all these years."[184] Mass violence is also increasing in other countries though not to the same degree as in the United States, a pattern that is likely due to not only particularly high rates of social isolation but also easy access to guns.[185]

The increase in depression, anxiety, and/or social isolation not only leads to increased suicide, drug addiction, and certain types of violence, but also leads to sickness and death. The health sciences have indicated over the past three decades that social isolation is as damaging to the body as smoking fifteen cigarettes a day.[186] Social isolation has also been shown to weaken our immune system and to make us more susceptible to diseases such as Alzheimer's, diabetes, high blood pressure, heart disease, and cancer.[187] In an examination of over 148 studies, health researchers Julianne Holt-Lunstad, Timothy Smith, and J. Bradley Layton concluded that individuals with strong social networks have a 91 percent greater likelihood of survival from various types of diseases compared to those with weak social networks. The risk of death for those with poor social networks is comparable to well-established risk factors such as smoking and excessive alcohol consumption, and this risk exceeds the influence of other factors such as physical inactivity and obesity.[188]

Researchers have also found that those who have close friendships or strong social support networks are less likely to experience physical illnesses and more likely to live longer lives. In a six-year study of 736 middle-aged men, attachment to a single person (almost always a spouse) did not lower the risk of heart attack and fatal coronary heart disease, whereas having a strong social support network did.[189] Smoking was the only risk factor comparable to a lack of social support. Researchers find that physical wounds heal more quickly when the person is embedded in a strong support network and/or in a positive and affirming marriage. In contrast, being in a hostile marriage or being isolated slows down the healing process.[190] Isolation and loneliness have been found to increase the likelihood of death by 26 percent and to lower the likelihood of and lead to a faster decline in physical activity participation over a two-year follow-up period. Loneliness also boosts rates of smoking, coronary heart disease and stroke, high blood pressure, the onset of disability, cognitive decline, clinical dementia (with lonely people having a 64 percent increased chance of developing it), and death.[191] Loneliness ranks above excessive drinking, obesity, and air pollution in increasing chances of early death by 45 percent.[192]

Additional evidence of the negative effects of disconnection from self and others comes from decades of research on self-silencing and depression.[193] Self-silencing, described initially in the Harvard Project with girls and women, is the act of choosing not to voice one's thoughts and feelings in relationships. Psychologist Alisha Ali found that self-silencing among psychotherapy clients predicted poorer clinical outcomes at the end of therapy relative to those who did not self-silence. The Framingham Offspring Study of over five thousand participants found that women who silenced themselves in their relationships were four times more likely to die over the course of the ten-year study, even after controlling for other known risk factors such as smoking, blood pressure, and age.[194] These findings demonstrate that silencing one's authentic voice can be psychologically damaging and physically lethal.[195]

Underscoring the importance of social relationships, Malcolm Gladwell, in *Outliers*, tells the story of Roseto, Pennsylvania—a tight-knit community of Italian immigrants. A physician, Dr. Wolf, in the 1950s became fascinated by this town because the rates of various health problems were extremely low, as were the rates of suicide, drug addiction, alcoholism, and crime when compared to the rest of the state and nation. He and his team set out to understand the reasons for such healthy outcomes. They looked at nutrition, genetics, and the environment, but none of these factors appeared to tell the story. Finally, after years of investigation, they realized that the answer lay in the tight-knit quality of the community. In Gladwell's words:

> What Wolf slowly realized was that the secret of Roseto wasn't diet or exercise or genes or the region where Roseto was situated. It had to be the Roseto itself. As Bruhn and Wolf walked around the town, they began to realize why. They looked at how the Rosetans visited each other, stopping

to chat with each other in Italian on the street, or cooking for each other in their backyards. They learned about the extended family clans that underlay the town's social structure. They saw how many homes had three generations living under one roof, and how much respect grandparents commanded. . . . Wolf and Bruhn had to convince the medical establishment to think about health and heart attacks in an entirely new way: they had to get them to realize that you couldn't understand why someone was healthy if all you did was think about their individual choices or actions in isolation. You had to look beyond the individual. You had to understand what culture they were a part of, and who their friends and families were, and what town in Italy their family came from. You had to appreciate the idea that community—the values of the world we inhabit and the people we surround ourselves with—has a profound effect on who we are.[196]

In sum, decades of research across the sciences have revealed the critical nature of relationships and communities and underscored that our social and emotional needs and capacities are not simply feel-good issues; they are matters of life and death.

Part 5: Solutions to the Crisis of Connection

The fifth and final part of the five-part story evident in the science of human connection, especially in the developmental research with girls and boys, demonstrates our human potential to resist harmful ideologies and their corresponding stereotypes that disconnect us from ourselves and each other.[197] Thus, the solution to the crisis of connection is to foster resistance to disconnection in our homes, schools, workplaces, and communities. The authors in this volume provide numerous examples of strategies of resistance. Their techniques are varied, but their underlying goals are the same: helping people connect to themselves and each other and build stronger and more inclusive communities. The solutions offered reinforce the belief that the problems we face cannot be solved simply at the individual level, but must be addressed through individual and collective actions that resist ideologies that dehumanize, with a focus on affirming our common interests and goals and recognizing each other's full humanity.

SCHOOL-BASED SOLUTIONS

School-based solutions to the crisis of connection include the love pedagogy described in this volume by educator Lisa Arrastia. The foundation of schools that counter alienation and "othering" is a pedagogy that builds and reinforces connection, that promotes deep social and intellectual engagement, and that cultivates genuine relationships between teachers and students and among students themselves. Using her own university-based classroom and her teacher's institute for K–12 educators as examples, Arrastia shows that relationship is at the center of any effective and humane educational practice and that a love pedagogy is a significant educational methodology that radically resists the criminalization of poor and working-class young people within and outside of schools. Similarly, Pedro Noguera, in this volume, shows that such strategies can produce schools that are safe and conducive to learning.

Another example of a school-based solution is Mary Gordon's Roots of Empathy, an international nonprofit organization that helps children develop and nurture their own empathy in a classroom setting, with the help of a baby and parent as a model. The program aims to help children understand that they belong, no matter what label society has imposed on them. As a result of their classroom-based interventions, classroom aggression goes down, prosocial behavior goes up, and students become kinder, more caring, and more focused on learning. Roots of Empathy is now in eleven countries and has touched the lives of more than eight hundred thousand children.[198]

The work of Niobe Way and Joseph D. Nelson in a middle school for boys of color in the Lower East Side of New York City offers another example of a school-based solution. In their Listening Project, boys and their teacher at George Jackson Academy are trained in transformative interviewing and interview each other, their teachers, and their family members, to foster their curiosity and connection to others. The aim of the training is to promote listening to the self and others and asking questions that challenge the "Black box" of stereotypes by which we see ourselves and each other. Boys in the school are encouraged to bring forward their own natural curiosity and allow their interviewees to reveal their full humanity rather than simply confirm stereotypes. Drawing from their interviews, the boys are then asked to write biographical essays and present their work in public settings. These activities not only serve to reconnect boys of color to their own humanity but also help them to see the humanity of others in their communities.

Victoria Rhoades illustrates still another school-based solution with her discussion of working with Shakespeare in the classroom. She demonstrates how her approach allows youth to transcend the stereotypes that often divide them—stereotypes rooted in static notions of gender and race—and to find connection and meaningful relationships through a love of verse and performance. Rhoades's project is unique in presenting a way of working with young men and women together that integrates the insights gained from developmental research with a pedagogy of voice and relationship. She found that encouraging the women to free their natural voices and stay present in their bodies freed the men to open their hearts and resist dehumanizing codes of masculinity.

The school-based pedagogy presented in Judith Dorney's chapter directly addresses the crisis of connection and illustrates the transformative power of cross-generational connections between women and girls in school settings. She demonstrates the effectiveness of a curriculum based on a five-step progression from silence and remembering to artistry and birthing, with mourning a crucial middle step. The curriculum hinges on women educators connecting to the vision and passion that led them into education in the first place and also provides an opportunity for them to reflect on the forces that have disconnected them from themselves, from one another, and from the girls in their classrooms. In the course of the retreats, led by Dorney and her colleagues, the women recognize the importance of encouraging girls to work through strong disagreement and emotional conflict.

We hear a similar message about the importance of genuine relationships in the school-based work presented by Michael Reichert and Joseph D. Nelson. The authors critique the current "boy crisis" that bemoans the state of boys and their achievements to emphasize the need for relational teaching. Their powerful message on the importance of developing strong bonds with boys, especially during adolescence, illuminates the shortcomings of a system that does not allow them to embrace their full potential as caring, compassionate, emotional human beings. To address the crisis of connection in classrooms, Reichert and Nelson offer concrete solutions to the traps inherent in traditional forms of masculinity.

COMMUNITY-BASED SOLUTIONS

Moving from school-based to community-based solutions, Dana Edell describes a theatrical intervention that is transformative not only for the girls, but also for teaching artists, the audience, and the broader community. By empowering girls to write and perform their own stories, this work connects them to themselves and to each other and reveals their humanity to the audience. Theater provides an avenue through which they uncover the common experiences shared by so many girls and young women in a culture that defines femaleness in narrow terms of beauty and femininity, and that assumes that girl versus girl competition is natural. Through theater, they create bonds that enable them to overcome their sense of alienation and affirm their deep connections.

Gary Barker's chapter offers community-based initiatives and provides additional insights into ways that we can transcend the pervasive and limiting binaries that divide us as humans. His nonprofit organization Promundo started the MenCare campaign in 2011 that challenges the binary of women as caregivers and men as not. The campaign, in more than forty countries, engages men as active, nonviolent partners and caregivers and has led to changes in family leave policies in various countries around the world.

In his work with military veterans, Stephan Wolfert uses theater to address the crisis of connection evident among members of the military. In his chapter with Alisha Ali, Wolfert discusses the development of the DE-CRUIT program that was designed to treat the effects of trauma among military veterans by using Shakespeare and the power of human connection. The strategies used include group cohesion, communalization of trauma, and therapeutic embodiment in supporting veterans' transition from military life into civilian life. Emphasis is placed on the therapeutic effects of veterans working together to help each other through this transition and toward personal and interpersonal growth and shared healing.

Khary Lazarre-White's chapter describes his nonprofit organization, New York City–based Brotherhood/Sister Sol, which is redefining
norms of manhood and womanhood and speaking out for full freedom
and access. Bro/Sis provides support, guidance, and love to youth to help
them develop their minds, bodies, and spirits in a healthy manner and
to connect to their own humanity as well as to the humanity of others.
Bro/Sis reaches more than 1000 youth a year.

Focusing on policy-based options, Hirokazu Yoshikawa discusses
the needs of undocumented children and the children of undocumented parents. He presents policy initiatives that can address the
crisis of connection by recognizing the humanity of immigrants (both
documented and not). Such a recognition makes it possible to transform the delivery of services to refugees, immigrants, and the poor
from acts of charity to acts of solidarity. Yoshikawa's chapter underscores the importance of addressing public attitudes in tandem with
changing public policy debates around such issues as immigration and
unauthorized migration.

Finally, love as a solution to the crisis of connection is discussed by
Rabbi Burton Visotzky, Reverend Chloe Breyer, and Dr. Hussein Rashid.
Quoting scripture and its interpretation over the past millennia, these
three religious leaders together wrestle with the relationship of love with
justice. While all three religions command love of God's fellow creatures
to promote our common humanity, each tradition offers a different interpretation of love. These leaders suggest a way forward to creating meaningful connections once we move past platitudes. They demonstrate that
it is possible to have difficult conversations to deepen a sense of community and belonging.

Even with such remarkable work being done by the practitioners and
policymakers, whose work is showcased in this volume and by countless
others, there remain significant barriers with which we must contend
as we attempt to resist dehumanization and build human connection.
Most daunting among these are the overriding cultural assumptions that
situate individual success and wellness at an oppositional pole to communal success. The belief that individuals can thrive only at the expense
of collective growth runs counter not only to the prevailing scientific
evidence on the human condition, but also to the significant strides
made by groups who foster positive change in even the most vulnerable

individuals, by embracing the principles of empathy, kindness, and the recognition of our common humanity.

Conclusion

By drawing from the five-part story evident in the science of human connection that tells us what lies at the root of our crisis of connection, its consequences, and its solutions, the contributions to this volume demonstrate the need for a paradigm shift—the elevation of a different voice. This is a voice not bound by the opposition of dependence to independence, girl to boy, Black to White, rich to poor, straight to gay, or Christian to Muslim, but one that recognizes interdependence as the human condition and the condition in which all humans thrive. The emerging consensus in the human sciences makes it clear that, within ourselves, we have the potential to solve our seemingly insoluble conflicts and to create a thriving society. Yet we live in a society that devalues or ignores the very qualities and experiences that are integral to our ability to meet these challenges and solve our collective problems. Rather than engaging in ideological disagreement, we can draw from the science of human connection to better understand the consequences of the culture and society that we have created and maintained. As we recognize both our shared capacity for empathy, caring, and cooperation and our tendency to create false and hierarchical stories of ourselves and each other that disrupt those capacities, what previously seemed insurmountable becomes possible.

In many respects, the 2016 election of Donald Trump in the United States illuminated and magnified the divisions that exist among us, making it impossible to ignore the crisis of connection. Trump's election held up a mirror and forced us to look at ourselves and recognize how deep the crisis is. Writing about the election and what it represented, political theorist Naomi Klein suggests that

> in so many ways, Trump is not a rupture at all, but rather the culmination— the logical end point—of a great many dangerous stories our culture has been telling for a very long time. That greed is good. That the market rules. That money is what matters in life. That white men are better than the rest. That the natural world is there for us to pillage. That the vulnerable

BRESCIA UNIVERSITY
COLLEGE LIBRARY

deserve their fate, and the 1 percent deserve their golden towers. That anything public or commonly held is sinister and not worth protecting. That we are surrounded by danger and should only look after our own. That there is no alternative to any of this.[199]

Yet when the pursuit of our common humanity seems most remote and hope seems to have evaporated completely, Klein reminds us that a glimmer of new possibilities is emerging in the resolve many are taking to "spend a few more hours a week in face-to-face relationships, or to surrender some ego for the greater good of a project, or to recognize the value of so much in life that cannot be bought or sold—we might just get happier."[200]

Experiencing the crisis of connection for themselves, people are now creating projects that bring us together in innovative ways. An example includes Brandon Doman's Strangers Project, in which he asks people in public settings to answer the question "What's it like being you?" Brandon writes, "I ask people to write about anything they want—as long as it's true. Whether about love or loss, joy or fear, what they all have in common is an honest voice of the human experience. . . . When people share their stories, we can explore the connections that make us human." He has collected over twenty-five thousand handwritten responses that he displays in galleries, at pop-up exhibitions in parks, in books, and online.[201] Other community projects that seek to underscore our common humanity include Leslie and Sam Davol's Uni Project, a nonprofit organization that brings learning and enrichment opportunities to public spaces in New York City. Using custom-designed installations, they offer reading, drawing, and hands-on activities that let people of all ages and living in all types of neighborhoods learn and create together. They have found that connections are often made between people who might otherwise have passed each other by.[202] The We Are Human Project, a campaign created by the Project for the Advancement of Our Common Humanity (PACH; www.pach.org) at New York University,[203] asks people around the world to answer five questions that underscore their commonalities. The researchers find that questions about fears, hopes, and trust often evoke responses that are similar across race, ethnicity, class, gender, nationality, and religion. The Radical Listening Project, which joins Carol Gilligan's Radical Listening Project at NYU, Columbia

University's program in narrative medicine, Narrative4's story exchange for empathy, and Narrativ's storytelling, teaches the art of radical listening as a first step toward healing the destructive divides that afflict our country and our world.[204] While these projects are not by themselves solutions to the crisis, they collectively remind us of commonalities in the midst of a world that focuses only on our differences and promotes ideologies that lead to a crisis of connection.

Our final story in this introduction is one of hope and solidarity and reminds us of what is possible. For some time now, AIDS and HIV rates have been rising among gay and bisexual Black men even as they have been declining among the rest of the population. In fact, the incidence of HIV/AIDS and morbidity from the disease is so high that, if treated as a nation, Black gay and bisexual men in the United States would have the highest rate of affliction in the world.[205] The problem is particularly severe in small rural communities where health care services are nonexistent and those afflicted with the disease are shunned by family, friends, and social institutions. Yet despite the severity of the problem, hope is emerging in the form of new "families" comprising community health workers and others who have contracted the disease, who have learned to cope with it effectively, and who now provide care and education to others. These communities offer care and comfort even as governmental agencies and biological families turn their backs on this population. Regarding the creation of the groups that have risen, Linda Villarosa writes:

> Black, gay, and bisexual men and the organizations and activists that support them have come to the painful realization that the nation and society have failed them and that they must take care of themselves and one another. Their group names and slogans reflect a kind of defiant lift-as-we-climb self-reliance: *My Brother's Keeper, Us Helping Us . . . Saving Ourselves Symposium, Our People, Our Problem, Our Solution*, the tag line for the Black AIDS Institute. . . . They are finding ways to provide love and support.[206]

By pursuing our common humanity even in the face of devastating illness or other threats that at times seem overwhelming, we see that solidarity and strong bonds of reciprocity can counter fear and hatred.

It is not in our nature to abandon the sick, to turn our backs on those in need, or to pretend that everything will be all right, as long as we as individuals are safe and comfortable. Turning to each other rather than on each other may sound trite when put forward as a solution, but it is nonetheless the best path forward if we are to reclaim our common humanity.

As author Arundhati Roy wrote, we must "redefine the meaning of modernity" so that our individual and collective rights and responsibilities are given equal weight in the search for solutions. We must reimagine and work toward re-creating a modern society that embeds the self in relationships and communities and that does not privilege one core human capacity or one type of human over the other. In her book *Deepening Darkness* with David Richards, Carol Gilligan writes, "The opposite of patriarchy is democracy."[207] The goal, in other words, is not to flip the hierarchy so that what was on the bottom is now on the top but to create a society that is premised on the fundamental humanness of all and work toward articulating and recognizing that humanity. From the science of human connection, we now know the root of the crisis of connection, the prevalence of the crisis, the consequences, and the solutions. The time to act is now.

NOTES

1 Maia Szalavitz, "Social Isolation, Not Just Feeling Lonely, May Shorten Lives," *Time*, March 26, 2013; Robert Putnam, *Bowling Alone: The Collapse and Revival of American Community* (New York: Simon & Schuster, 2000); Sherry Turkle, *Alone Together: Why We Expect More from Technology and Less from Each Other* (New York: Basic Books, 2011); Thomas L. Friedman, "Where Did 'We the People' Go?," *New York Times*, June 21, 2017; David Brooks, "The Golden Age of Bailing," *New York Times*, July 7, 2017; David Brooks, "Our Elites Still Don't Get It," *New York Times*, November 16, 2017; Susan E. Rice, "We Have Met the Enemy, and He Is Us," *New York Times*, January 25, 2018; Rebecca Mead, "What Britain's 'Minister of Loneliness' Says about Brexit and the Legacy of Jo Cox," *New Yorker*, January 26, 2018.

2 Dov Seidman, quoted in Friedman, "Where Did 'We the People' Go?"

3 Jane Jacobs, *The Death and Life of Great American Cities* (New York: Random House, 1961).

4 Putnam, *Bowling Alone*.

5 Ibid.

6 We have created the phrase "the science of human connection" to include the research from across a wide range of scientific disciplines that addresses who we

are as humans, what disrupts our humanity, what causes a crisis of connection, and what are solutions.

7 E. Bruce Goldstein, *Encyclopedia of Perception* (Thousand Oaks, CA: SAGE, 2010), 492.

8 Sarah Blaffer Hrdy, *Mothers and Others: The Evolutionary Origins of Mutual Understanding* (Cambridge, MA: Harvard University Press, 2009); Frans de Waal, *The Age of Empathy: Nature's Lessons for a Kinder Society* (New York: Crown, 2009); Matthew D. Lieberman, *Social: Why Our Brains Are Wired to Connect* (New York: Crown, 2013); Carol Gilligan, *Joining the Resistance* (Cambridge: Polity Press, 2011); Lyn Mikel Brown and Carol Gilligan, *Meeting at the Crossroads: Women's Psychology and Girls' Development* (Cambridge, MA: Harvard University Press, 1992); John T. Cacioppo and William Patrick, *Loneliness: Human Nature and the Need for Social Connection* (New York: Norton, 2009); Carol Gilligan, *In a Different Voice: Psychological Theory and Women's Development* (Cambridge, MA: Harvard University Press, 1982); Niobe Way, *Deep Secrets: Boys' Friendships and the Crisis of Connection* (Cambridge, MA: Harvard University Press, 2011); David Brooks, *The Social Animal: The Hidden Sources of Love, Character, and Achievement* (New York: Random House, 2012); Carol Gilligan, *The Birth of Pleasure: A New Map of Love* (New York: Knopf, 2003).

9 This image of man as savage unless contained by a social contract comes from philosophy (e.g., Thomas Hobbes) and literature (e.g., *Lord of the Flies*).

10 De Waal, *Age of Empathy*; Michael Tomasello, *Why We Cooperate* (Cambridge, MA: MIT Press, 2009); Hrdy, *Mothers and Others*.

11 Gilligan, *Joining the Resistance*; Brown and Gilligan, *Meeting at the Crossroads*; Gilligan, *In a Different Voice*; Hrdy, *Mothers and Others*; de Waal, *Age of Empathy*; Lieberman, *Social*; Cacioppo and Patrick, *Loneliness*; Way, *Deep Secrets*; Gilligan, *Birth of Pleasure*; Tomasello, *Why We Cooperate*.

12 De Waal, *Age of Empathy*, 7.

13 Hrdy, *Mothers and Others*; Gilligan, *In a Different Voice*; Gilligan, *Joining the Resistance*; Way, *Deep Secrets*.

14 Marc Lamont Hill, *Nobody: Casualties of America's War on the Vulnerable, from Ferguson to Flint and Beyond* (New York: Simon & Schuster, 2016); Naomi Klein, *The Shock Doctrine: The Rise of Disaster Capitalism* (New York: Picador, 2007); Jane Mayer, *Dark Money: The Hidden History of the Billionaires behind the Rise of the Radical Right* (New York: Doubleday, 2016); Prudence L. Carter, "The Multidimensional Problems of Educational Inequality Require Multidimensional Solutions," *Educational Studies* 54, no. 1 (2018): 1–16; bell hooks, *Bone Black* (New York: Henry Holt, 1996); bell hooks, *Ain't I a Woman?* (New York: Routledge, 1981); Gilligan, *Joining the Resistance*; Ta-Nehisi Coates, *Between the World and Me* (New York: Spiegel & Grau, 2015); Michelle Alexander, *The New Jim Crow: Mass Incarceration in the Age of Colorblindness* (New York: New Press, 2012); George Monbiot, "Neoliberalism Is Creating Loneliness: That's What's Wrenching Society Apart," *Guardian*, October 12, 2016.

15 Niobe Way and Leoandra Rogers, "Resistance to Dehumanization during Childhood and Adolescence: A Developmental and Contextual Process," in *New Perspectives on Human Development*, ed. Nancy Budwig, Elliot Turiel, and Philip David Zelazo (Cambridge: Cambridge University Press, 2017), 209–228; Niobe Way, "Getting to the Root of the Problem," *Feminist.com*, June 24, 2014; Pedro Noguera, *The Trouble with Black Boys: And Other Reflections on Race, Equity, and the Future of Public Education* (San Francisco: Jossey-Bass, 2008); David Kirkland, *A Search Past Silence: The Literacy of Young Black Men* (New York: Teachers College Press, 2013); Leoandra Onnie Rogers and Niobe Way, "Stereotypes as a Context for the Social and Emotional Development of Marginalized Youth"; Way and Rogers, "Resistance to Dehumanization"; Nour Kteily, Emile Bruneau, Adam Waytz, and Sarah Cotterill, "The Ascent of Man: Theoretical and Empirical Evidence for Blatant Dehumanization," *Journal of Personality and Social Psychology* 109, no. 5 (2015): 901–931; Nour Kteily and Jennifer A. Richeson, "Perceiving the World through Hierarchy-Shaped Glasses: On the Need to Embed Social Identity Effects on Perception within the Broader Context of Intergroup Hierarchy," *Psychological Inquiry* 27, no. 4 (2016): 327–334; National Coalition of Anti-Violence Programs, "Lesbian, Gay, Bisexual, Transgender, Queer, and HIV-Affected Hate Violence in 2016" (New York: Emily Waters, 2016); Williams and Cave, "Australia Grapples with Campus Assaults"; Niobe Way, Jessica Cressen, Samuel Bodian, Justin Preston, Joseph D. Nelson, and Diane Hughes, "'It Might Be Nice to Be a Girl . . . Then You Wouldn't Have to Be Emotionless': Boys' Resistance to Norms of Masculinity during Adolescence," *Psychology of Men & Masculinity* 15, no. 3 (2014): 241–252; Claude M. Steele and Joshua Aronson, "Stereotype Threat and the Intellectual Test Performance of African Americans," *Journal of Personality and Social Psychology* 69, no. 5 (1995): 797–811; Way, *Deep Secrets*; Gilligan, *Joining the Resistance*; Claude M. Steele, *Whistling Vivaldi: How Stereotypes Affect Us and What We Can Do* (New York: Norton, 2011).

16 Jean M. Twenge, *Generation Me: Why Today's Young Americans Are More Confident, Assertive, Entitled—and More Miserable Than Ever Before* (New York: Simon & Schuster, 2014); Richard G. Wilkinson and Kate Pickett, *The Spirit Level: Why Greater Equality Makes Societies Stronger* (London: Bloomsbury Press, 2009); Robert Putnam, *Our Kids: The American Dream in Crisis* (New York: Simon & Schuster, 2015); Fred Harris and Alan Curtis, "The Unmet Promise of Equality," *New York Times*, February 28, 2018. Craille Maguire Gillies, "What's the World's Loneliest City?" *The Guardian*, April 7, 2016.

17 While there are numerous consequences to the crisis of connection, in addition to the ones mentioned in this chapter, we focus here on the consequences that have been empirically examined as correlates of the crisis of connection (e.g., lack of trust, empathy, depression, anxiety, isolation).

18 Dhruv Khullar, "How Social Isolation Is Killing Us," *New York Times*, December 22, 2016; World Federation for Mental Health, "Depression: A Global Crisis" (October 10, 2012), www.who.int.

19 Sally C. Curtin, Margaret Warner, and Holly Hedegaard, "Increase in Suicide in the United States, 1999–2014" (Atlanta: Centers for Disease Control and Prevention, April 2016); Vanessa Coppard-Queensland, "Globally, 1 in 13 Suffers from Anxiety," *Futurity.org*, September 5, 2012; Julianne Holt-Lunstad, Timothy B. Smith, Mark Baker, Tyler Harris, and David Stephenson, "Loneliness and Social Isolation as Risk Factors for Mortality: A Meta-Analytic Review," *Perspectives on Psychological Science* 10, no. 2 (2015): 227–237.

20 Wilkinson and Pickett, *Spirit Level*.

21 Antonio Damasio, *Descartes' Error: Emotion, Reason, and the Human Brain* (New York: HarperCollins, 1994).

22 Émile Durkheim, *Suicide: A Study in Sociology*, trans. John A. Spaulding and George Simpson (1897; repr., Glencoe, IL: Free Press, 1951).

23 Sigmund Freud, *Civilization and Its Discontents* (London: Hogarth Press, 1930).

24 Gilligan, *In a Different Voice*; Gilligan, *Joining the Resistance*; Brown and Gilligan, *Meeting at the Crossroads*; Lyn Mikel Brown, *Girlfighting: Betrayal and Rejection among Girls* (New York: New York University Press, 2003); Deborah Tolman, *Dilemmas of Desire: Teenage Girls Talk about Sexuality* (Cambridge, MA: Harvard University Press, 2002); Carol Gilligan, Janie Ward, and Jill McLean Taylor, eds., *Mapping the Moral Domain: A Contribution of Women's Thinking to Psychological Theory and Education*, no. 2. (Cambridge, MA: Harvard University Press, 1988); Carol Gilligan, Nona P. Lyons, and Trudy J. Hanmer, eds., *Making Connections: The Relational Worlds of Adolescent Girls at Emma Willard School* (Cambridge, MA: Harvard University Press, 1990); Carol Gilligan, Annie G. Rogers, and Deborah L. Tolman, eds., *Women, Girls, and Psychotherapy: Reframing Resistance* (New York: Routledge, 1991); Jill McLean Taylor, Carol Gilligan, and Amy M. Sullivan, *Between Voice and Silence: Women and Girls, Race and Relationship* (Cambridge, MA: Harvard University Press, 1997); Gilligan, *Birth of Pleasure*.

25 Way, *Deep Secrets*; Judy Y. Chu, *When Boys Become Boys: Development, Relationships, and Masculinity* (New York: New York University Press, 2014); Way et al., "'It Might Be Nice to Be a Girl.'"

26 Paulo Freire, *Pedagogy of the Oppressed*, trans. Myra Bergman Ramos (New York: Herder & Herder, 1968).

27 Gilligan, *In a Different Voice*.

28 Brown and Gilligan, *Meeting at the Crossroads*; Carol Gilligan and Lisa Machoian, "Learning to Speak the Language: A Relational Interpretation or an Adolescent Girl's Suicidality," *Studies in Gender and Sexuality* 3, no. 3 (2002): 321–341; Gilligan, *Joining the Resistance*; Gilligan, Ward, and Taylor, *Mapping the Moral Domain*; Gilligan, Lyons, and Hanmer, *Making Connections*; Gilligan, Rogers, and Tolman, *Women, Girls, and Psychotherapy*; Taylor, Gilligan, and Sullivan, *Between Voice and Silence*; Gilligan, *Birth of Pleasure*; Carol Gilligan, "The Centrality of Relationship in Human Development: A Puzzle, Some Evidence, and a Theory," in *Development and Vulnerability in Close Relationships*,

ed. Gil G. Noam and Kurt W. Fischer (Mahwah, NJ: Lawrence Erlbaum, 1996), 237–261.

29 Gilligan, *Joining the Resistance*, 131–132.

30 Ibid.

31 Gilligan, *Birth of Pleasure*; Brown and Gilligan, *Meeting at the Crossroads*; Gilligan, *Joining the Resistance*.

32 Brown and Gilligan, *Meeting at the Crossroads*.

33 Taylor, Gilligan, and Sullivan, *Between Voice and Silence*.

34 Gilligan, *Birth of Pleasure*.

35 Ibid.

36 Gilligan and Machoian, "Learning to Speak the Language"; Gilligan, Ward, and Taylor, *Mapping the Moral Domain*; Gilligan, Lyons, and Hanmer, *Making Connections*; Gilligan, Rogers, and Tolman, *Women, Girls, and Psychotherapy*; Brown and Gilligan, *Meeting at the Crossroads*; Taylor, Gilligan, and Sullivan, *Between Voice and Silence*; Gilligan, *Birth of Pleasure*; Gilligan, Rogers, and Noel, this volume; Dorney, this volume.

37 Bonnie J. Ross Leadbeater and Niobe Way, eds., *Urban Girls: Resisting Stereotypes, Creating Identities* (New York: New York University Press, 1996).

38 Way, *Deep Secrets*; Way et al., "'It Might Be Nice to Be a Girl'"; Niobe Way, "Boys' Friendships during Adolescence: Intimacy, Desire, and Loss," *Journal of Research on Adolescence* 23, no. 2 (2013): 201–213; Way and Rogers, "Resistance to Dehumanization."

39 Michael Kimmel, *Guyland: The Perilous World Where Boys Become Men* (New York: HarperCollins, 2008).

40 Way, *Deep Secrets*. All of the quotes, and some of the text describing the research, are taken from Way, *Deep Secrets*. Other parts of this text have also been published in Way, "Boys' Friendships during Adolescence."

41 Way, *Deep Secrets*, 1.

42 Ibid., 2–3.

43 Ibid., 91, 94; Way, "Boys' Friendships during Adolescence."

44 Way, *Deep Secrets*, 96.

45 Ibid., 97.

46 Ibid., 183.

47 Ibid., 20.

48 Maurice Sendak, *Pierre: A Cautionary Tale in Five Chapters and a Prologue* (New York: HarperCollins, 1991).

49 Scottye J. Cash and Jeffrey A. Bridge, "Epidemiology of Youth Suicide and Suicidal Behavior," *Current Opinion in Pediatrics* 21, no. 5 (2009): 613–619.

50 Way, *Deep Secrets*, 97.

51 Ibid., 24–25.

52 Joseph P. Allen and Deborah Land, "Attachment in Adolescence," in *Handbook of Attachment: Theory, Research, and Clinical Applications*, ed. Jude Cassidy and Phillip R. Shaver (New York: Guilford, 1999), 319–335; Robert L. Selman,

The Growth of Interpersonal Understanding (New York: Academic Press, 1980); Gilligan, *In a Different Voice*; Gilligan, *Joining the Resistance*; Joseph P. Allen, Bert N. Uchino, and Christopher A. Hafen, "Running with the Pack: Teen Peer-Relationship Qualities as Predictors of Adult Physical Health," *Psychological Science* 26, no. 10 (2015): 1574–1583.

53 Judy Y. Chu, "A Relational Perspective on Adolescent Boys' Identity Development," in *Adolescent Boys: Exploring Diverse Cultures of Boyhood*, ed. Niobe Way and Judy Y. Chu (New York: New York University Press, 2004), 78–104; Chu, *When Boys Become Boys*.

54 Allison Reynolds (portrayed by Ally Sheedy), *The Breakfast Club*, directed by John Hughes (Universal Pictures, 1985).

55 Evidence of the consequences of the crisis include: Centers for Disease Control and Prevention, "Fact Sheets—Underage Drinking" (October 20, 2016), www .cdc.gov; Sonja A. Swanson, Scott J. Crow, Daniel Le Grange, Joel Swendsen, and Kathleen R. Merikangas, "Prevalence and Correlates of Eating Disorders in Adolescents: Results from the National Comorbidity Survey Replication Adolescent Supplement," *Archives of General Psychiatry* 68, no. 7 (2011): 714–723; Kathryn R. Puskar, Lisa Bernardo, Mary Hatam, Samantha Geise, Jeanne Bendik, and Beth R. Grabiak, "Self-Cutting Behaviors in Adolescents," *Journal of Emergency Nursing* 32, no. 5 (2006): 444–446.

56 Way and Rogers, "Resistance to Dehumanization."

57 This section of the chapter covers a wide range of research from dozens of disciplines. The goal is not to provide a comprehensive review of each topic (e.g., stereotypes, the empathy gap, the decline in trust, social isolation) but to briefly review some of the key findings in each of these areas that reveal the five-part story in the science of human connection. Extensive reviews of the literature exist on each of these topics, and it is beyond the scope of this chapter to provide a review on any one of these individual topics.

58 Hrdy, *Mothers and Others*; de Waal, *Age of Empathy*; Tomasello, *Why We Cooperate*; Lieberman, *Social*; Cacioppo and Patrick, *Loneliness*; Gilligan, *In a Different Voice*; Gilligan, *Joining the Resistance*; Way, *Deep Secrets*.

59 De Waal, *Age of Empathy*, 205.

60 Hrdy, *Mothers and Others*, 4.

61 Ibid.

62 John Bowlby, *Attachment* (New York: Basic Books, 1969); John Bowlby, *Separation: Anxiety and Anger* (New York: Basic Books, 1973); John Bowlby, *Loss: Sadness and Depression* (New York: Basic Books, 1980).

63 Carol Gilligan and Naomi Snider, *Why Does Patriarchy Persist?* (Cambridge: Polity Press, 2018).

64 Mary S. Ainsworth and John Bowlby, "An Ethological Approach to Personality Development," *American Psychologist* 46, no. 4 (1991): 333–341; Bowlby, *Attachment*.

65 Cassidy and Shaver, *Handbook of Attachment*.

66 Ibid.

67 Tomasello, *Why We Cooperate*.

68 Ibid.; Abraham Sagi and Martin L. Hoffman, "Empathic Distress in the Newborn," *Developmental Psychology* 12, no. 2 (1976): 175–176.

69 M. Katherine Weinberg and Edward Z. Tronick, "Infant Affective Reactions to the Resumption of Maternal Interaction after the Still-Face," *Child Development* 67, no. 3 (1996): 905–914; Edward Tronick, Heidelise Als, Lauren Adamson, Susan Wise, and T. Berry Brazelton, "The Infant's Response to Entrapment between Contradictory Messages in Face-to-Face Interaction," *Journal of the American Academy of Child Psychiatry* 17, no. 1 (1978): 1–13.

70 See Gilligan and Snider, *Why Does Patriarchy Persist?*, for further discussion of the still face experiment and its significance.

71 Simone Schnall, Kent D. Harber, Jeanine K. Stefanucci, and Dennis R. Proffitt, "Social Support and the Perception of Geographical Slant," *Journal of Experimental Social Psychology* 44 (2008): 1246–1255.

72 Ibid.

73 Lieberman, *Social*, ix, 5.

74 Ethan Kross, Marc G. Berman, Walter Mischel, Edward E. Smith, and Tor D. Wager, "Social Rejection Shares Somatosensory Representations with Physical Pain," *Proceedings of the National Academy of Sciences* 108 (2011): 6270–6275, doi:10.1073/pnas.1102693108.

75 Michael Kimmel, *Angry White Men: American Masculinity at the End of an Era* (New York: Nation Books, 2013); Lamont Hill, *Nobody*; Klein, *Shock Doctrine*; Mayer, *Dark Money*; Carter, "Multidimensional Problems of Educational Inequality"; hooks, *Bone Black*; hooks, *Ain't I a Woman?*; Gilligan, *Joining the Resistance*; Coates, *Between the World and Me*; Alexander, *New Jim Crow*; Monbiot, "Neoliberalism Is Creating Loneliness"; Way and Rogers, "Resistance to Dehumanization."

76 Wilkinson and Pickett, *Spirit Level*.

77 David Brooks, a columnist for the *New York Times*, has spent over a decade writing about the increasingly isolated and self-focused society that has sacrificed community for the sake of the individual's need. David Brooks, "The Golden Age of Bailing," *New York Times*, July 7, 2017; David Brooks, *The Social Animal*; also see Friedman, "Where Did 'We the People' Go?"; Putnam, *Bowling Alone*.

78 David Brooks, "What Our Words Tell Us," *New York Times*, May 20, 2013; Jean M. Twenge, W. Keith Campbell, and Brittany Gentile, "Increases in Individualistic Words and Phrases in American Books, 1960–2008," *PLOS ONE* 7, no. 7 (2012): e40181; Twenge, *Generation Me*.

79 Pelin Kesebir and Selin Kesebir, "The Cultural Salience of Moral Character and Virtue Declined in Twentieth Century America," *Journal of Positive Psychology* 7, no. 6 (2012): 471–480.

80 Patricia M. Greenfield, "The Changing Psychology of Culture from 1800 through 2000," *Psychological Science* 24, no. 9 (2013): 1722–1731; Twenge, *Generation Me*.

81 Twenge, *Generation Me*, 96; John Tierney, "A Generation's Vanity, Heard through Lyrics," *New York Times*, April 25, 2011.

82 Twenge, *Generation Me*.

83 Ibid.; Tierney, "Generation's Vanity."

84 Antonio Damasio, *The Feeling of What Happens: Body and Emotion in the Making of Consciousness* (Orlando: Harcourt, 1999).

85 Negin Ghavami and Letitia Anne Peplau, "An Intersectional Analysis of Gender and Ethnic Stereotypes: Testing Three Hypotheses," *Psychology of Women Quarterly* 37, no. 1 (2013): 113–127; Way and Rogers, "Resistance to Dehumanization."

86 Way and Rogers, "Resistance to Dehumanization."

87 Na'ilah Nasir, *Racialized Identities: Race and Achievement among African American Youth* (Stanford, CA: Stanford University Press, 2011).

88 Prudence L. Carter, *Keepin' It Real: School Success beyond Black and White* (Oxford: Oxford University Press, 2005); Erin McNamara Horvat and Carla O'Connor, *Beyond Acting White: Reframing the Debate on Black Student Achievement* (New York: Rowman & Littlefield, 2006); Nasir, *Racialized Identities*; Cyndy R. Snyder, Niral Shah, and Kihana Miraya Ross, "Racial Storylines and Implications for Learning," *Human Development* 55, nos. 5–6 (2012): 285–301; Rogers and Way, "Stereotypes as a Context"; Way and Rogers, "Resistance to Dehumanization."

89 Way and Rogers, "Resistance to Dehumanization"; Leoandra Onnie Rogers and Niobe Way, "'I Have Goals to Prove All Those People Wrong and Not Fit into Any One of Those Boxes': Paths of Resistance to Stereotypes among Black Adolescent Males," *Journal of Adolescent Research* 31, no. 3 (2016): 263–298; Niobe Way and Leondra Onnie Rogers, "'[T]hey Say Black Men Won't Make It, But I Know I'm Gonna Make It': Ethnic and Racial Identity Development in the Context of Cultural Stereotypes," in *Oxford Handbook of Identity Development*, ed. Kate C. McLean and Moin Syed (New York: Oxford University Press, 2015), 269–285.

90 John Gray, *Men Are from Mars, Women Are from Venus* (New York: Harper-Collins, 1992).

91 There is a large literature on the negative impact of stereotypes on academic outcomes, physical health, and social and emotional well-being. See Steele, *Whistling Vivaldi*; Faye K. Cocchiara and James Campbell Quick, "The Negative Effects of Positive Stereotypes: Ethnicity-Related Stressors and Implications on Organizational Health," *Journal of Organizational Behavior* 25, no. 6 (2004): 781–785; Richard J. Contrada, Richard D. Ashmore, Melvin L. Gary, Elliot Coups, Jill D. Egeth, Andrea Sewell, Kevin Ewell, Tanya M. Goyal, and Valerie Chasse, "Ethnicity-Related Sources of Stress and Their Effects on Well-Being," *Current Directions in Psychological Science* 9, no. 4 (2000): 136–139; Cleopatra M. Abdou and Adam W. Fingerhut, "Stereotype Threat among Black and White Women in Health Care Settings," *Cultural Diversity and Ethnic Minority Psychology* 20, no. 3 (2014): 316–323; Cleopatra M. Abdou, Adam W. Fingerhut, James S. Jackson, and

Felicia Wheaton, "Healthcare Stereotype Threat in Older Adults in the Health and Retirement Study," *American Journal of Preventive Medicine* 50, no. 2 (2016): 191–198; J. Thomas Kellow and Brett D. Jones, "The Effects of Stereotypes on the Achievement Gap: Reexamining the Academic Performance of African American High School Students," *Journal of Black Psychology* 34, no. 1 (2008): 94–120; Claude M. Steele, "A Threat in the Air: How Stereotypes Shape Intellectual Identity and Performance," *American Psychologist* 52, no. 6 (1997): 613–629; Steele and Aronson, "Stereotype Threat"; Claude M. Steele and Joshua Aronson, "Stereotypes and the Fragility of Academic Competence, Motivation, and Self-Concept," in *Handbook of Competence and Motivation*, ed. Andrew J. Elliot and Carol S. Dweck (New York: Guilford, 2005), 436–455; Steele, *Whistling Vivaldi*; Cocchiara and Campbell Quick, "Negative Effects of Positive Stereotypes"; Contrada et al., "Ethnicity-Related Sources of Stress"; Abdou and Fingerhut, "Stereotype Threat"; Abdou et al., "Healthcare Stereotype Threat"; Kellow and Jones, "Effects of Stereotypes."

92 Kimmel, *Guyland*; Kimmel, *Angry White Men*.

93 Noguera, *Trouble with Black Boys*.

94 Ibid., 16.

95 Lise Eliot, *Pink Brain, Blue Brain* (London: Oneworld, 2010), inside cover.

96 Programme for International Student Assessment, "PISA Data Explorer" (Organisation for Economic Co-operation and Development, 2015); Hannah Fairfield and Alan McLean, "Girls Lead in Science Exam, but Not in the United States," *New York Times*, February 4, 2013.

97 Brown and Gilligan, *Meeting at the Crossroads*; Chu, "Relational Perspective"; Kirkland, *Search Past Silence*; Niobe Way, *Everyday Courage: The Lives and Stories of Urban Teenagers* (New York: New York University Press, 1998); Way, *Deep Secrets*; Noguera, *Trouble with Black Boys*; Monique W. Morris, *Pushout: The Criminalization of Black Girls in Schools* (New York: New Press, 2015); Ritch Savin-Williams, *The New Gay Teenager* (Cambridge, MA: Harvard University Press, 2006); sj Miller, "(Un)becoming Trans*: Every Breath You Take and Every . . . ," in *Educators Queering Academia: Critical Memoirs*, ed. sj Miller and Nelson M. Rodriguez (New York: Peter Lang, 2016).

98 Bret Stephens, "How Twitter Pornified Politics," *New York Times*, June 23, 2017.

99 Lindy West, "Save Free Speech from Trolls," *New York Times*, July 1, 2017.

100 Twenge, *Generation Me*.

101 Ibid.; Esteban Ortiz-Ospina and Max Roser, "Trust" (2016), http://ourworldin data.org.

102 Ortiz-Ospina and Roser, "Trust"; Twenge, *Generation Me*; Jean M. Twenge, W. Keith Campbell, and Nathan T. Carter, "Declines in Trust in Others and Confidence in Institutions among American Adults and Late Adolescents, 1972–2012," *Psychological Science* 25, no. 10 (2014): 1914–1923.

103 Twenge, *Generation Me*, 48.

104 Wilkinson and Pickett, *Spirit Level*.

105 Ortiz-Ospina and Roser, "Trust."

106 Oliver Wright, "Levels of Trust between People in Britain on the Decline, Senior Government Adviser Warns," *Independent* (London), November 13, 2015.

107 Roman Krznaric, "Is Australia Losing Its Empathy?," *Guardian* (London), February 25, 2014.

108 OECD, "Trust in Government" (2017), www.oecd.org. The Organisation for Economic Co-operation and Development (OECD) is a group of thirty-four member countries that discuss and develop economic and social policy. OECD members are democratic countries that support free market economies.

109 Ortiz-Ospina and Roser, "Trust."

110 Sara H. Konrath, Edward H. O'Brien, and Courtney Hsing, "Changes in Dispositional Empathy in American College Students over Time: A Meta-analysis," *Personality and Social Psychology Review* 15, no. 2 (2011): 180–198.

111 Lori W. Malahy, Michelle A. Rubinlicht, and Cheryl R. Kaiser, "Justifying Inequality: A Cross-Temporal Investigation of US Income Disparities and Just-World Beliefs from 1973 to 2006," *Social Justice Research* 22, no. 4 (2009): 369–383.

112 David M. Ramey, "The Social Structure of Criminalized and Medicalized School Discipline," *Sociology of Education* 88, no. 3 (2015): 181–201.

113 Ann Arnett Ferguson, *Bad Boys: Public Schools in the Making of Black Masculinity* (Ann Arbor: University of Michigan Press, 2000); Russell J. Skiba, Robert H. Horner, Choong-Geun Chung, M. Karega Rausch, Seth L. May, and Tary Tobin, "Race Is Not Neutral: A National Investigation of African American and Latino Disproportionality in School Discipline," *School Psychology Review* 40, no. 1 (2011): 85–107.

114 Aneeta Rattan, Cynthia S. Levine, Carol S. Dweck, and Jennifer L. Eberhardt, "Race and the Fragility of the Legal Distinction between Juveniles and Adults," *PLOS ONE* 7, no. 5 (2012): e36680.

115 Sandra Graham and Brian S. Lowery, "Priming Unconscious Racial Stereotypes about Adolescent Offenders," *Law and Human Behavior* 28, no. 5 (2004): 483–504.

116 Krznaric, "Is Australia Losing Its Empathy?"

117 Robyn Dixon, "Why Somali Convenience Store Workers Are the Targets of Political Violence in South Africa," *Los Angeles Times*, November 7, 2016; Nina Lakhani, "Mexican Kidnappers Pile Misery on to Central Americans Fleeing Violence," *Guardian* (London), February 21, 2017; Azam Ahmed, "Forced to Flee Dominican Republic for Haiti, Migrants Land in Limbo," *New York Times*, December 12, 2015.

118 Maggie Fox, "One in 6 Americans Take Antidepressants, Other Psychiatric Drugs: Study," *NBC News*, December 12, 2016; Thomas J. Moore and Donald R. Mattison, "Adult Utilization of Psychiatric Drugs and Differences by Sex, Age, and Race," *JAMA Internal Medicine* 177, no. 2 (2017): 274–275.

119 World Federation for Mental Health, "Depression."

120 Twenge, *Generation Me*, 145.

121 Coppard-Queensland, "Globally, 1 in 13 Suffers from Anxiety"; A. J. Ferrari, A. J. Somerville, A. J. Baxter, R. Norman, S. B. Patten, T. Vos, and H. A. Whiteford, "Global Variation in the Prevalence and Incidence of Major Depressive Disorder: A Systematic Review of the Epidemiological Literature," *Psychological Medicine* 43, no. 3 (2013): 471–481.

122 A. J. Baxter, K. M. Scott, T. Vos, and H. A. Whiteford, "Global Prevalence of Anxiety Disorders: A Systematic Review and Meta-regression," *Psychological Medicine* 43, no. 5 (2013): 897–910.

123 Miller McPherson, Lynn Smith-Lovin, and Matthew E. Brashears, "Social Isolation in America: Changes in Core Discussion Networks over Two Decades," *American Sociological Review* 71, no. 3 (2006): 353–375.

124 Khullar, "How Social Isolation Is Killing Us"; Niina Savikko, Pirkko Routasalo, Reijo S. Tilvis, Timo E. Strandberg, and Kaisu H. Pitkälä, "Predictors and Subjective Causes of Loneliness in an Aged Population," *Archives of Gerontology and Geriatrics* 41, no. 3 (2005): 223–233.

125 Twenge, *Generation Me*, 150.

126 C. Wilson and B. Moulton, "Loneliness among Older Adults: A National Survey of Adults 45+" (Washington, DC: AARP, 2010), www.assets.aarp.org.

127 Eric Klinenberg, *Going Solo: The Extraordinary Rise and Surprising Appeal of Living Alone* (London: Penguin, 2013).

128 Jo Griffin, *The Lonely Society?* (London: Mental Health Foundation, 2010).

129 Haroon Siddique, "Half a Million Older People Spend Every Day Alone, Poll Shows," *Guardian* (London), March 20, 2017.

130 Orsolya Lelkes, "Archive: Social Participation Statistics" (Eurostat: European Centre for Social Welfare Policy and Research, 2010).

131 Haroon Siddique, "Three-Quarters of Older People in the UK Are Lonely, Survey Finds," *Guardian* (London), January 6, 2017.

132 Siddique, "Half a Million Older People."

133 Wilkinson and Pickett, *Spirit Level*; Keming Yang and Christina R. Victor, "The Prevalence of and Risk Factors for Loneliness among Older People in China," *Ageing & Society* 28, no. 3 (2008): 305–327; Ye Luo and Linda J. Waite, "Loneliness and Mortality among Older Adults in China," *Journals of Gerontology Series B: Psychological Sciences and Social Sciences* 69, no. 4 (2014): 633–645.

134 Yang and Victor, "Prevalence of and Risk Factors for Loneliness"; Luo and Waite, "Loneliness and Mortality."

135 Yang and Victor, "Prevalence of and Risk Factors for Loneliness"; Luo and Waite, "Loneliness and Mortality."

136 While there are numerous and wide-ranging consequences to the crisis of connection, we focus in this chapter on those for which there are empirical data linking a symptom of the crisis (e.g., isolation, depression) with consequences.

137 Wilkinson and Pickett, *Spirit Level*.

138 Ibid.

139 Elena Holodny, "Here's What Income Inequality Looks Like around the World," *Business Insider*, July 14, 2014, www.businessinsider.com; OECD Centre for Opportunity and Equality, "Inequality" (OECD, 2017), www.oecd.org.

140 Putnam, *Our Kids.*

141 Wilkinson and Pickett, *Spirit Level.*

142 Ibid., 18.

143 Ibid., 62.

144 James Gilligan, *Why Some Politicians Are More Dangerous Than Others* (Cambridge: Polity Press, 2013).

145 Akisha R. Jones, "For Equity, Build Relationships," *Usable Knowledge*, June 30, 2017, www.gse.harvard.edu.

146 Jason A. Okonofua and Jennifer L. Eberhardt, "Two Strikes: Race and the Disciplining of Young Students," *Psychological Science* 26, no. 5 (2015): 617–624; Skiba et al., "Race Is Not Neutral"; Jacob Hibel, George Farkas, and Paul L. Morgan, "Who Is Placed into Special Education?," *Sociology of Education* 83, no. 4 (2010): 312–332; Ramey, "Social Structure."

147 Adrienne Green, "How Black Girls Aren't Presumed to Be Innocent," *Atlantic Monthly*, June 29, 2017; Rebecca Epstein, Jamilia J. Blake, and Thalia González, "Girlhood Interrupted: The Erasure of Black Girls' Childhood" (Washington, DC: Georgetown Law, Center on Poverty and Inequality, 2017).

148 Sam Dillon, "Large Urban-Suburban Gap Seen in Graduation Rates," *New York Times*, April 22, 2009; Christopher B. Swanson, *Closing the Graduation Gap: Educational and Economic Conditions in America's Largest Cities* (Bethesda, MD: Editorial Projects in Education, 2009).

149 Noguera, *Trouble with Black Boys.*

150 National Association for the Advancement of Colored People, "Criminal Justice Fact Sheet" (2017), www.naacp.org; Sentencing Project, "Report of the Sentencing Project to the United Nations Human Rights Committee: Regarding Racial Disparities in the United States Criminal Justice System" (August 2013), http://sentencingproject.org; Saki Knafo, "1 in 3 Black Males Will Go to Prison in Their Lifetime, Report Warns," *Huffington Post*, October 4, 2013.

151 Jim Sidanius and Felicia Pratto, *Social Dominance: An Intergroup Theory of Social Hierarchy and Oppression* (Cambridge: Cambridge University Press, 2001); National Association for the Advancement of Colored People, "Criminal Justice Fact Sheet."

152 Phillip Atiba Goff, Jennifer L. Eberhardt, Melissa J. Williams, and Matthew Christian Jackson, "Not Yet Human: Implicit Knowledge, Historical Dehumanization, and Contemporary Consequences," *Journal of Personality and Social Psychology* 94, no. 2 (2008): 292–306.

153 Phillip Atiba Goff, Matthew Christian Jackson, Brooke Allison Lewis Di Leone, Carmen Marie Culotta, and Natalie Ann DiTomasso, "The Essence of Innocence: Consequences of Dehumanizing Black Children," *Journal of Personality and Social Psychology* 106, no. 4 (2014): 526–545.

154 Williams and Cave, "Australia Grapples with Campus Assaults"; RAINN, "Campus Sexual Violence: Statistics" (2018), www.rainn.org.

155 World Health Organization, "Violence Against Women: Intimate Partner and Sexual Violence Against Women" (2016), www.who.int; Olga Khazan, "Nearly Half of All Murdered Women Are Killed by Romantic Partners," *Atlantic Monthly*, July 20, 2017.

156 Margaret Renkl, "The Raw Power of #MeToo," *New York Times*, October 19, 2017; Jessica Bennett, "When Saying 'Yes' Is Easier Than Saying 'No,'" *New York Times*, December 16, 2017; Lili Loofbourow, "The Female Price of Male Pleasure," *Week*, January 25, 2018.

157 Rae Sibbitt, "The Perpetrators of Racial Harassment and Racial Violence" (London: Home Office, 1997); Natalie Wilkins, Benita Tsao, Marci F. Hertz, Rachel Davis, and Joanne Klevens, "Connecting the Dots: An Overview of the Links among Multiple Forms of Violence" (Atlanta: National Center for Injury Prevention and Control, Centers for Disease Control and Prevention, 2014).

158 The *New York Times* has been tracking hate crimes and harassment since the election of Donald Trump in their weekly opinion column, "This Week in Hate." See Anna North, "The Scope of Hate in 2017," *New York Times*, June 1, 2017; Anna North, "When Hate Leads to Depression," *New York Times*, April 17, 2017; Audra D. S. Burch, "Facing a Void Left by Hate," *New York Times*, July 9, 2017; Patrick McGreevy, "Hate Crimes Rise in California, State Report Says," *Los Angeles Times*, July 3, 2017.

159 Muslim Advocates, "Map: Recent Incidents of Anti-Muslim Hate Crimes" (2017), www.muslimadvocates.org; Bill Chappell, "Man Charged with Terrorism-Related Murder in Attack at London Mosque" *NPR*, June 23, 2017.

160 Mark Potok, "The Year in Hate and Extremism" (Southern Poverty Law Center, February 15, 2017).

161 Hawes Spencer and Matt Stevens, "23 Arrested and Tear Gas Deployed after a K.K.K. Rally in Virginia," *New York Times*, July 8, 2017.

162 Andrew Markus, "Australians Today: The Australia@2015 Scanlon Foundation Survey" (Victoria: Monash University, 2015), www.scanlonfoundation.org.au.

163 Jason Horowitz, "Italy's Populists Turn up the Heat as Anti-migrant Anger Boils," *New York Times*, February 5, 2018; Alissa J. Rubin, "A New Wave of Popular Fury Could Hit Europe in 2017," *New York Times*, December 5, 2016.

164 Alia E. Dastagir, "2016 Was the Deadliest Year on Record for the LGBTQ Community," *USA Today*, June 12, 2017.

165 Henry O'Connell, Ai-Vyrn Chin, Conal Cunningham, and Brian A. Lawlor, "Recent Developments: Suicide in Older People," *BMJ* 329, no. 7471 (2004): 895; Wilkins et al., "Connecting the Dots."

166 Rajiv Radhakrishnan and Chittaranjan Andrade, "Suicide: An Indian Perspective," *Indian Journal of Psychiatry* 54, no. 4 (2012): 304; Curtin, Warner, and Hedegaard, "Increase in Suicide."

167 Jenni Miller, "The Percentage of Suicidal Teens and Kids Has Doubled since 2008," *New York Magazine*, May 8, 2017; Curtin, Warner, and Hedegaard, "Increase in Suicide."

168 Office for National Statistics, "Suicides in the United Kingdom, 2013 Registrations" (London: National Archives, February 19, 2015).

169 World Health Organization, "Suicide Fact Sheet" (2017), www.who.int.

170 Johann Hari, "Everything You Think You Know about Addiction Is Wrong" (TED Global London, June 2015); Johann Hari, *Chasing the Scream* (London: Bloomsbury, 2015); Paul R. Robbins, "Depression and Drug Addiction," *Psychiatric Quarterly* 48, no. 3 (1974): 374–386; Pier Vincenzo Piazza and Michel Le Moal, "The Role of Stress in Drug Self-Administration," *Trends in Pharmacological Sciences* 19, no. 2 (1998): 67–74; Johann Hari, "The Likely Cause of Addiction Has Been Discovered, and It Is Not What You Think," *Huffington Post*, April 18, 2017.

171 Josh Katz, "Drug Deaths in America Are Rising Faster Than Ever," *New York Times*, June 5, 2017.

172 Brett Wolfson-Stofko, Alex S. Bennett, Luther Elliott, and Ric Curtis, "Drug Use in Business Bathrooms: An Exploratory Study of Manager Encounters in New York City," *International Journal of Drug Policy* 39 (2017): 69–77; Martha Bebinger, "Public Restrooms Become Ground Zero in the Opioid Epidemic," *NPR*, May 8, 2017.

173 "Statistics on Opium Use and Abuse Around the World" (2017), www.opium.org.

174 Youth who are socially isolated (i.e., "socially disinterested") are more likely to engage in violent delinquency and report depressive symptoms. Michael Niño, Gabe Ignatow, and Tianji Cai, "Social Isolation, Strain, and Youth Violence," *Youth Violence and Juvenile Justice* 15 (2017): 299–313.

175 Wilkins et al., "Connecting the Dots."

176 Gilligan, *Why Some Politicians Are More Dangerous Than Others*. See also James Gilligan, *Violence: Reflections on a National Epidemic* (New York: Putnam, 1997).

177 Gun Violence Archive, "Mass Shootings—2015" (2015), http://gunvio lencearchive.org; Sharon LaFraniere, Sarah Cohen, and Richard A. Oppel Jr., "How Often Do Mass Shootings Occur? On Average, Every Day, Records Show," *New York Times*, December 2, 2015; Editorial Board, "511 Days. 555 Mass Shootings. Zero Action from Congress," *New York Times*, November 6, 2017; Max Fisher and Josh Keller, "What Explains U.S. Mass Shootings? International Comparisons Suggest an Answer," *New York Times*, November 7, 2017; "Mass Shootings in the U.S.," *New York Times*, October 2, 2017; Alan Blinder and Daniel Victor, "School Shooting in Kentucky Was Nation's 11th of Year. It Was Jan. 23.," *New York Times*, January 23, 2018.

178 Michael M. Grynbaum, "A Familiar Editorial Split after Parkland Shooting, but Not Everywhere," *New York Times*, February 16, 2018.

179 Audra D. S. Burch, Patricia Mazzei, and Jack Healy, "A 'Mass Shooting Generation' Cries Out for Change," *New York Times*, February 16, 2018.

180 Peter Langman, *Why Kids Kill: Inside the Minds of School Shooters* (New York: Macmillan, 2009).

181 Ibid.

182 Niobe Way, "Why Are Boys So Violent?," *Huffington Post*, May 22, 2013.

183 Benjamin Mueller and Al Baker, "Before Arrests in Bomb-Making Case, a Fascination with Conspiracies," *New York Times*, February 16, 2018.

184 Megan Garvey, "Transcript of the Disturbing Video 'Elliot Rodger's Retribution,'" *Los Angeles Times*, May 24, 2017.

185 Adam Lankford, "Public Mass Shooters and Firearms: A Cross-National Study of 171 Countries," *Violence and Victims* 31, no. 2 (2016): 187–199; Taya Basu, "Why the U.S. Has 31% of the World's Mass Shootings," *Time*, August 24, 2015.

186 Holt-Lunstad et al., "Loneliness and Social Isolation."

187 Louise C. Hawkley and John T. Cacioppo, "Loneliness and Pathways to Disease," *Brain, Behavior, and Immunity* 17, no. 1 (2003): 98–105; Cacioppo and Patrick, *Loneliness*.

188 Julianne Holt-Lunstad, Timothy B. Smith, and J. Bradley Layton, "Social Relationships and Mortality Risk: A Meta-analytic Review," *PLOS Medicine* 7, no. 7 (2010): e1000316.

189 Kristina Orth-Gomér, Annika Rosengren, and Lars Wilhelmsen, "Lack of Social Support and Incidence of Coronary Heart Disease in Middle-Aged Swedish Men," *Psychosomatic Medicine* 55 (1993): 37–43.

190 Courtney E. Detillion, Tara K. S. Craft, Erica R. Glasper, Brian J. Prendergast, and A. Courtney DeVries, "Social Facilitation of Wound Healing," *Psychoneuroendocrinology* 29, no. 8 (2004): 1004–1011; Theodore F. Robles and Janice K. Kiecolt-Glaser, "The Physiology of Marriage: Pathways to Health," *Physiology and Behavior* 79, no. 3 (2003): 409–416.

191 Holt-Lunstad et al., "Loneliness and Social Isolation"; Louise C. Hawkley, Ronald A. Thisted, and John T. Cacioppo, "Loneliness Predicts Reduced Physical Activity: Cross-Sectional & Longitudinal Analyses," *Health Psychology* 28, no. 3 (2009): 354–363; C. Nathan DeWall and Richard S. Pond Jr., "Loneliness and Smoking: The Costs of the Desire to Reconnect," *Self and Identity* 10, no. 3 (2011): 375–385; Aparna Shankar, Anne McMunn, James Banks, and Andrew Steptoe, "Loneliness, Social Isolation, and Behavioral and Biological Health Indicators in Older Adults," *Health Psychology* 30, no. 4 (2011): 377–385; Nicole K. Valtorta, Mona Kanaan, Simon Gilbody, Sara Ronzi, and Barbara Hanratty, "Loneliness and Social Isolation as Risk Factors for Coronary Heart Disease and Stroke: Systematic Review and Meta-analysis of Longitudinal Observational Studies," *Heart* 102, no. 13 (2016): 1009–1016; Louise C. Hawkley and John T. Cacioppo, "Loneliness Matters: A Theoretical and Empirical Review of Consequences and Mechanisms," *Annals of Behavioral Medicine* 40, no. 2 (2010): 218–227; Rikke Lund, Charlotte Juul Nilsson, and Kirsten Avlund, "Can the Higher Risk of Disability Onset among Older People Who Live Alone Be Alleviated by Strong Social Relations? A Longitudinal Study of Non-disabled Men and Women," *Age and Ageing* 39,

no. 3 (2010): 319–326; Bryan D. James, Robert S. Wilson, Lisa L. Barnes, and David A. Bennett, "Late-Life Social Activity and Cognitive Decline in Old Age," *Journal of the International Neuropsychological Society* 17, no. 6 (2011): 998–1005; Tjalling J. Holwerda, Aaartijan T. F. Beekman, Dorly J. H. Deeg, Max L. Stek, Theo G. van Tilburg, Pieter J. Visser, Ben Schmand, Cess Jonker, and Robert A. Schoevers, "Increased Risk of Mortality Associated with Social Isolation in Older Men: Only When Feeling Lonely? Results from the Amsterdam Study of the Elderly (AMSTEL)," *Psychological Medicine* 42, no. 4 (2012): 843–853; Cacioppo and Patrick, *Loneliness*; Luo and Waite, "Loneliness and Mortality"; Andrew C. Patterson and Gerry Veenstra, "Loneliness and Risk of Mortality: A Longitudinal Investigation in Alameda County, California," *Social Science & Medicine* 71, no. 1 (2010): 181–186; Brenda W. J. H. Penninx, Theo Van Tilburg, Didi M. W. Kriegs-man, Dorly J. H. Deeg, A. Joan P. Boeke, and Jacques Th. M. van Eijk, "Effects of Social Support and Personal Coping Resources on Mortality in Older Age: The Longitudinal Aging Study Amsterdam," *American Journal of Epidemiology* 146, no. 6 (1997): 510–519; Sharon Shiovitz-Ezra and Liat Ayalon, "Situational versus Chronic Loneliness as Risk Factors for All-Cause Mortality," *International Psychogeriatrics* 22, no. 3 (2010): 455–462; Reijo S. Tilvis, Mervi H. Kähönen-Väre, Juha Jolkkonen, Jaakko Valvanne, Kaisu H. Pitkala, and Timo E. Strandberg, "Predictors of Cognitive Decline and Mortality of Aged People over a 10-Year Period," *Journals of Gerontology Series A: Biological Sciences and Medical Sciences* 59, no. 3 (2004): M268–M274; Campaign to End Loneliness, "Threat to Health" (2017), www.campaigntoendloneliness.org.

192 Holt-Lunstad et al., "Loneliness and Social Isolation"; Cacioppo and Patrick, *Loneliness*.

193 Dana Crowley Jack, *Silencing the Self: Women and Depression* (Cambridge, MA: Harvard University Press, 1991).

194 Ealine D. Eaker and Margaret Kelly-Hayes, "Self-Silencing and the Risk of Heart Disease and Death in Women: The Framingham Offspring Study," in *Silencing the Self across Cultures: Depression and Gender in the Social World*, ed. Dana Crowley Jack and Alisha Ali (New York: Oxford University Press, 2010), 399–414.

195 The research on self-silencing also reveals the risks of relying on stereotypes and binary notions of constructs like gender. In their 2010 edited book *Silencing the Self across Cultures*, Dana Jack and Alisha Ali brought together scholars from thir-teen different countries to describe and reflect on their research related to gender, depression, and self-silencing.

196 Malcolm Gladwell, *Outliers: The Story of Success* (Boston: Little, Brown, 2008), 9–11.

197 Brown and Gilligan, *Meeting at the Crossroads*; Gilligan, *Joining the Resistance*; Way et al., "'It Might Be Nice to Be a Girl'"; Way and Rogers, "Resistance to Dehu-manization"; Way, *Deep Secrets*.

198 See also Miriam Raider-Roth, *Trusting What You Know: The High Stakes of Class-room Relationships* (San Francisco: Jossey-Bass, 2005).

199 Naomi Klein, "Daring to Dream in the Age of Trump," *Nation*, June 13, 2017.

200 Ibid.

201 Brandon Doman, *What's Your Story? True Experiences from Complete Strangers* (New York: HarperCollins, 2015).

202 The Uni Project, "Make a Place for Learning" (2017), http://theuniproject.org.

203 Project for the Advancement of Our Common Humanity, "Using Science to Transform How We See Each Other" (2017), http://pach.org.

204 Narrative4 and Narrativ are global organizations that include renowned and influential authors, artists, and community leaders who have come together to promote empathy through the exchange of stories. The groups came together in May 2017 under the umbrella of radical listening to respond to our current crisis of connection. See, for example, Kripalu, "Radical Listening, Healing Conversations" (May 31–June 3, 2018). See also New York University, "Radical Listening Project," https://wp.nyu.edu; Carol Gilligan, "The Listening Guide Method of Psychological Inquiry," *Qualitative Psychology* 2, no. 1 (2015): 69–77; Carol Gilligan and Jessica Eddy, "Listening as a Path to Psychological Discovery," *Perspectives on Medical Education* 6, no. 2 (2017): 76–81.

205 Centers for Disease Control and Prevention, "Lifetime Risk of HIV Diagnosis" (Atlanta: CDC, 2016).

206 Linda Villarosa, "America's Hidden H.I.V. Epidemic," *New York Times Magazine*, June 6, 2017.

207 Carol Gilligan and David A. J. Richards, *The Deepening Darkness: Patriarchy, Resistance, and Democracy's Future* (New York: Cambridge University Press, 2009). See also Carol Gilligan and David A. J. Richards, *Darkness Now Visible: Patriarchy's Resurgence and Feminist Resistance* (New York: Cambridge University Press, forthcoming).

The Crisis of Connection in Human Development

1

Cartography of a Lost Time

Mapping the Crisis of Connection

CAROL GILLIGAN, ANNIE G. ROGERS, AND NORMI NOEL

At the edge in development when childhood falls into adolescence, we came to a place with girls that illuminates a lost time. Following girls' development through a series of studies, we had witnessed the onset of some of the more puzzling aspects of women's psychology: the tendency for women to become selfless or voiceless in relationships, to care for others by diminishing themselves, to use their gifts for empathy and relationship to cover over their own feelings and thoughts, and to begin not to know what they want and know.

Girls at seven, eight, nine, and ten generally do not cover what they want and know in relationships; in the absence of physical or psychological threat, they are able to act on the basis of what they know and feel. Moving forward in time, girls by age thirteen often shift away from this clarity and outspokenness into confusion and paralysis. By age fifteen, many girls have learned to hide what they want and know. Having made these moves out of relationship, paradoxically for the sake of having "relationships," girls in adolescence begin to show the same psychological patterns that are familiar to many women and well documented in the psychological literature on women's lives. Our studies with girls led us to name this turning point a crisis of connection and to describe this crisis as a crossroads in development.

The cartography of a lost time we present in this chapter maps an era in women's lives that women tend to forget or look away from. Our project, Strengthening Healthy Resistance and Courage in Girls, grew out of a longitudinal study with girls between the ages of seven and seventeen that involved interviewing them annually over a period of years.[1] We noticed that in approaching adolescence, girls do not anticipate the crisis of connection and that as they come into it, they quickly begin to cover over or forget what they had felt and known as children. Thus we became aware of the limitations of our interview method and the difficulty in charting the moves into dissociation or not knowing that we observed. This difficulty was compounded by our realization that women often live on the other side of this dissociation, so that maps of women's development often unwittingly occlude or obscure this time. We also discovered that for us to stay with what we learned from girls often meant that we had to become aware of and undo dissociative processes within ourselves. For these reasons, our method of working at this juncture changed in important ways.

In addition to annual interviews, we began to meet with girls in intensive and enduring relationships and to self-consciously explore our experience with the girls, both within ourselves and with one another. Our work, designed as a three-year prevention project and an exploration of girls' development as they reach adolescence, thus initiated and encouraged a process of remembering for us as women. Over the course of this project, we saw girls who had been keenly observant of the relational world and very direct in naming or playing out problems in relationships, including problems in our relationship with them, begin to cover things over and act as if problems that existed were not happening or were not problems. At this time, we saw girls still insisting on relationships but changing their expectations or wishes for honesty within them. Initially, we came up against our discomfort with the starkness of girls' perceptions and the directness of their voices, yet we also found ourselves experiencing relief to be in the presence of their clarity and courage. Our attempts to join girls at a time when their strengths were readily apparent and to encourage their resilience have led us to a different understanding of what love and caring mean in relationships between girls and women.

The crisis of connection or relational impasse that lies at the center of our developmental work with women arises precisely because women's knowing often seems to threaten their relationships. In illuminating this crisis, *Meeting at the Crossroads* (the book published by Lyn Mikel Brown and Carol Gilligan in 1992) highlighted the pressures girls face as they enter adolescence not to say what they feel and see and know.[2] And yet for women or girls to dissociate themselves from what they feel and know means to give up authentic relationship. Our work with preadolescent girls clearly documents girls' resistance to making this dissociation and their fight to stay in authentic relationship as they move from childhood into adolescence. Love and caring for girls mean joining their resistance and then staying with them as they experience the psychological and political ramifications of their struggle.[3]

Our work with girls took place in two settings that differed in significant ways: a small, experimental, private elementary school and an urban, public kindergarten through eighth grade school. In both settings, our project included all or most of the girls in a given class. In the private school, we worked with sixth graders for one intensive week following their graduation from the school and then for a weekend in June during the following two years. At the public school, we met with the girls from a combined fourth and fifth grade class weekly during the fall and continued to meet with them weekly in the fall of the next two years. In both settings, we referred to our work together as a Theater, Writing, and Outing Club. The public school girls were diverse in race, culture, and social class. Most of the parents had divorced, some had remarried. The private school girls were mostly white and middle-class; two of the girls had experienced the accidental or violent death of their fathers, the others lived with both parents.

In the course of this work, we found that poetry, the discussion of dreams, theater and voice work, artwork, and writing were essential sources of data for us in our attempts to map a time in women's psychological development that has been lost or forgotten by many women.

Both the girls and we engaged in keeping journals as well as in theater and voice work and the writing of poetry as part of this project. In drawing on this range of work to provide a detailed map of the changes that occur in girls at the edge of adolescence, this chapter explores possible ways of averting the crisis of connection and thus preventing psychological suffering and illness in women. Through a series of writing and theater exercises, we aimed to strengthen girls' voices and encourage them to speak and by doing so to stay in connection with what they are taking in as they go out into the natural and cultural worlds. We also sought to create authentic relationships between girls and women, and our relationships with the girls in our study became the laboratory for this exploration.

We, the three women researchers, are white women from culturally diverse and different social class backgrounds. In this project, we joined our expertise as psychologists and artists. We chose deliberately to work together as three women because doing so seemed essential to staying with our own experiences and sorting out the confusion that accompanies a process of remembering that we found surprising and unsettling. We were charting a history and also the process through which this history comes to be rewritten.

Remembering

Meg's poem, written at age twelve, gives voice to girls' knowing of relationships and feelings. As we three women researchers set out to learn from girls about girls' experiences, so the girls learned from watching us that their lives touched us as well. Watching us, they also saw both the intention and the limitations of our work: we were trying to come with them to a place where they were, which they would leave soon, a place that once left is difficult to reenter.

> What do they learn from watching us?
> Their eager eyes taking in every move.
> Watching us as we talk,
> Joining in with our laughter,
> Yet not really being there.
> Half in, half out of their world of dreams,
> Remembering when they used to be young.
> Like us but different . . .
> Wanting to be with us, but knowing
> Can't really be with us. They can't,
> Go back in time.

Meg's voice at twelve saying women can't go back in time then comes into counterpoint with researcher Annie's voice speaking of making that journey:

> I am going back for her the way I remember her
> Standing on a flat rock in the rain

Rain pouring down her upturned face,
Running into her wide open mouth
She is myself and twelve-years-old.

The process of remembering was key to the discoveries of this project and underscores its relational nature. Our involvement in this process individually and with one another differentiates our work with girls from projects in which women experience themselves solely as providing services for girls or helping them. At the same time, the work we did for ourselves and with one another in the course of this project differs from other psychological work that takes place solely among women, in that the presence of girls was crucial to our experience and our understanding of ourselves. The physical sounds of girls' voices, the kinesthetic presence of girls' bodies, and the daily realities of our activities and conversations with them were the touchstones for our remembering. It was as we came into deeper connection with ourselves and one another that we were able to stay more fully in connection with the girls, to see better what they were doing, and to hear better what they were saying.

Our method, then, was a clinical method of knowing through relationship. Taking our own experience in these relationships as sources of data was essential to understanding ourselves, to making sense of what was happening with the girls, and to explicating the psychological processes of dissociation and also the manifestations of girls' resistance to losing voice and relationship.

In a paper titled "Signposts: Watching for Fainting Canaries," researcher Normi describes her experience in joining this project. Trained as a theater director, actor, and voice teacher, she was very much at home in this work, which centered on girls' voices and outspokenness in relationships. At the same time, she experienced vertigo in coming to remember through taking in the voices of girls. As Normi began to write about this experience, she immediately divided her text into two alternating parts: one called "Facts" and the other called "Story." The facts are the touchstones—the events of her work with the girls and with Annie and Carol. The story is also about the work but encompasses those aspects of it that are commonly denied facticity—the parts that are sensed, that are felt but often unspoken, or if spoken discredited, dismissed as poetry.

Facts

We gather in the gym, ten girls, Annie, Carol and me, preparing for a journey. I find myself unusually nervous at this first meeting. Working with actors to develop their speaking voices is my job. I have never worked with eleven-year-old girls. There are no maps. We have come to draw some.

Story

We stand at the entrance to the underground, itemizing what will be needed to chart the lost country of our girlhood. We three women take hands and enter the small opening in the earth. We move down into what seems to be an abandoned mine shaft. My inner voice is deafening: who has been here before, has anyone remembered the canary cage? The two women move ahead of me in the darkness, and I remember that Carol is a brilliant translator and Annie has paid the boatman on the river Styx.

Facts

Driving home from a day in the country, we are in three cars. The girls bellow to each other, calling from car to car. Voices are huge, bellies responding effortlessly across traffic, wind, space. Raucous laughter: the girls are wild, contagious. These voices are not damaged.

Story

For some time now, we have been moving through the underground in silence. Why did we come here? Are we going back for someone? There is a terrible danger up ahead, but I can't remember why.

Facts

All the girls at times mirror the defenses I see in adult actors. Erin habitually draws down her soft palate to smother sound, Joan uses two notes in her voice. Then Nina reads her poem, and I am stunned by the subtlety and beauty her voice reveals.

Story

A terrible deafening blast. The earth explodes. Everywhere there are cries for help. The wounded lie scattered and broken in darkness. The canary is lying very still on the bottom of her cage, unconscious or dead. Where are the women?

Facts

Rachel in a rage calls her teacher Ted "pig" for not taking them on an outing with him. Her voice is clear, direct; her feelings are powerful. This is a living, breathing, upset, unrestricted girl. The room is charged. She excites and awakens all of us. The circle grows quiet, attentive. I begin to remember.

Story

Above ground, we stumble to safety. I numb the pain by thinking about other things. The sunlight, my dog, the sea. We must be in shock. I hold my breath. A dense fog moves in. There is weeping underground. This is not a place I ever want to return to.

Facts

In the final year, the girls, now in different schools and most of them thirteen, return for a last outing. They all seem confident, easy, relaxed, adjusted. They have come back onto their speaking voices. I am lulled, tricked.

Story

In this final year, I dream I am on top of an enormous mountain of sand. A few eleven-year-old girls are weaving their bikes skillfully in and out of what I gradually realize are half-buried skeletons. We do not make eye contact. In this strange, ominous burial ground, the girls seem at home, and at ease, calling out to each other, moving among the skulls. There is a tacit, sensory agreement that we are not to name what this place is. In code, they speak the language of the senses. Poetry.

I wake weeping.

The Meaning of Love and Relationships

The move from facts to story aims to capture the process of our working, the sometimes dizzying descent into knowing and memory that follows from being with girls. Washing Tess's feet one day in the school sink after playing outside in the park, Normi remembers her meeting with Tess over the rabbit cage in the classroom. Above the cage, a sign says "Animal Rights." Tess asks Normi to take the rabbit out of the cage for her. The rabbit struggles. Normi tells Tess that he does not want to come out. Tess disagrees.

Over his cage, girl and woman face off. Their meeting is complex, clear, familiar, and inaudible to the outer ear. This is not conceptual or logical: this syntax is carried by the breath. Tess wins: Normi reaches for the rabbit. In this silent conversation, Normi overrides her own knowledge—that the rabbit does not want to come out, that the cages are too small, that these animals have no rights—in the name of love and caring for Tess.

The question of what love and relationship mean is pressing for girls in preadolescence. It arose recurrently in the course of our weekly meetings with girls: What was the nature of our relationship with them? Did we really care about them? Did we prefer other girls to them? The girls were especially persistent in their efforts to establish what is real in relationship, who really listens to them, and who are real friends. Issues of trust and of reality repeatedly arise for girls in relational contexts.

Anita, who was scapegoated by other girls in the first year of our meetings because they felt that she—a new girl in the class—had "stolen" the teacher from them, says in her second-year interview with Annie:

> I told them I didn't want to join them, to join their musketeer club. . . .
> Okay, there's the three of them. . . . They were mad at me. Or mad at

each other. I don't know why because they don't like tell me any of their secrets. No. They were mad at me. So I'm going off with the other girls in the classroom. So okay. Tess comes out and starts playing with me. And she says, "I'm sorry I was mad at you." Just to ummm . . . just to like ummm, make Elisa and Maria mad. Then Tess went in, and I went into the bathroom. And Maria came into the bathroom and said, "Anita, I'm not really mad at you." Then I came out and I was walking down the hall and Eliza said she wasn't really mad at me. [laughs] They ride the bus together but they didn't talk to each other on the bus. . . . Just to fool each other, like make each other mad, they said that to me. But Tess. Tess always, now Tess really likes me. But Maria and Elisa, they kind of really don't like me.

In this passage, Anita describes what each girl says to her about not being angry with her and then by watching the girls on the bus, realizes they are saying this to her "just to fool each other"—that they really were not speaking to her at all. She differentiates clearly between Tess who really likes her and Maria and Elisa who "really don't like me" and decides not to join their three musketeers club. However painful that must be, Anita is clear about what she knows and sees. She is taking in a complex relational reality, analyzing intricate patterns of voice and alignment. And she relies on what she knows through experience in judging who really likes her and deciding what to do. In these preadolescent years, girls are not confused by idealized images of relationships or readily taken in by the way people talk about liking or love.

Listening to girls talking about relationships, we get the sense that what care means to them is someone who will stay with them, including someone who will struggle with them in the face of conflict and will voice and listen to strong feelings. Care means someone who cares enough to work things through. When Annie asks twelve-year-old Rosa about a time in her life when she was not listened to, Rosa begins with a story about her parents not listening and her response.

I actually felt sorry for them because my Mom was like, "Rosa come here," and I go, "No." And she goes, "Rosa come here." And I go, "No, I don't have to if I don't want to." And she grabs me by the arms and says, "Why are you doing this to me?" And I go, "Because you don't pay attention to me. When I want to say something, you just ignore me." And she goes, "What?" And I go, "Yes. You pay attention to Joanna, Stephen and Jeff, and that's it. You just don't even notice me that much." And then she goes, "Okay." And then my father was listening and he goes, "So this is the reason you're acting this way?" And I go, "Yes, anyways, I'm twelve years old, going on thirteen, and I'm going to be a teenager. When I'm a teenage [sigh], I'm going to treat your life like hell." And they are like "What?" And I go, "Yes, I'm going to torture you guys so much." And then my Mom started laughing. And I'm like, "I'm not kidding." And my father, he started laughing. And I was like, "What's the matter?" And he goes, "The fact is, this is funny. This is how we acted when we were children." And I started laughing, and it was like, "Oh my God." And then they really got it. They actually listened to me.

While on the one hand Rosa's account can be dismissed as a somewhat superficial if not rude and petty argument with her parents about not listening, when closely read the back-and-forth of it illustrates that both she and her parents are involved. At bottom, this is an argument about caring. To Rosa, caring means listening—actually listening. And her parents, in her experience, were not listening to her. Her outrageous refusal to respond to her mother's request to come here and her mother's response, "Why are you doing this to us?" begin to expose the underlying problem. Strong and angry feelings are voiced, thus coming to the surface. Once the rift in the relationship is exposed, Rosa and her parents can laugh together because, as she says, "they really got it."

In her relationship with her friend Janet, Rosa persists in the same way her mother persisted with her. Responding to Annie's question about how girls handle disagreements with one another, Rosa describes fights that break out among girls over boys:

Oh sometimes we get into fights a lot about the stupidest reasons. Like this week, Janet got mad at me because Janet likes Matthew. Matthew gave me a piece of paper and I said, "Thank you," in a real way. And then looked at her to give her a piece of paper, which she made a face and walked away. And I was like, "What's the matter?" And she said, "Oh, nothing." And I was like, "Is it because Matthew gave me the paper?" And she goes, "Yes." And I was like, "You're not supposed, why are you getting mad at this?"

And she goes, "Well, it seems like you like him and he likes you." And I'm like, "We're just good friends. We broke up last year. So why, we're going to go together?" And she goes "Oh." And I said, "Are you still mad at me?" And she said, "No." And we made up.

Taking in the expression on Janet's face, Rosa does not accept Janet's answer to her question because clearly something is the matter. Rosa's willingness to pursue this matter with Janet leads Janet to voice her fear that Rosa likes Matthew and Matthew likes Rosa rather than her. Rosa then can respond to Janet's fear and jealousy, and Janet, taking in Rosa's response, lets go of her anger, enabling them to make up. This process of working through conflicts in relationships is key to girls' ability to maintain and even strengthen their relationships with one another in the face of the inevitable tensions and misunderstandings that come up.

Just as Rosa knows how to argue in order to connect with her mother, so Janet, speaking of her mother, says that they fight. "I don't like it, but I don't see any way to stop it because it just happens. I mean, we always find one little thing to fight about, or something." Carol says, "You know, when relationships are changing, fights are the only way they can change." Janet asks, "Changing for better or worse?" Carol says, "Actually when I said that, I meant for the good. . . . How do you understand that?" Janet says,

Well, maybe me and my Mom are finding more understanding of one another. WHAT PART DO YOU THINK THE FIGHTS PLAY IN THAT? Getting it out. Getting our inside feelings out, so we can understand each other more. . . . WHAT DO YOU KNOW ABOUT HER INSIDE FEEL-INGS? She loves me [laughs]. DO YOU HAVE A SENSE OF WHAT GOES ON INSIDE HER? I think she just wants to make the family work.

Janet describes fighting as a way of getting inside feelings out, including her mother's feelings of love for Janet. Working through conflicts in relationships, or as Janet says, "finding more understanding of one another," is the way that the family works.

Girls' interest in the question of how to maintain relationships leads them to focus on what to do in the face of conflict. Much of girls' play at this time, including the intricacy of their friendships, can be understood as their attempts to discover how to face and resolve conflicts that threaten love and relationships. The meaning of love and relationship for girls therefore centrally involves girls' questions about how to listen, and how to stay with difficult feelings that may arise and thus come to understand and love one another more.

A Cartography of Lies

What make it impossible to work through conflict and in that sense to maintain real relationships are the various blinds that people create to protect themselves and one another. In the presence of these blinds or lies, it becomes impossible to know what is going on. The girls in our studies often name or play out what is happening in the relational world, and this play can be understood as an invitation into authentic relationship. The very nature of children's thinking—the frame-by-frame recounting of what is happening, the specificity of their feelings, and the "concreteness" of their observations of the external and internal world—makes it possible for girls to take in the full spectrum of their experience and feelings without having to eliminate seeming inconsistencies or frank contradictions. Therefore, girls are able to take in and hold within themselves a rich, complex, sometimes contradictory relational reality. And as they will often name a full range of feelings and thoughts in commenting on the relational weather, so too they name the various ways in which people hide their inner feelings and tell lies.

"I know all about lies," Elisa tells Annie one day. "My house is wallpapered with lies." The girls were discussing when it is good and not good to lie. This question goes to the heart of girls' desire for authentic relationship and also conveys girls' realization that, as Tess says, "people always mask their feelings," which is not always a bad thing. Yet given girls' relational knowing, the question of lies takes on different dimensions.

In her interview with Carol at the end of the second year of the project, Elisa responds to Carol's question, "How can you tell what your Mom is feeling?" by saying,

Depressed. She looks depressed. She's like [six-second pause, sigh, six-second pause] and that's depressed. And happy is: "Come on little bunny, let's go happy-bouncy shopping." WHAT OTHER MOODS DO YOU NOTICE IN YOUR MOTHER? Hmmm . . . there's her normal mood: come on, let's go happy-bouncy shopping. THAT'S HER NORMAL MOOD? Yup, that's her happy mood, where she's ultra, let's go happy-bouncy shopping and I'll buy Maria a dress and you a dress and Jessica a dress. . . . I SEE. THAT'S HOW HAPPY SOUNDS? Yah. WHAT OTHER FEELINGS, WHAT OTHER FEELINGS DO YOU KNOW? Well, there's a lot. [eight-second pause] Some of your questions don't make any sense at all to me.

Elisa's comment that her house is wallpapered with lies sounds implicitly through this passage as she speaks with Carol about the inner world of her mother's depression and replicates its sighs and silences. She has also taken in what seems to be her mother's cover: a "happy-bouncy shopping" persona that Elisa, by her very exaggeration of it, presents as false. Yet Elisa names this persona as her mother's "normal mood," and when asked to name other moods or feelings, she finally says, "Some of your questions don't make any sense at all to me."

It is not clear from this passage whether Elisa is coming up against feelings in her mother that she cannot know or something that does not make any sense to her. But the fact that she can lay out, side by side, her astute observation of her mother's depression and her description of her mother as a "normal," "happy-bouncy-shopping" person suggests that she has taken in a series of feelings and realities that in fact may not make sense at all to her.

Girls' encounters with confusing relational realities arose in the very process of our research, drawing us into questions about that practice that we had not previously asked.

Carol begins the interview with Elisa by asking her if she remembers what the study is about. "Girls developing or something," Elisa says. Carol goes on to explain the reason for interviewing: "To learn from you about what you know, like to be yourself at eleven, about your life, that becomes part of the study." She then tells Elisa that the interview will be "confidential, meaning it's just between you and me."

"And your tape recorder," Elisa adds.

"And the tape recorder," Carol agrees.

Carol then goes on to explain how confidentiality works. "And the tape when it gets transcribed, there are no names on the transcription. And then the transcription is only read by people in our group, working on this project." Elisa says: "Then why don't they just all come in here?"

Clearly Elisa does not know the conventions of psychological practice, but she sees the lies in these conventions: confidentiality both does and does not mean "just between you and me." When Carol continues to explain what is common practice within psychology—the use of disguise to protect people's privacy—Elisa immediately gets it: "Change their name or something?" she asks. And when Carol asks if she wants to choose the name we will call her, she says "Elisa," and thus enters into our framework.

The consequences of this entry, however, are clear. Carol asks if Elisa has any other questions that she wants to ask. "Not really," Elisa says. Carol pursues Elisa's hesitation, asking how she feels about being involved in this research project. "Odd," Elisa says. "It's just odd, peculiar, strange. I don't know. . . . Hmm, I don't know."

Elisa holds onto her sense of the oddness or peculiarity of this relationship. At the same time, she does not know or is unwilling to say what she in fact seems to know about why it feels odd or strange to her.

Several questions arise for us at this juncture: Is she willing to enter into the framework in order to protect Carol from what she knows about the relational structure that Carol is maintaining? Does she want this relationship with Carol and therefore is willing in some sense to override her sense of its peculiarity? Given the beginning—her clarity and insistence on naming what in fact is happening (there is a tape recorder present, her interview will be listened to or read by others whom she cannot see or know)—does she give up the hope for a relationship that she wants, a relationship that is just between her and Carol?

After the interview, Carol observed that Elisa seemed depressed. Was this impression of a damping down of Elisa's vitality a response on Elisa's part to her sense of having given up what she wanted in this relationship? Elisa's final comment, "I don't know," at the end of the opening conversation about the relationship suggests that Elisa was driven into not speaking or not knowing in response to a reality that she could not change.

Our impression that girls at times may protect women from seeing realities that disturb their practice of relationship, whether in the family or in schools or in psychological settings, grew in the course of this work.

We became aware of how readily women including ourselves become complicit in this and in this way unwittingly undermine girls' trusting what they feel and know. Working with girls, we began to ask ourselves new questions about practices that previously we had taken for granted.

For example, the existence of a group of researchers working with the data of this project, although standard practice in doing research, raises a question about relationship: If they are working with the girls' interviews, artwork, poetry, and journals and thus are in some sense in relationship with the girls, why don't they—as Elisa asks—just come into the room? Girls' desire to be in clear relationships with those who are involved with them seems reasonable and also desirable from many points of view. Conversely, it does not seem beneficial to encourage girls to look away from the relational realities they are involved in, however problematic it is to think through the implications of what they want and see and feel and know.

Maria, for example, listens carefully to the world around her, taking in the register of people's voices and recording them within herself. She also is adept at covering her feelings, acting friendly with a group of girls when she really feels mad. "Tell me about this business of acting friendly when you really feel mad: How do you do it?" Carol asks, and Maria demonstrates the shift in her voice as she explains:

> You just don't want everyone to know that you're mad because then they'll all get mad at you, and you wouldn't want them all to be mad at you be- cause then—a big group of people who are mad at you, and you—one lone. You really wouldn't want that to happen, so you just sort of act friendly. . . . You go up to them and say, "So hi, what's up?"

Maria's voice rises to the falseness of this presentation of herself as cheer- ful and friendly when she is really feeling angry and sad. The others have not listened to her, will not listen to her, she believes; it will only make matters worse to get angry, she thinks. Carol asks whether the girls could tell that she was mad. "Not really," Maria says. When asked whether she can tell when others are acting friendly but are really mad, she says, "I can with my Mom. I've seen her all my life." The way she tells with her mother is because she hears it in her voice. Carol asks: "What do you say?" Maria says with emphasis, "'It seems like you're mad at me.'" And then she goes (imitates a high, false voice) "'No, I'm not mad at you.' So okay. . . ." "And then what?" Carol asks. "Just sort of forget about it."

Maria hears her mother's voice as disconnected from her mother's feelings. The relationship reaches an impasse. Maria does not have direct access to how her mother feels. "Do you believe her?" Carol asks. "Sometimes I do and sometimes I don't."

When Annie asks Tess "Have you ever been in a relationship where you had to do something courageous because it was important to you?" Tess says,

> A boyfriend. [four-second pause] If they say to you, "Don't hang up, don't hang up, don't hang up," and you're really pissed off at them, you should hang up. Because they're saying "don't hang up," like everything is alright. . . . If you don't hang up, they're going to say, "Okay, good." And then they try to soften you up and then you realize, "God, I really hated that." [Annie and Tess laugh] So, you've got to kind of take courage and go, while they're blabbing on and on, and say, "Wait a minute." You just, you need to take some power from that.

Annie asks, "How would they be trying to soften you up?" Tess says, "Like, 'I'm sorry. I didn't mean it . . . I wasn't thinking.' It's like, 'Shut up, you were, you knew what you were doing. Now just shut up and listen to my side of the story.'"

In order to protect herself from taking in what she does not believe to be true, or in Tess's terms "being softened up," she must stand firmly in what she knows—what she calls "my side of the story." In staying with the truth of her experience, Tess risks being called hurtful or rude. Her awareness of these risks is evident as she explains how she does not speak what she feels to her relatives because of her wish not to hurt their feelings. When she feels like saying "Shut up" to them, she

> Just goes into the other room and says, "Shut up, shut up, shut up." Then I [slaps her mouth] that, and I give myself a little bit [*sic*] hit on the mouth, and then I walk out with a smile. [laughs] And I kind of do like this through my hair, and I just of sit there like, "Yah." And I don't say anything . . . 'cause I know I would really hurt some people's feelings if I did.

While she stops herself from speaking (by hanging up or leaving the room), Tess at twelve still knows what she feels and why she feels she can't say it. In our research, we have repeatedly seen a pattern whereby girls at eleven and twelve describe silencing themselves as a strategy of self-protection and also a way of not hurting other people's feelings or provoking retaliation. Initially, this strategy is overt and self-conscious; girls know what they feel and why they are not speaking. But then, after girls stop speaking, the description of the strategy (the reasons for not speaking) disappears and with it their awareness of the need to protect themselves and to act wisely in relationships.

At this point, what remains is often only the selfless justification for not speaking—the wish not to hurt other people's feelings. Concerns with honesty or authenticity in relationships have been occluded by idealized images of relationships and of self, as well as conventional understandings of what it means to be a good woman. Concerns with others are now pitted against concerns about oneself. Our research identifies adolescence as the time when this move out of relationship is both enacted and enforced among girls. This crisis of connection can explain the heightened signs of psychological distress at this time (the sudden high incidence among girls of depression, eating disorders, cutting, and other forms of destructive behavior). Without mapping the time just before adolescence, this loss of connection cannot be understood as a loss or its seeming inevitability questioned.

Deep Pools of Truth

What would it mean to rid this relational geography of its accepted lies? Our research project began to seem like a microcosm of a larger cultural reality—deceptions and lies about relationships that are especially dangerous for women. The meaning of care, like the meaning of love and relationship, became more complex. What does it mean to care for girls at the time of their adolescence? The practices of caring that have long been associated with the work and the worlds of women have been at once idealized and denigrated. Preadolescent girls push women beyond both the idealization and the denigration of women's caring into deep pools of truth about relationships. And out of this experience comes a new understanding of what it means truly to care.

In the second year of our three-year project, the girls taught us two games and insisted that we play these games with them. Both games speak to girls' need to voice painful feelings and to join with one another and with women in confronting confusing realities. The first game was "Agony Tag." It involved giving voice to agony in concert with others who had been tagged until the whole group—girls and women—is writhing on the floor moaning or shrieking. The second game was "Killer." Killer hones one's eye for false relationship. In the game, the group walks in a circle shaking hands as they meet and exchanging friendly greetings. One person, secretly designated the killer, uses her index finger to tap someone whose hand she is shaking. The "killed" person then has to shake hands with one more person before collapsing melodramatically. The others have to guess: Who is the killer? To spot the killer requires careful scrutiny of the relational scene.

As we played these games with the girls, we came to see their wisdom. They were playing out with us precisely those issues that seem most treacherous and most central in their development: the ability to join with other girls and women in expressing painful or agonizing feelings, and the ability to see beneath the surface of conventional politeness, to discern under the cover of friendly greetings which relationships are safe and which are deadly. The girls, we realized, were teaching us how to care for them.

As girls becoming women face conventions of love and relationship that will encourage them not to speak and eventually not to know their feelings of sadness and anger, jealousy and hurt, and also not to see the lies and the treachery of false relationship, so they lead women back into these feelings and into knowledge that women may have suppressed. A surprise of our work lay in the discovery of how readily this knowledge is both retrieved and recovered.

> In the cartography of this lost time I roll down hills, come in red-cheeked laughing, snow boots puddle up the hallway, vision sun-spotted with bright light, the light white into blackness stops time. . . . I sit with women writing . . . deep pools of truth glaze up, freeze, thaw and clear up with anger. Love? What is love in the lost time?
> —Annie's journal

Covering loss with words. Embroidering beauty over the ragged hole of loss. An inner sadness and a sign: do not touch. I am touched so directly, so immediately by these girls . . . I begin to move directly in their presence, to speak without hesitation, to find a kind of freedom and pleasure that I relish with Annie and with Normi. To leave this is to face the sadness of its loss, also to feel the hopelessness, the lure of the culture.
—Carol's journal

Carol Writes

On the last day of the first year of the theater, writing, and outing club, the public school girls file out of the school in a straight line rather than running pell-mell into our cars to greet us in the way they usually do. Something is amiss. As we drive and then walk to the place of our meeting, I see unfolding before me a dramatization of what in fact is happening: the girls are separating themselves from the women who are leaving them. Like a dumb show, without words they are enacting the ending.

They keep to themselves. Admonishing one another to stay in line and be quiet, they dramatize feminine goodness. In doing so, they reveal how closely they have observed the conventions of good woman behavior. But their script turns out to be very different.

Like gazelles they move across the quadrangle and enter the building. In the room, they form a circle. We—the three women—are the audience to what follows. The girls who have not acknowledged our presence are in fact performing for us. One by one, each girl enters the center of the circle and the group tunes to the cadence and pitch of her voice, going with her where she wants to go. The accuracy of ear is extraordinary and the range of their joining extends from one girl's echoing question, "Is it going to snow?" because it is December and the air is heavy, to another's humorous "cha-cha-cha," to another's intricate dance steps, and then into more serious questions, revealing an array of feelings and an intention whose point is not yet clear. The girls' concentration on what they are doing suggests that the audience is irrelevant and its composition inconsequential until another woman, familiar to us but not to the girls, enters the room and joins us in quietly watching. Then the conversational nature of this drama becomes clear as the girls insist on her leaving.

The girls break the circle after everyone has been in the center, and they organize games that move across the length of the room. Two stand on chairs at one end, keeping a tally on the board. Still, it is as though we are not present, and yet our presence is clearly essential. As the time begins to run out, we decide we must talk with the girls about the ending. And at this point, their point becomes clear.

They have been revealing the ending—dramatizing the fact that we are leaving them—and when we begin to talk about the ending, the girls who are now sitting in a row begin singing and effectively drown out our voices.

On the way back to the cars, they speak for the first time. A dead squirrel lying frozen in a yard we are passing becomes the occasion for the girls to say that we do not care, we have no feelings. They insist that the squirrel is alive and in need of resuscitation. They want to summon the Animal Rescue League. Their shouting summons the neighbors. And as their voices become louder and they become more insistent, I want to shut them into a dark closet at the same time as I want to cheer them. They will not paper over the ending or talk with us about our leaving them or speak with us about our relationship in the face of the break that we have imposed. Rejecting the conventions of good woman behavior, the orderly silence and staying in line that they dramatized at the outset, they have created a ritual, using their voices and their bodies, to reveal and give form to what they feel and know. What they have done is to show us what we are doing and also what we are missing by leaving them. These courageous and wild and irreverent knowing girls, whose affections run deeper than we had imagined and who insist on honesty in our relationship with them.

Annie Writes

Pandemonium. Anger. Shouts. Screaming, punctuated by high-pitched squeals. The girls race around the classroom, out to the bathroom, and come back in slamming the door. It is near the end of the second year of the project. Frustrated, I wonder: "Is there no way in?" Then listening more carefully, "You are leaving us, and we have no choice." They step away, turn away. The room with its dirty carpet and school desks does not feel like a place for such intense feelings. But their feelings pour into the room. They go into the closet and come out one by one, displaying anger, sadness, contempt, hope, hopelessness. I search their faces, and find a way in. Flickers of hunger waken in me, hunger for something like truth between us, among us. I am afraid to enter this within myself. It has been building like a storm over the weeks—their protests, their singing, the rituals gone awry, the unspoken in the room—and now this storm has broken over us. Within us. The girls accuse us: "You don't want to be with us," "You've wanted to leave us since the first day," "You can't leave us without our consent." A pause. "Oh yes they can."

We fight back. We say, "We can't work with you like this," "Why should we speak if you don't want to listen?" Across the circle, we shout to them. Their eyes drop, whispers break out among the girls. Janet kicks over a juice bottle while Libby lies flat on her belly and pounds the rug, chanting, "I hate them."

Suddenly my body aches with love and admiration for these girls. But how will we go on, into this second ending? In the midst of this, Normi begins an old camp song: "Rise Up O Flame." Several of the girls laugh but Janet begins to sing with Normi. Then, as a group, the girls rush out to the bathroom. They come back gradually, quiet. Hairbrush in hand, Rosa stands behind Libby and brushes her hair into a ponytail. Maria sits down on top of a desk. I meet her eyes. She grimaces, looks away, looks back, those dark eyes. . . . Everything is fragile after the storm, everything new.

The girls take sheets of paper from us to create plays and scurry under the tables to write out their plans. Suddenly they are back to borrow clothes. Normi's scarf, my black hat, Carol's long coat. During their impromptu plays, I sit on a desk swinging my feet. Tess comes up, moves another desk over and sits next to me, her whole body leaning into mine. I pat her knee, she glances at me once, briefly. Suddenly there is Elisa, leaning on the other side against my shoulder.

At the end of the third year, Libby asks: "Why would we end this?" Our project is over, we explain, we have no more money. "We can have a bake sale, we will have a car wash, we can set up a toll." The girls are insistent. Why would we end this?

Normi Writes

Facts

Kelly cannot climb the water tower to see the view. The other girls scamper up and down the tower ladder for the vista of the New Hampshire mountains. Kelly, the oldest, is the only one who cannot do this. Loss of balance.

Carol has a strong memory of a point when she could no longer climb the high ladder to hang lights in the theater. I think of my dizziness in entering and leaving this work with the girls. It is culture shock.

Kelly has now, at thirteen, almost completely fallen off her speaking voice. She is polite, attentive, quiet, ready to please, more grown up. More like me. Carol throws up a red flag. Kelly is no longer outspoken, direct like Amy or Rachel. Where has her voice gone? Is this the disappearance of the language of the senses, a deafening of the inner ear? Vibrations must have sympathetic surfaces in order to strengthen and re-sound, in order not to die out.

Story

Many of us are still in shock. The girls are powerful and often delicate guides. They guard their world savagely, for as long as they can.

Coda

The relational strengths of girls—their capacity for empathy, their knowing what goes on moment by moment within the relational surround—protect them from entering false relationships but also place them at risk in cultures where the truths of relationship are for the most part guarded and unspoken. The complexity of these truths and the depth of feeling that surround relational experiences in girls' and women's lives led us to work through theater exercises and writing—art forms that could hold the layering of psychological experience. We do not know if this work can prevent the losses of connection many women find familiar. In creating a map of the crisis, however, we wish to invite others into the places we have been with girls and to document for girls, for women, and also for men what is at stake.

NOTES

1 Lyn Mikel Brown and Carol Gilligan, *Meeting at the Crossroads: Women's Psychology and Girls' Development* (Cambridge, MA: Harvard University Press, 1992).

2 Ibid.

3 For further reading, see Carol Gilligan, "Joining the Resistance: Psychology, Politics, Girls and Women," *Michigan Quarterly Review* 24, no. 4 (1990): 501–536; Carol Gilligan, *Joining the Resistance* (Cambridge: Polity Press, 2011); Carol Gilligan and Annie Rogers, "A Paradigm Shift in Psychology: Reframing Mothering and Daughtering," in *"Daughtering" and Mothering*, ed. Janneke van Mens-Verhulst (New York: Routledge, 1993); Annie Rogers, "Voice, Play and a Practice of Ordinary Courage in Girls' and Women's Lives," *Harvard Educational Review* 63, no. 3 (1993): 265–295; Carol Gilligan and Naomi Snider, *Why Does Patriarchy Persist?* (New York: Polity Press, 2018).

2

Boys' Nature, Boys' Culture, and a Crisis of Connection

JUDY Y. CHU

As a parent of a thirteen-year-old, I have spent a fair amount of time observing kids and talking to other parents about kids. As a researcher who studies boys' development, I am especially inclined to notice how boys behave and how adults view them. I have found that when adults talk about boys, regardless of the context or the particular boys involved, someone will usually remark at some point that "boys will be boys." If the boys are young, this remark is often a response to their rowdy and rambunctious play (e.g., when they are running around, being loud, or otherwise brimming with energy). If the boys are older, this remark typically follows displays of emotional detachment (e.g., when they act callous or aloof). Regardless of whether adults buy into gender stereotypes, there is a tendency to focus on behaviors that confirm gender-based assumptions. I have rarely, if ever, heard adults say that "boys will be boys" when boys are, for instance, quietly reading, snuggling with a parent, or expressing concern for a friend who is sad. Although boys can also be calm, affectionate, and considerate, we are less likely to acknowledge these "feminine" qualities in boys, much less count them among the attributes that constitute masculine identities. Nevertheless, these qualities are a part of boys' (as well as girls') humanity and enable them to establish the kinds of relationships that are crucial to their healthy development.

Along with the other chapters in this volume, this chapter seeks to uncover the truth about boys. The point is not to suggest that there is one right way to be for everyone everywhere. Rather, the idea is to acknowledge a fuller range of what boys are capable of knowing and doing in relationships, and thereby expand their possibilities. This chapter builds upon feminist research that revealed how girls' socialization toward patriarchal constructions of femininity can hinder their ability to have a voice within their relationships with others.[1] These empirical studies of girls at early adolescence documented how they struggle to choose between having a voice and having relationships, when societal pressures to conform to norms of feminine behavior make these incompatible.[2] Faced with this dilemma, girls astutely view both options—when mutually exclusive—as resulting in loss.[3] If they choose to preserve their voices and forsake their relationships, they lose the sources of validation and support that enable their healthy self-expression. If they choose to preserve their relationships and forsake their voices, they diminish their chances of developing genuine, close connections.[4] Evidence of girls' healthy resistance against pressures that threaten their connections to themselves and to others has challenged patriarchal values and raised questions about whether boys' gender socialization could also be detrimental to their relationships and well-being, despite the social advantages of acting masculine.[5]

This chapter describes how boys' socialization toward patriarchal constructions of masculinity can result in disconnections from themselves and from others. It highlights boys' relational capabilities, which are often overlooked and underestimated in the literature on boys and in their everyday lives. One reason why we may overlook boys' relational capabilities is that we do not expect to see them. To the extent that our expectations are influenced by gender stereotypes, we are more likely to view, for instance, boys' rough or unruly behaviors as normal. Likewise, when boys are gentle, sensitive, or shy, we may view those instances or those boys as exceptions. One reason why we may underestimate boys' relational capabilities is that they are not always apparent, in part because boys' gender socialization forces a split between what boys know and what boys show.

This chapter traces a shift in boys' relational presence during early childhood that reflects how they are responding to intensified pressures to display gender-appropriate behaviors. By focusing on boys at this age, we gain insight into a critical period of transition when they are still able and willing to reveal their relational capabilities but are also beginning to cover them up as they become savvy in their social interactions. As boys spend increasing amounts of time interacting with peers and adults at school, they discover that their masculinity can be questioned, and that therefore it must be continually proven. In what is considered a socially adaptive move, boys learn to accommodate their behaviors to group norms. Yet, this accommodation comes at a cost, as constraints on their self-expression and a more guarded (albeit self-protective) approach to relationships inadvertently sabotage boys' chances of developing the close connections they seek.

This chapter draws on a study of boys at early childhood that explored how they negotiate their identities, behaviors, and relationships in light of culturally constructed messages about masculinity and societal pressures to conform.[6] Participants in the study were all six boys in the pre-kindergarten class at an independent elementary school in New England. Four of the boys are Caucasian, one is Asian American, and one is African American. They grew up in single- and dual-parent families living in middle- and upper-middle-class suburban neighborhoods. All of the boys were four years old when I met them in the fall of their pre-kindergarten year. This exploratory study involved working closely with these boys over a two-year period. Using a relational, voice-centered approach to psychological inquiry, my research methods centered on developing trusting relationships in which the boys could share their insights in their words and on their terms.[7] I began with ethnographic observations that provided opportunities for the boys and me to get to know each other, and continued with semi-structured interviews wherein the boys could opt to meet with me in groups or on their own.

Boys' Relational Capabilities

Through focusing on their perspectives to understand how they experience their gender socialization, I found that boys possess certain relational capabilities. They can be articulate in the sense that they express their views in a clear and coherent manner. They can be direct in the sense that they come right out and say what they mean. They can be authentic in the sense that their behaviors reflect what they are thinking and feeling. They can be attentive in the sense that they listen carefully and respond thoughtfully when interacting with others. Consistent with studies that show adolescent boys to be self-aware, emotionally perceptive, and socially astute,[8] the four-year-old boys in my study demonstrated the ability to be fully present and genuinely engaged in their relationships.[9] For example, during my first attempt to interview the boys—when they were not yet sure of my intentions—Jake asked me, "What exactly do you want to learn?" When I replied, "I want to learn what it's like to be a boy," Jake turned to consult Mike, who asked Jake, "Do you think we should trust her?" Jake glanced at me, then turned back to Mike and, with a smile on his face, shook his head slowly from side to side to indicate no. I appreciated that these boys engaged me only when they felt ready and only in ways that felt comfortable to them. In fact, it was because these boys were honest in expressing their initial doubts that I felt I could believe them when they eventually decided to show and tell me things.

The boys' parents also appreciated the boys' relational capabilities. When asked what they cherished most in their sons ("What makes you think, 'I hope he never loses that'?"), the boys' fathers mentioned the boys' "spunk" and "exuberance," their ability to be "out there," "imaginative," "joyful," and "friendly"—qualities that made the boys "charming" and "endearing." The boys' mothers additionally mentioned the boys' "loyalty" and "protectiveness" and how their sons were "paying close attention to [them]" and "tuned in to how things affect [them]." The parents expected that things would change as the boys grew older and began to pull away from them physically and emotionally. Nevertheless, the parents were hopeful that they might find a way to maintain the tenderness and affection that they were experiencing (and enjoying) in their relationships with their young sons.

Boys' relational capabilities are not surprising in light of infant studies showing that all humans are born with a fundamental capacity and primary desire for close, responsive relationships.[10] People are not only born *into* relationships, they are born *ready for* relationships. Moreover, it is human nature to seek connections and resist disconnections. Yet, within cultures that emphasize individuation and separation as indicators of maturity, health, and, for boys, masculinity, boys are often taught to view their capacity and desire for meaningful connections—which are stereotypically associated with femininity—as a liability. This tendency to associate boys' identity development with a move away from relationships may explain why older adolescent boys and adult men report fewer close friendships and lower levels of intimacy within their friendships, as compared with girls, women, and younger boys.[11]

Boys' Gender Socialization

Despite progress made in recent decades toward gender equity, boys and girls continue to encounter different expectations in society today. Starting soon after they are born, most boys are exposed to messages about masculinity (i.e., what it means to be a "real" boy or man) and pressures to conform to norms of masculine behavior. Whereas cultural constructions of femininity have expanded to represent a fuller range of girls' and women's abilities, cultural constructions of masculinity remain narrowly focused on toughness, indifference, and self-sufficiency, even though studies have revealed this archaic image of masculinity to be ultimately unattainable, unsustainable, and/or dysfunctional.[12] Accordingly, the content of boys' gender socialization has not changed much. Even boys whose families encourage a range of qualities, interests, and skills may nevertheless feel compelled to align with conventions of masculinity, as a result of their exposure to media and social influences outside the home.

A key theme in boys' gender socialization is that masculinity must be proven.[13] It is not enough simply to be anatomically male; a boy must establish his masculine identity publicly, for instance by displaying gender-appropriate attitudes and behaviors.[14] Moreover, because a boy's masculinity can be called into question at any time and by anyone, boys must always be prepared to defend it.[15] In cultures where masculinity is defined as the opposite of femininity, proving masculinity involves not only aligning with masculine norms but also differentiating from femininity.[16] In the absence of formal initiations into manhood, any deviation from masculine norms can raise doubts about a boy's (or man's) masculinity and also his sexuality.[17] So long as the need or wish for emotionally close relationships is associated with femininity, a boy's desire for this kind of intimacy will be at odds with his masculinity and may be regarded as a weakness.[18] Consequently, boys who want to show that they are not "sissies" or "mama's boys" learn to downplay their relational capabilities and inclinations.[19]

Early childhood has been identified as a critical period of transition in boys' socialization when gendered norms of behavior are introduced and reinforced.[20] On one hand, boys at this age have the cognitive capacity to verbalize their thoughts and feelings, and they are still free to express themselves in ways that older boys have learned can be unsafe. In other words, young boys are able and willing to show what they know. On the other hand, boys at this age are also becoming more selective about what they reveal about themselves and to whom, as they encounter new pressures to demonstrate maturity (e.g., that they are big kids, not babies) and to prove masculinity (e.g., that they are boys, not girls). Whereas demonstrating maturity is not a gender-specific expectation (e.g., most kids are encouraged to take pride in their ability to behave in ways that are age-appropriate), proving masculinity appears to be more important for boys—in the sense that deviance from gender norms is more strictly policed and more harshly punished—than proving femininity is for girls.

However, the need to prove masculinity was only a part of what motivated the boys in my study to align their behaviors with masculine norms. In fact, it was primarily a means to another end. What the boys really wanted was to be able to identify with and relate to each other. They were not seeking social approval in general. Rather, they sought to feel accepted and valued within specific relationships, and they were led to believe that their conformity to group norms would help them to achieve this goal.

The Mean Team

For the boys in my study, the ways in which socialization messages and pressures manifested within their peer interactions, and also the boys' motivation to comply, were best illustrated by their involvement with the Mean Team—a club created by the boys, for the boys, for the stated purpose of acting against the girls. In many ways, the Mean Team was a microcosm of the cultural context in which these boys learned to align with norms of masculine behavior. Most obviously, the Mean Team emphasized the boys-versus-girls dynamic that had emerged in their class. In addition to acting *against* girls, the Mean Team reinforced the notion that boys should act *differently from* girls (who composed the Nice Team). The Mean Team also formalized the hierarchy among the boys, so that the most domineering of the boys became its leader while the other boys became his subordinates. When Rob told me that Mike was the boss of the Mean Team, he explained:

ROB: [Mike] leads the whole gang. He decides *every*thing. We don't get
   to say *any*thing.
JUDY: What do you think about that?
ROB: [casually] It's okay with me.
JUDY: What happens if [Mike] tells you to do something that you don't
   want—
ROB: [cutting me off and stating firmly] I do it.
JUDY: Even if you don't want to?
ROB: [seriously] Yeah, I'm 'posed to do it.

Like Rob, the other boys learned through their participation on the Mean
Team that being a part of the group requires obedience, regardless of
their own preferences.

Once established, the Mean Team became the primary way to identify
with the boys (e.g., be one of the boys). For instance, when I asked the
boys what I would have to do if I wanted to learn how to be a boy, Tony
replied instantly, "Be on the Mean Team." Membership in this boys' club
also provided a means to relate to the boys and could instill a sense of belonging (e.g., being with the boys), as Jake and Tony demonstrated when
they referred to themselves as being Mike's "men" and "in [Mike's] army."
Moreover, being on the Mean Team provided some assurance of support.
As Rob explained, "If we can't do [something that Mike tells us to do], we
all group together and do it." Drawn by this promise of camaraderie, the
boys willingly joined the Mean Team and followed Mike's lead.

There were also conditions, however, to being a member of the Mean
Team. Although it was expected that all of the boys would be on the
Mean Team, their membership was not guaranteed. For example, when
Dan accused Rob of breaking one of Mike's rules, Dan swiftly and suc-
cinctly meted out the punishment.

DAN: [to Mike] So he has to go all by himself.
MIKE: Yeah, fired.
DAN: [to Rob] You're fired from the Mean Team. You're on the Nice
   Team. You're a girl.

The possibility of being fired from the Mean Team (and losing their status as boys) meant that it was no longer safe for the boys just to say or

do what they wanted, particularly if it involved disobeying Mike and/or deviating from group norms. To the extent that they wished to retain their group membership and avoid negative consequences, the boys became more self-conscious and careful to maintain at least the appearance of upholding the status quo. For instance, during a private meeting with Jake, he revealed that

> JAKE: All of the girls in the class are my friends, but I act as though they aren't.
> JUDY: How come?
> JAKE: Well, because if Mike finds out . . . that I like the girls, he'll fire me from his club.
> JUDY: The Mean Team?
> JAKE: Yeah. That would be a real bummer 'cause then I won't be on a team.

Similarly, Tony, who liked to play with dolls, learned to deny it when he was in the company of his peers (who said they would not like a boy who plays with dolls). One of the boys' mothers—referring to the wariness with which the boys were negotiating their peer interactions—noted that what looks to adults like fun is actually work for the boys.

As the costs of participating on the Mean Team began to outweigh the benefits, some of the boys became disenchanted with this arrangement. For instance, whereas Rob had been willing at first to go along with the group, by the end of the year he had changed his mind about the Mean Team and told me, "I don't feel like it anymore. . . . They make me go places, but I want to go where I want to, not where they tell me." After thinking through his options, Rob concluded solemnly,

> ROB: There's no way to get off the Mean Team.
> JUDY: What would happen if you tried to quit?
> ROB: [The boys] would *just* be mean to me.
> JUDY: Do you want to be off the Mean Team?
> ROB: I sort of do, but sort of don't.

Perhaps with age and experience, Rob would discover ways to remain a part of the group *and* have some say in matters. But at the time, he felt compelled to choose between the two. Eventually, Rob broke away from the Mean Team and ended up alone, which he said he did not mind. And, recalling girls' dilemma at adolescence wherein the decision to withhold their genuine thoughts and feelings effectively compromised the quality of their relationships,[21] it occurred to me that if Rob stayed in relationships in which he had no voice, he might nevertheless end up feeling alone.

A Shift in Boys' Relational Presence

As the boys became more strategic about how they conducted themselves with others, there was a notable shift in their relational presence. It is not that the boys were in relationship and then out of relationship, nor that they were present and then not present, but that the quality of their presence in relationships changed as they learned to accommodate their behaviors to masculine norms. The boys did not tell me about the shift. Rather, I observed it in their interactions with each other and experienced it in their interactions with me. For example, when I first met Jake (when he was four years old), there had been no need to second-guess his meaning because he would say exactly what he was thinking and feeling, usually in a straightforward manner. However, over the course of his pre-kindergarten year, Jake found that speaking his mind (which his parents encouraged at home) could get him into trouble with adults and peers at school. Jake adapted to his situation by becoming more cautious about what he expressed and how he expressed it. Sure enough, by regulating his self-expression, Jake was better able to avoid trouble. But this adaptation also made it harder to discern his true intentions, and put a damper on his otherwise outgoing spirit.

In addition to regulating their self-expression, the boys also began to posture more. This typically involved displaying masculine bravado and nonchalance—like a tough guise or cool pose—to shield their vulnerability and impress their peers.[22] For instance, when I asked the boys what they wanted to be when they grow up, Rob said proudly, "I'm going to be in the army." When Mike warned him, "Then you'll get killed," Rob feigned indifference, "I don't care" and Jake joined in, "Yeah, I don't care. That's what I want." When I asked Jake, "You want to be in the army?" Jake replied emphatically, "Yeah, and I want to get killed." As the boys' outward behaviors became separated from their inner worlds, their public personas felt more contrived and their relational capabilities became less apparent. Whereas these boys had demonstrated a remarkable ability to be articulate, direct, authentic, and attentive, they began to appear inarticulate, indirect, inauthentic, and inattentive. And as the boys' pretense gradually overshadowed their presence, they could seem disengaged, disinterested, or even defensive in their interactions. That is, they began to look more like stereotypical "boys," or how boys are often said to be. One of the boys' fathers noted how it was ironic that "in trying to make a good impression," the boys began to "cover up" their innermost qualities, because "actually, [those qualities are] what's most appealing" about the boys.

Although regarded as socially adaptive, the boys' emerging self-restraint could make them seem indifferent. Likewise, their masculine posturing could make them seem inaccessible. As a result, it became more difficult for the boys to engage with others (and for others to engage with them) in ways that are conducive to developing close relationships. However, despite becoming more guarded in their interactions, the boys did not lose their relational capabilities. In contrast to stereotypes that depict boys (particularly older boys) as incapable of or uninterested in emotionally intimate relationships, empirical studies indicate that boys' capacity and desire for meaningful connections persist beyond infancy, through early childhood, and into adolescence.[23] Thus, the shift in the boys' relational presence during early childhood is neither complete nor irreversible.

By observing boys at the age when they begin to shift their relational presence in response to their gender socialization, I saw how they learn to project an image of masculinity that is familiar (especially within our "boys will be boys" culture) but misrepresents boys by distorting, or portraying only a fraction of, what they are capable of knowing and doing in relationships. My study also revealed how, as boys become adept at assuming the guise of masculinity, it becomes easy to mistake culture for nature. What is often viewed as "natural" for boys actually reflects boys' adaptation to a culture of masculinity that centers on hierarchy and competition and emphasizes the need for boys and men to be (or at least appear) tough, indifferent, and self-sufficient. As Kimmel points out, if masculine qualities were inherent and masculine behaviors came naturally to boys, then the many social mechanisms that are currently in place to ensure boys' gender conformity would not be necessary.[24]

The significance of these findings is that they outline ways that boys' socialization toward patriarchal constructions of masculinity can result in disconnections from themselves and from others. Given that relationships depend on presence, constraints on boys' self-expression can decrease their chances of developing relationships wherein they feel truly known and accepted. In turn, as presence depends on relationships, boys' constricted relationships leave them without the support they need to feel confident being themselves. Although boys are motivated to conform by their desire to identify with and relate to their peers (e.g., be one of the boys and with the boys), their alignment with masculine norms sets them upon a developmental trajectory that ultimately compromises their presence, their relationships, and their ability to be fully present in their relationships.

Boys' Healthy Resistance

While individuals may experience pressures to display gender-appropriate attitudes and behaviors, as prescribed within their particular social and cultural contexts, their internalization of prevailing gender ideologies is not inevitable. As active participants in their learning, individuals can mitigate the impact of their socialization on their developmental outcomes, for instance through the ways they make meaning of cultural messages and respond to societal pressures. Just as researchers observed in adolescent girls and adolescent boys, boys at early childhood demonstrate the capacity to resist as well as comply with societal expectations that are intended to curb their impulses, guide their behaviors, and shape their identities.[25]

There may be age-related differences, however, in the focus of boys' resistance. For instance, in adolescent boys (and girls) who are exploring their individual identities, healthy resistance seems mainly directed at conventions of gender that conflict with their own sense of who they are and how they want to be. Resistance can be explicit, as when individuals speak out against stereotypes, or implicit, as when individuals take pride in their differences, especially qualities that are deemed deviant.[26] When reconciling *how they are said to be* with *how they experience themselves to be*, boys at early childhood may similarly resist gender norms that misrepresent them. However, the young boys in my study were more concerned with not being bossed around than with challenging cultural constructions of gender. Sometimes, the boys did not mind going along with the group (and conforming to gender norms). For example, when Rob first told me about the Mean Team and I asked if he liked being on it, he replied casually, "Yeah, 'cause I like being mean," which for these boys, at this age, meant being boisterous and stirring up harmless mischief.

Among these younger boys, healthy resistance seemed mainly directed at impositions that precluded them from feeling like they had a voice and a choice. Although the boys were mostly willing to comply with rules of the classroom and even rules set by the boss of the Mean Team, all of them vehemently refused to be told what they could or could not do, especially by peers whom they perceived to be their equals or subordinates. For instance, when Dan made a suggestion while playing with Mike and immediately proceeded to carry out his proposal, Mike responded angrily, "You are not the boss of us!" and undid Dan's work. On another occasion when Min-Haeng implied that his view about the identity of a comic book character was the only possibility, Jake asserted his right to have his own opinion.

MIN-HAENG: It's his mom and dad.
JAKE: [disagreeing] It's a helper.
MIN-HAENG: [insisting] It's his dad. He disguised himself.
JAKE: [matter-of-factly] You may think that, but I don't.

The boys also resisted being placed in situations that left them feeling uncertain about their relationships. For example, Mike, whose parents had recently separated, created the Mean Team and appointed himself the boss, which (at least among his peers) enabled him to punish anyone who tried to leave him. And when Tony felt that the other boys were trying to exclude him from their activities, he became even more determined to join them.

Above all, younger as well as older boys instinctively resist, at least initially, anything that threatens to undermine their connections to themselves and to others. Their connections to themselves are reflected in their sense of integrity and agency, and rest on their ability to realize (even when they do not express) a full range of thoughts, feelings, and desires (i.e., know what they know). Their connections to others include interpersonal relationships that are characterized by trust, respect, and understanding, and are bolstered by their ability to express themselves honestly with others (i.e., show what they know). These are the connections for which boys strive and that boys struggle to preserve when they feel pressured to conform and to compromise for the sake of fitting in.

Reminiscent of the relational dilemma that girls face at adolescence, boys' gender socialization during early childhood sets them up for what appears to be a choice between being true to themselves and having relationships with others, but is in fact a choice-less choice, or a lose-lose situation, because choosing *either* self *or* others leads to disconnections from *both* self *and* others. Boys' resistance—against constraints on their self-expression and against rules of engagement that leave them feeling isolated—is important because it means that they, too, are invested in preserving a version of themselves that feels honest and whole to them, and interested in relating to others in ways that feel mutually supportive. Boys' resistance is illuminating because it shows that socialization toward patriarchal norms that privilege masculinity and discount femininity, along with societal expectations that conflate gender and biological sex, can lead to a crisis of connection not only for girls but also for boys.

Supporting Boys

Given that connections to self (e.g., as indicated by voice and presence) and connections to others (e.g., as indicated by the quality of one's relationships) are interdependent, it could be said that the crisis of connection that boys face during early childhood centers not on choosing between self and relationships but on choosing between connection and disconnection. The possibility that the preservation of one's probity and relationships can conflict with the establishment of one's social status indicates a systemic problem that leaves everyone at a significant disadvantage. Therefore, in resisting the influence of their gender socialization, boys (and girls) are choosing connection over disconnection and also rejecting the cultural ideologies and societal infrastructures that perpetuate the crisis.

This raises the question of how we can best support boys in developing their relational capabilities and resisting disconnections from themselves and from others. With boys' best interests at heart, parents may worry that deviating from masculine norms will put boys at risk (e.g., for ridicule and rejection). This fear of not preparing boys to survive in the world of boys and men can serve to rationalize pressures that we place on boys to conform. However, to enable boys to thrive (not merely survive) psychologically and socially, it is also important to foster qualities and skills that will enable them to navigate through all of life's challenges (e.g., exploring their identities, discovering their purpose, working toward their goals) with their integrity intact.

Research has shown that boys can tell us what they feel they are up against and what they need to overcome it, when they believe that we are truly interested in understanding and supporting them.[27] In order to be effective, an intervention must therefore begin with listening. Listening for understanding involves taking a developmental, rather than a diagnostic, approach that starts from a place of not knowing (or not presuming to know) and seeks to learn about boys' experiences from their own perspectives. Without this, we risk simply testing our preformed assumptions and imposing solutions that may not be practical or relevant to boys' lived realities. Listening that is supportive rather than judgmental involves valuing what boys know, validating how boys feel, and trusting that there are reasons (often good ones) for why boys act the ways they do. Without this, boys are unlikely to share their stories with us, much less seek our advice and accept our help.

Research has also shown that having access to close, confiding relationships is the single best protector against psychological and social risks.[28] For instance, adolescent boys who have close friendships refer to a sense of being in it together that gives them courage to speak up when they feel misunderstood and to try to show people who they really are.[29] Likewise, four-year-old Jake's ability and willingness to speak his mind was enabled by his parents, who taught him to be comfortable with differences and gave him language and permission to follow his instincts (e.g., reminding him, "If you don't like it, don't do it"). Positive, reliable relationships can play a protective role in boys' (and girls') development by providing the reassurance they need—particularly when daunted by their self-doubts and/or other people's skepticism—to persevere in their efforts to remain true to themselves and to be valued members of their communities.[30]

To help boys develop protective relationships, we must first enable them to retain their relational capabilities. So long as relationships—along with qualities and skills that are crucial to establishing emotional closeness—are stereotypically associated with femininity, boys may feel compelled to devalue, for instance, their capacity for empathy. In order for change to be possible, it is important for boys to understand that their relational capabilities are not "feminine" weaknesses but human strengths and essential to their well-being. Fostering boys' relational capabilities is not asking boys to be something they are not (e.g., girls) nor teaching boys anything new, but enabling them to preserve their humanity by developing abilities they already possess. By framing these issues in terms of becoming good men and strong leaders, we can teach boys to trust their instincts, take responsibility for their actions, ask for assistance when they need it, and offer assistance when they can give it, without jeopardizing their masculinity. By honoring boys' (and girls') relational capabilities through the examples we set and the guidance we provide, we can enable them to remain grounded in what they know, even when they choose not to show it.

In order for change to be sustainable, however, it is not enough to empower individuals; it is also necessary to improve their circumstances. Although individuals may resist debilitating gender norms, the struggle is likely to continue for each successive generation if our cultures and societies remain the same. As sociologists and social psychologists have long emphasized, contexts matter.[31] Cultural institutions and societal norms can impede or facilitate progress. Even individuals who are willing to express themselves openly and honestly may hesitate to do so in situations that they perceive to be competitive and antagonistic. If socialization toward patriarchal constructions of gender leads to a crisis of connection, then our efforts to help boys (and girls) preserve connections and prevent disconnections must address society's role in perpetuating the problem as well as the individual's role in overcoming it.

NOTES

1 Lyn Mikel Brown and Carol Gilligan, *Meeting at the Crossroads: Women's Psychology and Girls' Development* (Cambridge, MA: Harvard University Press, 1992); Carol Gilligan, *In a Different Voice: Psychological Theory and Women's Development* (Cambridge, MA: Harvard University Press, 1982); Carol Gilligan, *Joining the Resistance* (Cambridge: Polity Press, 2011); Carol Gilligan, Nona P. Lyons, and Trudy J. Hanmer, eds., *Making Connections: The Relational Worlds of Adolescent Girls at Emma Willard School* (Cambridge, MA: Harvard University Press, 1990); Jill McLean Taylor, Carol Gilligan, and Amy M. Sullivan, *Between Voice and Silence: Women and Girls, Race and Relationship* (Cambridge, MA: Harvard University Press, 1997).

2 Brown and Gilligan, *Meeting at the Crossroads*.

3 Gilligan, *In a Different Voice*.

4 Gilligan, Lyons, and Hanmer, *Making Connections*; Taylor, Gilligan, and Sullivan, *Between Voice and Silence*.

5 Gilligan, *Joining the Resistance*; Carol Gilligan, "Remembering Iphigenia: Voice, Resonance, and a Talking Cure," in *The Inner World in the Outer World*, ed. Edward Shapiro (New Haven, CT: Yale University Press, 1997), 143–168.

6 Judy Y. Chu, *When Boys Become Boys: Development, Relationships, and Masculinity* (New York: New York University Press, 2014).

7 Carol Gilligan, "The Listening Guide Method of Psychological Inquiry," *Qualitative Psychology* 2, no. 1 (2015): 69–77.

8 Judy Y. Chu, "A Relational Perspective on Adolescent Boys' Identity Development," in *Adolescent Boys: Exploring Diverse Cultures of Boyhood*, ed. Niobe Way and Judy Y. Chu (New York: New York University Press, 2004), 78–104; Judy Y. Chu, "Adolescent Boys' Friendships and Peer Group Culture," *New Directions for Child and Adolescent Development* 107 (2005): 7–22; Niobe Way, *Deep Secrets: Boys' Friendships and the Crisis of Connection* (Cambridge, MA: Harvard University Press, 2011).

9 Chu, *When Boys Become Boys*.

10 E.g., Colwyn Trevarthen, "The Concept and Foundations of Infant Intersubjectivity," in *Intersubjective Communication and Emotion in Early Ontogeny*, ed. Stein Braten (Cambridge, UK: Cambridge University Press, 1998), 15–46; Edward Tronick, "Emotions and Emotional Communication in Infants," *American Psychologist* 44, no. 2 (1989): 112–119.

11 Way, *Deep Secrets*; Niobe Way, Jessica Cressen, Samuel Bodian, Justin Preston, Joseph D. Nelson, and Diane Hughes, "'It Might Be Nice to Be a Girl . . . Then You Wouldn't Have to Be Emotionless': Boys' Resistance to Norms of Masculinity during Adolescence," *Psychology of Men & Masculinity* 15, no. 3 (2014): 241–252; Stuart Miller, *Men and Friendship* (Los Angeles: Jeremy P. Tarcher, 1992).

12 James M. O'Neil, "Summarizing 25 Years of Research on Men's Gender Role Conflict Using the Gender Role Conflict Scale: New Research Paradigms and

Clinical Implications," *Counseling Psychologist* 38 (2008): 358–445; Joseph H. Pleck, "Gender Role Strain Paradigm: An Update," in *A New Psychology of Men*, ed. Ronald F. Levant and William S. Pollack (New York: Basic Books, 1995), 11–32; William S. Pollack, *Real Boys: Rescuing Our Sons from the Myths of Boyhood* (New York: Random House, 1998).

13 Margaret Mead, *Male and Female: A Study of the Sexes in a Changing World* (New York: Morrow Quill, 1949).

14 Sigmund Freud, "Family Romances," in *The Freud Reader*, trans. Peter Gay (1908; repr., New York: Norton, 1989), 297–300.

15 Paul Kivel, "Acting Like a Man," in *Men's Work: How to Stop the Violence That Tears Our Lives Apart* (Center City, MN: Hazelden, 1998).

16 Robert Brannon, "The Male Sex Role: Our Culture's Blueprint for Manhood and What It's Done for Us Lately," in *The Forty-Nine Percent Majority: The Male Sex Role*, ed. Deborah Sarah David and Robert Brannon (Reading, MA: Addison-Wesley, 1976); Michael S. Kimmel, *The Gendered Society* (New York: Oxford University Press, 2000).

17 Michael S. Kimmel, *Guyland: The Perilous World Where Boys Become Men* (New York: HarperCollins, 2008); C. J. Pascoe, *Masculinity and Sexuality in High School* (Berkeley: University of California Press, 2007).

18 Chu, "Adolescent Boys' Friendships"; Way, *Deep Secrets*; Way et al., "'It Might Be Nice to Be a Girl.'"

19 Chu, *When Boys Become Boys*; Way, *Deep Secrets*.

20 Jean Piaget, *The Construction of Reality in the Child* (New York: Basic Books, 1954); Lev S. Vygotsky, *Mind and Society* (Cambridge, MA: Harvard University Press, 1978).

21 Brown and Gilligan, *Meeting at the Crossroads*.

22 Jackson Katz and Jeremy Earp, *Tough Guise: Violence, Media, and the Crisis in Masculinity*, directed by Sut Jhally (Media Education Foundation, 1999); Richard Majors and Janet M. Billson, *Cool Pose: The Dilemmas of Black Manhood in America* (New York: Touchstone, 1993).

23 Chu, *When Boys Become Boys*; Chu, "Relational Perspective"; Deborah L. Tolman et al., "Getting Close, Staying Cool," in Way and Chu, *Adolescent Boys*, 235–255; Way, *Deep Secrets*; Way et al., "'It Might Be Nice to Be a Girl.'"

24 Kimmel, *Guyland*.

25 Gilligan, *Joining the Resistance*; Chu, "Relational Perspective"; Way, *Deep Secrets*.

26 Way et al., "'It Might Be Nice to Be a Girl.'"

27 Chu, "Relational Perspective"; Chu, "Adolescent Boys' Friendships"; Chu, *When Boys Become Boys*; Way, *Deep Secrets*.

28 Michael D. Resnick et al., "Protecting Adolescents from Harm: Findings from the National Longitudinal Study on Adolescent Health," *Journal of the American Medical Association* 278, no. 10 (1997): 823–832.

29 Chu, "Relational Perspective."

30 Carol Gilligan, "The Centrality of Relationship in Human Development: A Puzzle, Some Evidence, and a Theory," in *Development and Vulnerability in Close Relationships*, ed. Gil G. Noam and Kurt W. Fischer (Mahwah, NJ: Lawrence Erlbaum, 1996), 237–261; Carol Gilligan, Lyn Mikel Brown, and Annie G. Rogers, "Psyche Embedded: A Place for Body, Relationships, and Culture in Personality Theory," in *Studying Persons and Lives*, ed. Albert I. Rabin, Robert A. Zucker, Robert A. Emmons, and Susan Frank (New York: Springer, 1990), 86–147.

31 E.g., Erving Goffman, *The Presentation of Self in Everyday Life* (Edinburgh: Anchor Books, 1956); Lee Ross and Richard Nisbett, *The Person and the Situation: Perspectives in Social Psychology* (London: Pinter & Martin, 2011).

3

Staying Woke

Raising Black Girls to Resist Disconnection

JANIE VICTORIA WARD

It was called a local summit for black women and girls. There we were, an intergenerational community of attendees: little girls coloring quietly on the floor, teenaged women talked into attendance by an energetic high school teacher, policewomen, clergy, nurses and public health officials, older civil rights activists. African American, Caribbean, Afro-Latina, African immigrants—so many different looking women in the room. All were there to share their perspectives on what life is like for black women and girls in the city. This diverse group of attendees revealed long lists of environmental concerns. Women complained about safety issues and lamented that no black children are presumed innocent or in need of protection in their communities. "Emotional, psychological and physical," explained one woman, "it's unsafe to be who we are." The adult world of teachers and administrators, school counselors, even after-school program directors that black children have to navigate came under scrutiny. "Lots of things happen in school that teachers turn a blind eye to. Some school rules matter, others don't," a high school girl explained, and the penalties meted out are unequal and unfair. The young women spoke of a toxic masculinity that touches all aspects of their lives. They said boys are given far more options, freedom, and choices than girls, and that youth programming is seldom designed to serve girls and their needs. Adult women talked about how their communities have changed. Rising rents across the city are forcing familiar residents out. They said things like the new people moving in don't look like me, and even those who do look like me don't speak the same language, or share the same traditions. Moreover there's a great deal of wariness and suspicion, fear that "they" look down on "us" and "our" children. This increasing diversity in the black community evoked for some a deep sense of isolation—people moving away from rather than making connections with each other.

The expressions of anger and frustration were palpable. Young and older black women spoke of having to navigate the host of racial and gender stereotypes that negatively affect how they are treated in their schools, in their communities, and sometimes in their own homes. They spoke of the need to resist internalizing these negative stereotypes lest they destroy their sense of self-worth and positive identity. Moreover, as the populations of their communities shift, they struggle to stay connected to their neighbors in ways that foster strong social interactions and build alliances across differences.

In previous works I provided examples illustrating the centrality of resistance in the psychological development of African American girls. This work is built on two theoretical foundations: the research of psychologists studying women's psychology and girls development and that of social and clinical psychologists studying racial and ethnic socialization in families. Carol Gilligan and her colleagues have argued that for women and girls the recovery of voice and using this knowledge of the social world to resist false authority are essential to the work of resisting patriarchy.[1] Additionally, scholars in social and clinical psychology have expanded our understanding of the role of parental messages regarding the preparation for and resistance to race-related bias and discrimination in their studies of racial socialization in youth.[2] I argued that the refusal to allow oneself to become stifled by victimization or to accept an ideology of victim blame requires the development of a critical perspective on the world, one that is informed by the particular knowledge gained from one's social and political position. Such knowledge mitigates self-abnegation, fosters self-esteem, and enables African Americans' resistance to disconnection and to racial oppression.

Not all resistance strategies adopted by African Americans are liberatory, nor are they all psychologically healthy. Some strategies are what my colleague Tracy Robinson and I call *resistance for survival*.[3] These strategies tend to be transient, crisis-oriented, and short-term solutions that black teenagers adopt in an effort to endure the stressful effects and consequences of their subordination. These survival strategies are often evoked in reaction to black girls' sense that they are being attacked, demeaned, or psychically wounded and are evident in attitudes and behaviors that stem from anger, fear, or guilt. Although they may feel appropriate at the time, resistance strategies that are survival-oriented are seldom in the black child's long-term self-interest. Academic underachievement, black-on-black violence, the quick fixes of substance abuse, overeating, and irresponsible sexual behavior are examples of survival-oriented resistance strategies adopted by African American girls in this culture. While many black parents believe they must talk to their children about their racial realities, a distinction can be made between angry and mean-spirited race-based messages emanating from "tongues of fire truth-telling" and messages that are "resistance-building truth-telling."[4] Tongues of fire truth-telling is defined as the harsh tell-it-like-it-is negative critique of the world some black mothers inflict on their daughters to unmask illusions and ostensibly build character and psychological strength. In contrast, resistance-building truth-telling strategies emphasize constructive, critical affirmation of the individual and the collective and encourage black girls to think critically about their selves and their place in the world. Resistance-building truth-telling can be employed to understand and address the escalating rates of violence and relational disconnection in urban black female populations. In other words, this form of truth-telling can be used to help black parents construct psychologically strong and socially smart resistance strategies for their daughters.

Resistance for liberation strategies promote the search to discover people and activities in black girls' environment that affirm and support that their belief in themselves is greater than anyone's disbelief. In other words, resistance for liberation is an oppositional lesson in self-determination. These strategies, which are drawn from knowledge produced within the consciousness of African Americans' victimization, hold the emancipatory interests of a subordinated people. As such, resistance for liberation provides the requisite perspective, vision, and ultimate wisdom black folks need to live in ways that are self-defined, are in one's own best interest, and allow us to live out our full humanity.

This chapter explores the roots of resistance to disconnection—that is, the disconnection to self, brought on by the internalization of negative stereotyping and the effects of racial bias and discrimination, and the disconnection to others, including non-blacks, as well as other blacks who may not share the same cultural or social background.

The present-day realities that were raised in the summit—a lack of safety, unresponsive schools, social messages built on stereotypes that demean some groups and privilege others—erode the bonds of authentic relationship and create the conditions for alienation. This chapter explores how black girls deal with these issues, by way of strategies that stress short-term survival or those that emphasize the importance of liberating oneself from the shackles of oppression. I argue that lessons of resistance are about staying connected to the knowledge that keeps you alive and that this knowledge is essential for black girls as it allows them to stay true to who they are, as opposed to who others say they are or believe them to be. When effective these optimal resistance strategies allow black girls to navigate the social pressures that promote disconnection in schools, with peers, and with adults. This chapter focuses attention on (1) disconnections in school through the use of harsh policies and punitive disciplinary actions that push black girls out; (2) intraracial colorist violence among children and youth in school often operating under the teacher's radar (but sometimes with her participation as well); (3) the difficulties young black women face in creating and maintaining cross-racial relationships with non-black women; and (4) a model for teaching the strategies of resistance that black parents and other adults can pass down to black girls that foster resistance to alienation and disconnection. Throughout the chapter I highlight the two forms of resistance—resistance for survival and resistance for liberation—and illustrate how, as black girls navigate school policies and disciplinary actions, react to skin color bias with their peers, and engage in cross-racial relationships with non-black women, these strategies can either support or derail black girl's healthy psychosocial development. In highlighting the effective strategies of resistance undertaken in response to these conditions that serve to promote psychosocial resilience, I argue that there are critical lessons passed down in black families and from other adults in the lives of black girls that urge their daughters to "stay woke." These messages emphasize the importance of staying connected to self and to one's cultural knowledge and legacy by interpreting and, when necessary, challenging mainstream knowledge claims. These optimal strategies of resistance identify what black girls need in order to sustain fortitude and persistence in school, promote understanding and attachment to peers, and tap the energy and persistence required to connect across racial lines.

Promoting Resistance through Racial Socialization

Resistance is the development of a critical consciousness that is invoked to counter the myriad distortions, mistruths, and misinformation perpetrated about the lives of black women and men, their families, and their communities. Black feminist bell hooks referred to this process as the development of an oppositional gaze.[5] According to Mansbridge and Morris,

> Oppositional consciousness as we define it is an empowering mental state that prepares members of an oppressed group to act to undermine, reform, or overthrow a system of human domination. It is usually fueled by righteous anger over injustices done to the group and prompted by personal indignities and harms suffered through one's group membership. At a minimum, oppositional consciousness includes the four elements of identifying with members of a subordinate group, identifying injustices done to that group, opposing those injustices, and seeing the group as having a shared interest in ending or diminishing those injustices.[6]

The African Americans I interviewed indicated that the strength of the oppositional consciousness that they drew upon was forged in a common history of moral and political indignation at oppression. The lessons of resistance and authority passed down from parent to child are informed by the strength, power, and clarity gained from holding fast to a social and political perspective that allows a subjected people to know what the truth is. Knowing comes from being told the truth and learning how to interpret one's own experience, trust one's own voice, and give legitimacy to one's own perspective. Most important, being an effective resister demands that black individuals be responsive to and responsible for this knowledge. In essence, resistance is a body of knowledge and requisite skills that can help black children and youth read, interpret, and oppose racial bias and animosity, as well as affirm the self and one's cultural group.

The stories I have collected over the past twenty-five years from black parents illustrate why and how conversations about race take place in their families and what was learned in these discussions. In semi-clinical as well as less formal interviews I've engaged black mothers and fathers on topics that explore generational differences in perceptions of racial matters, racial identity, gender socialization, and race-related moral development. My book, *The Skin We're In: Teaching Our Children to Be Emotionally Strong, Socially Smart and Spiritually Connected*, presented research from a core set of qualitative interviews conducted in four cities across the United States. The primary focus of the interviews centered on the question "Do you speak to your black daughters/sons (or do your parents speak to you) about racial matters and why?" The one-on-one interviews of black mothers and fathers and teenaged boys and girls were audiotaped and later transcribed for analysis. A wide range of parenting experiences was represented in this data set as those parenting ranged from thirty-five to more than sixty-five years old and included grandparents and teenage women who were also mothers themselves. Parents' educational and socioeconomic status was similarly diverse, ranging from high school dropouts to university doctorates, welfare recipients to upper-income earners.

In analyzing the interviews, I employed a grounded theory approach in which I looked for trends and patterns in interviewee responses that I thought might contribute to an understanding of how parents of black teenage children and teenagers themselves understand, enact, and communicate the experience of race-related socialization in African American families.[7] Adopting an integrative approach, I sought to uncover the respondents' interpretations and understandings of racial socialization expressed in their own words and on their own terms, using a process of cross-participant analysis in which I compared participants' responses to reveal what I call narratives of resistance. These are a compilation of stories, directives, and pronouncements about the importance of resistance to the psychological and social well-being of black children and youth.

Over the years I've continued to collect data from African American, Afro-Caribbean, and African girls as they reflect on growing up in the skin they are in. The young women I have taught in my role as a college professor have contributed a variety of written materials to my studies of resistance, including autobiographical statements and essays and reports based on their own research findings exploring the topic of racial socialization in black families.[8] More recently, along with interviews of black undergraduate and graduate students, I have been in conversation with black girls (and other girls of color) in urban, community-based afterschool and sports programs. These preadolescent and adolescent girls have broadened my understanding and appreciation of the constructive connections made between adults and girls that enable girls to interpret dominant, mainstream knowledge claims about race, gender, and social class and to challenge them when appropriate.

The past few years have seen a marked increase in research on racial socialization in black families. Findings suggest that black parents, feeling vulnerable to racism and its effects, have long adapted to this reality by engaging in child-rearing practices that provide their children with the tools to cope with life in a hostile racial context. Racial socialization refers to the messages passed down within families that become integrated into a child's self-concept and that shape attitudes and behaviors. Researchers in racial socialization often focus on parental messages that emphasize preparation for bias, racial affirmation and pride, and discussions that highlight gender-specific concerns (for example, the vulnerabilities of black boys in regard to policing practices) as well as messages about cultural history, traditions, and heritage. Racial socialization messages have been found to improve mental health.[9] Bowman and Howard observe a positive relationship between racial barrier awareness and academic achievement.[10] Davis and Stevenson discuss the relationship between depression and the negative messages about race that black youth and young adults often receive via mainstream socialization.[11] Their findings suggest that black youth who receive messages about racial identity that were designed to counter the prevailing mainstream narrative of racial inferiority are psychologically better prepared to cope with bias and discrimination. To be forewarned is to be prepared. Thus when taught an awareness of racism, black children who are confronted by messages (explicit and implicit) that label them "less than" and say that they don't matter will hear those voices in their heads that remind them of their value, their humanity, and their strength to fight against and stand up for that which is fair and right. These socializing messages assist black teens as they develop social and psychological coping strengths and strategies for dealing with the effects of racism.

It is important to note that not all black parents engage directly in racial socialization practices. Some parents choose not to talk about race with their children; they de-emphasize the role racial bias may play in their children's success, and they may push their children to uncritically adopt mainstream values and beliefs.[12] For some black parents their cultural or national identity (e.g., being Haitian or African) or being middle-class or low-income holds greater importance than their racial status. Then, of course, the conditions of the lives of some black parents render them too overwhelmed to teach about these matters as they struggle to keep themselves and their families afloat.

Then there are the adults who teach black youth the importance of fighting back with whatever weapon is available, even if it is suboptimal and may ultimately put that child at risk. These are the messages that prompt what I refer to as resistance for survival strategies. We see these acts of resistance across a wide variety of settings. They appear in schools where black girls, feeling overlooked and discounted by their teachers, choose to slack off and underachieve. And we see them enacted in interpersonal relationships where black girls, feeling demeaned and disrespected, choose to physically or verbally fight back to preserve their self-image. This kind of oppositional behavior is shortsighted—it might make them feel better for the moment, but in the long run they are set up for school failure or injury and possible arrest. Healthy resistance strategies, those that go beyond mere survival, encourage black girls to embrace the liberatory elements of academic achievement, self-determination, positive identity (individual, racial/ethnic and gender), and racial pride.

Waking Up to Resistance

Americans were jolted awake watching the protests and subsequent riots unfold in response to the shocking death of Michael Brown, a young black man in Ferguson, Missouri, at the hands of the police. Tragically this was not an isolated incident. Media coverage surrounding even more horrific incidences of police brutality against young black and brown men made household names of Trayvon Martin, Eric Garner, Freddie Gray, and Tamir Rice. Less well publicized, though equally alarming, were the increasing numbers of black women killed during police encounters—a total of fifteen women in 2015 alone.[13] The racialized tragedies of the past few years reveal a predictable pattern—anger and frustration, protests taken to the streets, followed by violence and more arrests. The Black Lives Matter protest movement with its call for changes at the national and local levels in policing practices, policy, and law enforcement legislation illuminates three essential truths. First, the protesters are intergenerational and often multiracial. People from a wide spectrum of social identities are outraged at these events and have joined the resistance to voice their dismay. Second, the protests provide evidence of the dialectic between resistance and resilience in that resistance fosters resilience. Fueled by frustration and sorrow, the protesters rallied to march, chant, sing, and cry out to anyone who would listen. Through it all and amid the pain is the motivation to act. Explained one protester, "The more demonstrations I see, the less rage I feel." His resilience allows him to negotiate these hard times by resisting effectively in social protest, and that successful negotiation facilitates further resistance. Resistance for liberation in the black community and family provides a preventive psychosocial intervention that boosts hardiness and psychological resilience of black family members. Resisters for liberation are, in turn, resilient. That dialectic is an integral part of the African American tradition.[14]

Last, the high visibility of widespread police brutality and judicial injustice has led to a growing awareness of the necessity of "the talk," particularly in black families. As mentioned earlier, "the talk" refers to those conversations between black adults and black children intended to convey an understanding of race and place. Parents share with their children social and political perspectives that explain and inform an analysis of what it means to be black in today's society, and the importance of knowing how to stay safe on the streets as well as how to behave when confronted by law enforcement personnel. Along with fearing for their child's physical safety, black parents worry too about the psychological damage racial bias and discrimination can inflict. Everyone seems to have a cell phone these days, and photos of each tragic event spread electronically across multiple media platforms like wildfire. Psychologists warn that to repeatedly view and relive the images of violence and police misconduct on TV and in social media, and to later see police repeatedly indicted but not convicted, can evoke strong feelings that may overwhelm, traumatize, frighten, and depress children who struggle to make sense of the events they witness. Talk of "the talk" invites non-black people into conversations about topics many Americans prefer to avoid. White America may debate when or whether to talk with their children about racism. Black parents don't have such luxuries.

Vulnerabilities of Disconnection

Children pick up the ways in which whiteness is normalized and privileged in US society, and black girls learn early in life that the way they look, how they act, and who they are is inferior and not good enough. The developmental work of black adolescence is to resist internalizing the racial and gender oppression that would lead a black girl to succumb to stereotypic beliefs about black women and disbelieve who she is and what she can do—disconnection from the self. Similarly more black girls than ever are growing up in communities that are changing demographically. Resistance for black girls in these situations includes seeing the self in the other, thereby refusing to disconnect from other black and brown-skinned people and those who may look different, have a different gender orientation, speak a different language, or practice different cultural traditions.

Recent research on black girls suggests that there are three areas of particular vulnerability of disconnection that are faced by these young women. They include excessive discipline and school suspension, colorist violence in the form of skin color bullying and favoritism, and, among college-age women, confronting a color-blind ideology that prevents honest and authentic interracial relationships with white women.

Disconnections in School Settings

In the past decade attention has shifted to the plight of black and Latino boys (i.e., President Barack Obama's My Brother's Keeper initiative). As Dierdre Paul writes, "Blacks girls [have become] a footnote in the discourse on the endangered Black male."[15] It is not that black girls are doing so much better, but that black boys are simply doing that much worse. But are they? Recent studies document that more than any other racial or ethnic group black girls' experiences in public schools are as troubling as those of their male counterparts. Often seen as disruptive, deviant, and dumb, black girls, according to author Monique Morris, are "disproportionately represented among those who experience the type of discipline that renders children vulnerable to delinquency and future incarceration."[16] In her book *Pushout*, Morris meticulously details a host of disturbing institutional policies in elementary and secondary schools as well as disruptive educational practices inflicted on incarcerated girls in correctional facilities, all of which result in black girls being disciplined more often and more harshly than any other group of girls. Based on analyses of school narratives from a wide range of black girls—those who are straight, gay, and transgender, girls who are mothers themselves, girls who are locked up or in foster care, girls who are high-achieving, and those who struggle academically—Morris describes educational institutions as "structures of dominance that can either reinforce negative outcomes and ghettoize opportunity or actively disrupt conditions that render black girls vulnerable to criminalization." Her findings show that "black girls are 16 percent of girls in schools, but 42 percent of girls receiving corporal punishment, 42 percent of girls expelled with or without educational services, 45 percent of girls with at least one out-of-school suspension, 31 percent of girls referred to law enforcement, and 34 percent of girls arrested on campus."[17]

Still reeling from the problematic outcomes associated with the national educational reforms of No Child Left Behind and Race to the Top, schools serving black girls employ harsh zero-tolerance school-based policies that criminalize and push girls out. The penalties levied against loud, sassy, and assertive black girls, who possess and enact qualities of femininity that are seen as inferior, nonconforming, inappropriate and unworthy of a fair and equitable education blocks pathways to school success and diminishes the possibility for future social mobility. Those "loud black girls" challenge the sense of teachers (who are most often white and female) of what a good student should look like and how she should behave. Gender-normative behavior of women and girls is reinforced every day in school settings, and black girls' bodies (and voices) are policed, shamed, and silenced, particularly when they stand in opposition to those who would deny them the freedom to be who they are.

Arguably, engaging in school-based oppositional behavior is, for some black girls, an act of resistance—an attempt to push back and stand up for what they want or think that they need. However while their interests may be race-, gender-, and class-specific, it is also true that some oppositional behavior, though perceived to be acts of resistance, may be little more than the unmindful, desperate behavior of subjugated individuals beaten down by the conditions of life.[18] Such *survival-oriented* resistance lacks "radical significance" and is often shortsighted and ineffective for black girls in the long run as it ultimately reinforces the conditions that keep them trapped in the subordinate position they were initially trying to avoid.

It is also the case that many black girls are growing up in families that are floundering and struggling to survive. Black unemployment in America is nearly twice the national average. According to the Institute for Women's Policy Research, in 2014 African American women, often bearing the sole or primary financial responsibilities for their families, had the highest unemployment rate among women—twice as high (10.5 percent versus 5.2 percent) as that of white women.[19] Moreover, in the workplace black women face a variety of barriers to upward mobility including race and gender discrimination, high rates of underemployment, wage discrimination, and workplace discrimination. For unemployed female heads of households at the other end of the economic spectrum, TANF (Temporary Assistance for Needy Families, also known as welfare reform) has pulled the rug out from under their families, forcing black mothers into the workforce to hold down one, two, or three minimally paying jobs. Mothers have less time and energy for child rearing, and daughters are frequently left to pick up the slack.

In the social science literature black children are often described by a persistent and pathologizing narrative of crisis, and adults who work with black children are often preoccupied with sounding the alarm about all the problems black girls face. While these problems are formidable, they can blind us to the strengths girls may develop under conditions of adversity. Taking responsibility for their actions along with learning how to interpret, evaluate, and react to racially charged situations helps girls to develop optimal resistance sensibilities and fortifies their ability to withstand and rebound when the going gets tough. More important, seeing these girls as deficient and their problems as wholly unique to their racial or economic status prevents us from making the kinds of connections to these girls that truly matter.

In a discussion group with urban secondary school teachers, one white female teacher explained to my research group that she just cannot get that jazzed up about gender issues. She said she knew she should, being female and all, but it just does not excite her to work for gender-based causes. Soon afterward her colleague offered another story that illustrated the importance of gender role socialization in their students' lives. Days earlier a poetry slam had taken place in the school's auditorium. A young black student read a poem in which one black woman was chastising another for dating a man who had callously mistreated and abused the speaker just a short time before. In the poem she anguished over why "sisters" can be so caring, so understanding, and so strong when it comes to helping one another pick up the pieces after a heart has been broken, yet the same women will knowingly turn around and walk right back into a similar mess if the right man draws them in. As women, the poet explained, we have to love ourselves enough to make better decisions in our lives, and we must trust ourselves enough to believe the warnings we disclose. At the end of the poem the auditorium exploded in loud and raucous applause, especially from the young women present. It was, explained the teacher, a powerful moment, at least for the girls. Her female students stood together in solidarity, recognizing the vulnerabilities they share as women in the (dating) world.

What was curious to me was the inability of the adult women teachers in the lives of these girls to see themselves connected in any way to the expressed concerns. Overlooking the insights and strengths inherent in black and Latina girls' reflections upon their social world, these adult women miss an essential moment to connect meaningfully to the lives of these girls. Moreover, this lack of connection prevents women from being in the position to teach the requisite skills of effective resistance and to offer the support that these girls of color may need to find their way.[20]

Resisting Skin Color Bias

My colleagues and I recently published a chapter based on stories shared by black teens about their experiences with colorism in school settings.[21] Colorism is the internalized bias and favor for a distinct set of phenotypical characteristics that include lighter skin, Eurocentric facial features (e.g., thin nose and lips), and "good" hair texture (i.e., hair that is long and straight or wavy, rather than tightly coiled and/or kinky). As a system of inequality, social privileges and disadvantages are allocated based on biases held about skin coloration.[22] We heard from black girls that they have been victimized by three discriminatory forms of skin color attitudes and behaviors that children and sometimes teachers and administrators engage in during school: exercising favoritism and using colorism as a weapon, and expressing and acting on skin color preferences in interpersonal dating relationships.

The roots of colorism are deep and have a very long history in the United States. From the earliest centuries of slavery through today, skin color has operated as a form of social capital and reflects a form of social power and unearned privilege that both produces and reproduces inequality.[23] Black girls told us of the direct and indirect messages about skin color preferences they heard when growing up, and they had plenty to say about the pervasiveness of light skin bias in the images and messages disseminated from the entertainment, beauty, fashion, and advertising industries, particularly aimed at women and girls. These attitudes surfaced in the classroom and on the playground where black girls shared horrifying stories of favoritism shown toward some girls and outright bullying behavior toward other girls based on how they look. It didn't matter where the girls grew up—the patterns are disturbingly similar. Light-skinned black girls are assumed to be prettier, smarter, better behaved, and worthy of special treatment in comparison to dark-skinned black girls.[24] Conversely, dark-skinned girls are assumed to be less intelligent, loud, ill-mannered, and disagreeable. Teachers were hardly immune from acting on these perceptions. For example, recent studies using data from the National Longitudinal Survey of Youth and the National Longitudinal Study of Adolescent Health show evidence of a form of "racial profiling" in that dark-skinned children are disciplined, suspended, and disproportionately referred for special educational services.[25] Remarkably, the effect was driven not by black boys, but by the school experiences of black girls; that is, darker-skinned girls are disciplined more harshly than girls who have a lighter skin color.[26]

Many black girls can easily recall episodes of name-calling and colorist bullying provoked by color envy or dislike. They've described to us and to other researchers how children use skin color as a weapon against those who are afforded colorist privileges, that is, the kids who are considered pretty, valued, and worthy, and against those who are considered dark, unattractive, mean, and irredeemable. School personnel are familiar with and sensitive to teasing and name-calling associated with harassment based on race, gender and sexual orientation, physical challenges, and relational aggression, but fewer teachers are aware of the violence inflicted by children based on something as immutable as skin color. Teacher favoritism, where some students receive more attention and privileges, are disciplined less often and are held in higher regard than others, distorts a child's sense of who they are and the value of their achievements. Disfavored students know when teachers dislike them. They feel judged and ignored. Their self-esteem suffers, their relationships are impaired, and their academic performance can suffer.

Black teens also speak openly about the role of skin color preference in the choices black people make of whom to date and whom to marry. "Lighten the line" is a message many black adolescents heard growing up advising them to intentionally date blacks who are lighter, presumably in order to gain social power and/or produce lighter offspring.[27] Black teens are quick to identify what they see as color preferences in the dating and mating practices of black celebrities and sports stars as contemporary manifestations of this phenomenon. The choice of whom one chooses to marry and why is of course highly personal and generally related to much more than perceptions of attractiveness and social acceptability. Yet the issue becomes complicated for black girls in adolescence, the period in the life cycle when body image and self-esteem become entangled, and the desire for social approval and acceptance becomes a driving force in the work of identity development. Black girls who feel rejected or are made to feel unlovely and unlovable may fall victim to a host of negative influences and questionable choices.

In black families where lessons of resistance are modeled and taught judiciously, parents often share their own personal experiences of colorism with their children as a way to understand and resist skin color bias. Mindful of the role that sexism, racism, and social class bias play in shaping our attitudes, beliefs, values, and behaviors, these adults fortify girls from within by helping them to develop a critique of domination and subordination as it relates to skin color bias. They teach black girls to interpret and challenge mainstream knowledge claims like society's preferences for lighter skin color and its demonization of darker skin colors. They encourage resistance for liberation strategies that help girls to replace colorist attitudes with those that celebrate the wide and beautiful diversity of skin colorations that exist throughout the black community. This can be done through the judicious selection of magazines and social media sites that celebrate skin color diversity, through the encouragement of media critique that interrogates images of bias, and through the purchase of black dolls and other racially diverse toys and artifacts.

Cross-Racial Disconnections between Women

> I grew up with white girls. We went to middle and high school together, played on sports teams, went to proms, celebrated together at graduation. I've shared some pretty important aspects of my life with my white girl friends. But here at college it's different. I don't really know these girls and they certainly don't know me. WHY DO YOU SAY THAT? Because most of them haven't had any real experiences with black people before. We're living in close quarters in the dorm and that's where you really see how they see us.

Paulina, an undergraduate at a predominately white college in New England went on to explain that she and her black friends deal with racial stereotypes, microaggressions, and what is now called "hipster racism" on a daily basis. In class they are expected to be experts on all things black, and outside of class the white students either act as though they know all there is to know about race, or acknowledge that they don't know much and that's fine with them.

> In high school I talked more with the white girls. Here I think there's lots to talk about. There's stuff happening all the time. We're having lots of important experiences that you just want to talk about. But they don't want to. WHAT DON'T THEY WANT TO TALK ABOUT? Race . . . racial stuff. I'm studying to be a nurse. And like I've noticed that when stuff comes up, like something happens in clinic with people of color, I'll be like. . . . wow did you see that? And they be like silent. They don't want to talk. Something comes up in class, same thing. They pretend it didn't happen, didn't hear it. WHY IS THIS IMPORTANT TO YOU? This stuff is

important to me. There's not many black girls in my program. I wanna talk to someone. The racial stuff is real! It's very important to me. I'm a black nurse-that's who I am. I want to be good at what I do. You're supposed to talk, and learn, and share perspectives with other students, right? But not about race. They don't wanna talk about it. So I just don't talk to them. Not about anything meaningful, not about the stuff that matters to us black girls. We don't have those kinds of conversations with the white girls. . . . [We don't have] those kinds of relationships.

These black undergraduate women described feeling stereotyped, judged, and tokenized in their college settings. Moreover, they are tired of teaching white women, tired of being silent about the racial realities that matter to their individual and professional development, and tired of feeling the need to carefully dance around "white fragility" and the fear of race talk.[28] The young women are weary of integration. That is, despite all of the campus diversity training and the institution's touting of diversity's educational benefits, black students, at least those whom we've talked to, feel that colleges are not doing enough to promote real, honest, and deep conversations about race across racial groups. These conversations are not easy, yet they are essential for the kinds of engagement that lead to authentic, growth-fostering relationships between students as they increase relational competencies over the life span.[29]

Research has investigated the role that interpersonal relationships play during the college years and has found that relationships are pivotal to identity formation, feelings of belonging, and psychological and physical well-being, provide a buffer to stress, and may even play a role in encouraging retention.[30] Women's friendships, particularly cross-racial friendships during students' undergraduate years, may increase access to valuable academic and professional success networks that women can build on and benefit from. Thus it is particularly disturbing to hear black undergraduate women say that their resistance to the silence of their white counterparts is to disengage themselves from the hard work of cross-racial relationship building. While this resistance for survival strategy may make sense in the moment, in the long run it is good for neither black women nor white women to opt out of the work of relationship because it is too hard, is too scary, or takes too much time. In addition and equally problematic is that for black undergraduate (and graduate) students in predominately white institutions who fail to make friends across racial groups, the process of completing a degree can be a very lonely experience. Students who feel isolated and disconnected from other students, faculty, and the institution itself can suffer in ways that lead to alienation, anxiety, and depression.

Stepping toward Healthy Resistance: Lessons in Staying Woke

Based on what I learned from the respondents in my studies, I constructed a four-step model (Read it, Name it, Oppose it, Replace it) that is designed to help adults assist their children, youth, and young adults in developing critical thinking skills to effectively resist damaging racial and gendered realities. The model emphasizes the need for parents and other adults to foster girls' capacities to generate safe, creative, and effective internal (psychological) and external (social) strategies of resistance. Central to this process is the need for adults to listen to and learn from these girls who are, in fact, crucial informants of their own cultural contexts (such as peer cultures, school cultures) and developmental needs.

To illustrate the model, I will share what I learned from black mothers as they described how they talk to their daughters about hip-hop and other popular music videos produced for and consumed by American children and teens. The concerns I heard again and again centered on the women in these videos. "Half-naked video hoochie mamas," as one mom put it, "gyrating to a seductive back beat." Mothers who struggle to instill in their daughters the characteristics they would like them to possess—self-respect, respect for others, independence, and pride—feel undermined by these video messages. The mothers worried about the extent to which black girls internalize these narrow, objectifying stereotypes before they are old enough to resist their appeal. They believe it is essential that their daughters learn to bring a critical eye to the images they consume.

"Reading it" refers to analyzing a situation for the dynamics of race, gender, and class. This requires that girls think carefully about what they see, hear, think, believe, and feel. Central to the process of reading situations and events is the ability to identify patterns, covert and overt, that reveal the routines and rituals of everyday racism and sexism. These "isms" evoke strong emotional responses, particularly in children and teens, and these emotions are key survival signals in that they indicate something important is happening. It is essential to stay in touch with the feelings that surface. Do these images make girls feel sad? Mad? Hurt? Afraid? Despite the fact that these media images portray our nation's obsession with sex and materialism in (what some might argue) the worst of ways, black mothers say that it is hard for their daughters to invoke a critique of music videos because it looks like the women are enjoying themselves. When adults help black girls to read a situation, they give girls the skills to analyze whose interests are privileged, favored, and legitimized and whose are discounted, silenced, and ignored.

"Naming it" refers to the process of establishing criteria for determining if racism (or sexism) is, or is not, at play. After all, not everything is about race, and not everything that involves race is racist. However, if racism is involved, naming it becomes very important, to figure out socially smart strategies to oppose the injustices perceived. Naming it requires practical, accessible words whose meanings are shared and understood. It means bringing the existence of injustice and inequity into full consciousness, "telling it like it is." Girls need guidance, particularly from adult women, to determine what constitutes racism and sexism and to identify the dynamics at play in what they are seeing. Lacking guidance, girls passively and uncritically consume the media products marketed to them, and, failing to see them as problematic, many lack the ability to resist these images.

In the area of skin color bias, adults can read and name colorist violence too. First, they can listen more closely for evidence of colorist bullying between children. What are black children saying about each other's appearance and why? Teachers and school administrators can periodically review their disciplinary records, searching carefully for patterns of bias—which girls are most often disciplined, suspended, or expelled? What do they look like in terms of skin coloration, hair, and facial features? Similarly, what do the girls who get the awards, the best roles in school plays, the special attention of the teachers look like? Are some children being favored, preferred, and supported more than others, and what can school personnel do to change these attitudes and behaviors in themselves and in the children they teach?

"Opposing it" is about finding smart and effective ways for black girls to respond to racism and sexism. This means standing up, fighting back, speaking up, and asserting moral authority in the face of injustice, intolerance, and ignorance. The resistance that black girls employ (i.e., the calculated steps that a girl might take in response to a situation that she feels is demeaning, constraining, and diminishing of her sense of self and her opportunities) requires an awareness of where they are now and where they want to be in the future. These strategies must also be mindful of the consequences of missteps.

Opposing it demands an acute recognition of the unique circumstances of black girls' lives such that we can work closely with them to craft effective and efficient resistance strategies tailor-made for their specific circumstances. For example, the rising numbers of black girls who get pushed out or drop out of school before completion suggest the need for teachers, administrators, school counselors, program developers, and policymakers at all levels to recognize how gender plays out in the school-to-prison pipeline. Adults need to know that for girls, the educational pathways that lead to harsh disciplinary practices, criminalization, and confinement are often connected to girls' histories of victimization, exploitation, and abuse.[31] Ultimately the adults who are most effective at helping black girls to design effective resistance strategies are those who are trained in culturally competent, gender-responsive, and trauma-informed practices that are relevant to and effective with this population. We know what is needed; we just need the will to make it happen.

Who Is There to Help?

For black girls much of the work of adolescence is to explore and integrate the multiple identities of race, class, and gender while they simultaneously battle multiple gendered and race-based stereotypes. To do this they look to their mothers, grandmothers, aunts, and other adult women for help in shaping the personal characteristics that support positive psychosocial development. Black women's power lies in their ability to encourage their daughters to use their social knowledge to calculate their strengths and weaknesses and to deal with the limitations they face.

Recognition of this common cultural experience unites black women and girls as partners in the same struggle.

I have argued here that this work is not limited to black parents, nor can it be the sole responsibility of black adults. White (and other non-black) adults too must become acutely attuned to the sociopolitical context of gender and race in America. They must understand and acknowledge the need for resistance in the lives of black women and girls. If nothing else they should respect this work. When we come to recognize that the work of self-creation, with its salience in the adolescent years, necessitates that black girls actively design and produce strategies that are appropriate to their life goals and demands, we will begin to see elements of transcendence and the emancipatory possibilities needed to *keep staying woke* despite all odds.

NOTES

1 Carol Gilligan, *Joining the Resistance* (Cambridge: Polity Press, 2011).

2 E.g., Michael C. Thornton et al., "Socio-demographic and Environmental Correlates of Racial Socialization by Black Parents," *Child Development* 62 (1990): 401–409; Phillip Bowman and Cleopatra Howard, "Race-Related Socialization, Motivation, and Academic Achievement: A Study of Black Youth in Three-Generation Families," *Journal of the American Academy of Child Psychiatry* 24 (1985): 132–141; Curtis W. Branch and Nora Newcombe, "Racial Attitude Development among Young Black Children as a Function of Parental Attitudes: A Longitudinal and Cross-Sectional Study," *Child Development* 57 (1986): 712–721; Diane Hughes et al., "Parents' Ethnic-Racial Socialization Practices: A Review of Research and Directions for Future Study," *Developmental Psychology* 42, no. 5 (2006): 747–770, doi:10.1037/0012-1649.42.5.747; Sheree Marshall, "Ethnic Socialization of African American Children: Implications for Parenting, Identity Development, and Academic Achievement," *Journal of Youth and Adolescence* 24, no. 4 (1995): 377–396doi:10.1007/bf01537187; Robert M. Sellers et al., "Racial Identity Matters: The Relationship between Racial Discrimination and Psychological Functioning in African American Adolescents," *Journal of Research on Adolescence* 16, no. 2 (2006): 187–216, doi:10.1111/j.1532-7795.2006.00128.x; Margaret B. Spencer, "Children's Cultural Values and Parental Child Rearing Strategies," *Developmental Review* 3, no. 4 (1983): 351–370, doi:10.1016/0273-2297(83)90020-5; Margaret B. Spencer and Carol Markstrom-Adams, "Identity Processes among Racial and Ethnic Minority Children in America," *Child Development* 61 (1990): 290–310; Margaret B. Spencer, Dena P. Swanson, and Alvin Glymph, "The Prediction of Parental Psychological Functioning: Influences of African American Adolescent Perceptions and Experiences of Context," in *The Parental Experience in Midlife*, ed. Carol D. Ryff and Marsha M. Seltzer (Chicago: University of Chicago Press, 1997), 339–382.

3 Tracy Robinson and Janie V. Ward, "'A Belief in Self Far Greater Than Anyone's Disbelief': Cultivating Healthy Resistance among African American Female Adolescents," in *Women, Girls, and Psychotherapy: Reframing Resistance*, ed. Carol Gilligan, Annie G. Rogers, and Deborah L. Tolman (New York: Routledge, 1991), 87–103.

4 Janie V. Ward, "Raising Resisters: The Role of Truth Telling in the Psychological Development of African American Girls," in *Urban Girls: Resisting Stereotypes, Creating Identities*, ed. Bonnie Leadbeater and Niobe Way (New York: New York University Press, 1996), 85–99.

5 bell hooks, *Black Looks: Race and Representation* (Boston: South End Press, 1992).

6 Jane Mansbridge and Aldon Morris, *Oppositional Consciousness: The Subjective Roots of Social Protest* (Chicago: University of Chicago Press, 2001), 4–5.

7 Juliet M. Corbin and Anselm L. Strauss, *Basics of Qualitative Research: Techniques and Procedures for Developing Grounded Theory* (Thousand Oaks, CA: SAGE, 2015).

8 See Andrew Garrod, Janie V. Ward, Tracy L. Robinson, and Robert Kilkenny, *Souls Looking Back: Life Stories of Growing Up Black* (New York: Routledge, 1999).

9 Callie H. Burt, Ronald L. Simons, and Frederick X. Gibbons, "Racial Discrimination, Ethnic-Racial Socialization, and Crime a Micro-sociological Model of Risk and Resilience," *American Sociological Review* 77, no. 4 (2012): 648–677; Enrique W. Neblett Jr. et al., "Racial Socialization and Racial Identity: African American Parents' Messages about Race as Precursors to Identity," *Journal of Youth and Adolescence* 38 (2009): 189–203; Howard C. Stevenson et al., "Development of the Teenager Experience of Racial Socialization Scale: Correlates of Race-Related Socialization Frequency from the Perspective of Black Youth," *Journal of Black Psychology* 28 (2002): 84–106.

10 Bowman and Howard, "Race-Related Socialization."

11 Gwendolyn Y. Davis and Howard C. Stevenson, "Racial Socialization Experiences and Symptoms of Depression among Black Youth," *Journal of Child and Family Studies* 15, no. 3 (2006): 293–307.

12 Michael C. Thornton, "Indigenous Resources and Strategies of Resistance: Informal Caregiving and Racial Socialization in Black Communities," in *Resiliency in African American Families*, ed. Hamilton I. McCubbin, Elizabeth A. Thompson, Anne I. Thompson, and Jo A. Futrell (Thousand Oaks, CA: SAGE, 1998), 49–66.

13 Kate Abbey-Lambert, "These 15 Black Women Were Killed during Police Encounters: Their Lives Matter, Too," *Huffington Post*, May 26, 2016, www.huffingtonpost.com.

14 Janie V. Ward, *The Skin We're In: Teaching Our Children to Be Emotionally Strong, Socially Smart and Spiritually Connected* (New York: Fireside/Free Press, 2000).

15 Dierdre Paul, *Talkin' Back: Raising and Educating Resilient Black Girls* (Westport, CT: Praeger, 2003), 29.

16 Monique W. Morris, *Pushout: The Criminalization of Black Girls in Schools* (New York: New Press, 2015), 13.

17 Melinda D. Anderson, "The Black Girl Pushout," *Atlantic*, March 15, 2016, www.theatlantic.com.

18 Henry A. Giroux, *Theory and Resistance in Education: A Pedagogy for the Opposition* (London: Heinemann Educational, 1983).

19 Nia Hamm, "Against All Odds: Economic Inequities for Black Women Cripple Communities," *NBC News*, July 8, 2015, www.nbcnews.com.

20 Janie V. Ward and Beth C. Benjamin, "Women, Girls and the Unfinished Work of Connection," in *All about the Girl: Power, Culture and Identity*, ed. Anita Harris (New York: Routledge, 2004), 15–28.

21 Janie V. Ward, Tracy L. Robinson-Wood, and Noreen Boadi, "Resisting Everyday Colorism in Schools: Strategies for Identifying and Interrupting the Problem That Won't Go Away," in *Race and Colorism in Education*, ed. Carla Monroe (New York: Routledge Press, 2016), 5–23.

22 Margaret L. Hunter, "If You're Light, You're Alright: Light Skin Color as Social Capital for Women of Color," *Gender & Society* 16 (2002): 175–193; Margaret L. Hunter, *Race, Gender and the Politics of Skin Tone* (New York: Routledge, 2005); Kerry Ann Rockquemore, "Negotiating the Color Line the Gendered Process of Racial Identity Construction among Black/White Biracial Women," *Gender & Society* 16 (2002): 485–503; JeffriAnne Wilder and Colleen Cain, "Teaching and Learning Color Consciousness in Black Families: Exploring Family Processes and Women's Experiences with Colorism," *Journal of Family Issues* 32 (2011): 577–604.

23 Margo Okazawa-Rey, Janie V. Ward, and Tracy L. Robinson, "Black Women and the Politics of Skin Color and Hair," *Women and Therapy* 6 (1987): 89–102; Ward, Robinson-Wood, and Boadi, "Resisting Everyday Colorism."

24 Kathy Russell-Cole, Midge Wilson, and Ronald E. Hall, *The Color Complex: The Politics of Skin Color in a New Millennium* (New York: Random House, 2013).

25 Lance Hannon, Robert DeFina, and Sarah Bruch, "The Relationship between Skin Tone and School Suspension for African Americans" (California State University, Northridge, June 2013), www.csun.edu.

26 Ibid.

27 Ward, Robinson-Wood, and Boadi, "Resisting Everyday Colorism."

28 Robin DiAngelo, "White Fragility," *International Journal of Critical Pedagogy* 3, no. 3 (2011): 54–70.

29 Judith V. Jordan, "The Role of Mutual Empathy in Relational-Cultural Therapy," *In Session: Psychotherapy in Practice* 55 (2000): 1005–1016.

30 Tracy L. Robinson-Wood, "The Relevance of Non-colorblind Talk between White Women and Non-White Children in the United States: A Discussion," *International Journal of Child, Youth and Family Studies* 6, no. 4.1 (2015): 646–661.

31 Morris, *Pushout*.

4

The "Black Box"

Identity Development and the Crisis of Connection among Black Adolescent Boys

LEOANDRA ONNIE ROGERS

It takes courage to grow up and become who you really are.
—E. E. Cummings

Society has its boxes for everybody, and they don't like it when you like jump outside of it. . . . The well-you're-never-going-to-be-anything 'cause you're in the Black box and I don't think you can do this cause you're Black. . . . Like Black kids are always doing the drugs . . . and they're always doing sports, or always the one that's just tryin' to shoot somebody up. . . . You're not supposed to be a bookworm, be feminine, be gay. Oh, you're Black, you're not supposed to be gay, you're supposed to have like 50 women and get a lot of people pregnant and then leave them all. . . . So yeah, my plan in life is to be as unique and extraordinary as possible. I have goals to prove all those people wrong and not fit into any one of those boxes.
—Marcus, Black boy, Grade 9

The Black box in American culture is imposed upon Black boys and girls whenever questions about what they can and cannot do and who they should and should not be arise. In the case of Black boys, they *can be* athletes and thugs or rappers and drug dealers, but they *cannot be* scholars and scientists or engaged fathers and partners. They *should be* tough, independent, and aggressive, but they *should not be* vulnerable, relational, and sensitive. The Black box, in other words, constrains the humanity of Black people; it splits Blackness from goodness, and embeds homophobia into the Black male identity.[1] These impositions are not simply about race, as Marcus reveals, but also about its mutually constitutive relationship to gender, sexuality, and social class concepts. When Black boys and young men accommodate to society's box of intersectional stereotypes, they disconnect from what they know about themselves—that they are thinking and feeling human beings—and disconnect from others as fellow human beings within and outside of their communities. The consequences of this crisis of connection in the identity development of Black boys and young men are increasingly evident: rising rates of depression and suicide, startling homicide rates that involve Black males as both victims and perpetrators.[2] Yet there are also Black boys, such as Marcus, who resist this disconnection. Marcus asserts that he will "not fit into any one of those boxes" that undermine his humanity and potential to thrive.[3] While the study of racial identity development among Black adolescents has been rich in its depth and breadth,[4] rarely have researchers investigated the processes of accommodation *and* resistance in the construction of identities among Black boys.

My own research with a small group of Black boys attending an all-Black, all-boys school suggests that there are at least three identity pathways that Black adolescent boys take in the search for who they are and who they want to be in the world.[5] Each pathway engages with and responds to the Black box of stereotypes in different ways. Those adhering to the first pathway, the "accommodators," respond to society's impositions and expectations by accommodating to both racial and gender stereotypes, resulting in disconnection from the self and others. The boys adhere to the box, and their sense of self appears to be constrained by it. The second and most common pathway I find in my research is the "exceptions." These boys resist the racial stereotypes of the Black box for themselves while at the same time applying both the racial and gender stereotypes to other Black boys. In other words, they do not challenge that the stereotypes they face are untrue, they simply say they do not fit into the stereotype. In their effort to remain connected to what they know about themselves, the "exceptions" disconnect from what they know about their peers. The final identity pathway, the "resisters," illustrates how Black boys reject the Black box entirely, explaining that society's racial, gender, and sexuality stereotypes are indeed stereotypes and not accurate representations of Black people. These boys appeared to develop a strong sense of self and stay connected to others. Over the next few pages, I first describe identity development and then reveal what these pathways sound like from the boys themselves, and conclude with ways to foster resistance to help Black boys stay connected to themselves as well as to others.

Identity Development and the Crisis of Connection

Psychologist Erik Erikson proposed a theory of *psychosocial identity*, describing development as "a process of simultaneous reflection and observation" whereby adolescents integrate their past, present, and future roles, along with their collective experiences into a coherent "sense of sameness and continuity."[6] The messages, images, and stereotypes from parents, peers, teachers, and society act as "social mirrors," guiding this identity process by reflecting to youth who and what they should be. How the adolescents respond to such messages as they construct their identities shapes the ways in which they understand not only how others see them but also how they see themselves.[7] According to Erikson, a positive identity will develop in a society that sends positive messages to adolescents about their possible roles in society; a negative identity will result when society communicates negative messages. Because Black adolescents live in a society that is saturated with negative messages that stereotype them as ignorant, lazy, and violent, they are at risk for developing negative identities as these messages or expectations seep into their identities and limit their understanding of their "role" possibilities.[8] These expectations are further complicated by the intersectional nature of racial stereotypes about Black boys. For example, they are "expected to be" heterosexual and hypermasculine, physically tough and emotionally stoic.[9] Therefore, rather than become who they really are, Black boys may "become exactly what the careless and fearful community expects" of them.[10]

Developmental psychologist Margaret Beale Spencer and colleagues reveal that many of the "negative identities" or hypermasculine "bravado" styles that Black boys develop are coping strategies that they use to contend with a racist society defined by violence and disconnection.[11] Black boys, in response to this hostile context, try to protect themselves from experiencing a sense of hypervulnerability by adopting aggressive behaviors and a stoic emotional stance. According to Spencer, this particular coping strategy, though protective, is counterproductive to developing a strong, positive sense of self. Sociologists Richard Majors and Janet Billson also reveal in their research that Black males embrace what they call the "cool pose," an identity defined by autonomy and stoicism, to protect themselves from the stress of racism, poverty, and violence.[12] Similar to Spencer and her colleagues, Majors and Bilson argue that the cool pose is not simply a "negative identity" but a self-protection strategy. Research suggests that while these poses, stances, and styles may offer short-term protection, they also make the boys prone to risky behaviors such dropping out of school, joining gangs, doing drugs, and perpetrating violence.[13] The Black box of stereotypes, in other words, leads some Black boys to experience a crisis of connection that has dire consequences.[14]

Yet research has found that Black youth not only accommodate to society's negative stereotypes but also resist them.[15] Developmental psychologists Tracy Robinson and Janie Ward outline two paths of resistance to stereotypes and racial oppression: *resistance for survival* and *resistance for liberation*.[16] The first strategy, *resistance for survival*, refers to short-term solutions, or "quick fixes," in response to oppressive systems, such as joining a gang or dropping out of school. These strategies focus on the individual and might make him or her feel better in the moment, but in the long run they are counterproductive because they ultimately perpetuate stereotypes and result in "emotional isolation and self-alienation" rather than positive identity and community building.[17] When Black boys adopt "hypermasculine" or "negative" identities to cope with contextual stressors, they are employing "resistance for survival strategies," or strategies of accommodation that disconnect them from themselves and others. The counterpoint to resistance for survival is *resistance for liberation*, a pathway of resistance that is rooted in an "inner strength" of hope. Unlike resistance for survival, the focus is on nurturing a sense of connectedness to the self and others. These strategies can be as abstract as maintaining strong spiritual and community ties or as concrete as challenging a school system that is improperly educating its students. The result of these types of strategies is that they empower Black youth by confirming positive self-conceptions and strengthening connections to the broader Black community; they are a pathway of connection.[18] Examples of resistance for liberation among Black boys include Niobe Way's work on boys' friendships. In her research over many decades, she finds that many boys insist on having emotionally intimate male friendships, especially during early adolescence, as they perceive these friendships to be critical to their mental health. They resist a culture, in other words, that frames these types of relationships as "girly" and "gay" and thus not "normal" for straight boys, especially boys who are stereotyped as hypermasculine.[19]

The constructs of accommodation (or resistance for survival) and resistance for liberation are useful in the investigation of the identity development of Black boys precisely because they allow for not only the disruption of passive narratives about Black boys, but also monolithic representations of Black boys as "bad" and "troubled." They underscore the agentic nature of identity development and the ways in which context and culture shape, and are shaped by, the meaning and expression of identities.

Three Paths of Identity Development among Black Adolescent Boys

My three-year, mixed-method study of the ways in which Black boys resist and accommodate to racial and gender stereotypes in their identities followed the entering cohort of 183 ninth-grade boys at an all-Black, all-male high school in the Midwest.[20] The data I present here are from the in-depth, one-on-one interviews that I conducted with twenty-one boys during their ninth- and tenth-grade years.[21] The interviews were designed to discuss, "what it is like being a young Black male in society today." During each hour-long interview, I asked the boys questions about their family and friends, their school and future aspirations, and their ideas about what it means to be Black and male. I was particularly interested in examining their awareness of racial and gender stereotypes, and their perceptions of discrimination.

My analysis of the interviews revealed three paths of identity development. Each path illustrates a different way by which Black boys navigate the crisis of connection in their identity development. The "accommodators," who composed 24 percent ($n = 5$) of the interview sample, reinforced the racial and gender stereotypes that define the Black box. The "exceptions," who made up 57 percent ($n = 12$) of the interview sample, also reinforced, or accommodated to, gender stereotypes, but saw themselves as exempt from those stereotypes (i.e., exceptions to the race and gender stereotypes that define the Black box). Finally, the "resisters," who composed 19 percent ($n = 4$) of the sample, rejected or resisted racial and gender stereotypes both about themselves and for others. Mapping these identity pathways onto Robinson and Ward's framework, the accommodators and the exceptions demonstrate resistance for survival strategies that ultimately lead them toward disconnection, while the resisters represent resistance for liberation strategies that ultimately lead them to forge pathways of connection with themselves and others.

The Accommodators

The accommodators were those boys who, on the whole, reinforced gender *and* racial stereotypes in their identity narratives. The accommodators speak like a stereotype—the independent and hypermasculine, "tough Black male" who is ready to fight and more focused on getting with girls than learning in school. Their identity narratives thread together stereotypes about race, gender, and sexuality and mirror many of the hypermasculine identities outlined in prior research.[22] But, contrary to the pervasive cultural narrative of hypermasculinity that Black boys inevitably go on to develop disconnected, accommodating identities, this group represented only 24 percent of the boys in my interview sample. In fact, most of the Black boys in my sample do not describe developing their identities in this way.

Omar, one of the accommodators, describes himself as "the hood guy" who is "trying to make it." When asked what some of the good things are about being Black, he responded:

> OMAR: Oh, like a lot of people are scared of us; that's great.
> ROGERS: Okay, and why is that a good thing?
> OMAR: Because sometimes it's kinda funny to see that fear in people, "Oh no, I walked in to the wrong neighborhood." [laugh] They're shaking; it's funny to me. Almost everything be funny to me. [laugh] I could be in the craziest situation and still be laughing.

Omar's enjoyment of the fact that the stereotypes of dangerous Black men create fear in others suggests a disconnection from what he knows about himself, which is that he is not dangerous or scary. His laughter at the "people" who are scared suggests not only a masculine stoicism, but an acknowledgment of the "fear" that others project on him is not justified. He worries, however, that one day he will become exactly what society expects:

> ROGERS: When you think about your future, what do you worry about?
> OMAR: Man, I think I'll worry about me being bad; I don't know. I'll be kind of tempted sometimes, like 'man, you need that money dog'; I'm trying to be good now. . . . I ain't trying to be locked up. [laughs] I can't do that, no, no, no. I'm too little to go to jail.

Omar articulates who he does not want to be, but fears who he will become. His response indicates a vulnerability that was rarely expressed among the accommodators because, as Margaret Beale Spencer and her colleagues have shown us, those who feel the *most* vulnerable often appear to be the *most* stereotypical.[23] Omar fears losing who he is, thus, it is his *hypervulnerability* that he masks with accommodation (and laughter).

The accommodators appeared to disconnect not only from who they know themselves to be but from others. Unlike the boys in the other two groups who spoke of having one or two close friends, Omar says he only has "acquaintances" and that his friends are a group of "about fifty or more of us that kick it."[24] Using hypermasculine language to describe his friendships suggests not only accommodation to gender stereotypes but also a lack of intimacy in his friendships.[25] Though the accommodators did not necessarily believe in the veracity of the various stereotypes they repeated, nonetheless they integrated both gender and racial stereotypes into their identities and relationships, and thus disconnected from both self and others.

The Exceptions

The most common identity pathway, the exceptions, were those Black boys who *resisted* racial stereotypes for themselves but saw the stereotypes as generally true for other Black people and *accommodated* to gender stereotypes. Like all of the boys in my study, "the exceptions" were acutely aware of society's negative stereotypes and expectations, but rather than challenge the Black box they viewed themselves as exceptions. When I asked Jaire, one of the exceptions, to describe himself, he said: "I would say that I'm a very intelligent, articulate young man. . . . And someone who is genuinely a well-behaved person, a well-dressed or groomed person." Jaire's general self-description stands in direct opposition to how he says *other people* view Black people: "Just lazy and acting out and don't care about their educations." The exceptions, in other words, tried to resist racial stereotypes by separating themselves from *other* Black people.

> ROGERS: What do you like most about yourself?
> JAIRE: I love the fact that people think of me to be a more complex individual and a more intelligent individual. Because there's no fourteen-year-old—let's be real, no fourteen-year-old *African American male* that can use different words in different situations and give his opinion about Barack Obama or the state the economy is in, the Iraq war, and different situations or the lesbian movement.

Jaire resists the idea that because he is a Black male, he is unintelligent and uninformed, which is, of course, an important counternarrative. However, he establishes this sense of identity by viewing himself as an *exception* to the stereotype, thereby leaving the stereotype intact. He essentially says, *other Black boys are dumb, but I'm not.* Caught in the false choice of choosing between the self *or* the other, Jaire effectively disconnects from the other in an effort to connect with the self. Yet, because the self and the other are inextricably linked, the path leads to disconnection.

The disconnection of the exceptions is also explicitly evident in their accommodation to gender stereotypes, endorsing masculine autonomy, dominance, and stoicism. Jaire explains what he likes about being a "young man":

> Um, the best part about being a young man is that we get to, like we're, um, the trendsetters of the world. You know what I'm saying? Like the government, the world is run by men. Men run the world, you

know what I'm saying. . . . And I don't think that a woman is fit to run a world. . . . Because men make hard decisions without emotion. And the women get emotional in certain situations. . . . Like their emotions are too high.

Jaire reiterates the stereotype that women are emotional and thus incompetent whereas men are stoic and thus competent. By doing so, Jaire disconnects from his own capacity for emotion and, more broadly, from girls and women. This disconnection from others is also evident in Jaire's friendships with other boys, whom he separates into "good" and "bad" influences. His closest friends are a group of Black boys who share his academic aspirations; and together they distance themselves from "regular Black guys."[26] By referring to this latter group as "regular," he is suggesting that the *stereotype* of Black boys as having no academic aspirations reflects the true reality of most Black boys. His response is striking, in particular because most of the boys in Jaire's all-male and all-Black high school have high academic aspirations.[27] This identity strategy disconnects Jaire not only from what he knows about himself and his close friends—who are Black boys with high academic aspirations—but from what he knows about the other Black boys around him.

In contrast to the accommodators who placed themselves inside the Black box, the exceptions placed *themselves* outside the Black box by defining their identities in opposition to the stereotypes that define the Black box. However, as seen in Jaire's response, they ultimately reinforce the very stereotypes they want to resist and thus disconnect from themselves and each other.[28]

The Resisters

The final identity pathway is the resisters, who confronted both racial *and* gender stereotypes using resistance for liberation strategies. They viewed stereotypes about race, gender, and sexuality as a system of oppression that threatens entire groups rather than specific individuals and refused to disconnect from themselves or from others in service of these stereotypes. As suggested by Marcus, one of the resisters who is quoted at the beginning of this chapter, "Society has its boxes for everybody, and they don't like it when you like jump outside of it." The boys in this group recognize the broader social context and are determined to resist it in ways that maintain connections both to themselves and to others.

Marcus explains how he feels when he thinks about the stereotypes:

> I actually get kind of mad but I try to keep that anger under wraps [be]cause, you know, you don't want that anger coming out in the wrong way. So, I try to focus it in, do my schoolwork, so I can break the stereotype. . . . So I guess you could say that I'm kind of inspired, but then again I'm kind of like pissed off. That's kind of how I feel about it.

Unlike the accommodators who tended to laugh off stereotypes or the exceptions who simply separated themselves from the stereotypes, the resisters acknowledged the impact of stereotypes on the self and others. Marcus names his own emotions—"mad," "angry," "inspired," "pissed off"—and explains how he harnesses each emotion to resist the stereotypes.

The resisters were also characterized by actively contesting the gender hierarchy.

> ROGERS: Are there things you feel like you're supposed to do or ways you're supposed to act just because you're a boy?
>
> MARCUS: Well, it's not things that *I think* I'm supposed to do, it's things that people think I'm supposed to do. Like guys aren't supposed to be feminine or guys aren't supposed to be sensitive or show their feelings, or cry. That's a big one, like guys aren't supposed to cry. . . . It's like but if you get hit or you get a bone broken or your mama or someone close to you dies like, you know, of course you gonna cry cause that's like human nature, you're supposed to cry, that's why you have tear ducts in your body.

Marcus first distinguishes between who he really is and who society says he should be ("not things *I* think . . . things that people think I'm supposed to do"). Then, in claiming his own humanity and the humanity of others, he rejects the stereotype that emotion is feminine, asserting that emotion is "human nature." When I ask Marcus to explain where this conflict comes from, he threads together the racial, gender, and sexuality stereotypes that define the Black box:

I guess society thinks that if men or boys act feminine that they're gay or they just assume that they're gay. And I think that's a bad stereotype because guys need to express their feelings too. I'm not going to say that guys are supposed to be tough all the time . . . and they're supposed to like man up and like cover that up with hardness or whatever. It's okay to let yourself cry and be heartbroken. I don't think that's a good stereotype because that's like telling kids not to care about anything that happens.

Marcus *refuses* to disconnect from himself or other boys and men ("I'm not going to say that guys are supposed to be tough all the time") and underscores the importance of caring, which is an explicit rejection of the masculine dictate not to care.[29] Marcus cares deeply and expresses this quality throughout his interviews, describing his close relationship with his mother and explaining that close friends are a necessary "support system" for Black males who "always get pushed down and have to work harder." His identity, in other words, is fully integrated into his relationships, suggesting the presence of a resistance for liberation strategy in which he insists on staying connected to himself and to others.[30] The resisters reveal an identity pathway that allows Black adolescent boys to care, feel, and know themselves and each other. These identities are rooted in their recognition of a racist, sexist, homophobic context, and they understand that this context leads to a set of stereotypes that are deeply damaging to themselves and each other.

It would be easy to glorify the resisters and conclude that they have it figured out, relative to the accommodators and the exceptions. But ethnographer Ann Arnett Ferguson cautions against categorizing these three groups as entirely distinct. In her study of Black boys, the boys' responses fell on a continuum where the "schoolboys" resisted racial stereotypes about academic competencies and the "troublemakers" accommodated or used resistance for survival strategies by disrupting the class or acting out in other ways. Ferguson argues that these different responses to stereotypes represent two ends of a continuum with "the 'schoolboys' always being on the brink of being redefined into the 'troublemakers' . . . due to the force of racial and gender stereotypes working against them."[31] In other words, these processes of resistance and accommodation occur both within and in response to an *active* context of oppression and thus may change due to the extent to which the resistance for liberation of Black youth is supported.

Discussion

My study suggests that Black boys forge at least three types of pathways for themselves in their search for understanding who they are and want to be. Moreover, these identity pathways that these Black boys navigate are related to the crisis of connection with themselves and others. The accommodators exemplify boys who struggle the most with their identities, because they align themselves with society's presentation of images and expectations, the stereotypes, that define the Black box. These boys have forgotten who they really are, and have taken up the "negative identity" that society presents to them. The accommodators are the Black boys we hear most about in novels (e.g., *Native Son*), in the research literature, and in national conversations that frame Black boys as "endangered" and "in crisis."[32] Omar's narrative aligns with previous research on the "cool pose" and "bravado" identities, illustrating how the Black box disrupts positive identity development among Black boys.[33] The disconnection that the accommodators experience in their sense of self is expressed through their lack of close relationships with others as well. Without a secure sense of self, they struggle to form intimate relationships with others.[34] Yet, this story, which often pervades our understanding of what it means to be a Black boy (and man), is not the only story. The accommodators represented only a quarter of the boys in my research sample; the rest of the boys were navigating different pathways of identity development.[35]

The second, and most common, pathway of identity development was the exceptions. Faced with a crisis of connection, the exceptions attempt to save themselves at the high cost of sacrificing their connections to others by continuing to believe in, and perpetuate, the stereotypes that plague the members of their own racial community. For example, although Jaire steps outside of the Black box to establish his identity, he leaves the Black box intact. Like society, Jaire believes that "other Black boys" fit within the box, and thus fosters his own disconnection with others. In the Harvard Project, a longitudinal study of girls' development, researchers discuss the false choices that girls are asked to make in a patriarchal culture in sacrificing themselves for the sake of "relationships" in which they cannot speak what they really think and feel.[36] Like the adolescent girls, the Black boys are asked to make a false choice between their own sense of humanity (i.e., *I am not* a stereotype) and the humanity of others (i.e., *other* Black people *are* the stereotype). In a racist and sexist culture, Black boys seem to make a similar sacrifice when they surrender their connection to others, including, in the case of Jaire, girls and women, for the sake of saving themselves as "exceptions."

Black boys in the resisters pathway fight to hold on to what they know about themselves—that they are allowed to think and feel—and others, or that the stereotype of Black people is, in fact, not a universal truth but just a stereotype. Marcus not only steps outside of the Black box, he tries to "break" it so that the box will not disconnect him from himself or from his peers. He maintains that friends are his "support system" rather than bad influences to distance himself from. His resistance, in other words, is a resistance for liberation strategy that helps to pave the pathway for others to also resist and (re)connect with their own "human nature," as he describes it.[37]

Knowing that resistance for liberation is a human capacity and necessity for Black youth to thrive, the pressing question becomes how to foster such resistance. Janie Ward demonstrates how Black mothers teach resistance for survival or liberation through their conversations with their children.[38] In order to cultivate resistance among youth, adults—including parents, teachers, coaches, and community leaders—must assess their own identities and ask themselves how they are resisting disconnection. These identity assessments must give consideration to the types of strategies the adults themselves use to connect with who they really are and those around them.[39] Fostering healthy identity pathways also entails helping adolescents to develop an "oppositional gaze" so that they can see the boxes of society.[40] Marcus was able to name the stereotypes: he could see the "Black box." But invisibility and silence are often the tools that power social hierarchy. The systems of racism and sexism are shrouded in normativity and can therefore advance unquestioned. Yet adults can foster within youth the ability to see systems of oppression so they are equipped to "oppose ideas that are disempowering to the self."[41] "Resistance-building truth-telling" is needed in order to foster within youth resistance for liberation that builds up the sense of self.[42]

Schools also play a role in fostering resistance and supporting identity development. Although schools often reproduce inequality,[43] they can also provide spaces for Black males to thrive and (re)connect with themselves and others in meaningful ways.[44] Education scholar Theresa Perry refers to such schools as "counterhegemonic communities" that deliberately resist hegemonic ideologies and practice liberation.[45]

My research at an all-Black male high school also demonstrates how a school's ideology and mission can foster resistance and forge paths of connection through identity development.[46] For example, the principal described the all-Black male high school this way:

> We want an environment where [students are] free to be who they are, where they don't have to live with these stereotypical ideas of what a Black man is, you know, I can only be a basketball player, I can only be a rapper, or a lot of machismo. We intentionally build . . . an environment where they really want to achieve and not feel like someone will call them lame or a nerd if they are achieving academically.

This school aspired to *create* a space for boys to be "free to be who they are" beyond the limiting boxes. Teachers at the school expressed similar goals to *teach* and instill positive identities:

> [Society] has created an image for us: that Black males are irresponsible . . . that we're sexual creatures that just spread our seed irresponsibly, that we deal drugs, that we're not educated, those things. We have to fight that image. That we're rappers and basketball players and not scholars. These are the images that we have to tell them [the students], no, that's not the reality of who we are. (English teacher, Black male)

Through ritualized culture, counternarratives and counterimages, high expectations, and support, schools can help support boys in becoming who they really are.[47] Projects such as the Listening Project (see Way and Nelson, this volume) offer boys of color the opportunity to reimagine themselves as being as emotionally astute and socially competent as their female peers. They also offer an opportunity for teachers to explicitly foster resistance for liberation among boys of color by nurturing boys' natural curiosity and capacity to ask and answer their own questions and connect more deeply with those around them.

While fostering resistance among youth is critical, it is equally important that we pay attention to the ways in which youth are already questioning and resisting oppressive norms and expectations. When adolescent boys express sadness and vulnerability, when they express the value of cultivating their relationships with other boys,[48] we must notice and support their resistance by normalizing and creating space for our sons' social and emotional desires and vulnerabilities in the same ways that we do for our daughters. We must normalize talking with our sons and organizing playdates and sleepovers instead of dismissing their desires as unimportant or pathologizing their requests as "gay" and "girly."[49] When a young girl questions why teachers say the "girls team needs a boy" to make the game "fair," or rejects the assumption that her interest in science somehow makes her unique or exceptional, it is important that we notice and affirm her identity as a physically and intellectually capable young person. When gender-nonconforming teens resist the label of abnormal or disturbed and insist on being who they are, it is important that we embrace rather than doubt, shame, or marginalize them.[50] Noticing the ways in which youth resist, in other words, is a critical part of fostering resistance.

In a society predicated on social hierarchy, it takes courage for Black children to grow up and become who they really are. Yet the potential to resist the Black box is, as shown by the boys in my study, a human quality and must be nourished to effectively address the crisis of connection in identity development. While the constraints of dehumanizing stereotypes make it extremely difficult for Black boys to develop positive identities,[51] boys such as Marcus show us that it is not only possible to resist for liberation but also urgent to nurture such resistance so that Black children can stay connected to their own humanity as well as to the humanity of others, and find the communities that they want and need in order to thrive.

NOTES

1 James Earl Davis, "Transgressing the Masculine: African American Boys and the Failure of Schools," in *What about the Boys? Issues of Masculinity in Schools*, ed. Wayne Martino and Bob Meyenn (Buckingham: Open University Press, 2001),

140–153; Michael Dumas and Joseph D. Nelson, "(Re)imagining Black Boyhood: Toward a Critical Framework for Educational Research," *Harvard Educational Review* 86, no. 1 (2016): 27–47; Negin Ghavami and Letitia Anne Peplau, "Urban Middle School Students' Stereotypes at the Intersection of Sexual Orientation, Ethnicity, and Gender," *Child Development*, published ahead of print, March 6, 2017, doi:10.1111/cdev.12763.

2 Jeffrey A. Bridge et al., "Suicide Trends among Elementary School–Aged Children in the United States from 1993 to 2012," *JAMA Pediatrics* 169, no. 7 (2015): 673–677, doi:10.1001/jamapediatrics.2015.0465; Suicide Prevention Resource Center, "Suicide among Racial/Ethnic Populations in the U.S.: Blacks" (2013), www.sprc.org; Violence Policy Center, "Black Homicide Victimization in the United States: An Analysis of 2012 Homicide Data" (2015), www.vpc.org.

3 Leoandra Onnie Rogers and Niobe Way, "'I Have Goals to Prove All Those People Wrong and Not Fit into Any One of Those Boxes': Paths of Resistance to Stereotypes among Black Adolescent Males," *Journal of Adolescent Research* 31, no. 3 (2016): 263–298, doi:10.1177/0743558415600071.

4 Howard C. Stevenson, Jr., "'Missed, Dissed, and Pissed': Making Meaning of Neighborhood Risk, Fear and Anger Management in Urban Black Youth," *Cultural Diversity and Mental Health* 3, no. 1 (1997): 37–52; Ann Arnett Ferguson, *Bad Boys: Public Schools in the Making of Black Masculinity* (Ann Arbor: University of Michigan Press, 2000); Margaret Beale Spencer et al., "Vulnerability to Violence: A Contextually-Sensitive, Developmental Perspective on African American Adolescents," *Journal of Social Issues* 59 (2003): 33–49; Richard Majors and Janet Mancini Billson, *Cool Pose: The Dilemmas of African American Manhood in America* (New York: Lexington, 1992); bell hooks, *We Real Cool: Black Men and Masculinity* (New York: Psychology Press, 2004); Leoandra Onnie Rogers, Erika Y. Niwa, and Niobe Way, "The Friendships of Racial-Ethnic Minority Adolescents in Context: Identity and Discrimination," in *Handbook of Positive Development of Minority Children*, ed. Natasha Cabrera and Brigit Leyendecker (Amsterdam: Springer, 2017), 267–280; Niobe Way, *Deep Secrets: Boys' Friendships and the Crisis of Connection* (Cambridge, MA: Harvard University Press, 2011); Derrick R. Brooms, "Mapping Pathways to Affirmative Identities among Black Males: Instilling the Value and Importance of Education in K–12 and College Classrooms," *Journal of African American Males in Education* 5, no. 2 (2014): 196–214; Leoandra Onnie Rogers, Marc A. Scott, and Niobe Way, "Racial and Gender Identity Development among Black Adolescent Males: An Intersectionality Perspective," *Child Development* 86, no. 2 (2015): 407–424, doi:10.1111/cdev.12303; Rogers and Way, "'I Have Goals to Prove.'"

5 Rogers and Way, "'I Have Goals to Prove.'"

6 Erik H. Erikson, *Identity, Youth, and Crisis* (New York: Norton, 1968), 22.

7 Stevenson, "'Missed, Dissed, and Pissed'"; Carola Suárez-Orozco, "Formulating Identity in a Globalized World," in *Globalization: Culture and Education in*

the New Millennium, ed. Marcelo M. Suárez-Orozco and Carola Suárez-Orozco (Berkeley: University of California Press, 2004), 173–202.

8 Nick Haslam, "Dehumanization: An Integrative Review," *Personality and Social Psychology Review* 10, no. 3 (2006): 252–264; Nour Kteily, Emile Bruneau, Adam Waytz, and Sarah Cotterill, "The Ascent of Man: Theoretical and Empirical Evidence for Blatant Dehumanization," *Journal of Personality and Social Psychology* 109, no. 5 (2015): 901–931; Sophie Trawalter, Kelly Marie Hoffman, and Adam Waytz, "Racial Bias in Perceptions of Others' Pain," *PLOS ONE* 7 (2012): e48546; Adam Waytz, Kelly Marie Hoffman, and Sophie Trawalter, "A Superhumanization Bias in Whites' Perceptions of Blacks," *Social Psychological and Personality Science* 6, no. 3 (2015): 352–359.

9 Negin Ghavami and Letitia Anne Peplau, "An Intersectional Analysis of Gender and Ethnic Stereotypes: Testing Three Hypotheses," *Psychology of Women Quarterly* 37, no. 1 (2013): 113–127; hooks, *We Real Cool*; Niobe Way and Leoandra Rogers, "Resistance to Dehumanization during Childhood and Adolescence: A Developmental and Contextual Process," in *New Perspectives on Human Development*, ed. Nancy Budwig, Elliot Turiel, and Philip David Zelazo (Cambridge: Cambridge University Press, 2017), 209–228; Kate C. McLean and Moin Syed, "Personal, Master, and Alternative Narratives: An Integrative Framework for Understanding Identity Development in Context," *Human Development* 58, no. 6 (2015): 318–349; Na'ilah Nasir, *Racialized Identities: Race and Achievement among African American Youth* (Stanford, CA: Stanford University Press, 2011); Judy Y. Chu, "A Relational Perspective on Adolescent Boys' Identity Development," in *Adolescent Boys: Exploring Diverse Cultures of Boyhood*, ed. Niobe Way and Judy Y. Chu (New York: New York University Press, 2004), 78–104; Judy Y. Chu, *When Boys Become Boys: Development, Relationships, and Masculinity* (New York: New York University Press, 2014); Rogers, Niwa, and Way, "Friendships of Racial-Ethnic Minority Adolescents"; Way, *Deep Secrets*.

10 Erikson, *Identity, Youth, and Crisis*, 196.

11 Margaret Beale Spencer, Davido Dupree, and Tracey Hartmann, "A Phenomenological Variant of Ecological Systems Theory (PVEST): A Self-Organization Perspective in Context," *Development and Psychopathology* 9, no. 4 (1997): 817–833; Spencer et al., "Vulnerability to Violence"; Michael Cunningham, "African-American Adolescent Males' Perceptions of Their Community Resources and Constraints: A Longitudinal Analysis," *Journal of Community Psychology* 27, no. 5 (1999): 569–588; Michael Cunningham and Leah Newkirk Meunier, "The Influence of Peer Experiences on Bravado Attitudes among African American Males," in Way and Chu, *Adolescent Boys*, 219–232.

12 Majors and Billson, *Cool Pose*; Spencer et al., "Vulnerability to Violence."

13 Majors and Billson, *Cool Pose*; Pedro Noguera, *The Trouble with Black Boys: And Other Reflections on Race, Equity, and the Future of Public Education* (San Francisco: Jossey-Bass, 2008); Spencer et al., "Vulnerability to Violence."

14 Ferguson, *Bad Boys*; Noguera, *Trouble with Black Boys*; Spencer et al., "Vulnerability to Violence"; Jewelle Taylor Gibbs, *Young, Black, and Male in America: An Endangered Species* (Dover, MA: Auburn House, 1988); Noguera, *Trouble with Black Boys*; Tyrone C. Howard, *Black Male(d): Peril and Promise in the Education of African American Males* (New York: Teachers College Press, 2013).

15 Rogers and Way, "'I Have Goals to Prove'"; Way and Rogers, "Resistance to Dehumanization"; Rogers, Niwa, and Way, "Friendships of Racial-Ethnic Minority Adolescents in Context"; Way, *Deep Secrets*; Nasir, *Racialized Identities*; Niobe Way, María G. Hernández, Leoandra Onnie Rogers, and Diane L. Hughes. "'I'm Not Going to Become No Rapper': Stereotypes as a Context of Ethnic and Racial Identity Development," *Journal of Adolescent Research* 28, no. 4 (2013): 407–430.

16 Tracy Robinson and Janie V. Ward, "'A Belief in Self Far Greater Than Anyone's Disbelief': Cultivating Healthy Resistance among African American Female Adolescents," in *Women, Girls, and Psychotherapy: Reframing Resistance*, ed. Carol Gilligan, Annie G. Rogers, and Deborah L. Tolman (New York: Routledge, 1991), 87–103.

17 Ibid., 91.

18 Ibid., 91.

19 Way, *Deep Secrets*.

20 Full details of the study can be found in Rogers, Scott, and Way, "Racial and Gender Identity Development"; and Rogers and Way, "'I Have Goals to Prove.'"

21 Rogers and Way, "'I Have Goals to Prove.'"

22 Spencer et al., "Vulnerability to Violence"; Majors and Billson, *Cool Pose*.

23 Spencer et al., "Vulnerability to Violence."

24 Rogers, Niwa, and Way, "Friendships of Racial-Ethnic Minority Adolescents in Context."

25 Way, *Deep Secrets*.

26 Rogers, Niwa, and Way, "Friendships of Racial-Ethnic Minority Adolescents in Context."

27 The school was designed as an academy of academic excellence for Black boys. The school founders and leaders describe it as a space designed to provide students with "positive counter-images of successful Black men" and give them a "vision for college." They refer to the students as "scholars," and college graduation (not merely acceptance or attendance) defines the school's primary mission. They have an extended school day, built-in Saturday school for study hall, and college preparatory classes. For additional details, see also Rogers, Scott, and Way, "Racial and Gender Identity Development"; Rogers and Way, "'I Have Goals to Prove.'"

28 Robinson and Ward, "'Belief in Self.'"

29 Rogers, Niwa, and Way, "Friendships of Racial-Ethnic Minority Adolescents in Context."

30 Way et al, this volume; Way, *Deep Secrets.*

31 Ferguson, *Bad Boys*, 10.

32 Gibbs, *Young, Black, and Male in America*; Noguera, *Trouble with Black Boys*; Howard, *Black Male(d).*

33 Majors and Billson, *Cool Pose*; Spencer et al., "Vulnerability to Violence."

34 Erikson, *Identity, Youth, and Crisis.*

35 Brooms, "Mapping Pathways to Affirmative Identities"; Davis, "Transgressing the Masculine."

36 Lyn Mikel Brown and Carol Gilligan, *Meeting at the Crossroads: Women's Psychology and Girls' Development* (Cambridge, MA: Harvard University Press, 1992).

37 Robinson and Ward, "'Belief in Self.'"

38 Ward, this volume; Janie V. Ward, "Raising Resisters: The Role of Truth Telling in the Psychological Development of African American Girls," in *Urban Girls: Resisting Stereotypes, Creating Identities*, ed. Bonnie Leadbeater and Niobe Way (New York: New York University Press, 1996), 85–99.

39 Carol Gilligan, "Joining the Resistance: Psychology, Politics, Girls and Women," in *Beyond Silenced Voices: Class, Race, and Gender in United States Schools*, ed. Lois Weis and Michelle Fine (Albany: State University of New York Press, 1993), 164.

40 bell hooks, *Black Looks: Race and Representation* (Boston: South End Press, 1992); Ward, this volume.

41 Ward, "Raising Resisters," 87.

42 Ibid.

43 E.g., Jay MacLeod, *Ain't No Making It: Leveled Aspirations in a Low Income Neighborhood* (Boulder, CO: Westview, 1987); Pedro A. Noguera, *City Schools and the American Dream: Reclaiming the Promise of Public Education* (New York: Teachers College Press, 2003).

44 E.g., Gilberto Q. Conchas and Pedro A. Noguera, "Understanding the Exceptions: How Small Schools Support the Achievement of Academically Successful Black Boys," in Way and Chu, *Adolescent Boys*, 317–337; James E. Davis and Will J. Jordan, "The Effects of School Context, Structure, and Experiences on African American Males in Middle and High School," *Journal of Negro Education* 63, no. 4 (1994): 570–587; Dumas and Nelson, "(Re)imagining Black Boyhood"; Way and Nelson, this volume.

45 W. E. B. Du Bois, "Does the Negro Need Separate Schools?," *Journal of Negro Education* 4 (1935): 328–335; Theresa Perry, "Up from the Parched Earth: Toward a Theory of African American Achievement," in *Young, Gifted, and Black: Promoting High Achievement among African-American Students*, ed. Theresa Perry, Claude Steele, and Asa G. Hilliard (Boston: Beacon, 2003), 1–108; Nasir, *Racialized Identities.*

46 Rogers, Scott, and Way, "Racial and Gender Identity Development"; Rogers, Niwa, and Way, "Friendships of Racial-Ethnic Minority Adolescents in Context"; Rogers and Way, "'I Have Goals to Prove.'"

47 Perry, "Up from the Parched Earth."

48 Chu, "Relational Perspective"; Chu, *When Boys Become Boys*; Way, *Deep Secrets*.

49 Way, *Deep Secrets*.

50 Kristina R. Olson, Lily Durwood, Madeleine DeMeules, and Katie A. McLaughlin, "Mental Health of Transgender Children Who Are Supported in Their Identities," *Pediatrics*, February 2016, http://pediatrics.aappublications.org.

51 Violence Policy Center, "Black Homicide Victimization."

The Crisis of Connection in Society and Science

5

In Pursuit of Our Common Humanity

The Role of Education in Overcoming the Empathy Gap and the Crisis of Connection

PEDRO NOGUERA

If you assume that there is no hope, you guarantee that there will be no hope. If you assume that there is an instinct for freedom, that there are opportunities to change things, then there is a possibility that you can contribute to making a better world.
—Noam Chomsky

Throughout the ages we have to rediscover that our community is not only made of the highly motivated competing individuals . . . but that it includes fragile, vulnerable, suffering individuals who reveal to ourselves our own fragility, our own vulnerability. . . . This fundamental discovery is at the heart of our humanity.
—Xavier Le Pichon

As several of the contributors to this volume make clear, signs that we are in the midst of a crisis of connection are everywhere. They are present in our inability to prevent war, terrorism, and violence, whether perpetrated by gangs, the police, psycho killers, or the state. Signs that the crisis of connection is growing and becoming more severe are painfully obvious in our failure to respond effectively or adequately to hunger and disease, and in our inability to stop modern forms of slavery, now referred to as human trafficking. The crisis is detectable in the ineffectiveness of the response toward the global movement of refugees, some of whom are unaccompanied children who find themselves unwanted, endangered, and in some cases perpetually homeless. It is perhaps most present in the way we accept or respond with passive helplessness to the growing threat of global warming and climate change. Finally, the crisis of connection is present in our acceptance of growing inequality in incomes, in the fact that eight men now control more wealth and resources than the poorest 3.6 billion people on the planet,[1] and that problems related to the deterioration in the human condition are tolerated because they affect the marginalized, the dispossessed, and the "wretched of the earth."

The crisis of connection is not the sole cause of these problems, but it is often the critical factor and ingredient that abets their growth. Together with its twin, the empathy gap—a condition characterized by our growing inability to respond with compassion to the suffering of others—it serves as an obstacle that obstructs the search for creative solutions to human problems. To the degree that violence is accepted as "normal" when it occurs in Somalia, Afghanistan, El Salvador, or Chicago's South Side, to the degree that the signs of global warming are ignored because they are felt most directly on remote islands of the Pacific or in South America, or to the degree that we tolerate large numbers of mentally ill people living on our streets or filling our nation's prisons, it becomes clear that the crisis of connection is indeed a factor contributing to both the proliferation and the passive acceptance of these enormous problems.

The crisis of connection deludes us into believing that these problems are not "ours," and it lulls us into believing that we can ignore them until they affect us directly. Must we wait until one of our loved ones dies from a drug overdose to recognize the threat of pervasive heroin and opioid abuse? Can we afford to ignore gun violence until a school, movie theater, or shopping mall in our own community is the site of violence, or until one of our loved ones dies or is maimed in a mass shooting? Why does the slogan "Black Lives Matter" evoke anger and resentment rather than empathy and solidarity, particularly among those who believe "their" lives already matter? Creative, preventative actions and policies are difficult to enact when large portions of the population and those with the most power feel disconnected and lack the ability to empathize with the suffering of others. Indifference is invariably a source of sustenance to hardships that fester when ignored, that spread and become more severe because the crisis of human connection has stymied empathy and blocked the emergence of solutions, or even consideration of serious responses to problems large and small.

From Benign Neglect to Willful Ignorance: The Election of Donald Trump and the Widening of the "Empathy Gap"

In March 1970, Daniel Patrick Moynihan, former US senator and advisor to President Richard Nixon, wrote a memo to the president advising him that the nation might benefit from a period of "benign neglect" with respect to how it responded to conditions in impoverished Black communities. A year later, another Nixon aide, Patrick Buchanan, suggested that rather than ignoring the suffering the Republican Party would be better off exploiting the growing White resentment as a way to split the Democratic Party and the country in half, so that Republicans could inherit the "whiter part."[2]

In the election of 2016, the fruits of the Buchanan strategy were clearly on display and played no small part in the surprising electoral victory of Donald Trump. Fueled by the resentments of the White working class in rust belt states like Pennsylvania, Ohio, Wisconsin, and Michigan, Trump rode a wave of resentment to the White House, harnessing the anger with promises to his supporters that he would "build the wall," to keep immigrants out, and "lock her up," to imprison Hilary Clinton for deleting emails she claimed were private while serving as secretary of state. Since Trump's election, extreme polarization has led to further expansion across the empathy gap, particularly with respect to differences in race, gender, and sexual orientation, and contributed to the creation of an even more divided nation.

At the beginning of the Trump era, the "empathy gap" was already evident in matters pertaining to immigration, with a significant increase in ICE (Immigration and Customs Enforcement) raids and detentions of undocumented immigrants, and Trump's repeated efforts to ban Muslims from six nations from entry to the United States. Even before Trump's election Americans had demonstrated an extraordinary inability or willful unwillingness to respond to suffering when it occurred to an ostracized group or in a non-Western nation. Undoubtedly, this sentiment also provided fertile ground for Trump's campaign and subsequent election. It was, for example, strikingly evident when one compared the outpouring of concern after the shooting at the gay nightclub in Orlando in June 2016 to the muted response in the American media to the terrorist attack at the Istanbul airport less than two weeks later that resulted in even more deaths and injuries. Jalal Baig, a physician based in Chicago, called attention to the discrepancy in response to the two incidents:

> Though many reasons can be posited for this yawning gap, the most cogent explanation relates to expectations. Western societies often view areas like the Middle East, Africa or Pakistan as being unstable and perpetually embroiled in conflict. When viewed through this prism, violence and death are understandable and thus considered a *normal part of life* here. Though sad, it is merely seen as just another day in this part of the world. And so Beirut, Syria, Yemen and Nigeria become expected and we are automatically inured to their suffering, leaving our scarce stores of empathy intact.[3]

The crisis of connection, like the empathy gap, can be characterized as a condition, not unlike a form of myopia, in that it distorts our vision and prevents us from seeing the world as a coherent whole. It is also a form of self-centeredness commonly rationalized as a type of pragmatism that obstructs our ability to recognize our common humanity, especially when suffering occurs among people of a different race, religion, gender, sexual orientation, or nationality.

Clearly, these conditions are not new. Elie Wiesel, the Holocaust survivor and Nobel Laureate, understood the threat posed by the crisis of connection and made it his life's mission to call attention to suffering in all parts of the world. He did this work in part because he understood that the appeasement of Hitler and the blatant indifference exhibited in many parts of the world to the horrific violence of the Holocaust were made possible by the crisis of connection and the empathy gap. In his writing and speeches he made it clear that he saw the fractured and fragmented nature of modern society as a factor that contributed to mass killing in Germany. He also saw that the indifference that abetted the suffering of Jews and others in Nazi Germany continues and has contributed to various crimes against humanity that have occurred since.[4] Wiesel knew that when we define "our interests" in terms that exclude and negate the humanity of others, and when we accept the notions of "survival of the fittest" and "every man for himself" as sacrosanct principles, we create the moral and ethical basis for ignoring the suffering of others and valorizing the idea that some individuals or interest groups are inherently more important and valuable than others.

World history is full of examples of moral detachment, which is the essence of the crisis of connection. Such beliefs not only provided a rationale for the neutrality of some nations during the Holocaust,[5] but much earlier served as the philosophical premise that rationalized the transatlantic slave trade. Amoral reasoning by European merchants and states served as an effective cover for the brutality of slavery, and made it possible for the trade in human beings to serve as the cornerstone of the world economy for over three hundred years. Historian Blake Smith argues that the very idea of a laissez-faire economy, an economy unfettered by the constraints created of government regulations and moral considerations, emerged during the eighteenth century in relation to the slave trade. Today, the idea is intimately associated with the defense of liberalism and "free trade." Smith explains: "Modern capitalism is entangled with slavery in multiple, profound ways. Slave labour supplied the cotton, sugar and other vital commodities. The profits from the sale of slaves created fortunes on both sides of the Atlantic. And, in a disturbing paradox, the founding fathers of *laissez-faire* saw the slave trade as a showcase of liberty."[6]

Today, the crisis of connection shows up often in the prioritization of profits over environmental sustainability, as environmental concerns are frequently a lower priority than short-term economic growth and the "interests" of powerful economic elites. The public is presented with scenarios in which we are led to believe that we must choose between jobs, cheap goods, and economic growth on one side, and justice and environmental sustainability on the other. Faced with such choices, the environment and justice almost always lose out. This is especially likely to be the case when it is a group defined as the "other" who suffers— Native Americans opposing construction of the Keystone pipeline in South Dakota, or peasant farmers and fishermen who are forced to move from land they have occupied for centuries when the second largest lake in Bolivia dries up.[7] Environmental and health concerns were also clearly an afterthought among public officials in Michigan, who we now know were aware that the people of Flint were using lead contaminated water for years prior to the public outcry in 2014, while the consequences to them and their children were ignored.[8]

We have been conditioned to tolerate a high degree of hardship and suffering because we have trouble seeing our commonalties with other human beings, much less our interdependence. Our commonalities and common interests go unrecognized because we give greater priority to the group or place we belong to, or simply to ourselves. Our tendency is to compartmentalize, rationalize, or simply ignore the mistreatment or misfortune of the "other," and this allows us to treat incidents that might otherwise be seen as barbaric and inhumane as simply a normal part of everyday life. Mass shootings, defined as the killing of four or more people by a single shooter at the same time,[9] now occur with such frequency (at least 998 mass shootings since the killing of twenty-six schoolchildren in Newtown, Connecticut, in 2012) that they are increasingly treated as inevitable. The crisis of connection lulls us into accepting barbarism and human suffering as the "new normal," and prevents us from even considering or attempting to devise or propose solutions to horrific and extreme problems. This is not merely because the problems are perceived as complex but because there is a lack of political and social will, and a shortage of compassion and empathy. Without commitments to these moral and ethical principles the development of solutions to difficult problems is unattainable. Particularly for those of us who have the privilege to watch these incidents passively on television or simply divert our attention to something else—a convenient distraction offered by social media, sports, entertainment, or drugs and alcohol, so that we can be fooled into pretending the problems don't exist, or at least lulled into believing they won't affect us—the empathy gap is increasingly part of our everyday lives.

But what if we accepted Wiesel's argument that inaction in the face of brutality and injustice is a form of complicity? What would happen if we felt compelled to actively affirm our humanity when confronted with suffering or injustice, to do more than simply watch, shake our heads in disgust, or change the channel in the hope that not seeing the pain of others would remove feelings of guilt from our conscience? What if we saw the "other" as a member of our community, our tribe, our family, or our interest group, and acted on that premise? Is it conceivable that we might find a way to move to act in our collective interests if we believed that *our interests* were tied to the fate of others?

These are important questions. How we answer them will undoubtedly have tremendous bearing on our future. If the crisis of connection is simply a manifestation of what human beings have become in the twenty-first century, is it even reasonable to imagine that an alternative is possible? Though we may not see it, the crisis of connection poses an existential threat to our collective future.

From Alienation and Fear to Trust and Empathy

To answer these questions it is important to recognize that the crisis of connection is related to the forms of alienation and individualism that philosophers and social scientists have written about for many years. French sociologist Émile Durkheim documented its presence more than two hundred years ago in his seminal work *Suicide*.[10] Through careful study of incidents of suicide in mid-nineteenth-century France and Germany, Durkheim discovered interesting and unmistakable patterns: those who were most socially isolated were more likely than others to commit suicide. What is most remarkable about Durkheim's finding is that wealth and status do not reduce but increase the likelihood of suicide. Durkheim found that wealthy, single, Protestant men were more likely to commit suicide than married, working-class Catholic or Jewish women. He found that vulnerability to suicide increased with alienation and isolation, and that the correlates of success—income, education, and status—were actually factors that contributed to risk.

More than 150 years later, sociologist Eric Klinenberg found patterns that corresponded strikingly to those of Durkheim. Studying mortality patterns in the aftermath of a devastating heat wave in Chicago in July 1995, Klinenberg discovered a pattern that was quite revealing: while the elderly were generally more likely to die from the effects of extreme heat than others, their likelihood of dying was substantially greater if they lived alone or resided in a building where they were isolated from other residents. Klinenberg learned that it was actually not the heat that killed people but the lack of support from others and various forms of social breakdown—including the institutional abandonment of poor neighborhoods, and the retrenchment of public assistance programs—that contributed to the high fatality rates.[11]

Klinenberg's research reinforced a finding that social scientists have been aware of for some time now: people need people. Put differently, individuals who are rich in social capital—the resources and benefits one derives from participation in social networks—receive tangible benefits that are not available to those who lack social capital.[12] These benefits can include access to information, jobs, housing, safety, social support, and a variety of forms of material assistance. When individuals are embedded within social networks they generate and benefit from bonds of reciprocity with others who participate in the network. For example, a neighborhood watch group provides enhanced security to its members simply by watching each other's homes; parent groups provide access to valuable information about babysitters and schools; religious and civic organizations provide members with access to jobs and information about housing, health care, and a wide variety of other resources and services. Political scientist Robert Putnam has argued that when these ties whither and when people become more isolated, the social fabric that holds society together literally begins to fall apart.[13]

In his most recent book, *Our Kids*, Putnam argues that growing inequality, the shrinking of the American middle class, and the loss of secure union jobs has imperiled what is commonly known as the American Dream: the idea that America is a land where hard work and talent are rewarded with opportunity and social mobility. In the book, Putnam reflects on the state of his hometown, Clinton, Ohio, a small, blue-collar city that managed to send 80 percent of its children to college when he graduated in 1964. Today, the same town bears all the marks of race/class segregation, deindustrialization, and capital flight. Most of its residents are trapped in a perpetual cycle of poverty and downward mobility, ravaged by the effects of growing inequality. Only those with means, particularly those with high incomes who live in large homes along the shores of Lake Erie, consistently send their children to college today.[14]

What went wrong? Can it be reversed? Must we accept a society, or even a world, where suffering and despair are widespread, hopelessness festers, and prospects for change seem at best elusive?

Deploying Trust and Utilizing Education as a Resource to Promote Empathy

To the extent that we are able to see the crisis of connection not as the cause of many of our most pressing problems but as an impediment to the development and application of creative solutions, then we might also see that overcoming this crisis may be the key to a better future. Instead of waiting for technical or political solutions to problems like global warming, violence, and disease to be devised by political and economic elites, we might recognize that practical solutions can be conceived and acted upon if we focus on addressing the crisis of connection directly.

Such an approach might seem idealistic, but consider for a moment how the Ebola crisis was addressed and resolved in 2014–2015. In the summer and fall of 2014 Ebola was characterized in the media as a pandemic of epic proportions.[15] The World Health Organization projected that the disease would quickly spread beyond the borders of the three West African nations where it emerged—Sierra Leon, Guinea, and Liberia—and begin spreading throughout the world. Panic set in as health workers returning from the front lines of fighting the disease contracted the illness themselves, and fears that it would quickly spread to others proliferated.

But less than a year after the disease emerged it was contained. By the fall of 2015 no new cases were recorded in any of the three countries where the outbreak had occurred, and victory over Ebola was officially declared. How was this deadly disease contained, especially given that there still is no vaccine to inoculate people from the disease? How was the threat of Ebola abated, and what can we learn from this success story?

The story of how Ebola came to be contained without the development of a vaccine provides an important lesson for how we might think about overcoming the crisis of connection to address pressing, complex problems. While politicians like New Jersey governor Chris Christie and members of the US Congress called for health workers returning from West Africa to be quarantined,[16] dozens of health workers chose to risk their health and safety and voluntarily went to the countries most affected by the disease to address the crisis. One of these individuals was Dr. Masoka Fallah, an epidemiologist at MIT. Fallah, a Liberian who grew up in the poor neighborhood known as West Point in the capital

Monrovia that was at one point an epicenter of the Ebola outbreak, worked in concert with community activists to combat the disease. Fallah and other international health workers began educating Liberians on how to care for the sick and tend to the bodies of those who died from Ebola. Together with other health workers from organizations such as Doctors Without Borders, they created a rudimentary public health system where none existed. Describing the approach he used to counter the spread of the disease, Fallah explained: "If people don't *trust* you they can hide a body and you will never know and Ebola will keep spreading. They've got to *trust* you . . . we don't have the luxury of time."[17] If trust and education can be used as resources to stop the spread of a deadly disease, can similar strategies be deployed to solve other pressing problems?

The possibility of using trust to devise innovative strategies to address complex problems has in fact been applied elsewhere. For example, Richmond, California, was one of the most violent cities in the United States for many years. Despite being located in the Bay Area, one of the most prosperous regions in the United States, this small, impoverished city of a hundred thousand residents experienced high rates of poverty and unemployment, and neighborhoods that were impacted by high levels of environmental toxicity and industrial contamination, due to the proximity of oil refineries, for many years. In 2007, the homicide rate in Richmond reached a high of forty-seven per hundred thousand, one of the highest rates in the nation. After years of relying on traditional law enforcement strategies to curtail the violence, which had proven to be ineffective, Richmond finally took a radical step: it hired community activist Devone Boggan to work directly with the individuals most likely to commit violent crimes. Working with the Richmond police department and Dr. Barry Krisberg of the National Center on Crime and Delinquency, Boggan devised a novel plan. They identified the fifty individuals most likely to perpetrate acts of violence based on their profile and criminal record, and proposed to the pay them three hundred to a thousand dollars a month if they agreed to take anger management and life skills classes. They also offered assistance with finding jobs and housing and, if the individuals wanted, assistance in pursuing their education. The results were remarkable and unexpected. By 2014 the homicide rate declined by 77 percent and Richmond recorded its lowest number of deaths by handguns—eleven per hundred thousand—in decades. Krisberg explained how and why the strategy worked:

> We looked at who was committing the violence, who was doing the shooting and when . . . and it came down to a small number of people. . . . Violence tends to be concentrated in certain social areas, and most of the people who engage in criminal violence engage people they know, or are related to, and it spreads from generation to generation.[18]

While some criticized the Richmond plan, now known as the "shooters project," because they objected to the fact that individuals with criminal records were in effect paid to not commit crimes, what is perhaps most interesting is the way the issue was reported by the media. Like with the Ebola crisis, the media largely overlooked the most important factor influencing its success: the promotion of trust and empathy among those most likely to kill or be killed. As was true in the fight against Ebola, trust and some degree of courage proved to be the most effective means to counter fear. Boggan was able to convince the men in the group to work together to stop violence in Richmond. He did this by bringing them together to talk about their lives, to share their fears, their hopes, and their dreams. As they forged ties they began traveling throughout the community and eventually across the country sharing their experience in the hope that other communities faced with similar challenges might adopt similar strategies.

While the shooters project has generated some interest, it has still not yet been replicated in other places, though several municipalities have expressed interest.[19] Undoubtedly this may be because there are too many skeptics, individuals who present themselves as "pragmatists" who cling to the belief that trust and empathy are insufficient for solving a problem as threatening as violence. In part, this is because we have trouble believing that a different approach might work.

Psychologist James Gilligan produced similar results in his work among violent convicts at the San Francisco County Jail. From 1992 to 1998, he created support groups for men with a history of violence and found that when the men were given the opportunity to talk about their own experiences with violence, particularly the ways in which they had experienced shame and disrespect, they began to experience respect and empathy, in some cases for the first time in their lives. Through the trust developed in the support groups created by Gilligan the cycle of victimization and recidivism was substantially reduced.[20] He explains:

> I felt that certainly one thing that had been missing that had made it possible for them to commit serious harm to others was their lack of a capacity for empathy with the suffering of others, and a lack of the capacity to care about others or to love others. . . . What struck me was they couldn't respect other people or treat other people with esteem if they were lacking in self-esteem and self-respect. So helping them reach the point where they gained self-respect and self-esteem was really a prerequisite to their being able then to care about others enough so that they would not violate the rights or inflict harm on other people.

Given the results obtained from the small number of examples presented here, the question we must now consider is whether similar approaches can be applied to other pressing problems. The final section of this chapter focuses on the role of schools, because they can potentially play an important and unique role in addressing the crisis of connection and the empathy gap.

The Role of Schools in Overcoming the Crisis of Connection

As we contemplate how to address the larger problems we face—global warming, violence and terrorism, poverty, and inequality—without succumbing to the sheer sense of exasperation and resignation they generate due to their size, scale, and complexity, it may be helpful to start by considering the role that the crisis of connection plays in preventing the development of innovative responses. Focusing on the crisis of connection does not mean that we ignore the substantive challenges at the core of these large and complex problems, or that we lose our ability to think practically about what even partial solutions might consist of. To do so would be naïve and unrealistic. However, as the examples of the response to the Ebola crisis and the violence prevention project in Richmond suggest, it might be possible to devise creative responses if we were to take action locally, involving those most directly affected, and move forward in a strategic manner. My work over the past thirty years in the field of education has led me to believe that schools can play a significant role in addressing the crisis of connection, and that the strategies devised there can be applied in our larger society and in other parts of the world. What follows are three examples, two based on research and one based on an anecdote, that illustrate how this might be possible.

Overcoming Violence by Advancing Common Interests

In the fall of 1998, several schools in the San Francisco Bay Area experienced a series of incidents involving interracial violence. The violence involved different groups at different schools: Blacks versus Latinos at Castlemont High School in Oakland and Richmond High School in Richmond, Blacks versus Asians at Skyline High School in Oakland, and various groups (White, Black, Latino, and Asian) fighting each other at El Cerrito and Berkeley high schools. There seemed to be no consistent or single cause linking the violence across the five schools, but it was frequent and seemed to be spiraling out of control. On numerous occasions, dozens of police officers were deployed to quell what the police described as "riots" involving large numbers of students, at each of the schools.

The police complained to school district officials in all three communities that it was not their job to stop the violence and made it clear that they could not station police officers indefinitely at the schools. District officials were at a loss about what to do. They didn't understand what was causing the outbreak of violence and had no idea of how further violence could be prevented. After a third week of fighting two of the districts approached a community-based research firm—Arts, Resources and Curriculum (ARC)—for help in devising a strategy to respond to the violence. The firm came up with a novel idea: they would create multiracial student-run groups called Youth Together (YT) on each of the five campuses so that students could take the lead in addressing the issue. I was asked to serve as the evaluator for their efforts.

In approaching their work, YT devised a novel strategy. Rather than bringing young people together to talk about what had happened, they started out by bringing a multiracial group of students together to talk about their experiences at schools. The conversation quickly revealed a number of serious complaints about their schools, and within a short period students on each of the five campuses began to see that they had a great deal in common. YT decided that rather than simply airing their concerns the students should develop school change campaigns, and that they should organize with others to carry them out. The campaigns varied in focus, but in each case they were led by students and focused on issues that were of concern to students generally. At Richmond and El Cerrito high schools students marched to the school board to demand access to bathrooms, which were locked while classes were in session due to concerns about safety. At Berkeley and Skyline high schools students made demands for ethnic studies classes based on their belief that if they knew something about the history and culture of others they might be less likely to regard them as a threat. At Castlemont High School Black and Latino students marched together to demand that a new cafeteria be built (for over two years the students had been eating outdoors, even in the rain).

Our research team documented the YT efforts and evaluated the impact of their school change efforts on the schools. We conducted this assessment by surveying administrators, teachers, and students to measure how the climate of each school was affected by the change campaigns. Remarkably, not only did the violence subside within a short period of time (six to eight weeks) but the surveys revealed that perceptions of safety and the morale of students and staff at each of the schools improved. The following quote from a student at Richmond High School helps to explain the dramatic turnaround:

> Most of the fights were caused by stuff that happened outside of school and crept in. Because we didn't even know each other we didn't trust each other. When Youth Together brought us together we started to see that we had a lot in common. As we began working together to get access to the bathrooms we began to see that we were fighting over nothing. We had more in common than we realized. (November 15, 1998)

Similar responses were expressed at the other schools. One teacher at Berkeley High School acknowledged that adults had unintentionally helped to create a climate where violence was likely because they had done so little to bring students together.

We like to celebrate the diversity of this school but actually it's very segregated from within. Our classes are tracked and even the clubs and sports teams are mostly segregated. Our ESL students don't even attend classes with other kids. How can we expect kids to learn how to respect each when they aren't learning together? (February 3, 1999)

Our study found that through students working together to promote their common interests, the schools experienced a reduction in hostility, conflict, and fear and students from different racial backgrounds also began to forge bonds based on solidarity and trust.[21]

Listening to Students for School Improvement

In 2001, I was approached by the former superintendent of Boston Public Schools, Dr. Tom Paizant, who was looking for help in figuring out how to improve several of the high schools in the school district. Like most urban school districts across the country, Boston had experimented with a number of reforms in an attempt to raise achievement at its schools. After several years of effort it was clear that while some schools were getting better, others were not. Paizant wanted to know why progress was uneven and what could be done about it. After visiting several of the schools in the district I proposed what he and I considered a novel idea: we would study the reforms through the experience of the students. We opted for this focus because we wanted to know how students were affected by the reforms that had been carried out. We would conduct this study by shadowing fifteen students at ten different high schools. The groups would be representative of the schools with respect to race, ethnicity, and gender, and would include students with differing levels of academic achievement—five low, five medium, and five high.

Over the course of the next two years we followed our focal students to their classes, interviewed them, their teachers, and their parents periodically, and tracked their academic performance. We also collected school climate surveys, which allowed us to compare the responses of our focal students to the larger population of students at each school. Our goal was to understand how the students experienced the reforms that were undertaken: Did they develop closer, more supportive relationships with teachers as schools were made smaller? Did they receive better and more rigorous instruction as their schools prepared for high-stakes exams? Did charter schools or pilot schools have greater success at meeting the needs of students than traditional public high schools, and if so, why?

The questions we posed were central to the larger policy debates about education reform. However, missing from these debates were the voices of students. There seemed to be an unstated assumption that if the adults got the reforms right students would eventually achieve at higher levels. Our research at the schools allowed us to test the theories underlying the reform strategies. It also allowed us to elevate the voices of students so that their perspectives and experiences were considered, in many cases, for the first time.

Over the course of two years we began to see significant discrepancies at several of the schools between what the adults claimed they were doing and what the students were actually experiencing. We went into classrooms serving students who had failed the state exam and were at risk of being denied diplomas if they did not eventually pass. Expecting to see rigorous, highly focused instruction, more often than not we saw disorganization. For example, during one visit to a math class a student we had been shadowing informed us that he and his classmates usually played poker during class, but he suspected that because we were present, the teacher might make them do some work. Despite our presence, the students played poker anyway. Embarrassed by the obvious lack of educational focus, the teacher turned to us and said: "These kids refuse to do any work so I let them play. They're probably learning more math playing poker than they would from my lesson anyway."

Observations of this kind were not uncommon at several of the schools. We observed students chatting, brushing their hair, and putting on makeup in classes that were supposed to prepare them for high-stakes exams. At one school I saw the principal lock the front door to the school at 7:35 AM, preventing students who arrived more than five minutes late (7:30 AM was the official time start time) from entering until they could return with a note from their parents explaining why they were tardy. I pointed out sarcastically that his tough tardy policy had created a truancy problem. He failed to note the irony of my observation. At other schools we pointed out that many of the students lacked basic skills in literacy and math and were unlikely to pass the state's new high-stakes exam if the classes they took focused only on providing test-taking tips. Even after sharing our findings with the schools, the disconnect between what the adults asserted they were doing in the name of reform and what the students actually experienced remained striking and clear.

However, we also visited schools where relationships between students and teachers were strong, where students were able to clearly explain what they were learning in their classes and why it was important. What set these schools apart from the other more dysfunctional schools appeared to be what education scholars have called school culture. That is, the beliefs, values, and norms that guided the mission of the school were all aligned with its goals.[22] Students took their education seriously, both in word and in deed, not because they were afraid of failure but because they accepted the premise upon which the school operated.

In contrast with students at the dysfunctional schools, students in the higher functioning schools also accepted responsibility for their education and did their part to maintain a safe, orderly environment. As I have described elsewhere in more detail, the strong, positive relationships we observed contributed to higher levels of school safety and student achievement.[23] What is most important about these findings is that they run counter to official policies designed to promote school safety and higher achievement. Current education policies designed to promote safety generally emphasize the adoption of strict security measures including metal detectors, law enforcement, surveillance cameras, and zero-tolerance policies.[24] Similarly, the path to high achievement has relied primarily on high-stakes accountability (via standardized testing) and the elevation of academic standards.[25] Our research at the ten Boston high schools showed that the development of strong, positive relationships between teachers and students was more effective than heavy security measures at creating a safe and orderly environment. We also found that *hope* was more effective than *fear* in motivating students to achieve.

It is important to note that positive relationships cannot be imposed upon a school. It is easier to install a metal detector or surveillance camera than it is to improve the quality of relationships between children and the adults who serve them. However, if we fail to recognize that such an approach might actually work and be more effective in realizing the goals of education, it will never even be considered.

A Final Anecdote: Not Waiting to Act on Our Common Interests

In bringing this chapter to conclusion I end with a story, told to me by a teacher, that illustrates the power of trust and community and the need for the courage to act on our common interests. I share this anecdote because it serves as an excellent example of how we can overcome our fears through positive action that affirms the basic human values that are essential for living in a just, humane civil society.

The teacher's school was a small continuation high school, designed to serve students with a record of poor attendance, poor behavior, or both.[26] Many of the students at the school had criminal records, and most had a long record of poor academic performance. One of the students at the school was a known gang leader with a reputation for violence in the community. One morning he informed his counselor that starting the next day he was going to show up at school with a new identity as a young woman. He intended to change his name and to dress as a woman, and he wanted his choice to be respected. He informed the counselor that his parents had kicked him out of his house because they were unhappy with his transgender identity and that he expected a violent reaction to news of his transformation from members of his own gang, who felt betrayed by his decision.

The counselor reacted with alarm and immediately notified the school principal. The principal was also alarmed because he feared an outbreak of gang violence at his school. At the end of the day he called for a meeting with the faculty and staff to warn them and figure out what should be done. Fearful of the violence they thought might occur, the staff immediately decided that the police should be notified and the student should be banned from entering the school. However, while the adults were in the middle of their meeting a small delegation of students arrived and asked for an opportunity to speak. They wanted the staff to know that they were aware of their classmate's decision to change his gender identity, and on their own, they had devised a plan to support him. Since the student had been kicked out of his parent's home he would start living with another student at the school whose family was willing to take him in. The students also reported that they had organized themselves to take turns riding the bus with him to school each day to provide him with protection. Finally, they agreed that while he was in school everyone would accept and respect his decision, and begin calling *her* by *her* preferred name and pronoun.

The school staff was shocked by the news shared by the students. Several spoke up and said how proud they were that the students had come together to support their classmate. One announced how embarrassed she was because of the action they had proposed—calling the police and banning the student—prior to hearing from the students. After further deliberation the staff decided that they would support the students' approach, and that together they would support the transgendered student. The following day the plan was implemented as proposed. No violence occurred, and ultimately the student was able to complete the school year and graduate without any violent incidents occurring at the school.

* * *

I share this final story because it serves as a poignant way of reinforcing the larger point of this chapter and volume. While the crisis of connection is real, rooted in history, and reinforced by divisions that have led to deep distrust and disconnection based on race, language, sexuality, gender, nationality, and more, these examples show that it might be possible for the crisis of connection to be overcome. Each of the examples presented here—fighting Ebola in West Africa with trust and education, reducing homicides in Richmond by building community among those most likely to perpetrate or to be victims of homicide, listening to students and developing caring relationships to create safe schools where students are willingly engaged in learning, countering racial violence by focusing on the common interests of students, and countering fear with empathy and compassion—shows that possibilities for addressing complex problems may be more likely if we focus directly on the crisis of connection. While these examples don't serve as proof that countering the crisis of connection is easy or that the strategies can be applied to solve larger problems like terrorism and global warming, they do provide an inkling of how we might think about addressing the large, complex problems we face.

The news is often frightening and the problems often seem overwhelming. Because acts of mass violence occur with such frequency, often before we even have time to process and fully comprehend their meaning and implications, they can easily become the "new normal." As we become numb and inured to news of violence, whether it occurred across the globe or across town, we risk growing used to the idea that mass shootings are simply an unfortunate part of modern life.

But why should we accept such widespread human suffering? Normalization and complacency toward issues that deteriorate the quality of our lives and threaten our future can be resisted if we can find ways to take creative forms of action, actions that remind us of our common interests, that further and promote empathy, trust, and goodwill. The renown French geophysicist Xavier Le Pichon reminds us that "our humanity is not an attribute that we have received once and forever with our conception. It is a potentiality that we have to discover within us and progressively develop or destroy through our confrontation with the different experiences of suffering that will meet us throughout our life."[27]

Like Le Pichon, I am under no illusion that the problems we face can be solved by simple solutions or small acts of kindness. However, I do believe that the best way to counter hopelessness and despair, and the most effective way to revive a pragmatic form of optimism about the future of the planet and human society, is through deliberate actions that address our crisis of connection, and that remind us that our common interests as human beings are worth acting upon.

NOTES

1 Anna Ratcliff, "Just 8 Men Own Same Wealth as Half the World" (Oxfam, January 16, 2017), www.oxfam.org.

2 See Francis Wilkinson, "Benign Neglect," *New York Times*, June 11, 2008, www.campaignstops.blogs.nytimes.com.

3 Jalal Baig, "Istanbul and the Empathy Gap: Why Was the West's Response Muted Compared to Paris or Brussels?," *Salon*, July 3, 2016, www.salon.com.

4 For a discussion of Wiesel's ideas, see Elie Wiesel, *The Night Trilogy: Night, Dawn, the Accident* (New York: Hill & Wang, 1962).

5 Many nations, including Switzerland, Sweden, Portugal, and Spain, adopted a position of neutrality toward the war in Europe, and toward Germany generally. This position was maintained even after news of Jewish internment and the impending genocide was widely known. According to the *Holocaust Encyclopedia*, "Responding to pressure generated by the public revelation of the

'Final Solution' in late 1942, US and British representatives met in Bermuda on April 19, 1943, to find solutions to wartime refugee problems. Neither government initiated rescue programs and no significant proposals emerged from the conference." See www.ushmm.org. For a detailed discussion, see Richard Breitman and Alan Kraut, *American Refugee Policy and European Jewry, 1933–1945* (Bloomington: Indiana University Press, 1987); and Richard Breitman, *Official Secrets: What the Nazis Planned, What the British and Americans Knew* (New York: Hill & Wang, 1998).

6 See Blake Smith, "Slavery as Free Trade" (Aeon, June 29, 2016), www.aeon.co.

7 See Brian Clark Howard, "Bolivia's Second Largest Lake Has Dried Out: Can It Be Saved?," *National Geographic*, January 21, 2016, www.news.nationalgeographic .com.

8 For a detailed discussion of when public officials including the governor's office in Michigan knew about the water crisis in Flint, see Michael Martinez, "Flint Water: Governor's Office Knew of Legionnaires' Cases," *CNN*, February 27, 2016, www.cnn.com.

9 For a definition of mass shootings and a cataloguing of their occurrence in the United States, see Mark Follman, Gavin Aronsen, and Deanna Pan, "US Mass Shootings, 1982–2016: Data from Mother Jones' Investigation," *Mother Jones*, June 12, 2016, www.motherjones.com.

10 Émile Durkheim, *Suicide: A Study in Sociology*, trans. John A. Spaulding and George Simpson (1897; repr., Glencoe, IL: Free Press, 1951).

11 See Eric Klinenberg, *Heat Wave: A Social Autopsy of Disaster in Chicago* (Chicago: University of Chicago Press, 2002).

12 James S. Coleman, "Social Capital in the Creation of Human Capital," *American Journal of Sociology* 94 (1988): S95–S120; Michael Woolcock, "Social Capital and Economic Development: Toward a Theoretical Synthesis and Policy Framework," *Theory and Society* 27 (1998): 151–208.

13 Robert Putnam, *Bowling Alone: The Collapse and Revival of American Community* (New York: Simon & Schuster, 2000).

14 Robert Putnam, *Our Kids: The American Dream in Crisis* (New York: Simon & Schuster, 2015).

15 For examples of articles warning of the threat posed by Ebola, see "Why Is Ebola so Dangerous," *BBC News*, October 8, 2014, www.bbc.com; and "Are We Ready for a Global Pandemic of the Ebola Virus," *International Journal of Infectious Disease* 28 (November 2014): 217–218.

16 For an explanation for why New Jersey governor Chris Christie called for health worker to be quarantined near the New Jersey airport after returning from Liberia, see Sara Fischer, "Christie's Office: Quarantined Woman Headed to Maine," *CNN*, October 27, 2014, www.cnn.com.

17 For a detailed discussion on the strategy employed by Fallah and others in fighting Ebola, see Norimitsu Onishi, "Back to the Slums of His Youth, to Defuse the Ebola Time Bomb," *New York Times*, September 13, 2016, www.nytimes.com.

18 For a discussion of the Richmond violence prevention project, see Terrence McCoy, "The Controversial Method That Turned One of America's Most Violent Cities into One of Its Safest," *Washington Post*, June 1, 2015, www.washingtonpost.com.

19 Cities where officials are considering implementing the shooters project include Washington, DC and Chicago.

20 For a discussion of the strategy and the results, see James Gilligan, *Violence: Reflections on a National Epidemic* (New York: Putnam, 1997).

21 For a copy of the evaluation report, see Pedro A. Noguera and Miriam Bliss, "School Violence Reduction Initiative: Youth Together Project. Final Year Report" (Berkeley: Center on Diversity & Urban School Reform, University of California, Berkeley, December 1998).

22 Seymour Sarason, *The Culture of Schools and the Problem of Change* (Boston: Allyn & Bacon, 1971).

23 Pedro Noguera, "Transforming High Schools," *Educational Leadership* 61, no. 8 (May 2004); Pedro Noguera, "How Listening to Students Can Help Schools to Improve," *Theory into Practice* 46 (Summer 2007): 205–211.

24 Denise Gottfredson, *Schools and Delinquency* (Cambridge: Cambridge University Press, 2001).

25 Richard Elmore, "The New Accountability in State Educational Policy," in *Holding Schools Accountable: Performance-Based Strategies for Improving Schools*, ed. Helen F. Ladd (Washington, DC: Brookings Institution Press, 1996); Linda Darling-Hammond, "Standards, Accountability, and School Reform," *Teachers College Record* 106 (2004): 1047–1085.

26 Continuation high schools are alternative schools that are designed to serve students with a track record of poor attendance and poor academic performance.

27 Xavier Le Pichon, *Ecce Homo (Behold Humanity)* (Paris: Templeton Foundation, 2009).

6

Masculinity and Our Common Humanity

"Real" Men versus "Good" Men

MICHAEL KIMMEL

I.

"What does it mean to be a good man?" You know, you wake up in the morning and look in the mirror and say to yourself, "You are a good man." Or you imagine your funeral and you want it said of you: "He was a good man."

I have asked this question of several thousand young men and boys around the world, from single-sex schools in Australia to college class-rooms in the United States, a police academy in Sweden, and former soccer stars at FIFA. It's part of a workshop I do with them to explore the process of becoming a man—what are the rules, how they learn them, and how these rules structure their lives.

Their answers rarely vary. Here is what men believe it means to be a good man:

Integrity
Honor
Being responsible
Being a good provider
Doing the right thing
Putting others first
Caring
Standing up for the little guy

"Where," I ask, "did you learn this?" They look a bit confused. Eventually, someone will say, "well, it's everywhere." And he's right. It's

Shakespearean, Homeric. It's the Judeo-Christian heritage. It's the air we breathe; it's the water we drink. Pretty much everyone agrees that this is what it means to be a good man and that we learn it through osmosis in our respective cultures.

"Okay, fair enough," I say. "Now tell me if any of those ideas or words or phrases occur to you when I say 'Man the f*** up!' 'Be a *real* man!'"

The guys look startled. "No, that's completely different," they shout, almost instantly, and almost as one.

I ask what it means to be a real man, and this is a short list of what they say:

Never cry
Be strong
Don't show your feelings
Play through pain
Suck it up
Power
Aggression
Win at all costs
Be aggressive
Be responsible
Get rich
Get laid

"Hmm," I'll say. With one exception, "be responsible," it's a completely different list. "So," I ask, "where did you learn this?"

Here is what they say, in order:

1. Father
2. Coach
3. My guy friends
4. My older brother

If they mention women at all—and they rarely do—it's their mother, and she comes in at about number six or so. They sometimes even say "teacher" before they say mother.

Much of the rest of the workshop takes us inside that idea of being a real man, but in this chapter I address two central elements of this difference between being a good man and a real man. First, you will naturally have noticed that the characteristics of being a good man are really the characteristics of being a good person. The adjective "good" is the central word in the phrase, and both women and men can equally be "good." A good man is, in a sense, an ungendered term; it is synonymous with being a good person, a good citizen, a good parent.

But "real" is another category altogether. It is very specific to men, a most gendered term. It is demonstrated and proven before the evaluative eyes of other men. And for that reason, we often say that masculinity is "homosocial"—that it is other men who judge the effectiveness of our performance of it. We want to be a "man's man," not a "ladies' man." A "man among men."

And here is the lesson I hope that workshop participants will draw from the exercise: there are times in every man's life when he will be asked by other guys to betray his own values, his own ethics, his own idea of what it means to be a good man in the name of proving that he is a real man. That is, proving that we are "real men" to other men will ask—no, insist—that we sometimes do the wrong thing, fail to stand up for the little guy, behave dishonorably.

If this is true—and that every man reading these words knows exactly what I am talking about, that every man reading these words has had at least one experience in which he was asked to betray his own values to prove his masculinity to other guys—then this is the story we must tell our sons. That we have been there, that we know the pressures they face. Frankly, I would far prefer to tell my son how awesome I am. But the truth is that I, like everyone else, have betrayed that idea of being a good man.

For me, it was in eighth grade, when some bigger, more athletic, and more popular guys were bullying the guy whose locker was next to mine. I knew what to do, what you are *supposed* to do, when someone is being bullied. You're supposed to stand up for him, to intervene. There's good research that says that if one person stands up against the bullies, they often back down.

Oddly, though, at that moment, for some reason, my shoes became so utterly fascinating that I couldn't take my eyes off them. I looked down at my shoes for what felt like an hour. I moved my feet different ways, never taking my eyes from the ground.

In short, I did the wrong thing. I turned away from him. I was afraid that the other guys would come after me if I stood up for him. Even though I knew I was doing the wrong thing. I was too frightened to do anything else.

Today, thinking back on that day, I think I may have been right in my calculations of the likelihood that the bullies would have come after me. Yet that night—and every night since—I was so ashamed of myself. For days afterward, I avoided that guy who had been bullied. I avoided making eye contact with anyone who was there.

* * *

That's the story I think we grown men, we fathers, must tell our sons. I think we must tell them not only for their sakes, because it can help them acknowledge the ways that they, too, may feel pulled between those poles. But we have to tell them for our own sakes, so that we can finally acknowledge the damage done to us, done to our hearts, our souls, by the demands of trying to deny our humanity and be real men.

To prove you are a real man is to prove you exist *as a man*. Masculinity is not a given; it does not happen at a certain age, all by itself. We have to earn it.

Many cultures, and several religions, posit such a trajectory, a need to move from "not man" to "man" by means of achievement. You learn a passage of the Torah, go on a walkabout, or survive an initiation ritual. Remember what Simone de Beauvoir famously said about women: "One is not born, but rather becomes, a woman."

This is true for men in spades. Boys must become men, by undergoing a test, a challenge, a struggle. Masculinity is understood to be an achievement. As Norman Mailer famously quipped, "Nobody was born a man. You earned your manhood provided you were good enough, bold enough."

Rarely, though, do we ask where such a strange idea originated. Where did we learn that "good" and "real" are antithetical—indeed that the good man's masculinity is questionable? When did ethics become associated with femininity?

Surely not among the ancients, where honor and virtue were markers of masculinity. Certainly not in the Bible, where "real" men are unmasked as frauds before falling before the righteous.

I think the answer for us, in the industrial West, begins by shifting good and real from categories of existence to a developmental sequence, from mapping these qualities into a developmental trajectory. We move from good to real as we move from the world of women to the world of men. Virtue and morality are qualities in the worlds of women. This truly insane idea began with Freud. And it has become axiomatic in the world of developmental psychology: to achieve manhood, a boy must shift his identification from mother to father. That is, I believe, the single most damaging idea to boys that has ever been invented.

II.

Recently, a young black mother came up to me following a lecture I gave about boys. A social worker, she was concerned about a conversation she had had with her husband a few nights earlier. It seems that her husband had taken their son to the barber, which, she explained to me, was a very central social institution in the African American community. As the barber prepared the boy's hair for treatment, using apparently some heat and some painful burning chemicals, the boy began to cry. The barber turned to the boy's father. "This boy is a pussy," he said. "This boy has been spending too much time with his mama! Man," he said to the father, "you have got to get this boy away from his mother!"

That evening, the father came home, visibly shaken by the episode, and announced to his wife that from that moment on the boy would not spend so much time with her, but instead would do more sports and other activities with him, "to make sure he doesn't become a sissy."

After telling me this story, the mother asked what I thought she should do. Oh, did I mention that her son is not yet four years old? Do I need to mention that the natural reaction of any person—let alone a child—to pain is to cry?

* * *

We generally believe that the boy's path to manhood is a direct path away from mother and toward father. He achieves his masculinity by repudiation, dissociation, and then identification. It is a perilous path, but a necessary one if we want to be the sort of "real man" that our society—and by that I mean our homosocial world—expects us to be.

Such theories have been around for a very long time, of course. But it was Freud's particular genius to make this moment the centerpiece of his theories of both gender identity development and the origins of sexual orientation. Freud believed that from birth through about three to five years old, both boys and girls identified with their mothers; that is, they patterned their identity on their perception of their mothers. This notion was, of course, convenient to middle-class Viennese families, in which husbands were out of the home virtually all day, and mothers were the sole caregivers to their children. Children's views of the world were what they understood hers to be.

Around age five, though, boys' and girls' paths diverge. In this new stage of development, which Freud called the "phallic stage," boys and girls experience different crises of identity and desire, and seek different paths to resolve their anxieties and form stable identities. This process is more difficult for boys than it is for girls, because a girl learns to identify with her mother as a female, and her identification therefore remains continuous into adulthood. By contrast, a boy must detach himself from his identification with his mother, to "disidentify" with her, and identify with his father, a process that requires unlearning one attachment and forming a new one. This is made more difficult because mothers commonly offer a great deal of affection and caring, whereas fathers are often less affectionate and more authoritarian, and certainly more distant.

* * *

Boys experience a crisis during which they must renounce their mothers and identify with their fathers. The Oedipal crisis is a crisis of connection. It is, in the psychoanalytic literature, *the* crisis of connection, the necessary one. This is the crucial moment in a boy's development: *the boy achieves gender identity and sexual orientation at the same moment in time.* During the Oedipal stage, the boy desires sexual union with mother, but he also realizes that he is in competition with his father for her affections. With his sexual desire for his mother thwarted by his father, the little boy sexualizes his fear of the father, believing that if he were to compete sexually with his father, his father would castrate him. The boy's ego resolves this state of terror of castration by transferring the boy's identification from mother to father, so that, symbolically, he can have sexual access to mother. Thus the boy must break the identification with his mother, repudiate her, and identify with his father. This is a great shock—his mother has been the source of warmth and love, and is the object of his desire; his father has been a more distant source of authoritarian power, and is the source of the boy's terror. But by identifying with his father the little boy ceases being "feminine" (identified with his mother) and becomes masculine, as he simultaneously becomes heterosexual, symbolically capable of sexual relations with mother-like substitutes. Almost literally, as the 1930s popular song put it, he will "want a girl just like the girl that married dear old Dad."

For girls, Freud believed that the path was complementary, but not nearly as traumatic. Girls retain their identification with mother, but must renounce their sexual desire for her. They do this by acknowledging that they are incapable of sexual relations with their mother, because they lack the biological equipment that makes such relations possible. This is why Freud believed that women experience "penis envy." The little girl understands that her only chance for sexual gratification is to retain her identification with her mother and to be sexually possessed by a man who can satisfy her so that she can have a baby, which will be her source of feminine gratification. In the process, she transfers the location of sexual gratification from the clitoris (an "atrophied penis" in Freud's terms) to the vagina, that is, she develops feminine, passive sexuality. Again, gender identity and sexual organization go hand in hand.

Three issues are worth noting in this account of gender identity and sexuality. First, Freud dislocates gender and sexuality from the realm of biology. Gender identity and sexuality are psychological achievements—difficult, precarious, and full of potential pitfalls (an absent father may prevent a boy from transferring his identification from his mother, for example). Gender and sexuality are accomplished within the family, Freud argues, not activated by internal biological clocks. Second, Freud links gender identity to sexual orientation, making homosexuality a developmental *gender* issue rather than an issue of immorality, sin, or biological anomaly. Homosexuals are simply those who have failed either to renounce identification with their mother in favor of their father (gay men) or those who have failed to retain their ties of identification to their mother (lesbians). (This idea also served as the basis for therapeutic interventions designed to "cure" homosexuals by encouraging gender-appropriate behaviors.) Third, Freud restates with new vigor traditional gender stereotypes as if they were the badges of successful negotiation of this perilous journey. A boy must be the sexual initiator, and scrupulously avoid all feminine behaviors, lest he be seen as having failed to identify with his father. A girl must become sexually passive, wait for a man to be attracted to her, so that she can be fulfilled as a woman. Femininity means fulfillment not as a lover, but as a mother.

It's important to remember that though Freud postulated that homosexuality was the failure of the child to adequately identify with the same-sex parent, and was therefore a problem of gender identity development, he did not believe in either the criminal persecution or psychiatric treatment of homosexuals. In fact, when Freud was contacted by a woman whose son was homosexual, he patiently explained why he did not think her son needed to be "cured":

> Homosexuality is assuredly no advantage, but it is nothing to be ashamed of, no vice, no degradation; it cannot be classified as an illness; we consider it to be a variation of the sexual function. . . . Many highly respectable individuals of ancient and modern times have been homosexuals, several of the greatest men among them. . . . It is a great injustice to persecute homosexuality as a crime—and a cruelty too. . . .
>
> What analysis can do for your son runs in a different line. If he is unhappy, neurotic, torn by conflicts, inhibited in his social life, analysis may bring him harmony, peace of mind, full efficiency, whether he remains homosexual or gets changed.

It took another forty years before the American Psychiatric Association declassified homosexuality as a mental illness.

Today, popular stereotypes about homosexuality continue to rely on Freudian theories of gender development. Many people believe that homosexuality is a form of gender nonconformity; that is, effeminate men and masculine women are seen in the popular mind as likely to be homosexual, while masculine men's and feminine women's gender-conforming behavior leads others to expect them to be heterosexual.

Freud's theories have been subject to considerable debate and controversy. He based his theories about the sexuality of women on a very small sample of upper-middle-class women in Vienna, all of whom were suffering from psychological difficulties that brought them to treatment with him in the first place. (Freud rejected the idea that they had been the victims of sexual abuse and incest, although many of them claimed they had been.) His theories of male development were based on even fewer clinical cases and on his own recollections of his childhood and his dreams. These are not the most reliable scientific methods, and his tendency to make sexuality the driving force of all individual development and all social and group processes may tell us more about his own life, and perhaps contemporary Vienna, than about other societies and cultures. Some researchers have argued that many of Freud's patients were actually telling the truth about their sexual victimization and not fantasizing about it, and that, therefore, it is not the fantasies of children but the actual behaviors of adults that form the constituent elements in the construction of children's sexual view of the world.

Although many today question Freud's theories on methodological, political, or theoretical grounds, there is no question that these theories have had a remarkable impact on contemporary studies and on popular assumptions about the relationship between gender identity and sexual behavior and sexual orientation. If gender identity and sexual orientation were *accomplished*, not inherent in the individual, then it was the parents' fault if things didn't turn out "right." Magazine articles, child-rearing manuals, and psychological inventories encouraged parents to do the right things and to develop the right attitudes, traits, and behaviors in their children; thus, the children would achieve appropriate gender identity and thereby ensure successful acquisition of heterosexual identity. That's a lot for a little boy to carry, sitting in a barber's chair at age four.

III.

Recently a colleague told me about a problem he was having. It seems his seven-year-old son, James, was bullied by another boy on his way home from school. His wife, the boy's mother, strategized with her son about how to handle such situations in the future. She suggested he find an alternate route home, tell a teacher, or perhaps even tell the boy's parents. And she offered the standard "use your words, not your fists" conflict cooler.

"How can I get my wife to stop treating James like a baby?" he asked. "How will he ever learn to stand up for himself if she turns him into a wimp?"

The process of disidentification with mother and identification with father is fraught and far from easy. Nothing is given. What if father isn't there?

Historically, we've blamed this on mothers. What if mother holds the boy too tightly and refuses to let him go? Sissies are also called "mama's boy" for a reason. The model sees the boy as wriggling to get "free," to bond with father, and mother as clutching him, resisting, refusing to let him go.

This is particularly ironic because Freud's retelling of the Oedipus myth, from which he derived the classical template for the masculinity-as-achievement project, places all the agency on the shoulders of the boy, and virtually none on the shoulders of either mother or father. Now, it's all mother's fault for holding on too tight.

Remember how that story goes? The boy feels sexually attracted to mother in a genital way; he wants her. But he is frightened of the father, and experiences that fear as a fear of castration because the father is so much bigger and stronger, and because the father's penis is so much bigger than the little boy's. (Freud is the first theorist who tells us that size matters—to men.) The boy's anxiety about wanting mother and being unable to have the object of his desire is resolved by the boy repudiating the object of his desire (mother), and all she stands for (femininity), and instead identifying with the source of his terror (his father). Sounds a little like the Stockholm syndrome, doesn't it, where the victim of the torture comes to identify with his torturer.

So the driving force that sets all these processes in motion is the boy's sexual desire for his mother. Which might be interesting itself, but as a template it actually inverts the entire Oedipus story. Freud retells the Oedipal story backward, removing agency from grown-ups and locating it in little boys.

As philosopher Harry Brod reminds us, in the actual, original Oedipal story, it is the father, Laius, who banishes Oedipus because the Delphic oracle has presaged that Laius's son will one day kill him. It is the father's fear of the boy—the father's recognition of mortality, his fading strength, and his awareness that eventually his son will be more physically strong—that sets the story in motion. Thus when father and son meet at the crossroads, and neither will yield (the first recorded case of road rage in literature), they do not recognize each other. The boy has no reason to fear the father because he does not know the man is his father. And the father, in all his arrogance, does not recognize the boy is already stronger than he is. His arrogance costs him his life.

This should more accurately be called "the Laius complex"—the father's fear of the son's eventual ascension to power. This Laius complex highlights intergenerational conflict among men, and a status hierarchy in which age becomes a determinant of masculinity. "The power of the patriarch is not just that of men over women, but also that of older over younger men," Brod writes.

And what about Jocasta, the mother of Oedipus? How many mothers do you know who would so unquestioningly yield to some arrogant patriarch's insistence that her son be killed? What sort of mother refuses to protect her son from a tyrannical father?

IV.

> They fuck you up, your mum and dad.
> They may not mean to, but they do.
> They fill you with the faults they had
> And add some extra, just for you.
>
> But they were fucked up in their turn
> By fools in old-style hats and coats . . .

So wrote the great British poet Philip Larkin in "This Be the Verse" (1971). I think this is exactly what he had in mind.

In the 1990s, the mythopoetic men's movement, which led retreats and gatherings, connected with middle-aged men who were desperate to heal what the movement leader, poet Robert Bly, called the "father wound"—the painful search for acceptance and love from withholding, cold, distant, or even absent fathers. Many such men were brought to tears describing fathers who never told their sons they loved them, were proud of them. They ached from deep inside for validation from their fathers. Didn't the fathers realize the trauma they had undertaken? Didn't they realize what these boys had given up—connection with mother, connection to those emotions of dependency and vulnerability, the capacity to love and feel loved—in order to connect with their father?

So here is what the boy learns. He learns that no sooner does he understand that he has grown close to his mother, someone with whom he feels it is safe to feel dependent, vulnerable, and loved, that she abandons him, she pushes him away. Yes, she is forced to do so by the ideology that demands he identify with father. But she becomes complicit in the boy's eyes: she has abandoned him.

And what does he learn? That it is a terrible, traumatic mistake to ever trust a woman again, to ever get close, be vulnerable, dependent. That if he truly loves he will only get hurt. "I'll never make that mistake again!" he says, doubled over in his first experience of the pain of rejection. His sister, meanwhile, of course, has learned that if she loves she will be loved, and that is unbroken.

So, completely contrary to Freud, the boy comes through this Oedipal drama broken, traumatized, and determined never to open himself up to such possible abandonment again. This is what psychoanalysis calls "autonomy."

The girl, by contrast, comes through knowing that love will be reciprocated, that it is safe to be vulnerable and dependent, because one will be loved. And then she is, of course, abandoned by her future husband or lover because he is incapable of vulnerability or dependency. She is then traumatized, and is expected to be consoled by the devaluation of the mother's love, clearly secondary to the love of the father. After all, in patriarchy, it's men's love that matters.

It's easy to see why generations of Freudian psychologists have blamed mother for this. But, as we can see, she is simply following the dictates of a theory, a theory that prizes the achievement of masculinity, an ideology, over the concrete relationships the boy has already developed with his mother, and privileges his stoicism with his father over any possibility of warmth and vulnerability with his mother.

It is as if the boy is being offered a choice: Which will it be, young man: the ideology of masculinity, or the actual, visceral experience of love and connection? And to make it clear: both father and mother are telling him that they support the ideology. He learns not to trust his feelings, but to put faith in that ideology instead.

You want to know why it's so hard for men to commit, to open up, to be sensitive? Look no further. Why subject oneself to such a deeply painful trauma? Why risk it?

However, just in case he might even consider refusing to abandon love and connection in the name of this ideology we call masculinity, we sweeten the deal. We provide rewards, compensation. Here's the deal: if you agree to leave mother, join with the stoically shut-down father, and, in so doing, sacrifice all that nurture and connection, here's what you get in return: entitlement. You are entitled to power, to wealth, to sexual access to women. Why would you want to *be* like a woman when you can dominate them and have sexual access to them? You'll get rich, get laid, be in control. Be . . . wait for it . . . "independent," as if disconnection is the highest goal to be achieved. (Are you listening, Eriksonians?) You will have power over others, and no one will have power over you.

This was the point made so eloquently by feminist psychologist Carol Gilligan in her pathbreaking book, *In a Different Voice* (1982). (She makes a similar point elsewhere in this volume.) "Maturity" is defined by separateness. What gender could possibly have thought that one up? You know you live in a patriarchy when "maturity" and "masculinity" are synonymous.

* * *

It is through this process of repudiating the mother and seeking the approval of the father for having repudiated her that the boy comes to devalue everything she stands for—compassion, empathy, love, dependency, and vulnerability—and to value everything the father represents. He learns not only masculinity and heterosexuality, as Freud thought, but also that the price of patriarchal privilege is the renunciation of those very qualities that set us apart as humans, the capacity to empathize. The "healthy" psychological development of the boy, repudiating mother in the name of the father—or at least the father's entitlement—is the moment when patriarchy is reproduced at the micro level. Toddler patriarchs, filled with entitlement.

No wonder in the original story of Iron John, as recounted by Robert Bly in his best seller and countless mythopoetic retreats, the men who encountered the story identified only with one of the four male characters in the tale. These were the king, his son, the father of the girl that the prince desires, and Iron John himself (who also turns out to be a king). Three kings and a prince. And all those middle-aged, middle-class men identified not with any of the kings, but with the prince. With the boy! And why? Because the prince is not in power—but he will be. He is entitled, by birth, to be in power. It is only a matter of time. He has made his choice, and now sits and waits for his rewards, his compensation for hollowing out his heart.

There is anthropological evidence that earlier weaning of males makes boys more violent and aggressive. Perhaps, then, contra the mythopoetic "elders"—those male mothers who sought to rebirth those wounded men—we need to consider healing the mother wound, that rupture that turns boys into men by suppressing the capacity for empathy and the desire, the need, for connection. It was mother who embodied that, literally, in her nurturing body.

I remember feeling this pull when my own son hit age three or four. I had never seen anything more gorgeous in all the world than the special loving connection that had developed between my son and his mother. It made me weep to watch them together, cuddling. When he would sleep with us, he would sleep in between us, and wedge himself closer to Amy by sleeping horizontally (think of the letter H) and he would get closer to her by pushing against me with his feet. At the time, I was often tired, and sometimes grouchy. But to watch them together was to dispel any commitment I might have made to that ideology over their real human connection.

In retrospect, we didn't ruin him. We didn't break him, we didn't traumatize him by dangling the rewards of masculinity in front of him as compensation for renouncing his love for his mother. To reassure you, he's okay. He plays varsity sports and sings and dances in musical theater. He has deep friendships with both boys and girls. He does well in school, and is generally happy. We followed, I believe, the single most important rule of parenthood: we didn't fuck him up.

Maybe we can do more than not fuck our kids up. Maybe it's time to heal the mother wound, to channel and celebrate our inner mama's boy. Maybe, as Gary Barker argues elsewhere in this volume, we can help men connect back to their humanity by healing that father wound, the hunger for his approval. Maybe these reclaimed mothers and healed fathers are the route back to our common humanity.

V.

> But I reckon I got to light out for the territory, ahead of the rest, because Aunt Sally she's going to adopt me and sivilize me, and I can't stand it. I been there before.

Those are the last lines Huck Finn says in the novel that bears his name. When we read these lines, we are struck, of course, by the masculinity project, the sense that masculinity is to be proved, achieved, away from the feminizing, civilizing clutches of women, out in the wilderness, the woods, the territory.

But rarely do we pay much attention to the very last line of the book. "I been there before."

That is now, for me, the crucial line, the line that expresses the hope of reconnecting ideas of masculinity to connectedness, to embeddedness. We *have* been there before, in that nurturing pre-Oedipal world. We know what it feels like to be accepted and loved, without having to be relentlessly policed by other guys to make sure we are doing it right. We know what it feels like to exhale, have nothing left to prove.

Now all we have to do is remember. And come home.

7

Slut Shaming as a Crisis of Connection

Fostering Connections to Fuel Resistance

DEBORAH L. TOLMAN

Slut shaming is all over the news. Girls have been slut shamed into being completely socially isolated, switching schools, depression, and suicide.[1] Mainstream headlines, television news and specials, blogs, YouTube videos, and radio shows toggle between blaming and punishing adolescent girls for posting "inappropriate" pictures on social media and sexting boyfriends, and celebrating girls' sexual empowerment and freedom. Rumors of "outrageous" sexual behavior and dressing in a "shockingly sexy" way are addressed for accuracy rather than whether such rumors should exist, arrayed side by side with outrage about bullying, rape culture, and sexualization. Ironically, the burgeoning panic about slut shaming has the unintended consequence of normalizing it, rendering its use expected. Awareness is up, but why isn't slut shaming down? If girls are now supposed to embody sexiness, project sexual know-how, and claim sexual empowerment, how is it that slut shaming exists? Concern and outrage usually decry the effects rather than the causes of slut shaming. Even as some media offer a feminist analysis of how gender inequities continue to fuel slut shaming,[2] strategies for how to change or challenge it are, for the most part, rare, thus feeding a sense of "slut" intractability. The reality is that adolescent girls' sexuality—in particular their embodied sexual feelings—is still anathema, dressed up as desirable but ultimately devalued, denied, and punished.

This volume is predicated on an analysis of fundamental binaries, hierarchies, and resulting splits woven into our social fabric, happening in social and interpersonal relationships and embodied in individuals' psyches, creating, re-creating, and perpetuating crises of connection.[3] Importantly, the crisis of connection framework offered in this book recognizes that the dehumanizing requirements and effects of crises of connection damage both oppressed and oppressor. I suggest that slut shaming is such a crisis of connection, both created by and sustaining one of these key binaries: gender inequality, the still-beating heart of patriarchy, specifically, inequitable beliefs and practices of sexuality. Within this gender inequality are different forms of oppression for young women marginalized in other ways—by race and ethnicity, by class and nationality, by immigrant status and ability.[4] Conceiving of slut shaming as a crisis of connection is an innovative way to make sense of, and thus to intervene in, this relentless policing and punishing of girls and women. The term "slut" gains its power by creating and then leveraging disconnections from our bodies and psyches, and within relationships.

A crisis of connection framework invites us to consider that slut shaming is a form of everyday violence and violation experienced by adolescent girls.[5] It is pervasive and terrorizing; it can happen to anyone at any time, often without rhyme or reason. To shame is to use *disconnection* as a means of violence and damage, to cast an individual out of a community and/or to induce her to cast doubt on herself. The point of shaming is to separate someone from a group, from community, and, one could argue, from herself. Slut shaming is mobilized interpersonally—the mechanism is, in one form or another, relational. Slut shaming disrupts relationships and its effect is disruption of connection between girls and other girls, girls and boys, girls and social supports and communities. Recognizing that relational and psychological disconnects—the effects of structural barriers to empathy—are produced by societally sanctioned slut shaming underscores the importance of doing more than reporting on it. This chapter makes the case for slut shaming as a crisis of connection and articulates potential strategies to redress it by engaging in forms of resistance that a crisis of connection framework can offer.

What's in a Name?

How does the word "slut" have so much power? "Slut" is a social production, used both to assess and reduce girls to their sexual value while in fact obfuscasting their sexuality.[6] In various ways, adolescent girls' sexuality has been especially fraught and mobilized as a smoke screen or substitute for other social anxieties, a moral panic that underpins the current ostensible epidemic of slut shaming. The outsized concern with girls being "sluts" can be understood as a disconnection from what we are often worried about, and girls' bodies and behavior become both totem and vessel for those anxieties, covering up more complex, deeper, or insidious social problems.[7]

The word "slut" does "work"—it has discursive power to create and perpetuate a crisis of connection.[8] Recognizing how "slut" is a *mechanism* fueling disconnections, we can deconstruct how it does the work of patriarchy. When I put quotations around the word "slut," I am referring to it as representing a mechanism that does work rather than common usage. Patriarchy has been located in what Rich described as compulsory heterosexuality, the concept that a set of social practices and beliefs organize heterosexuality as an institution produced by oppressing and keeping women oppressed.[9] While it was not framed as such, she articulated what can be seen as *a series of disconnections* that produce and maintain patriarchy, including denying female desire(s), treating women as objects not people, keeping women separated from and out of relationship with one another, and obfuscating women's own history. Control and punishment of female sexuality is a primary target used to monitor and contain women's hungers, desires, knowledge about themselves, relationships with other women, gender inequality, and sense of entitlement.[10] Slut shaming and its threat is a mechanism of social control.

The gender inequity that compulsory heterosexuality produces and perpetuates is practicing, embodying, believing in, and performing conventional ideas about masculinity and femininity.[11] This inequity produces a split of fundamental dimensions of our humanity along gender lines into hierarchies, which privilege and value appropriately masculine men (heterosexual, sexually driven, assertive, aggressive, tough, protective, rational) *over* appropriately feminine women (heterosexual, sexually accommodating, desirable, contained, emotional, selfless and attentive to others). Slut shaming is punishment for girls' "failures" or refusals to comply, much like the historical public punishment of the stocks or wearing of the letter "A," mobilizing shame, isolation, and demonization that produce and sustain disconnection. Recognition of and theory about gender inequality highlight how women's and girls' positionalities within structural hierarchies—for instance, race, class, nationality, ability—intersect with these conditions, producing a plethora of forms and intensities of slut shaming, infused and shaped by other disconnections and dehumanizing social forces.[12] Gender inequality is predicated on the sexual double standard: boys are expected to be sexually voracious and uncontrollable, their sexual desires and satisfaction are prioritized, and girls are meant to keep boys under control and not recognize, give weight to, or privilege their own sexuality, especially outside of appropriate bounds (i.e., relationships with boys/men). If the sexual double standard were no longer at play, slut shaming would not exist. And without question, it does.

"Slut" accrues power by slipperiness and lack of accountability. Anyone can call anyone a "slut." There is no need to provide evidence or make a "credible" accusation. The slut moniker can be imposed for a variety of reasons—some having to do with sexuality, some having to do with perceptions about sexuality, some having nothing to do with sexuality but utilizing its power to diminish a girl. The very use of "slut," then, constitutes a disconnection from "reality," giving it a kind of ambient power. While sexuality is not actually always what motivates slut shaming, it is always what is leveraged by it. Anxiety, panic, and critique are directed toward social media, as if it is the cause of an "epidemic" of slut shaming, a red herring that covers up this crisis of connection. While social media in and of itself has been seen as a crisis of connection, often as a technology that further atomizes people from one another,[13] it is a *means* of slut shaming. Bullying of all sorts has been thrust out of the shadows by social media and new technologies—it is hard to deny when it has extended from hallways and to the internet. Yet reducing slut shaming only to bullying, which perhaps makes it more palatable, obfuscates what it has always been: the maintenance of patriarchy through disconnection.

While "slut" has always been a threat, at the *current time*, it is an even more pervasive, present, and complicated matter. As Tanenbaum observed, "the sexist mindset [remains] that boys will be boys, and girls will be sluts."[14] Updated somewhat, the sexual double standard persists under strange conditions. Potent postfeminist public discourse in Western contexts of sexual empowerment stands in contradiction to the ongoing practice of slut shaming.[15] *Both* its simultaneous persistence and the denial of its existence make its "work" more insidious. While previously thought of as not desiring or actively interested in being sexual, White (and to some extent Asian) elite girls are now having to navigate the contradictory burden of "compulsory sexual agency"[16]—the idea that girls *must* project a kind of sexual sophistication and empowered sexuality, and also to present themselves as sexually desirable, as "good" or "well done" sexual objects—but without overstepping an invisible line into "sluttiness." For poor girls and girls of color, current conditions have intensified a long-standing imposition of sexuality *onto* them—and their bodies—that they have to manage, an intensification of their "always already" assumed *excessive* sexuality.[17] Lesbian and bisexual girls are also subject to the effect and control of slut shaming in their experiences with same-sex desire.[18]

A key task in adolescence is constructing identities.[19] Slut shaming is implicated in how both boys and girls engage in this process, insinuating threats of disconnection.[20] Observing how slut shaming is utilized in boys' constructions of themselves as masculine, in their embodiments, in their relational interactions with others, and in their own psyches sheds light on *how* slut shaming "works." Boys can use the punishment of slut shaming girls to constitute themselves as masculine within a system that defines masculinity as not-girl, being "one of the boys," and treating girls as failed or excessive sexual objects.[21] This practice depends on the dehumanization and use of girls, or the performance of it, yielding disconnection from the self and boys' own feelings and from authentic relationships with girls and others.

The crisis of connection framework helps to explain the inexplicable: girls slut shaming other girls. Often described as "mean" or "vicious," relationally aggressive or jealous, the conditions of continued diminution of girls and their sexuality in relation to boys and male sexuality yield a practice of positioning oneself as "not a slut." This "othering" or mobilizing of "slut discourse" makes it possible to know and project oneself as acceptable in comparison with a girl who has been deemed spoiled.[22] It furthers the goal of keeping oneself disconnected from a "tainted" girl in the minds of others, enabling ongoing acceptance in a community. Tanenbaum observed that the idea of "good" and "bad" sluts has gotten some traction under the specter of girls' sexual empowerment;[23] however, a "good" slut is always at risk of becoming a "bad" slut in the ever-slippery terrain that in essence terrorizes girls. It is notable that girls rarely, if ever, use this label self-referentially.

Embodiment, Desire, and Slut Shaming: Recognizing Disconnection

Recognizing that sexual desire lies at the intersection of the physical and the social—that what we feel in our bodies is always mediated by language, ideas, and beliefs, which inform practices and policies (that is, discourses) and also by relationships—is key to understanding the ways in which individual girls' engagement with slut shaming produces a crisis of connection. Slut shaming can happen to adult women, but it is primarily a tool to control adolescent girls, and for them it is devastating and leaves long-term residues. Embodiment—the idea that (1) we live in physical bodies and (2) culture shapes our bodily experiences—is key to well-being and connection; embodiment is a form of knowing, an anchor in the body, and a compass for one's own perceptions. Disembodiment is one way to manage physical and psychological pain, fear and distress, and to literally dissociate from bodily sensations. Piran and Thompson and others have argued that girls learn to live in a patriarchal society by severing their connections from their bodies.[24] "Slut" aims at the heart of female adolescent sexual desire and pleasure; slut shaming is predicated on the notion that girls cannot be or should not have or express sexual desire, making it hard to act on or experience desire or pleasure. That is, under the sexual double standard, desire is always linked to "slut." If a girl is thus always at risk of being labeled slutty, it can yield disembodiment or vigilant management of one's own sexual desire.[25]

But how is it possible that girls struggle with their own sexual feelings at a time when there is the possibility of sexual empowerment—the idea of girls embracing their sexual agency to "do whatever they want" or be constantly "up for it"?[26] Adolescent girls' sexual desire may no longer be simply "missing";[27] it is hobbled and even more complicated than it was. Under the current pressure for girls to be sexually sophisticated and knowing but not *excessively* sexual, knowledgeable but not *too* knowledgeable, experienced but not *too* experienced, sexy but not *too* sexy, the question of girls' embodied sexual desire looms even larger. While it can be anathema to be a virgin or a prude, it is also problematic to have too much experience. The neoliberal mandate to "make good choices" does not give much weight to girls' own desires; being embodied becomes, in essence, crazy or crazy making. Girls are taking up the language of sexual empowerment, but there is almost no evidence that they feel an explicit entitlement to sexual feelings of their own or to connect to their own bodies; they do continue to worry about and be subjected to slut shaming.[28] Given the intense monitoring of how one looks—including looking sexy and sophisticated but not too sexy or too sophisticated— managing "slut" is a challenging task and is in part dependent on girls focusing on how they look rather than how they feel.[29] The contradiction may be leading to "performing" sexual desire and knowingness, which may fuel disembodiment and lack of connection in sexual encounters and relationships as well.[30] The current discourse and lessons in sexual empowerment are about how to act rather than having a sense of entitlement to embodied feelings, which can be meaningfully linked to the idea that girls have *the right* not to be slut shamed.

Fostering Resistant Connections

As many chapters in this volume have articulated so well, patriarchy and resulting gender inequality remains one of the most entrenched and fundamental crises of connection. The sexual double standard is one of the most reliable henchmen of patriarchy, keenly resistant even to diverse girls' and women's progress across so many dimensions of life.[31] Like the other potent, profound, and persistent crises of connection, when under pressure, patriarchy shape-shifts into alternative and more clandestine mechanisms while keeping the organizing hierarchies in place, less visible, and even well disguised, and that makes the task of eradicating slut shaming and its motor daunting. At the same time, there is a renewed desire for *collective action*—for resistant connection—as the Women's March of January 2017 demonstrated. It may have been a unique moment, a perfect storm of visibility, outrage, and desire to redress threats to our common humanity in general that could and should be leveraged. For slut shaming in particular to be undone, action requires recognizing rather than whitewashing gender inequality (and the unequal ways it manifests across race, class, and other dehumanizing binaries) that privileges male and denigrates female sexuality. There have been excellent efforts by feminist scholars and a plethora of activists, people who care about girls, and girls themselves that recognize and explain how the sexual double standard is at the heart of slut shaming. Yet while analysis and protests are necessary, they are not sufficient. The crisis of connection framework calls for fostering connections as a principle of resistance that resets its sights in both intensive short-term, individual, and relational strategic action, as well as slower, deeper, and longer-term movements.

Fostering Resistant Connections through Embodiment

Embodiment is a key to connecting with oneself, and it has been shown to be helpful with connecting to others. In a society that continues to subject diverse girls and women to male gaze(s), to further commodify, sexualize, and objectify female bodies and sexuality (e.g., the pervasiveness on the internet, easy access to pornography that presents unrealistic images of female and male bodies and sexuality), and sexualizes queerness, connecting with one's sexual body can be difficult, be dangerous, or seem unimportant. In this landscape, disregarding or protecting oneself from desire may in fact be a sensible response. Given that so many girls have learned how to disconnect from, guard, and not value their own sexual feelings and bodies, a three-part strategy of querying why they detach, devalue, or objectify their bodies, developing a sense of entitlement to their own bodies *and* literally learning how to connect may foster resistant connection.

Providing girls with critical tools (e.g., critical thinking techniques, feminist perspectives, and understanding of how female sexuality is demeaned, hamstrung, or made to seem unimportant, excessive, or even pornographic) is a first step. Having an understanding of these ideas about female (and male) sexuality and possibly even being angry or outraged (also forms of bodily arousal) are forms of and fuel for resistance. However, in the face of a culture of slut shaming, simply suggesting that or "giving permission to" girls to feel and accept their desires and use them for guidance is a setup. Telling girls that they can be embodied, even celebrating embodied sexual feelings, does not enable them in and of itself. Believing we are entitled to our bodies, desires, and rights is more elusive and fundamental. As Dorothy Aken'oa states in a radical proposition, a politics *of* the body can translate into politics *beyond* the body: feeling entitled to one's own embodied pleasure can instigate a sense of entitlement to fundamental rights.[32] *Feeling* entitled is a challenge. What can encourage this sense of entitlement? How we talk to and about girls, what we say to them about their bodies matters. Don't judge and disparage girls for *dressing* sexy; ask them about *feeling* sexy. Dressing sexy in and of itself is not the problem. Dressing sexy within a sense of entitlement to one's body, bodily feelings, and right to say yes (really) and say no and be respected, within a critical perspective, can be positive and even transformative. Differentiating between sexual feelings and choosing how and when to act on those feelings is critical as well. Feeling entitled to choose how to express sexual feelings, including not to act on them, is equally important. Embodiment and entitlement are reclamations of consent: when "yes" can be believed, then "no" can be as well. The ongoing public discourse about consent in rape culture, simplified as it is, may be wreaking havoc with these processes. Conveying the fuzziness, ambivalence, and fluidity of desire and sexual expression, even in a discrete sexual encounter, is a newly important conversation.

Practices that teach us to accept, live in, and feel our bodies, such as meditation, Pilates, and yoga, and to enjoy the pleasures that movement and body competence invite, such as flamenco, sports, and martial arts, may be indirect, but they may make a difference. These practices can be done with others to create connections through shared experience. They teach and provide practice for attuning to one's bodily feelings. While not directly about sexual feelings, developing that ability, that connection, can be built and extended to one's sexual body. Knowing about one's sexual body, through masturbation for instance, is a long-standing tool; some women who recall masturbating as children describe both embodied desires and pleasures and a sense of entitlement to them as adults. However, childhood masturbation can also be infused with shame and questions about one's sexual body, and so is not a panacea.[33] Women who are not girls' mothers or parents may be good people for girls to talk to about the "nitty gritty" of embodied sexual feelings (see below). It does indeed take a village: fostering relationships between young people and other adults who are not parents or guardians, whom we trust to keep confidences and encourage resistance, can be difficult but can make a difference. These practices show young people how relationships build networks and communities and also provide alternatives to the lone her-oine approach that the media loves.

For progressive, even feminist, parents, addressing slut shaming poses a dilemma. No parents ever want their daughter to be subjected to slut shaming, and we want them to be happy. However, under the current terms of these identity and social challenges, girls becoming young women must navigate this confounded scaffolding of seeming sexy—producing sexy and desirable bodies, in essence being good sexual objects—but not overstepping into the minefield of "slut." This contra-diction is not new but is intensified in the 24/7 presence and emphasis of surveillance:[34] how they and their friends appear and represent them-selves on social media, being captured constantly by iPhone videos, see-ing relentless representations of young women with jutting hip bones and perfectly toned but not overly muscular bodies. Looking sexy is currency in girls' lives, whether feminist parents or other adults like it or not; feeling sexual feelings, feeling entitled to them, particularly in heterosexual relationships, may be dangerous. Resistance is truly dif-ficult for individual girls; experiencing and knowing their bodies as competent and as fundamentally theirs, embracing and embodying their sexuality and sexual feelings as a resource and pleasure for them-selves are easier said than done.

Therefore *telling* our own (individual) girls to love their own bodies, not to worry about being popular, whether and how others, especially boys, judge them to be desirable, or even that they are entitled to their own sexual feelings, to sexual pleasure and sexual agency leaves girls in a quandary. In addition to the three-part strategy, engaging girls through authenticity and vulnerability ourselves may be helpful: finding (subtle!) ways to tell them about our own quandaries about and ongoing struggles with our bodies; our navigation of our own sexuality when we were teens (in a way that does not mortify them) and beyond. Revealing how we try to deal with the complexity of embodiment and entitlement, allow-ing ourselves hungers, bodily pleasures, and satisfaction in the face of pressures to "have it all" and yet still face the boundaries of femininity mandates as we age, how our material embodiment (race, class, fluid and same-sex desire, personal history) informs our struggles, how gender in-equities continue to challenge our ability to live in our bodies. Engaging in these conversations or other ways of sharing (through writing or art, for instance) requires that we recognize the need for and try to do this work ourselves. What are our successes? What are our failures? How do we understand what works and what doesn't?

Understanding slut shaming as a crisis of connection enables us to recognize that the threat of and being labeled slut is both ambient and personal. Research has shown that girls who refuse the terms of the sexual double standard, and embody and feel entitled to their own sexual feelings, can gut "slut" of its power to harm them.[35] This is a monumental task, and few girls are able to do it by themselves. Yet maybe they have a lesson for us. In my own research, some girls who have experienced violence and disembodiment work to get their bodies back. They have succeeded through some kind of relational process—therapy, family, or even community—and have been able to learn how to anchor themselves in their bodies and, most importantly, to have a sense of entitlement to their own humanity. Not only do they maintain their resistance for themselves, they enact it in social contexts by openly refusing to disconnect from other girls and being a voice of refusal in their communities. Recognizing that boys are not the only ones who have a right to sexual desire and agency is part of what they describe; critical thinking is necessary but not sufficient. Engaging with others from a position of connection to themselves has been effective for them as individuals, and they have made inroads into their immediate relationships and social circles. What they offer us is part of a mechanism toward connection that includes and goes beyond themselves.

The risks and possibilities of sexual embodiment and entitlement may differ for girls by race, class, citizenship status, sexual orientation, religion, or other marginalizing social forces[36]—sexual desire may be bundled with or simply seem less important than fundamental desires, for education and safety, what McClelland and Fine have called "thick desire."[37] When a girl's body is always already sexualized, when resources of all kinds are scant, when having material security is in question, what does it mean to be sexually embodied, and how does a girl manage sexual feelings under such conditions? Parents and other adults who worry about material consequences of sexual expression may find the suggestion that girls be encouraged to connect with their bodies anathema or dangerous. Engaging communities in the question of embodiment and sexual entitlement may be critical. Where can or do girls' sexual feelings fit in? If embodiment is an element of overall well-being, how can diverse communities engage with the resulting array of dilemmas of desire?

Fostering Resistant Connections through Community Building

Slut shaming is frequently represented as bad behavior, bullying, or meanness. It is rarely framed as an effect of the political (meaning both electoral politics and social practices) landscape or social policy. Political action in the streets and in the voting booth matters. Some efforts to redress and diminish several tenets of institutionalized heterosexuality have in fact worked, largely by fostering connections among individuals, within relationships, within communities, and for society. Revisiting these successes and how they happened is worthwhile. The movement to recognize and render domestic violence intolerable made significant inroads in the 1970s through an array of connections: women's consciousness-raising groups, helping women both recognize and criticize such violence and growing a sense of entitlement to their safety and bodily integrity, women banding together to create shelters and then advocate for them to be funded, organizing for changes in social policy and the law, and engaging and shifting public discourse to reframe it as unacceptable. Critiques of this movement as racialized, privileging White women's lives and issues, without recognizing the situations and barriers that these solutions overlooked for women of color and other marginalized women also provide guidance.

We should take a page from the playbook of the queer movement's efforts. People whose desires and gender embodiments do not comply with compulsory heterosexuality insisted on a community-*driven* and community-*creating* reclamation of "queer" that provided a large umbrella to grow its political power, as well as individuals' senses of entitlement to their bodies and desires. The lesson is not to suppress "slut" with school policies or parenting practices that forbid its utterance but to engage in the slow work of creating community—connections—to refuse it *collectively*. Some girls are calling their friends "slut" as a term of endearment or playing with it as a way to refuse it. Current efforts among girls to reclaim "slut" often do so without this kind of analysis; the results have been rocky at best and short-lived.[38] As "slut" functions to disband relationships and community, often already marginalized sexual citizens, creating communities of sexual entitlement may be more effective; when individuals make these attempts on their own, without organizing or a strategy predicated on understanding the negative and controlling uses of "slut," it is not surprising that time and again these efforts fall short. A collective process by which "slut" might be reclaimed is not clear but worth engaging or encouraging young people to consider.

When communities refuse the word "slut"—not suppress it but refuse it—"slut" will lose its power. When members of any institution and community can be persuaded to understand the "work" that slut does, the disconnection it causes for individual girls (and boys), in relationships and to society, to really question their perspectives on girls' sexuality and their values about girls' humanity, and then to voluntarily pledge in community not to ostracize a girl who gets called slut and call out people who use it, that makes a difference. It is hard to imagine "slut" ever becoming a positive word, but it is not hard to imagine engaging in community building to unlink what leads to the shaming that it induces. When leadership in communities, including religious, political, medical, even "the popular kids," shift practices, fostering resistant connections becomes more possible. In the case of slut shaming, trust in and respect of girls, resources to enable them to make the best decisions for themselves (material, educational, social), safety and commitment to their well-being are required; it is in connection that those values are made possible. Different communities will call for different strategies for shifts. Given what we have observed about the uneven acceptance of gay marriage and transgender people, the process is slow and demanding change is only a start.

Fostering Resistant Connections through Education

Another effort is making feminism, well, sexier. The developing movement of feminist clubs in high schools is an excellent example. These contexts are rich resources for engaging with girls about what girls' desire is like—and how girls' desire matters—not just its absence but also its presence. Fueling this movement is a way to foster connection. Some studies have found that sexual subjectivity is associated with resistance to the sexual double standard and with self-esteem.[39] Feminist clubs develop in a context in which girls' sexual subjectivity may be recognized as a right, reclaimed and solidified.[40] They may enable and support girls refusing to go along with slut shaming: girls who embody or value their desire may be more able to recognize and reject the "system" and refuse to repudiate other girls based on their (ostensible) desire or behavior. They are also a context in which girls and women can work together to challenge school policies and practices that may seem progressive by mandating a climate free of slut shaming but effectively suppress discussion or analysis of what slut shaming is, what is required to diminish it, and what girls and their allies can do to resist.

Fostering resistant connections has to involve boys as well as girls—and men as well as women. We know that slut shaming and the sexual double standard are possible only when everyone participates; the same is true for resisting these practices. Providing boys with the conditions and tools to recognize and resist stereotypes and harmful ideas about their sexuality and girls' sexuality is key; even more important is helping them understand and value what they are "trading" for toxic masculinity (knowledge and experience about their own emotions, even their own bodies, the pleasures of emotional connections, in essence, their entitlement to their full humanity). Boys are often motivated to embrace feminism and start to participate in feminist clubs when they recognize or witness someone about whom they care and love—to whom they are profoundly connected—experiencing the results of sexism, including slut shaming and its threat.[41] Encouraging girls and boys to participate in feminist youth organizations that are dedicated to resisting slut shaming, sexism, heterosexism, and racism—that are fueled by intersectional gender justice—provides them with a way to share their outrage and commitment to action. As we know from the past, engaging in these processes—of coming to know and of feeling entitled—can be more effective when girls and women work together in larger groups, and the same is true for boys. We also know, however, that those adults have to foster these connections and commitment to resistance themselves, and be willing to engage in what is often a painful process of listening to and taking seriously what girls (and boys) have to tell us about our complicity in maintaining gender inequality.[42]

Reducing slut shaming to bullying obfuscates its work and how to address it; when generalized anti-bullying strategies are "straight applied" without revealing the persistent and rotten roots of patriarchy, illuminating what "work" slut shaming does that is more than bullying, the effect is a misdiagnosis. When such interventions do not get to the heart of the matter—how gender is a system that upends our common humanity, that takes bodies from girls and women and feelings from boys and men—slut shaming resurfaces in whatever guises fit into the fissures that suppression forces rather than motivating all involved to challenge its purpose and recognize its effects. The development of anti-sexism curricula to address slut shaming will be more effective as it gets to what is actually driving the problem.[43]

There is variability in how the sexual double standard operates in girls' social worlds; it can be the culture of a school, for instance, that diminishes it or particular social groups.[44] However, culture and climate cannot be mandated; they must develop among young people and the adults in their lives. High school English teacher, activist, and popular blogger Ileana Jimenez shares examples of how to create awareness and a sense of collective demand among girls and boys in teaching feminism and also teaching English through an intersectional feminist lens.[45] She writes about how her students develop a kind of feminist nose for oppressive and unjust social processes. In a participatory research project on which she and I collaborated, a group of ten girls designed, implemented, analyzed, and reported on a study about slut shaming in their school—a question *they* wanted to investigate, because it affected them *and* they believed that, despite the official line, it was endemic in their school. This work moved the needle on slut shaming through awareness of its pervasiveness, instigating discussions of why girls are slut shamed in their school, and being included in action to reduce it.

Fostering Resistant Connections through Media

A critical mass of books, media, and Internet resources is burgeoning that leverages and challenges slut shaming in the public arena. Feminist blogs and articles about girls' rights to dress and present themselves however they please, even their right to be sexual and enjoy their own bodies, are more available than ever. There is a wider public discourse that reveals the persistence and harms of slut shaming, girls and women are telling their stories, articulating the brutality and "stickiness" of being called a slut, outing how headlines normalize slut shaming—all are resources. There is a new and readily available film, *Slut: The Documentary* by the UnSlut Project, complementing Emily Linden's publication of her own adolescent diaries documenting the effects on her of being called a slut.[46] An earlier book, *Slut!*, written by Leora Tanenbaum, utilized her own experience to unpack the phenomenon;[47] an updated analysis, *I Am Not a Slut*, illuminates how "slut" works in the current moment.[48] She writes an ongoing column for *Teen Vogue* to help girls deal with it. The intergenerational feminist activist initiative SPARK now has a deep archive of blogs written by girls, and research blogs on related issues, action histories and strategies, and training consultations are available.[49] Lyn Mikel Brown's book *Powered by Girl* outlines successful intergenerational activism—and the challenges that doing so entails.[50]

If observing and living sexual gender inequality is essentialized, change seems impossible. Films such as *Diary of a Teenage Girl*, for instance, offer alternatives and even scripts for entitlement to female adolescent sexual desire and pleasure. *Blue Is the Warmest Color*, a French film about a high school girl coming to know and explore same-sex desires, is another (very frank) example. The power of these films is evident in the resistance to and denigration of them in mainstream media.[51] Lacy Greene's YouTube sex education videos explain and illuminate both unfairness of slut shaming and girls' right to be sexual. The television shows *Girls* and *Chewing Gum* embrace the complexity of sexuality for White and Black young women, respectively. While watching "resistance" television with one's teenagers may be a bridge too far for everyone, adults can watch on their own (or with their own peers) and use the shows as a resource for raising questions about slut shaming in a way that is salient to girls. The website feministing.com is flush with blogs that make the case for young women's sexual entitlement and challenge slut shaming; everydayfeminism.com is particularly effective at illuminating the mechanisms that perpetuate slut shaming and strategies to resist it, with evocative and informed explanations and cartoons. Thought-provoking discussions of slut shaming can even be found on Reddit—which is also replete with outsized examples of slut shaming that can be fodder for critique and discussion. Girls can follow Twitter posts by GuerillaGirls on Tour, Bitch Media, Girls for Gender Equity and generate their own, make Tumblr pages creating alternative ways to express their desires and outrage, post audacious YouTube videos that can and have gone viral, critique and create Instagram feeds.

Fostering Resistant Connections in the Political Landscape

Being willing to have and engage in a long-term strategy starts with and is deeply anchored in connections with those who share the threat of "slut," but also those who perpetuate it out of fear and loathing. Dismantling slut shaming will never happen in a vacuum; we need more connections among the panoply of specialized interests that have proliferated into silos of protest and push back, to incorporate the human right of embodiment, well-being, and community. Social media and new technologies provide mechanisms by which connections can happen globally. It is critical to engage people who are in positions of power, who understand and are also outraged by the negative effects of this kind of crisis of connection (e.g., witness Joe Biden's successful efforts with the Violence Against Women Act). Informing them of the complexities that a crisis of connection model illuminates can make such efforts stronger and more effective (e.g., identifying shortcomings of VAWA).

The phenomenon of SlutWalks—both their effectiveness and their disappointment—offers lessons.[52] They have had enormous success in raising awareness of ongoing sexism, perpetuation of rape culture under conditions of mandated or desired sexiness. SlutWalks focus on girls' and women's right to dress as they wish—even as "sluts"—and not be targets of rape and to have freedom from sexual violence regardless of their appearance. They demand that boys and men are held accountable and that the criminal justice system takes it seriously. A strong positive of SlutWalks is a notable form of connection among women, girls, and their allies, creating community even for the short time of the walk that may (or may not) continue its power and voice. The enactment of Slut-Walks, like the protests of the second wave women's rights movement, refuses the separation of women and girls from one another that compulsory heterosexuality insinuates. Yet a crisis of connection framework illuminates that SlutWalks do not address or focus on girls' and women's rights and entitlement to their own sexuality, to gender equality within relationships, or to their own desires. They are a defense and a refusal, a strong one that gets attention. They are a good example of a fine way to take on the symptom and refute it, yet their effort and effect fall short of demanding more, including conditions that enable women's and girls' embodiment beyond the surface of how their bodies look and are treated. SlutWalks have encountered the question of the unevenness of diverse women's vulnerability to rape and sexual violence and also what it means for women of color to embrace "slut"—the ways in which "slut" operates not simply because of perceived bad behavior or egregious, excessive appearance, but in the very embodiment of Black and Brown and queer women's bodies.[53] Addressing this differential in both rejecting and taking back "slut" has remained elusive; creating connections across these differences requires hard conversations, understanding of and accounting for profound differences associated with "slut" and sexuality for women of color and queer women.[54] That SlutWalks (in the United States) have in essence become a commercial venture is worth recognizing.[55]

Pumping up the volume of the increasing recognition that girls are sexual people, that sexual desire(s) is normal and expecting them should be normative and should foster deeper connections between activists and institutions and organizations that have discursive power and political clout. In a world in which President Trump tweets incessantly, mobilizing social media is a way to foster connections. In what ways might the refusal to engage in or tolerate slut shaming "go viral"? Connections between young people and adults are critical in making this happen. We have observed the power that young people have in changing practices and values in their communities.[56] Supporting them, especially when they are in places that do not foster these connections, is worth our effort. If political parties can mobilize to change the outcome of elections, we can consider how to utilize those strategies. This idea raises the question of funds. Engaging people and institutions that have deep pockets is another factor that we often disregard.

Activism, particularly by girls working collectively and intergenerationally with women, has been effective in changing hearts and minds. Encouraging and supporting—and listening to—girls themselves without positioning them as lone saviors is key. A teen girl for the feminist girls' activist initiative SPARK blogged about how girls' saying "Love Ya, Slut!" to each other is premature; without a critical analysis of its power, "slut" just becomes a more easily mobilized word. Girls have also taught us that humor is a secret weapon that engages people rather than putting them on the defensive or yielding a dismissive response to a rant. Activism and resistance in the form of art and performances can be a visceral change agent.[57] Katie Cappiello has found that girls performing *Slut: The Play* have ignited awareness, outrage, action, and refusal to use the word and be more respectful of girls as sexual people in communities that perform it.[58]

Conclusion

In virtually all research that has been done on girls' sexuality from a perspective of sexual agency, slut shaming has played, and in some sense surprisingly continues to play, a fundamental shaping role.[59] It is always a point of reference and a backdrop. If we encourage, even demand, that each of us, and everyone to whom we are connected (and so on), asks the simple question—Why is it not okay for girls to be sexual?—we can begin to explore what benefits and costs are associated with this system for girls and for boys, and how they can be supported to push back against it. Asking questions that gently invite girls to query the contradictions that they are trying to manage, even as we manage our own distress and disappointment, is one way to enable them to develop and strengthen the muscles that entitlement and embodiment are: Why is it that boys can be, even have to be, sexual, and girls pay a price if they look too sexy or act too sexual? What does sexual pleasure feel like? In my own research, this question is almost unanimously met with "I don't know, that's just the way things are or have always been." Query essentialized gender inequality: Do (all) boys really just want sex, not relationships? Speak loudly in public venues. Build on the networks that social media and new technologies have created and enabled, like other political movements have done, because slut shaming is political and requires movement. Take time doing this. It is not easy. The crisis of connection framework situates slut shaming beyond bullying and as a mechanism by which the gender binaries undermine our humanity. Redressing slut shaming by fostering resistant connections provides a multidimensional map that can contribute to mending and ameliorating the crisis of connection.

NOTES

1 Emily Poole, "Hey Girls, Did You Know: Slut-Shaming on the Internet Needs to Stop," *USFL Review* 48 (2013): 221.

2 Nico Lang, "There's No Such Thing as a Slut," *Harper's Bazaar*, April 10, 2017, www.harpersbazaar.com.

3 Carol Gilligan, *Joining the Resistance: Psychology, Politics, Girls and Women* (Cambridge: Polity Press, 1991); Niobe Way, *Deep Secrets: Boys' Friendships and the Crisis of Connection* (Cambridge, MA: Harvard University Press, 2011).

4 Elizabeth A. Armstrong, Laura T. Hamilton, Elizabeth M. Armstrong, and J. Lotus Seeley, "'Good Girls': Gender, Social Class, and Slut Discourse on Campus," *Social Psychology Quarterly* 77, no. 2 (2014): 100–122; Amy M. Fasula, Monique Carry, and Kim S. Miller, "A Multidimensional Framework for the Meanings of the Sexual Double Standard and Its Application for the Sexual Health of Young Black Women in the US," *Journal of Sex Research* 51, no. 2 (2014): 170–183.

5 Elizabeth Stanko, *Intimate Intrusions: Women's Experience of Male Violence* (New York: Routledge & Kegan Paul, 1985); Deborah L. Tolman, "Object Lessons: Romance, Violation, and Female Adolescent Sexual Desire," *Journal of Sex Education and Therapy* 25, no. 1 (2000): 70–79.

6 Feona Attwood, "Sluts and Riot Grrrls: Female Identity and Sexual Agency," *Journal of Gender Studies* 16, no. 3 (2007): 233–247; Maddy Coy, "Milkshakes, Lady Lumps and Growing Up to Want Boobies: How Sexualisation of Popular Culture Limits Girls' Horizons," *Child Abuse Review* 18, no. 6 (2009): 372–383; Leora Tanenbaum, *I Am Not a Slut: Slut-Shaming in the Age of the Internet* (New York: Harper, 2015).

7 Deborah Tolman, "Afterword. Insisting on 'Both/And': Artifacts of Excavating Moral Panics about Sexuality," in *The Moral Panics of Sexuality*, ed. Breanne Fahs, Mary Dudy, and Sarah Stage (New York: Palgrave, 2013), 244–255.

8 Michel Foucault, *The History of Sexuality: An Introduction*, vol. 1 (New York: Random House, 1978).

9 Adrienne Rich, "Compulsory Heterosexuality and Lesbian Existence," *Signs: Journal of Women in Culture and Society* 5, no. 4 (1980): 631–660.

10 Ibid.; Carole S. Vance, *Pleasure and Danger: Exploring Female Sexuality* (London: Routledge & Kegan Paul, 1984).

11 Judith Butler, *Bodies That Matter: On the Limits of "Sex"* (London: Routledge & Kegan Paul, 1993).

12 Elizabeth R. Cole, "Intersectionality and Research in Psychology," *American Psychologist* 64, no. 3 (2009): 170–180; Patricia Hill Collins, *Black Feminist Thought: Knowledge, Consciousness and the Politics* (New York: HarperCollins, 1990); Emma Renold and Jessica Ringrose, "Regulation and Rupture: Mapping Tween and Teenage Girls' Resistance to the Heterosexual Matrix," *Feminist Theory* 9, no. 3 (2008): 313–338.

13 Sherry Turkle, *Alone Together: Why We Expect More from Technology and Less from Each Other* (New York: Basic Books, 2011).

14 Tanenbaum, *I Am Not a Slut*, 115.

15 Laina Y. Bay-Cheng, "The Agency Line: A Neoliberal Metric for Appraising Young Women's Sexuality," *Sex Roles* 73, nos. 7–8 (2015): 279–291; Deborah L. Tolman, "Female Adolescents, Sexual Empowerment and Desire: A Missing Discourse of Gender Inequity," *Sex Roles* 66, nos. 11–12 (2012): 746–757.

16 Rosalind Gill, "Empowerment/Sexism: Figuring Female Sexual Agency in Contemporary Advertising," *Feminism & Psychology* 18, no. 1 (2008): 35–60.

17 Michelle Fine, "Sexuality, Schooling, and Adolescent Females: The Missing Discourse of Desire," *Harvard Educational Review* 58, no. 1 (1988): 29–54; Deborah L. Tolman, *Dilemmas of Desire: Teenage Girls Talk about Sexuality* (Cambridge, MA: Harvard University Press, 2002).

18 Elizabethe Payne, "Sluts: Heteronormative Policing in the Stories of Lesbian Youth," *Educational Studies* 46, no. 3 (2010): 317–336; Jane M. Ussher, "The Meaning of Sexual Desire: Experiences of Heterosexual and Lesbian Girls," *Feminism & Psychology* 15, no. 1 (2005): 27–32.

19 Erik H. Erikson, *Identity, Youth, and Crisis* (New York: Norton, 1968).

20 Cheri Jo Pascoe, *Dude, You're a Fag* (Berkeley: University of California Press, 2011); Deborah L. Tolman, Brian R. Davis, and Christin P. Bowman, "'That's Just How It Is': A Gendered Analysis of Masculinity and Femininity Ideologies in Adolescent Girls' and Boys' Heterosexual Relationships," *Journal of Adolescent Research* 31, no. 1 (2016): 3–31.

21 Michael Bamberg, "Form and Functions of 'Slut Bashing' in Male Identity Constructions in 15-Year-Olds," *Human Development* 47, no. 6 (2004): 331–353; Michael Kimmel, *Guyland: The Perilous Place Where Boys Become Men* (New York: HarperCollins, 2008).

22 Eivind G. Fjær, Willy Pedersen, and Sveinung Sandberg, "'I'm Not One of Those Girls': Boundary-Work and the Sexual Double Standard in a Liberal Hookup Context," *Gender & Society* 29, no. 6 (2015): 960–981.

23 Tanenbaum, *I Am Not a Slut*.

24 Niva Piran and Sarah Thompson, "A Study of the Adverse Social Experiences Model to the Development of Eating Disorders," *International Journal of Health Promotion and Education* 46, no. 2 (2008): 65–71.

25 Tolman, *Dilemmas of Desire*.

26 Gill, "Empowerment/Sexism"; Angela McRobbie, *The Aftermath of Feminism: Gender, Culture and Social Change* (Thousand Oaks, CA: SAGE, 2009).

27 Fine, "Sexuality, Schooling, and Adolescent Females."

28 Nicola Gavey, "Beyond 'Empowerment'? Sexuality in a Sexist World," *Sex Roles* 66, nos. 11–12 (2012): 718–724; Tolman, "Female Adolescents, Sexual Empowerment and Desire."

29 Danielle R. Egan, *Becoming Sexual: A Critical Appraisal of the Sexualization of Girls* (New York: John Wiley, 2013); Deborah L. Tolman, Stephanie

M. Anderson, and Kimberly Belmonte, "Mobilizing Metaphor: Considering Complexities, Contradictions, and Contexts in Adolescent Girls' and Young Women's Sexual Agency," *Sex Roles* 73, nos. 7–8 (2015): 298–310.

30 Lisa M. Diamond, "'I'm Straight, but I Kissed a Girl': The Trouble with American Media Representations of Female-Female Sexuality," *Feminism & Psychology* 15 (2005): 104–110; Gill, "Empowerment/Sexism."

31 Panteá Farvid, Virigina Braun, and Casey Rowney, "'No Girl Wants to Be Called a Slut!' Women, Heterosexual Casual Sex and the Sexual Double Standard," *Journal of Gender Studies* (2016): 1–17.

32 See Sara I. McClelland and Michelle Fine, "Rescuing a Theory of Adolescent Sexual Excess: Young Women and Wanting," in *Next Wave Cultures: Feminism, Subcultures, Activism*, ed. Anita Harris (London: Routledge, 2008), 83–102.

33 Christin P. Bowman, "Persistent Pleasures: Agency, Social Power, and Embodiment in Women's Solitary Masturbation Experiences" (PhD diss., City University of New York, 2017).

34 Sandra Lee Bartky, *Femininity and Domination: Studies in the Phenomenology of Oppression* (New York: Routledge, 1990).

35 Tolman, *Dilemmas of Desire.*

36 April Burns and María Elena Torre, "IV. Revolutionary Sexualities," *Feminism & Psychology* 15, no. 1 (2005): 21–26; Michelle Fine and Sara I. McClelland, "The Politics of Teen Women's Sexuality: Public Policy and the Adolescent Female Body," *Emory Law Journal* 56 (2007): 993–1038.

37 McClelland and Fine, "Rescuing a Theory of Adolescent Sexual Excess."

38 Jessica Ringrose and Emma Renold, "Slut-Shaming, Girl Power and 'Sexualisation': Thinking through the Politics of the International SlutWalks with Teen Girls," *Gender and Education* 24, no. 3 (2012): 333–343.

39 Sharon Horne and Melanie J. Zimmer-Gembeck, "The Female Sexual Subjectivity Inventory: Development and Validation of a Multidimensional Inventory for Late Adolescents and Emerging Adults," *Psychology of Women Quarterly* 30, no. 2 (2006): 125–138.

40 Sienna Ruiz and Cammy, "How to Run an Intersectional Feminism Club," *Rookie Mag*, November 18, 2015, www.rookiemag.com.

41 Lynn Chandok, personal communication, November 8, 2013.

42 Lyn Mikel Brown, *Powered by Girl: A Field Guide for Working with Girl Activists* (Boston: Beacon, 2016).

43 Marisa Ragonese, Christin P. Bowman, and Deborah L. Tolman, "Sex Education, Youth, and Advocacy: Sexual Literacy, Critical Media, and Intergenerational Sex Education(s)," in *The Palgrave Handbook of Sexuality Education*, ed. Louisa Allen and Mary Lou Rasmussen (London: Palgrave Macmillan, 2017), 301–325.

44 Heidi Lyons et al., "Identity, Peer Relationships, and Adolescent Girls' Sexual Behavior: An Exploration of the Contemporary Double Standard," *Journal of Sex Research* 48, no. 5 (2011): 437–449.

45 Ileana Jimenez, June 6, 2017, www.feministteacher.com.

46 Emily Linden, *The Unslut Project: A Diary and a Memoir* (San Francisco: Zest Books, 2015).

47 Leora Tanenbaum, *Slut! Growing Up Female with a Bad Reputation* (New York: HarperCollins, 2000).

48 Tanenbaum, *I Am Not a Slut.*

49 See the SPARK Movement's website, www.sparkmovement.org.

50 Brown, *Powered by Girl.*

51 Jennifer F. Chmielewski, Deborah L. Tolman, and Hunter Kincaid, "Constructing Risk and Responsibility: A Gender, Race and Class Analysis of News Representations of Adolescent Sexuality," *Feminist Media Studies* 17, no. 3 (2017): 412–425, doi:10.1080/14680777.2017.1283348.

52 Jessica Valenti, "SlutWalks and the Future of Feminism," *Washington Post*, June 3, 2011, www.washingtonpost.com.

53 Jo Reger, "The Story of a Slut Walk 1: Sexuality, Race, and Generational Divisions in Contemporary Feminist Activism," *Journal of Contemporary Ethnography* 44, no. 1 (2015): 84–112.

54 bell hooks, *Sisters of the Yam: Black Women and Self-Recovery* (Boston: South End Press, 1993).

55 Amber Rose Foundation, June 6, 2017, www.amberroseslutwalk.com.

56 Sinikka Aapola, Marnina Gonick, and Anita Harris, *Young Femininity: Girlhood, Power, and Social Change* (Houndmills: Palgrave Macmillan, 2005); Brown, *Powered by Girl.*

57 Dana Edell, "'Say It How It Is': Urban Teenage Girls Challenge and Perpetuate Stereotypes through Writing and Performing Theatre," *Youth Theatre Journal* 27, no. 1 (2013): 51–62.

58 Katie Cappiello, personal communication, May 21, 2017.

59 Claire Maxwell and Peter Aggleton, "The Bubble of Privilege: Young, Privately Educated Women Talk about Social Class," *British Journal of Sociology of Education* 31, no. 1 (2010): 3–15; Tolman, Anderson, and Belmonte, "Mobilizing Metaphor."

8

Humanizing the Scientific Method

ALISHA ALI AND CORIANNA E. SICHEL

"Madeleine" is a research participant in one our studies on depression in women. The study begins with a straightforward questionnaire listing symptoms of depression. Halfway through the questionnaire, she looks up and says, "I'm going to say 'True' to a lot of these. After all, I'm a depressive." After completing the questionnaire, she takes part in an individual interview conducted by a research assistant. The research assistant asks her about her use of the term "depressive" to refer to herself. Madeleine responds, "I guess it's just something I was born with, something I've always been." Forty-five minutes later—after describing when she first felt something like depression (as a teenager after the death of her grandmother and her parents' divorce)—she states that the interview questions have allowed her to think differently about her depression. She is beginning to understand her depressive experiences as being grounded in life traumas rather than something biologically inherent to her. At the end of the interview, she explains that the empathic listening on the part of the research assistant made her feel comfortable to respond to the interview questions in a manner that encouraged her own self-reflection and self-examination. This is an example of the transformational potential of scientific research.

Scientific inquiry has traditionally been construed through a lens of detachment that values objectivity above all else. This approach places a primacy on objective analysis of observable phenomena. However, over the past several years, theorists and scientists have argued that this emphasis on objectivity is problematic, and they have described the many ways in which an objective stance is not only unattainable but also a hindrance to research in such areas as the social and health sciences.[1] In the continuing reliance of objectivity as an ideal in scientific analysis, we see the dominant crisis of connection in the scientific community.

The emphasis on objectivity is grounded in the assumption that being too "close" to one's subject or subject matter interferes with the usefulness and validity of the resultant data. This crisis has resulted in a proliferation of blind spots and biases that shape the very nature of scientific knowledge. This chapter aims to resituate human curiosity and compassion at the root of the scientific method. Its goal is to redefine the meaning of scientific understanding. It illuminates the ways in which our blind spots contribute to the crisis of connection by taking us out of relationship and into the false realm of detachment. The result of this detachment is the perpetuation of stereotypes that appear to be validated by research because the research itself is biased against human connection.

Compounding these problems is a lack of attention to existing research approaches that are more *relational* in nature—research that allows us to understand human experience through methods that themselves function through connection and listening between researcher and participant. Niobe Way and Joseph D. Nelson's wonderful chapter in this book provides direction for listening-based methods that can reflect participants' experiences through recognition of the experiential and emotional common ground that exists between interviewer and interviewee. The need for such approaches in research is a pressing issue not only because our methods shape the questions we ask, but also because the answers we generate often go on to influence decisions made across such sectors as health care, education, policy, and social services. Moreover, the impact of these decisions can be far-reaching, given that the processes involved in conducting and evaluating work in these sectors then feeds the development of new research questions and research approaches, thereby creating an iterative pattern that dictates both practice and empirical work in the sciences and beyond.

A drastic reenvisioning and transformation of research methods and empirical assumptions are necessary to challenge the rampant alienation and disconnection in modern culture and to underscore our common humanity. The implications of such transformation can have benefits not only in generating questions that acknowledge the workings of connection and disconnection in research itself and in the communities we study, but also in allowing scientists to forge connections through their work that can make their research more meaningful personally and in its reach. That process can involve rediscovering the experiences, events, and beliefs that led to the desire to become a scientist in the first place.

The process of humanizing scientists' work can be beneficial as well for those who already actively integrate humanistic elements into their work. For instance, even within more progressive approaches to conducting research, we see the pitfalls of assuming that doing research *on* oppressed people is enough. We continue to predominantly conduct research that focuses on person-level variables, ignoring the overarching social context as well as the relationship between the individual research participant and the participant's context, the researcher and the research participant, and the researcher and context. To address these challenges, this chapter advocates a methodological stance premised on the notion that person-level variables cannot be understood without acknowledgment of structural and contextual forces. It outlines an approach that integrates principles from a model called the *structural competency paradigm* and from the practice of *anti-oppression advocacy* to shift the dominant empirical focus away from the sole emphasis on person-level factors and toward an examination of the underlying structures and processes at play in the lives of groups and individuals. Such a focus can bring us closer to a more relational understanding of scientific inquiry that counters the perpetuation of false stereotypes and biases that masquerade as objectivity.

The Fallacy of Scientific Objectivity

In their 2001 article titled "To Be of Use," psychologists Michelle Fine and Ricardo Barreras wrote that it is "the responsibility of social scientists to study critically 'what is,' to imagine 'what could be' and to contribute responsibly to a mobilization toward 'what must be.'"[2] Since Fine and Barreras wrote those words, well over a decade has passed, marked by increasing global socioeconomic stratification, heightened racial tensions domestically and abroad, and ongoing threats to the rights of marginalized groups including women, immigrants, and sexual and religious minorities. Yet, despite these pressing issues, research in the health and social sciences has not adequately addressed social needs. This lack of progress is in part the result of a deep-seated bias toward the belief that research and those who conduct it must be objective and thus "untainted" by societal factors. The challenge of attempting to address this bias is certainly evident, for instance, in psychological research, where we see a long-standing devaluation of qualitative research that aims to capture phenomenological experience from the point of view of research participants. Rather than acknowledging the perspective of our participants, we choose to privilege the viewpoint of the scientist. This privileging is hidden in the language and assumptions of objectivity.

Objectivity emerged as a force in the scientific community in the late nineteenth century as a way of distilling the "truth" by removing all individual idiosyncrasies, interests, and viewpoints. It came to prominence with the proliferation of positivist and postpositivist epistemologies, which are built around the assumption that there exists a single, discoverable truth. Scientists coming from this epistemic stance claim that their work is unbiased, apolitical, and value-free.[3] Daston described this type of objectivity as "aperspectival." According to Daston, "aperspectival objectivity was the ethos of the interchangeable and therefore featureless observer."[4] Obviously, no such observer exists because to observe necessitates being located in a relationship to the phenomena under observation, thus making the notion of not having a perspective absurd. Critics of the objectivity of science assert that the emphasis on objectivity provides those already in power with an excuse to ignore the voices of the oppressed, thus serving to further subjugate marginalized groups. For instance, pertaining to gender and the oppression of women, philosopher Sandra Harding wrote,

> Mind vs. nature and the body, reason vs. emotion and social commitment, subject vs. object and objectivity vs. subjectivity, the abstract and general vs. the concrete and particular—in each case we are told that the former must dominate the latter lest human life be overwhelmed by irrational and alien forces, forces symbolized in science as the feminine.[5]

Thus, critics of objectivity have called for alternative epistemologies that emphasize understanding group memberships and individual identities as products of social interactions and reflections of societal structure.[6] Such understandings emphasize the contextualization of individual lives and encourage us, as researchers, to engage in reflexivity, considering our own positionality in relation to our work and its subjects.[7] To this end, psychologist Aida Hurtado suggests that the constituencies for whom and about whom the research is being produced should be the ones to determine if the research product is indeed important and worthwhile. By emphasizing accountability in this way, she recognizes the interconnectedness of human social relations, and the ways in which our interconnectedness determines our subjectivity, with the aim of ensuring that "knowledge production is intended for transformation and achieving social equity."[8] Stressing the inevitability of the "embeddedness" of science and scientific knowledge in specific political and cultural moments, scholars create opportunities for sophisticated, intersectional analyses of systemic oppression and multiple marginalities.[9]

There is also a growing need for researchers and theorists to move beyond the mere description of oppression toward an understanding of the dynamics undergirding oppression and the realities of living within oppression. Additionally, there is a need to empirically document the effects of resistance against oppression. Science has an essential role to play in proving that the results of resistance benefit all of us by moving us toward recognition of our common humanity and our shared goals. These endeavors will require us to draw upon the scientific method in ways that avoid the traditional focus on individual outcomes and instead allow us to engage in an analysis of context and process. However, in this work, we are faced with a unique challenge: much of the current research that aims to study oppression in marginalized groups involves examination of person-level variables and thus runs the risk of "othering" research participants by construing the effects of oppression as individual traits and—even worse—as individual pathologies. The challenge in this work is to advance an understanding of the complex interactive, iterative processes occurring between individuals and their contexts while simultaneously acknowledging the researcher as being in relation to both individuals and contexts. To meet this challenge, we propose that the concept of *structural competency* can be adopted as a method of un-othering research participants and explicitly identifying and addressing the oppressive forces shaping human lives. By focusing on societal configurations, the structural competency paradigm addresses the direct role of oppression as built—sometimes intentionally—into societal institutions.

The Structural Competency Paradigm: Humanizing Methodology

The structural competency paradigm is a framework that began in the field of medicine and medical training and has recently been applied to the social sciences.[10] According to this paradigm, both mental and physical health conditions can be understood as "downstream implications of upstream decisions."[11] Upstream decisions include inequitable institutional and social practices such as workplace discrimination and unequal access to housing, health care, and other resources. The downstream implications of these practices include the elevated rates of illness, which emerge in oppressive contexts. This approach emphasizes the environmentally constructed nature of illness and health within a socially informed frame that provides an alternative to dominant reductionist biomedical approaches.

The structural competency framework aims to represent the workings of oppression and illness in a manner that recognizes that pathology can originate and reside in environments and institutions rather than individuals. This framework further captures the reality that oppression itself can be the cause of illness. In work that closely parallels writings in structural competency, psychologist Laura Smith describes the notion of *oppression as pathogen* in which illness is constructed socially and environmentally through forces that can not only make a person physically or mentally ill, but also restrict access to sources of care and support that could alleviate suffering.[12] Taken together, these ideas have great transformative potential for how we understand and theorize illness and disease.

Although the model of structural competency was developed for use in the training of physicians, and adapted for use in the training of counseling psychologists, the structural competency paradigm has important implications for social science research in general, and particularly for research that aims to describe and address the psychological and physical effects of oppression. To be structurally competent as a practitioner is to acknowledge the role that individual and collective agency can play in bringing about positive change. For practitioners, this means transcending the hierarchy of the conventionally construed practitioner-client relationship to join in collective resistance. This true alliance disrupts the dominant dynamic of the expert and the ill, who require "treatment," and instead invites practitioners to partner with clients and colleagues in challenging and transforming existing systemic inequities in ways that can holistically advance the wellness and well-being of oppressed individuals and groups. Structurally competent approaches to treatment are foreshadowed by Rogerian, relational approaches to psychotherapy, which conceptualize the therapist-client relationship as defined by unconditional positive regard and prioritize such relationships as imperative for psychological well-being, underscoring and upholding the common humanity of both the "treaters" and the "treated."[13] Similarly, structurally competent practitioners take an emancipatory, liberatory stance that locates the etiology of "illness" outside of the ill, that is, by engaging in anti-oppression advocacy, and partnering *with* clients to counteract overreliance on decontextualized treatments. Participating in structurally competent practice means that practitioners must approach "treatment" as something that is done *with* and not *to* patients and clients.

Exemplifying such work is the chapter in this volume by theater artist Victoria Rhoades in which she describes the ways in which theater can be used as an antidote to serious social and psychological issues confronting young people. Similarly, the theater-based works described in this volume by military veteran Stephan Wolfert and by drama educator Dana Edell illustrate that the arts can be a bona fide treatment for mental health problems such as traumatic stress by addressing mental struggles through forms of expressive creativity that allow young people, adults, and military veterans to heal through connection and through the dramatized telling of their lived stories. Also in this volume, education scholar Janie Ward describes the role of resistance in the psychological development of African American girls. Through such work, we see that acts of creativity and acts of resistance are not superfluous self-indulgences; rather, they are necessary acts of self-preservation and indeed of survival for those at risk for chronic disenfranchisement and suffering.

Below we propose three principles, derived from structural competency, as touchstones for the development of a socially responsive methodological stance that acknowledges the respective relatednesses of researchers, research participants, and contexts. Each of these principles is aimed at transforming both basic and applied research, laying the foundation for reenvisioning empirical work through an anti-oppressive lens that emphasizes our common humanity.

The "Un-othering" of Research Participants

The research process in social sciences such as psychology and sociology typically involves studying patterns of actions, behaviors, or thoughts of research "subjects" or participants. The participants are studied by experts—that is, trained scientists with expertise in the domains that are relevant to making sense of the particular patterns under study. In this traditional model, the participants are observed and studied as scientific subjects that are scrutinized and essentially "objectified." The interpretations and observations made by the scientists are privileged and assumed to be bias-free; the thoughts and actions of the participants are perceived through the lens of scientific objectivity. A research participant is assumed to be a nonreflective "other." The process of "othering" involves dehumanizing groups or individuals by deeming them objects of observation, frequently distinguished as different from or "other than" the conventionally accepted norm. In this process, "different from" is generally equated with "less than." The othering of research participants also perpetuates a false binary between the "knower" and the "known." This binary excuses researchers from recognizing the power differential between being the one who "discovers" knowledge and the one who is known about. It ignores the fact that researchers and human subjects are inevitably engaged in a process of *co-creating* meaning and knowledge, obfuscating the common humanity of the researcher and the researched, and deepening the crisis of connection. Structurally competent research aims to disrupt this process by privileging the self-knowledge of the research participant through an acknowledgment that participants are experts in knowing, living, and understanding crucial aspects of the working of oppression and other social forces in their lives. This acknowledgment can be seen as a process of "un-othering."

In addition to opening up largely uncharted intellectual and scientific territories, un-othering is a first step in bridging the chasm created by the crisis of connection. Specifically, the process of un-othering allows us to address disconnection by fostering a view of research itself not just as a constellation of methods, but as a way of thinking about and participating in the world. The more we allow ourselves to see the world as full of potential for transformative change and interconnection, the more we as scientists can see the potential of research as a means of connecting to our topics of inquiry as well as research participants.

Humanizing Scientists

Structural competency in research requires an openness to methodologies that recognize the many blind spots and sources of bias that color our work as researchers. Such approaches must involve privileging transactions of inquiry that are informed by human compassion, curiosity, and empathy. To challenge the myth of scientific objectivity, it is not enough to say that we know we are biased or that we are subjective; we must admit that we are *human*, with our own constellations of experiences and understandings. Scientists are fallible: we often do not see or appreciate the realities of the lives of those we study or even the experience of being studied. Additionally, we may fail to fully acknowledge the role of our own life stories in guiding our areas of, and approaches to, inquiry. A structurally competent approach to research necessitates that we, as scientists, critically engage and exhume our own epistemologies. A structurally competent approach to research can reduce some of the risks of our blind spots by acknowledging scientists' own subjectivities and allowing scientists to trust and rely on the experiences and knowledge of the people and communities under study, seeing our research and its questions and methods through their eyes. We need to design and conduct studies that humanize scientists and research participants to each other, and explicitly recognize the co-created nature of scientific findings. Such a stance fosters mutual understanding in the research process by creating a valid space for research aimed at exposing and counteracting the effects of oppression in the lives of research participants, while additionally helping scientists avoid the pitfalls of allowing our work to inadvertently distance, marginalize, and further oppress participants.

Contextualizing Oppression

In addition to the need to humanize research participants and scientists, a structurally competent approach to research actively builds considerations of power and privilege into research methods, not just into the topics we study. This is a challenging task because it involves contextualizing oppression by moving beyond simply the description of oppression toward an understanding of oppression as it is lived and understood by those who are marginalized and victimized. This approach necessitates an examination of context and the *effects* of context simultaneously. For example, structurally competent research on the legal system's treatment of women who report sexual assault can capture the suffering of the survivor and additionally expose the workings of a system that often fails to provide justice for survivors. It also becomes necessary in structurally competent research to resituate variables traditionally construed as individual in structural terms. For example, research on human agency can challenge the notion of agency as an individual attribute and instead offer a conceptualization of agency as a dynamic interplay between the environment and the individual's attempts to navigate and change the environment. Such work can generate theories and models of practice that address the effects of oppression in the lives of groups and individuals.

Research as Advocacy: Scientific Advancement through Human Connection

The notion of moving toward structurally competent empirical research holds promise for the recognition that research can capture some of the realities and consequences of oppression in the lives of marginalized individuals. Such work also allows us to see the ways in which research participants can resist oppression. However, the goal of socially just research can be further advanced by adopting a research lens that sees the transformational capacity of research itself as part of a process of actively creating positive change in the lives of research participants. We argue that such transformation is possible not only in actual intervention research, but additionally in more descriptive research that aims to better understand the lived experiences of members of oppressed groups. To this end, we propose the integration of principles from *anti-oppression advocacy*.[14]

Anti-oppression advocacy was initially developed and implemented as an approach to conducting psychological practice and direct intervention. However, the tenets of anti-oppression advocacy can readily inform socially just methodologies in research in the social sciences and allied disciplines. The anti-oppression advocacy approach is premised on the assumption that practitioners should use their practice and training to address underlying oppressive forces that shape the individuals and communities with which they work. Similarly, anti-oppression advocacy as a methodological lens presents the opportunity for scientists to use the research process to address the need for structural, systemic, and institutional changes. Thus, we outline the following guiding principles as a means of employing research as a form of advocacy.

Subverting Power Differentials in the Research Process

Part of the "un-othering" of research participants is the privileging of the participant's voice and vision throughout the research process. This entails acknowledging the subjugated knowledge of oppressed communities and marginalized individuals in ways that are often uncomfortable for researchers.[15] However, as a process, the benefits can be tremendous: if we subvert traditional models of power and emphasize what is known by those whose lives we aim to represent in our research, we can expand the realm of viable research topics and research questions that guide our work. This approach can be particularly effective in evaluation and intervention research where our methods too often reflect the "experts know best" mentality. Such a mentality leads to challenges in matching intervention goals to community needs and to what is traditionally labeled a "lack of buy-in" from the communities from whom we "recruit our samples." If we instead follow the lead of community members, we can understand not only the types of programs and treatments that could be the most effective, but also the types of offerings that community members will view as valuable and consistent with their own beliefs, values, and desires about health and wellness.

Reframing the Dissemination Process

The dissemination of research findings traditionally involves publications in empirical journals and presentations at scientific conferences. While these outlets are essential for communication between researchers, they do not allow for direct dissemination to communities. The practice of disseminating findings only through vehicles typically inaccessible and/or unknown to research participants constitutes an act of othering in itself. By communicating only with other "experts," researchers implicitly suggest that they deem research participants as undeserving of a voice in the broader project of inquiry. In the anti-oppression advocacy approach, dissemination focuses on the goal of using empirical findings to positively transform the lives of individuals and their communities in three crucial ways. Doing so, it reimagines the "other" (i.e., research participants) as deserving, and important in the process of further exploration and discovery. The first form of transformation involves public gatherings, events, and meetings in which findings from research projects conducted in partnership with those communities are discussed and presented through various forms, including flyers, presentations, student posters, and firsthand spoken narratives by community members who took part in the research. The second form of transformation includes neighborhood research forums in which community members meet with members of the research team to collectively brainstorm ideas to inform next steps for subsequent research studies connecting to the ongoing research. This process opens up exciting, creative opportunities that foster not only community involvement in the research process, but also crucial input in the development of socially relevant and structurally competent research questions and methods. The third form of transformation pertains to the lives of individuals. When research is undertaken as advocacy, the very process of research has the potential to change the life trajectory of participants. Participants may come away from research participation empowered to engage with their environments with a new sense of agency, which can reciprocally impact both individuals' lives and their environments. Viewed in this way, research participants are themselves disseminating research findings through their own insights and experiences.

Engaging Research Teams in Activism

A facet of anti-oppression advocacy that is highly compatible with integration of tenets from the structural competency paradigm is the requirement that members of research teams must engage in activism tied in some way to the research projects that are either planned or under way. This type of advocacy can take many forms, including working alongside community-based activists and practitioners to assist them in their work, developing and implementing campaigns (such as public awareness campaigns) around the rights of community members and available services that can support groups and individuals within their neighborhoods, and volunteering to help community members in meeting some of their daily challenges. On our own university-based research teams, we have found that these types of involvements help students and interns better understand the experiences of the communities and community members connected to our projects, thus informing the research process. These involvements also increase community engagement as well as trainees' knowledge and understanding of both the potential and the limits of the research we do.

Advocacy-Based Science: Some Examples of Structurally Competent Research

Although it is not explicitly termed as such, examples of structurally competent research are emerging from the research community, especially from scholars interested in race/ethnicity and gender. For example, psychologists Shelly Grabe, Rose Grose, and Anjali Dutt partnered with women's organizations in Nicaragua and Tanzania to investigate relationships between women's ownership of land, relationship power, and physical and psychological violence.[16] One aim of this multinational project was to examine if proposed links between women's land ownership and power and well-being were context- or country-specific or if they reflected more generalizable patterns. Their findings suggested that the relationship between structural dynamics (i.e., the institutional power that comes with land ownership) and women's violent victimization is explained through relationship power. Thus, individual women and men come to "embody" societal structures and processes. The researchers took a multilayered, structurally competent approach to understanding women's violent victimization, investigating individual-level processes and characteristics (e.g., land ownership, levels of victimization, relational power dynamics) across societal contexts to illuminate the potential role of social structures. Additionally, they subverted power differentials frequently found in the research process. By partnering with organizations already facilitating women's land owner-ship, the researchers were able to ensure community voices informed the research effort. Conventional power differentials between researchers and participants were additionally subverted through the research team's approach of establishing partnerships with these organizations through egalitarian dialogue with organization leaders. In contrast to conventional practice conceptualizing researchers as experts and community members as subjects, the research team stayed close to the communities in which they were working by creating and partnering with local research teams to develop and administer the research instruments. Interpreting their findings in a frame that acknowledged the danger of imposing a universal rights-based approach to social justice, they were able to incorporate structural considerations in their analysis. Doing so demonstrated that "macro-level processes involving resources and power may operate similarly across different contexts while at the same time allowing for the processes to be identified by local values."[17]

Psychologists Shabnam Javdani and Nicole Allen provide a second example of a research process reflecting a structurally competent approach.[18] Their research describes a strengths-based intervention focused on the provision of flexible services to girls at risk for juvenile justice system involvement. The intervention itself reflects an intervention-as-advocacy approach by pairing girls with highly trained advocates and working with girls within their home communities. Rather than adhering to the conventional approach of focusing on youth deficits, the intervention was oriented toward promoting positive development by leveraging the strengths of girls and their environments to access community resources. In the past this type of intervention has commonly been evaluated through researcher-determined metrics of success. Javdani and Allen subverted these paternalistic dynamics in their study design by allowing the girls themselves to inform the metrics by which intervention success was determined. They achieved this goal by allowing the girls, working with their assigned advocates, to both identify areas of unmet need and goals and decide which resources were pursued. Unlike conventional research studies requiring participants to come to the researchers' labs, Javdani and Allen further upended conventional power dynamics by conducting both intervention and assessment activities in the girls' natural environments. Finally, Javdani and Allen reframed the dissemination process by sharing study results with participants, advocates, and community partners through distribution of a community newsletter and presentations at community-based meetings.

Concluding Thoughts: The Challenges of Structurally Competent Research

Given the extent to which researchers are invested in and benefit from the existing power differentials in dominant research processes, the task of encouraging structurally competent research is a challenging one. In many ways, the challenges parallel the difficulties faced in the earlier days of qualitative research in psychology and related fields, wherein the processes, methods, and assumptions were at times met with hostility and, even after years of high-quality research, marginalized and derogated. Similarly, the goals of anti-oppression advocacy are at odds with prevailing assumptions about the role that research should play in academia and in society: research continues to be evaluated through a lens that privileges objectivity.

To remedy some of these ongoing biases, we propose that scientists consider the notion of structural competency as an ethical imperative. This notion is supported by scientists and theorists who use structural competency as a guiding value in their work. For instance, psychiatrist Mindy Fullilove and urban architect Michel Cantal-Dupart describe the ethics involved in structural competency in recognizing the fundamental human need for solidarity and fellowship with other human beings as key in informing theory and best practices in the area of urban renewal and restoration.[19] In moving forward with adopting structural competency and anti-oppression in our research, we are encouraged by practitioners who habitually privilege perspectives of the marginalized and oppressed in their work. These include activists, clinicians, and artists such as those represented in this volume, all of whom deliberately choose to emphasize human connection as a principle, a process, and a personal value. We argue that much can be learned from these experts about the ways in which mainstream research can be transformed. Socially relevant, structurally competent research is necessary not only to save our research from being out of touch with social realities but also to allow us as scientists to engage and expand our own capacities for human connection with those with whom we work and with the world around us.

NOTES

1 Alisha Ali, "A Framework for Emancipatory Inquiry in Psychology: Lessons from Feminist Methodology," *Race, Gender, and Class* 13, nos. 1–2 (2006): 1–14; Michelle Fine and Ricardo Barreras, "To Be of Use," *Analyses of Social Issues and Public Policy* 1, no. 1 (2001): 175–182; Jonathan M. Metzl and Helena Hansen, "Structural Competency: Theorizing a New Medical Engagement with Stigma and Inequality," *Social Science & Medicine* 103 (2014): 126–133.

2 Fine and Barreras, "To Be of Use."

3 Egon G. Guba and Yvonna S. Lincoln, "Competing Paradigms in Qualitative Research," in *Handbook of Qualitative Research*, ed. Norman K. Denzin and Yvonna S. Lincoln (Thousand Oaks, CA: SAGE, 1994), 105–117.

4 Lorraine Daston, "Objectivity and the Escape from Perspective," *Social Studies of Science* 22, no. 4 (1992): 597–618, 609.

5 Sandra Harding, *The Science Question in Feminism* (Ithaca, NY: Cornell University Press, 1986), 125.

6 Riger, "Epistemological Debates, Feminist Voices: Science, Social Values, and the Study of Women," *American Psychologist* 47, no. 6 (1992): 730–740, doi:10.1037/0003-066X.47.6.730.

7 Karen Barad, "Posthumanist Performativity: Toward an Understanding of How Matter Comes to Matter," *Signs: Journal of Women in Culture and Society* 28, no. 3 (2003): 801–831; Sandra G. Harding, *Whose Science? Whose Knowledge? Thinking from Women's Lives* (Ithaca, NY: Cornell University Press, 1991).

8 Aida Hurtado, "Multiple Lenses: Multicultural Feminist Theory," in *Handbook of Diversity in Feminist Psychology*, ed. Hope Landrine and Nancy Felipe Russo (New York: Springer, 2010), 29–54.

9 Banu Subramaniam, "Moored Metamorphoses: A Retrospective Essay on Feminist Science Studies," *Signs: Journal of Women in Culture and Society* 34, no. 4 (2009): 951–980.

10 Metzl and Hansen, "Structural Competency"; Alisha Ali and Corianna E. Sichel, "Structural Competency as a Framework for Training in Counseling Psychology," *Counseling Psychologist* 42 (2014): 901–918.

11 Matthew Schneider, "Structural Competency: Framing a New Conversation on Institutional Inequalities and Sickness" (presentation, MHS/NYU Structural Competency Conference, New York, March 2013).

12 Laura Smith, *Psychology, Poverty, and the End of Social Exclusion: Putting Our Practice to Work* (New York: Teachers College Press, 2010).

13 E.g., Carl R. Rogers, *Client-Centered Therapy: Its Current Practice, Implications, and Theory* (Boston: Houghton Mifflin, 1951).

14 Alisha Ali and Kristin E. Lees, "The Therapist as Advocate: Anti-oppression Advocacy in Psychological Practice," *Journal of Clinical Psychology* 69, no. 2 (2013): 160–169; Alisha Ali, Emily McFarlane, Robert Hawkins, and Ini Udo-Inyang, "Social Justice Revisited: Psychological Recolonization and the Challenge of Anti-oppression Advocacy," *Race, Gender, and Class* 19 (2011): 322–335.

15 Alisha Ali, "The Convergence of Foucault and Feminist Psychiatry: Exploring Emancipatory Knowledge-Building," *Journal of Gender Studies* 11, no. 2 (2002): 233–242.

16 Shelly Grabe, Rose Grose, and Anjali Dutt, "Women's Land Ownership and Relationship Power: A Mixed Methods Approach to Understanding Structural In-equities and Violence Against Women," *Psychology of Women Quarterly* 39 (2015): 7–19.

17 Ibid., 16.

18 Shabnam Javdani and Nicole Allen, "An Ecological Model for Intervention for Juvenile Justice-Involved Girls: Development and Preliminary Prospective Evaluation," *Feminist Criminology* 11 (2016): 135–162, doi:10.1177/1557085114559514.

19 Mindy Fullilove and Michel Cantal-Dupart, "Medicine for the City: Perspective and Solidarity as Tools for Making Urban Health," *Bioethical Inquiry* 13 (2016): 215–221.

School-Based Solutions

9

Love Pedagogy

Teaching to Disrupt

LISA ARRASTIA

Because love is an act of courage, not of fear, love is a commitment to others. No matter where the oppressed are found, the act of love is commitment to their cause—the cause of liberation.
—Paulo Freire, *Pedagogy of the Oppressed*

Basketball commentators talk about the strength derived from playing inside the paint. The paint is also known as "the key" for a reason. Inside the paint both dunks and blocked shots go down. Importantly, this is the space in which players are like lattice, woven together, connected; they are in spiritual, mental, and physical congruence. In his book *Sacred Hoops*, Zen Buddhist and NBA coach Phil Jackson describes the symbiosis of an athletic team this way: "Basketball is a sport that involves the subtle interweaving of players at full speed to the point where they are thinking and moving as one."[1] In a classroom, to think and to move in authentic unison like this with young people is the method and practice of teaching I call a love pedagogy. Inside a classroom, a school building, or whatever site becomes the key to teach for understanding, we're moving at full speed, we're vulnerable, and we're attentive to our individual and collective needs, hopes, and fears. In a Facebook post, my former student Yoshi Shimada, now a teacher in Japan, describes the essence of my love pedagogy. He writes, "One of my favorite teachers, Lisa Arrastia, used to tell us what she kept in mind when she entered the classroom—talking to herself she 'loves her students' and then opens the door. I must say, this has affected my career significantly, and it's still deep in my heart after I became a teacher in Japan. Nowadays, every time I walk into the classroom, I remind myself that all my students have immeasurable potential and bright futures ahead of them. 'I love my students,' and I vow to be the best teacher for them no matter what, who truly respects them, and can bring out their own missions for them to pursue to make this world a better place."

A love pedagogy recognizes, and uses as a part of its practice, a common humanity. The practice of love pedagogy sees this as a very intellectual and academic endeavor. Love pedagogy, then, requires presence, attention to emotional detail, and a keen focus on the twitches of intellect, the quiver of engagement, and spasms of understanding in young people. Because that's the way learning comes.

To teach inside the paint is to practice a love pedagogy; it is to be profoundly aware of all the mechanisms in the contemporary education economy that seek to divert our attention away from what every teacher I've ever coached tells me produces authentic and consequential learning: relationship. If we grade, we hide from students the process of our internal thinking, and we are not in relationship with the student. If we test or if the state tests, Narcissus appears seeking only his own reflection. If we focus solely on what we think a kid *should* know and never ask them what they *want* or *need* to know, we rob them of the process of critical inquiry, of learning how to critique their own sociopolitical lives; we neglect our democratic responsibility to provide young people opportunities to think, question, and create.

So to teach inside the paint is to be in a relationship, not just with the result of the lesson or quarter, the semester or the exam, but with the social life of the child, and the curiosities she wrestles. It is to ask and create whole units that allow young people to surface the dangers they know await them on the streets that stretch from home to school. It is to be brave enough to forgo a carefully structured lesson plan when a student seemingly moves you off course with some issue or query; it is to recognize that the issue or question raised is always already the course. If teaching and learning are to be in any way meaningful, in any way everlasting, in any way a disruption to the crisis of connection, as teachers we must be deeply affected by our students; we must feel an intense affection for them. As Maxine Greene once said in *The Dialectic of Freedom*, we must be genuinely *interested* in young people. To teach inside the paint is to think and move as one with your students, to plan and let go of every lesson so that this is assured; it is, ultimately, to seek to create and then fully inhabit spaces of love; it is, then, a love pedagogy. And the pedagogy is not some sentimental absurdity because love is not some "emotional bosh," as Martin Luther King Jr. once argued.[2] Within the context of the struggle against racism, gendered notions, and poverty, a pedagogy of love in the classroom is "something strong . . . that organizes itself into powerful direct action."

You might wonder what constitutes the syllabus for a love pedagogy and where you can download it. When talking with K–12 teachers and college professors about the Young People's Archive I started, which is a digital representation of my love pedagogy,[3] I'm often asked, "Can you email me your syllabus for how you get the kids to be so honest?" or "In what unit do you include the love part?" or "How do you scaffold the lesson to teach kids to be curious about their own lives and the lives of others? How do you get them to want to connect to themselves and others?" These are difficult questions to answer because they emerge from thinking of teaching and young people like cars in a garage awaiting repair by mechanics. No one ever likes hearing my real response to these kinds of questions because my responses don't involve special tools or anything that can be purchased from an online curriculum company. Instead, my answers point teachers right back to themselves. To practice a love pedagogy is to be in relationship with your own fragile state on Earth, your own pain, and your own suffering; it is to simultaneously be in relationship with students' pain and dissatisfaction, their innate desire to know and understand; it is to acknowledge openly to the kids not your stupidity, but your ongoing ignorance about the human condition; it is to design content that interests you, yes, but that provides ways for students to connect to themselves and witness others as both breakable and deserving of honor; it is to recognize teaching as a transdisciplinary art of social and intellectual engagement in which students grapple with the predicament of social dislocation, and social isolation, as well as conscious and subliminal social detachment. As teachers today, we must recognize that before now and after now we were and always will be the observers and the victims of a crisis of connection unlike any that human kind has experienced in education. It is a socially constructed crisis, and this means that it is a crisis that teachers can deconstruct, disrupt, then dismantle. So think of a pedagogy of love in the classroom as a horizontal act in which you don't look up to power and request or even demand from the public education system the return of your humanity in the liberation of young people. You just reclaim your humanity by liberating the kids. My disruption comes in the form of curricular content that is contextual; it emerges from students' own questions about their personal struggles—often in the moment of teaching. I ask students to produce projects (audio, visual, written, performative) that compel them to humanize even those they once deemed unworthy of respect, and I ask them to show the public how both they as young people and the people around them are trying to negotiate and make sense of larger American cultural values and beliefs. Maybe the philosophy of practice (PoP) I teach the SLiCk youth interns of the Young People's Archive Service Learning Collective can help you to understand the basic principles of a love pedagogy. Our interns and the young people they teach learn to internalize this practice. I think it makes sense to them on the inside. Some have said it helps them to reframe the message that young people are weak, irresponsible, distracted, and disconnected. Some have said this PoP gives them courage: We dare to ask questions. We are brave enough to listen. We place ourselves inside other people's words. We listen across difference. We are connected.

These may not be the nuts and bolts you seek, but this is the love pedagogy I've been forging in classrooms and schools, and which I've attempted to advance in organizations, programs, and even administrations for decades. A love pedagogy sees teaching as an act of investigation, exploration, self-discovery, and creative expression by the teacher and the student. As teachers, we are not perpendicular to our students' lived experience in the classroom. Instead, the students and we are a pair of parallel, self-intersecting sides. At first, it may appear that we are opposite angles facing each other, but through a love pedagogy we can discover that in reality we are coinciding exactly when superimposed. Indeed, the teacher-student relationship is the very possibility of congruence. As should be evident, the foundation of a love pedagogy comprises social engagement, self-reflection, and relationship. One way to thwart the crisis of connection in our contemporary education economy is to allow ourselves, and young people, to abandon, even repudiate convention. Another way: notice what young people do, what they say, what makes them begin to question, why they feel this and not that, and when their interest is genuinely piqued. Yet another approach? Pretty simple: connect.

Royce

Six, maybe eight students strewn all over my tiny office. They're on the floor, on top of the radiator. They're half hanging off padded stools. They're eating bad-for-you snacks. They're loud talking. They're laughing behind cupped hands while sharing YouTube videos on their cells. Not one of them is over eighteen. Not one of them except Royce. Royce is nineteen, a self-identified Afro-Caribbean computer science major in his sophomore year. Royce is also a graduate of Hutchinson Central Technical High School in Buffalo, New York. For me, Hutch Tech is more than just any public school. This is the school from which my father-in-law graduated half a century ago. With his vocational skills in technical drawing, Harry Nowak went from Hutch Tech straight to where every poor Polish immigrant in Buffalo landed after graduation: a factory. Decades later, he died of a kind of lung cancer that only such a history could cough up, all while his son Mark, appetite-less, sat beside him, honoring him by drinking Dad's favorite beer, eating Dad's favorite sub from Dagwood's until there was Dad's last breath.

Now Royce, he's hilarious. He's kind. He appreciates respectful razzing. He knows I love him, which means Royce knows I truly see him. Royce knows that I'm interested in his way of understanding ideas, his community, this country. I'm interested in what Royce has been taught to believe. I'm interested in how he processes information, and I'm interested in finding the most conducive learning structures and processes that work just for him. This kind of interest, this sort of desire to produce creative, individualized learning is a principle that guides a love pedagogy. Royce knows that I understand in what areas and exactly when he can use a good, but gentle push, a prod to step into an intellectual challenge. Royce is not my favorite student. I don't have favorites. What Royce intuits (and I think this is why he opens up this day) is that maintaining what artist Chris Johnson calls a zone of no consequences, in which all speech is met with interest and curiosity, is a significant working facet of the love pedagogy I practice with all students I teach, even the tough ones.

On this day with the kids scattered all over the room, Royce tells me about the villain of his high school, a police officer whose beat is Hutch Tech. Incredulous, Royce says, "There's actually a cop in Buffalo named Pac-Man. That's like the name for him."

Remember the 1980s video game Pac-Man out of Japan? Pac-Man is this yellow blob with a big mouth that goes around eating up pac-dots and dodging foes like Inky, Pinky, Blinky, and Clyde so it (you) can get to the next stage. After school at Hutch Tech, Royce says Pac-Man would "literally, like, terrorize high school students." In the actual game, Pac-Man's enemies turn blue; they reverse direction; their movements become slower; and an enemy's eyes remain even when it is eaten.

As he describes Pac-Man, everyone gets quiet because we all begin to understand that what Royce is describing is an intimate, daily experience of racism. Royce's stuttering as he tells the story allows us to hear how he is trying to make sense of something that he probably has never tried to describe before. As teachers, if we enable young people access to these seemingly—for kids—indescribable places inside their minds, we empower them to wrestle with the tangled complexities of self, other, and difference; we allow them to work out social dilemmas, social disconnections with the Other, which they've experienced but don't, and shouldn't, make any sense because racism doesn't make sense to a kid, not when he's been raised in a country that professes we're all equal and everyone is presumed innocent. But the dissonance Royce experienced at the hands of Pac-Man was like a short-circuiting of that message. If Royce were to hold in this internal confusion for a lifetime, he might hold judgments about the Other, he might distance himself from the Other, he might begin to believe the messages that some white people have about black and brown people, especially boys. As teachers, we are our students' attendants. A part of the practice of love in the classroom is to remain keenly aware of the moments when a student is emotionally and mentally ready to negotiate his internalized racial conflicts by comprehending his country's social and political contradictions.

Royce continues, "Pac-Man would go around like, *Oh you can't stay here . . . Oh you can't stand on, like, the street, you have to leave. You can't stay in the school.* In a couple of months, they started arresting kids or detaining kids for trespassing, but, you know, if you're coming out of school, let's say at 2:30, and your parents can't pick you up until 2:50 or like 3:00, you know, where can you go? You can't stay in school anymore, so what can you do?"

When an enemy comes into direct contact with Pac-Man, he loses a life. Enemies don't lose their whole lives, just a piece of life, and then they become known as "ghosts." Royce describes an apparitional, criminalized position of young brown bodies in which they are suspended by Pac-Men between notions of youth and adulthood. In a sort of stammer, Royce explains, "They look at you, like, you're not an adult but you're not a kid. And, you can't have the rights for some people. You can't have the rights as an adult, but you still can't have the rights as a kid, like, you just in the middle, like, they don't know what to do with you basically."

Love pedagogues listen closely. We listen for the truths kids like Royce can speak. We listen to understand by really noticing. We are vigilant in our attention to seeking what is beneath the words our students use to describe their experiences of social injury, social loss, self-doubt, economic and political challenges, and even achievements. The vocabulary for these experiences is not a regular part of the social lexicon, so young people, like adults, often don't recognize Pac-Man, for example, as racist. A part of working to disrupt social disconnection in the classroom is to provide students ways to name their experiences. For Royce, and for many of my students, racism, economic exploitation, even rape, as they say, "just is what it is." Sometimes in class, when I detect a student telling a story in which she was targeted because of her gender, race, religion, or sexuality, I'll stop everything to ask a different student to rewind and play back for his classmate what he has heard. Rarely does the student I've asked to retell the story miss the truth beneath the classmate's words. And in these instances, meaningful connections are made between students, as well as between the students and me. An important structure of a love pedagogy is relationship building across normative power relations in educational settings, especially when stories like these are shared. Often this means subverting conventional teacher-student hierarchies. In these moments, I, a black and brown woman, allow my own memories of racial or gendered injury to surface, then in these moments the students and I share a verified, communal truth. The truth becomes more comprehensible, and we experience a sense of reciprocal recovery. A love pedagogy is practiced not just for the benefit of young people because the practice of love isn't about saving the kids. Instead, through a practice of love, we as teachers can heal from our own traumas; we can reconnect to ourselves.

In "The Site of Memory," Toni Morrison contends that truth is random and stranger than fiction because it's odd.[4] Racism *is* odd, and its experience can feel unaccountable because it doesn't seem like it's really happening or true. We know racism as a noun. As such it stands still conceptually, but racism is, indeed, active—it's when, in an instant, we become a part of some aberrant whole. We're the direct and indirect object, but never the subject. Racism is illogical and feels inexplicable because it's incompatible with our innate hardwiring to connect, to empathize, to selflessly concern ourselves with the well-being of others.[5] Racism is like a neural short-circuiting of our inherent need to connect, and so we stumble over our words when we speak it. Within the incoherencies of racism, Royce sputters, "I just feel, like, maybe I just, like, grew up in, like, maybe like, like a semi like very, like, racist, like, police district, maybe, or like if it's just like cops in general, like I have no clue." The "They" to whom he refers are white people, white police. The "Us" are poor and working-class black and brown boys.

Philippe Ariès says of the medieval world, to which, perhaps in some ways, we have returned, "there is no place for childhood."[6] What is particularly true is that there is no place in America for poor, working-poor, and working-class black, brown, and white childhoods. There's that space that Royce describes with a nebulous and contradictory specificity. It's the lacuna in which boys like Royce and white cops just can't seem to meet. When Royce says police look at him like he's not an adult but not a kid, like he's just in the middle, he squarely identifies an interval in the black and brown person's development. It's a space between Royce's brown body and the police, between the police and the very fact of his humanity. This is what Michael Dumas describes as a "liminal space," a position young black and brown bodies occupy on both sides of a racialized boundary: still children yet at the threshold of adulthood. Dumas insists that this is a place in which they are "certainly not children but accorded none of the legitimacy or regard of those with adult status, only the culpability."[7]

Imagine trying to live openly while being made to feel responsible, even accountable for a mental and physical violence perpetrated against you because of America's perception of you. Young people experience this contradiction and often subsume it until, for them, "it just is what it is." Imagine this behavior involves physical force intended to hurt, damage, or kill your essential self. Then you get inside the school, beyond Pac-Man, inside the classroom where something as vulnerable and fraught as learning is supposed to occur, and it's nothing but worksheets and Scantron tests filled with blanks you're supposed to fill in. Nowhere is there a space for you to process—to describe, explicate, inquire, and then comprehend the rationale for why you are targeted. Instead you leave the school thinking it's just you. You believe that you are the crazy one, and you begin to take responsibility for the abuse and neglect. You take on the culpability of the abuser, which is your country.

I recorded Royce that day, with his permission. I then emailed him the recording. I asked him to listen to it like he was listening to a story being told by someone he loves very much. A few days later Royce said, "I heard myself talking about all that stuff you have us read in class . . . about capitalism and class, about how race is in our minds but has real effects." After another few days, with the help of his own recorded words, Royce changed his final project. He focused his final audio essay on black and brown boys, on cops, on the need for more humanity, on the need for justice. I think Royce began the process of healing himself. His audio essay engaged an intellectual, academic, and emotional analysis to understand the social, economic, and political complexities of racism and masculinity. In Royce's project we can hear him realize that he's surrounded by Pac-Men in an America that doesn't think he's as beautiful and capable as white kids. We hear him attempt to grapple with the idea of how America perceives him versus how he understands himself. In the eyes of Pac-Men, Royce is inadequate; he is aberrant; he is a biotic mistake against which others must be inoculated. And this malignant notion, juxtaposed with the American Alger work-hard, win-big myth that the nation still can't seem to dispel, wreaks havoc on a young, developing psyche. This lore, reinforced by the contemporary education economy, violates young people. It destabilizes their still developing belief that each one is not just a candidate for the good, but indeed is the good itself. It adds to the crisis of connection.

When we shut up and listen to students, when we renegotiate classroom hierarchies that are scaffolded by constant measurement, grading, and assessment, we become accountable to our students' humanity, and we reclaim our own. The classroom must be a space for memory, for truth-telling, for exposing the frailty of masculinity, for exploring and struggling with the cognitive dissonance of racism. The classroom must disrupt the violence of the contemporary education economy and close the relational gap between teacher and student. In this way, a love pedagogy is an active and radical resistance to the criminalization of young bodies, particularly poor and working-class black, brown, and white bodies. The contemporary education economy requires a radical disruption to the mechanization of teaching, the standardization of what's taught, and the dehumanization and violence of education in public schools. A part of shattering the contemporary education economy also requires that not only the humanity of the students but also the rights, needs, and humanity of the teachers—the K–12 educators, the adjuncts, and the contingents—be acknowledged and regarded. The contemporary education economy exploits us all in different ways; it attempts to disenfranchise us from the condition of being human, from our social connection with students, and from what and how to teach. Left unchallenged and unchanged, the crisis of connection will just continue to reproduce itself in schools and universities.

The practice of love in the classroom involves small acts, large acts, medium acts. For example, I have taught young people in grades K–16 autoethnography. Importantly, I fuse autoethnography with audio documentary. I call this qualitative research method audioethnography. This is what Royce practiced. It's an approach that can allow young people to expose and explore their experiences living inside social categories of difference. They become honest about what they feel and think, and they begin to inquire. They begin to ask about differentiated power structures, and they question why these structures exist and for whose benefit. Love pedagogy is fueled by these kinds of questions. And questions, as one student asserted, "inspire us to be brave."

The students I have taught in state universities are all working-poor and working-class. Many of them are first-generation college students who are recent or first-generation immigrants. They arrive to my college classroom thinking they have no voice. What that says to me is that before they got to me, the wire was pulled; they were disconnected from the importance of their own life histories and the significant social, economic, and political truths their lives can help the public to understand. They arrive disconnected from their own power to make social change. To unearth their life histories, there's a photo essay project I designed, which is based on the work of photographer Dawoud Bey. I call it "Outside-Inside" because the project requires students to write about how America sees them in terms of their identity and photograph a self-portrait (a selfie) of how they see their real selves. I assign Outside-Inside about four weeks after students have spent time reading and writing about the science of social connection, watching documentaries like *The Central Park Five*, and examining school websites. The intellectual process of comparing public and independent schools (through their websites) is also an emotional process. Students quickly understand that education is a political economy, especially once they become cognizant of the economic and social disparities between their own public high schools and the independent high schools like Phillips Exeter, which the founder of Facebook, Mark Zuckerberg, attended.

Once our Outside-Inside projects are completed, we hold a silent exhibit just for our class. During the exhibit, we quietly walk around exploring each other's work. There are no PowerPoint presentations, no fear-producing or embarrassing, memorized speeches that the students perform at the front of the class. Instead, we engage the power of silent and communal inquiry. After we've all taken in each other's work, no verbal words are exchanged. We immediately sit down and begin to write. The prompt that guides us is "What do you know now that you didn't understand before?" We sit. We write. Then we read our responses aloud to the class from our seats. We do not speak them. Then we write some more, but this time using a metacognitive approach. We reread what we last wrote and then write to describe what it was like to read our own words, hear ourselves in writing, and hear the experiences of others in the room. Through this process, we come together both intellectually and socially. The students say, "It's like we're now a family." At the end of one writing session, I asked eighteen-year-old Matt why he chose to be so honest in his photo essay. He answered me, but he looked out at his classmates, as though he wanted them all to recognize and record what he was about to say. He then responded, "You've always been so honest with us, it made me want to be honest back."

Tanya, and Josh and Je'meyah . . .

Love pedagogy is hard work. So much work that some of us who practice it sometimes sacrifice time with family and time at the rally or protest because every day of teaching means a night of changing things up to address the individual twenty, thirty, or forty kids we have in our rooms. A kid blinks her eyes differently one morning, by the afternoon you're changing the lesson you spent all weekend planning. You're calling her home to ask why so-and-so wasn't at school today. You are, then, like Tanya Hodge at South High in Minneapolis—you often skip lunch to make sure you get to talk to Malik.

Tanya is an English teacher. Annually, she teaches nearly a hundred fifty young people. She's got a strong principal. Like good principals do, he gets out of the way of teacher brilliance, but not so much that he can't actively support it with every dime and every tool he can muster. Tanya's got too many kids in one room, which makes teaching hard, so Tanya just teaches harder. She makes rooms at South seem like protected dens of knowledge and understanding. Tanya was a fellow in the Teacher's Institute, a professional development program for K–12 teachers I designed, which was facilitated by my consultancy, the Ed Factory. The Ed Factory uses the art of social engagement to transform the educational process and challenge notions of difference. The Ed Factory's Teacher's Institute provides opportunities for teachers to examine the social, economic, and political relationship among stereotypes, the larger culture, schools. It is a space in which teachers can grapple openly with the ways in which stereotypes obstruct the possibility for connection in the classroom and in the communities surrounding the school. In this respect, the institute is fundamentally different from cultural competency programs. The concept of cultural competency assumes that social categories of difference are physical, mental, or cultural conditions for which individuals can learn a particular language or cultural skill to help them "manage" difference. At the Teacher's Institute, fellows learn to understand race, social class, gender, religion, and sexuality stereotypes as symptoms of social disconnection. Through individual mentoring, online resources, seminars in social theory, and symposia with local and global innovators and trendsetters in the humanities, arts, (neuro)sciences, and mathematics, the Teacher's Institute provides fellows and their students a professional development experience rooted in the science and the art of social engagement. The institute provides programming in various cities, but it began in Minnesota and ran there, funded by Minneapolis Public Schools, for four years.

As a part of the institute's methodology for practicing love in the classroom, I assign fellows the task of choosing just one child on whom they will focus as if she or he is their own for the fellowship term. They are instructed to really notice their child, photograph their child, write about him or her, and ask the child to write about herself or himself, but also about the fellow as a teacher. Tanya Hodge is white and American. She chose as her child six-foot-three, seventeen-year-old Malik, who is black and American. One prompt I give fellows is "Ask your child how she or he sees himself, and how they think the world sees them." Here's Malik's response to Tanya:

> Well when most people see me for the first time, off back they think oh he's probably not a good kid, A "Gangbanger," He doesn't do good in school, He's trouble. I guess it's the way I come off to people, The way I dress, walk, My facial expressions, My "lango," it might all add up to a Gangbangers Mentality. But the best part about that, is when these people find out im the exact oppose. When people actually see how talented I am and how smart I am, they can't believe it. And I love that about myself. . . . So as some people might see me as a young black delinquent male from the hood, I think of my self as a slightly hood, Handsome, Educated, Loyal, Respectful young man.

Look at the photo of Malik that Tanya took while he was writing his answer to how the world sees him and how he sees himself. Makes me sick to think of all the Pac-Men waiting to eat him up like a pac-dot.

Throughout the institute, teachers worked hard to notice, to witness, and to listen to their "children." In the process, the student as concept and commodity evolved steadily and naturally into someone warm-blooded. Malik grew closer to Tanya because he knew she was watching and listening carefully to what he thought and felt. He became a more curious, intellectual, and socially engaged partner in his education. In fact, after graduation, Malik worked for a black male empowerment program facilitating workshops in public schools. As Tanya

Figure 9.1. Photo of Malik. ©The Ed Factory, LLC. Photo credit: Tanya Hodge.

observed and noticed, as Malik shared with Tanya more of his fears, hopes, weaknesses, and beliefs in his own strengths, Tanya felt safer to let down her "teacher" guard. Tanya began to reconnect with her own humanity and with Malik's. In the institute, fellows commit to actively defy *how* the state makes them teach and the sentinels of standardized learning that the state has made them become. They defy attempts to measure and assess and to be measured and assessed. Instead, fellows focus on individualized instruction and the construction of classrooms of collaboration—just like they do at Phillips Exeter Academy, but for about fifty thousand dollars less per year.

The institute's exercises, design strategies, and private and public seminars with artists, various types of scientists, psychologists, architects, and, of course, educators reinforce that both teaching and learning are processes of human understanding. Indeed, learning isn't something streamlined and fixed that is capable of objectification. What the PhD-MBAs of the offices of Institutional Research, Planning, and Effectiveness try to quantify in public K–16 education can't be measured with one-size-fits-all assessment tables. These measurements are like an anti-love pedagogy, and they distract from real learning. Real learning involves making the effort to perceive the intended meaning of a young person's ideas as well as the significance and source of those ideas through varied, often convoluted and unexpected interactions. Real learning is idiosyncratic. It's temporal.

In an interview with Barry Walsh, Katherine Merseth, a senior lecturer at Harvard's Graduate School of Education, contends that the "nature of improvement in teaching and learning is more uncertain than in other practitioner/client relationships. 'Success is difficult to define. What does it look like? What are we measuring?'"[8] Merseth has no answers to her queries. Instead, she provides insight into the difficulty of nailing down what learning is. This is exactly the gray area in which I want the institute's fellows to live as they teach because living inside the gray matter is another part of the foundation of love pedagogy. The fact is that learning resists being an exact measurable quantity. Learning is vague; often it materializes without structure or organization while sometimes it simultaneously emerges through both. Learning is slippery. It's a fish we teachers should never believe we can hook.

A part of the institute's design is to treat teachers as intellectual workers who practice the art of social engagement. Fellows learn to design classroom curricula grounded in transdisciplinary methods and content. Always central to their designs is the question, how do I build *relationship* in my classroom?, which means that fellows are inevitably designing classrooms founded on love. Getting teachers to be this honest and intimate with their practice entails giving them permission to reveal and discuss, in direct and indirect ways, their experiences of teaching under the fire of high-stakes testing and high-stakes accountability, all measures that they feel make it more difficult for them to see themselves and their students as anything more than automatons. Through our private seminars with national and international scholars and practitioners, fellows discuss how the contemporary education economy disconnects teachers from the feeling part of themselves, from their original purpose as educators, from themselves as intellectual workers—from the kids. Fellows share how they want to abandon the notion that school is a space reserved for judgment and accountability, and they argue that the system of public education produces small, indelible, unrelenting psychic violences.

During one term of the institute, I invited a friend, writer Claudia Rankine, to come to the institute to help us dig deeper into the effect of the contemporary education economy on teachers and students, but specifically through the lens of race-based microaggressions in schools. The fellows, like most teachers, wanted to find their way back to love, so in front of Claudia, upon her forthright and loving command, on the white-boarded walls of the institute, Minneapolis public school teachers confessed to the author of *Citizen: An American Lyric* the sins against young people that they'd been compelled to commit in school. One wrote, "I was surprised that 'Christian' scored all 4's on the FIRST unit exam. He gave me no reason to be surprised. In fact, he gave me evidence that he would do well." Another wrote, "Am I holding X accountable and upholding expectations and at the same time pushing him out [of the school]?" And yet another recounted, "I was in a discharge (from treatment meeting) 2 days after starting a job in North Carolina. The White counselor told the black student 'How can you be successful if you go back with your family?' I refused to accept this was about race → It was."

Later, I told fellows to return to their child and ask: "What's one fear you have for me as your teacher?" Marco told Tanya, "I fear I will disappoint you." Ben said bluntly, "Burn-out." What was the fear Tanya had for herself? "That I will, somehow, lose hope. I fear getting sucked into the vortex of negativity. The status quo of test scores, white privilege, categories of assumptions. I fear not fighting back, not disrupting at the right times." A hope Tanya has for herself? "That I can learn to be more uncomfortable. I hope to learn how to disrupt more. Question more answers than I accept."

The practices of the Teacher's Institute have made a scientifically empirical discovery, which is the essence of a love pedagogy: being in relationship with students improves everything. It improves the understanding of complex ideas; a willingness to work with large quantities of information; the ability to inquire, analyze, and synthesize; it even improves test scores, and especially attendance. Most important is the fact that a love pedagogy reconnects students and teachers to their own innate ability to connect, and connection reminds us that we are not ghosts. It reminds us that we are the living.

* * *

Josh Zoucha is the coordinator of Edison High School's SHARP program in Minneapolis. Josh describes SHARP as "a program for students who have fallen behind in credits and aren't on track to graduate. Our program allows students to stay at their current school and work to get college ready." Josh, white like Tanya, chose Je'meyah, a black child like Malik, as his child. Je'meyah was a senior when Josh was an institute fellow, and Je'meyah was fast on her way to *not* graduate. Josh recorded a conversation between them after he began implementing a love pedagogy. Below is a transcript of a recorded conversation that Josh and Je'meyah had about her school attendance. Making audio recordings of discussions between fellows and their students is a part of the institute's approach because we are training teachers to hear, listen closely, and notice, so we use recordings to share, reflect, and push our classroom practices as a group. Josh submitted his discussion with Je'meyah as an example of love pedagogy. The discussion provides a powerful example of how love in the classroom is very much a pedagogy of relationship. Notice that after just a few weeks engaging this practice, Je'meyah begins to call Josh "Dad." Je'meyah's words are in quotes.

Hi, Je'meyah. "Hi, Dad." So, I got a question for ya. "Um-hm." I've been going through all these people's credits like kinda tryin to figure out where they're at, where they've gone. Last fall, you had 48 absences from school. "Oh. And—Just the fall?" Just the fall. And you earned only 2.75 credits, and you had seven days of suspension with four referrals. [Je'meyah kind of chortles at this point] So, you wanna know what you have this year? "What?" This year you've earned 14.5 credits. "A miracle." A Miracle. Guess how many referrals you had in the fall? "0?" Yeah, 0. How many days of suspension have you had? "0." So, what's the difference between last year and this year? "Different? This might be a long answer." That's fine. "Um, it's just when you get to know people, and they make you want to come to school, and they make you wanna do right, then you start to do right, and you start to like it, and you start to enjoy comin to a place, and you don't wanna do nuthin to lose those people and make them stop liking you."

Unfortunately, in K–12 public education, the Common Core, and in colleges and universities the offices of accountability, are bent on measuring something different from what Josh measured here. Yes, he had the numbers, the measurements, so Josh retained for the state education system what it believes it needs to mark "success," but what the numbers here really represent is that a practice of love—of being socially connected to young people—is what changes the data.

Before Josh shared with Je'meyah her record of attendance, he followed a love pedagogy as "prescribed" by the institute. First, he spent time getting to know Je'meyah as a person, not as an academic pupil. He asked her questions about what she did outside of school. That's how he found out that sometimes Je'meyah lived in a shelter for people without homes. Like the other fellows in the institute, Josh wrote descriptively about "his child" Je'meyah. Josh and the other fellows shared descriptions of their days *noticing* their children. Josh wrote about what it was like to be Je'meyah's teacher. He wrote and photographed portraits of Je'meyah, and he recorded their conversations and played them back to Je'meyah so that she could hear and write about herself and her relationship to and with Josh.

As time progressed, Josh told me, Je'meyah became less of a character in the play that is school and more of an individual deserving of respect, intellectual challenge, and love. Josh always knew Je'meyah was human, but he never had the opportunity (or the prompting by the education system) to slow down and really see or understand Je'meyah. What's ironic (and might sound contradictory) is that despite all my objections to formalized accountability measures like standardized, high-stakes tests, Josh proved that, at least in one way, the effect of love in a classroom can, indeed, be assessed and measured. The formula being that when love is present, teachers are more committed to their practice and kids show up physically and mentally.

As Bill Ayers writes in *Teaching with Conscience in an Imperfect World: An Invitation*, "Every teacher must decide whether to trust students and approach them honestly as full and equal human beings with agency and capacity, with experiences and hopes and ideas that must be taken into account, or to assume that they are savages to be broken and tamed, their minds conquered and colonized."[9] The stories of Josh and Je'meyah, Tanya, Malik, and the other students are all stories of connection and love. The institute and my own classroom are sites in which it is presumed that each young person and every teacher has her own kind of good, his own kind of usefulness, their own absolute value.

NOTES

1 Phil Jackson and Hugh Delehanty, *Sacred Hoops: Spiritual Lessons of a Hardwood Warrior* (New York: Hyperion, 1995).

2 Martin Luther King Jr. interviewed by Dr. Kenneth Clark, "The Negro and the American Promise," *American Experience* (PBS, 1963).

3 Young People's Archive (YPA) is a digital archive of young people's experiences locally, nationally, and globally as they wrestle with notions of self, other, difference, and the crisis of connection. YPA is published by the Ed Factory.

4 Toni Morrison, "The Site of Memory," in *Inventing the Truth: The Art and Craft of Memoir*, ed. William Zinsser (Boston: Houghton Mifflin, 1987), 93.

5 See Matthew D. Lieberman, *Social: Why Our Brains Are Wired to Connect* (New York: Crown, 2013); and Frans de Waal, *The Age of Empathy: Nature's Lessons for a Kinder Society* (New York: Crown, 2009).

6 Philippe Ariès, *Centuries of Childhood: A Social History of Family Life* (New York: Knopf, 1962), 333.

7 Michael Dumas and Joseph D. Nelson, "(Re)imagining Black Boyhood: Toward a Critical Framework for Educational Research," *Harvard Educational Review* 86, no. 1 (2016): 27–47.

8 Barry Walsh, "Two-Way Learning," *Usable Knowledge*, January 26, 2016, www.gse.harvard.edu.

9 William Ayers, *Teaching with Conscience in an Imperfect World: An Invitation* (New York: Teachers College Press, 2016), 47.

10

Empathy as Strategy for Reconnecting to Our Common Humanity

MARY GORDON

Belonging. It's what drives us, mentally, spiritually, physically, no matter how hard we try to fit into the zeitgeist of independence, grit, and success. So many of our problems are fueled by the tension between our need to stand up, stake our ground, take what's ours, to win at all costs—and our need to care, to be kind, to nurture, to strive together, to belong. This book, every chapter, every nuanced angle explores this dilemma. At the core of our shared humanity, it's our sense of belonging and connection that drives our well-being—affects our health—influences our longevity.

You can't belong, or help someone belong, without empathy. Empathy has two overarching components: thinking (cognitive empathy) and feeling (affective empathy). Typically we talk about cognitive empathy—the ability to take another person's perspective. But there is also affective or emotional empathy—the ability to feel how another person feels. The phrase "walk a mile in my shoes" is born of affective empathy.

I like to say empathy isn't taught, it's caught. I founded Roots of Empathy, an evidence-based school program in 1996. It is about cultivating the capacity of children to understand first themselves, and then understand others. We started in Canada and we're now in eleven countries. When it comes to empathy, we've helped more than eight hundred thousand children catch it.

And it's needed more than ever. The global climate, politically, societally, culturally, seems to be built on suspicion and hatred of the "other." Roots of Empathy is an antidote. It helps children connect to our shared humanity, our shared feelings, breaking down the barriers that dehumanize others and embracing our commonalities.

Our research shows that it works. It works because children don't read about it, they experience it and experiential learning is the deepest learning there is. At the heart of Roots of Empathy is a parent and baby. Once a month, for the whole school year, the parent and baby visit "their" classroom. The children stand around the edge of the Roots of Empathy green blanket and sing the welcome song (we call it "the anthem" as it's sung on three continents in multiple languages) to their "tiny teacher." The parent holds the baby at eye level to the children for at least three seconds (yes, I ask the parent to count); the children touch the baby's feet, they lock eyes with the baby, and they sing hello.

It looks cute. But as I'll outline in this chapter, it's more than cute. Roots of Empathy is designed carefully, systematically, to help children build their capacity for empathy, inclusion, respect, care, resilience, problem solving, responsive parenting, responsible citizenship, participatory democracy, and peace. We do that by building children's understanding of attachment/attunement, emotional literacy, temperament, authentic communication, intrinsic pride and motivation, social inclusion, and even neuroscience. Our program is supported by scientific research—both informed research and our own studies. But it didn't start that way. It started when I followed my instinct—when I synthesized what I was seeing in the classroom, the living room, and the board room.[1] The science later confirmed it. And it confirmed our mission: nothing less than breaking the intergenerational cycles of violence, modeling responsive parenting, and building peaceful societies. Our motto is "changing the world, child by child."

The starting point is watching a parent and baby connect. The baby is anywhere from two to four months old at the beginning of the program, and a year old by the end. Every visit, as they sit together around the green blanket, the children pepper the mother (usually the mother) with questions about how things have changed with the baby since their last visit: Does she have her first tooth? Does she like vegetables? Can she roll over yet? Does she reach for a toy now when you show it to her?

They watch the baby figure out the boundaries of her world. They see the baby look for her parent, watch the eye contact, see the touch. Mom is safety. Mom is there. The children are witnessing the first and most primal bond we have—mother/child attachment and attunement.

Empathy is innate in all of us. Every child is born with empathy, but it either flourishes or fades in the attachment relationship. Science now firmly backs up what we've known from generations of experience: attachment is where empathy begins.[2]

Our society has missed the boat when it comes to attachment. We don't invest in it, and we've paid an enormous price in child development and therefore in the family, in our schools, communities, justice system, and society. Often early childhood programs are created to try to fill the gap.

Insecure attachment is a failure to connect. If we don't have the secure connection made in the earliest days, months, and years, the consequences are felt by the decade and by the generation.[3] We read about academic brain drain from countries, but this is brain drain as opportunity cost—by not nurturing a baby's brain development, that lost potential is lifelong and the costs are society-wide.[4] It means we let generations of children miss the boat when they don't have to.

Roots of Empathy is a lifeboat. It gives children who missed the first round of attachment in infancy an opportunity to develop empathy through experiential learning (as noted earlier, the deepest learning there is), bringing together the mind and the heart—cognition and emotion—with deep consequences that last beyond the end of the program.

It also gives teachers an opportunity to reposition their relationship with their students. I really believe to care is to teach. But to teach is to care. Our program gives teachers the chance to see the emotional vulnerability and courage in children outside the curriculum and performance-driven spotlight. Teachers tell us they have been changed by the experience—that they are more empathic toward their students and their students are more empathic toward them.

Attachment comes from the baby, but it is dependent on a parent's attunement. It's a dance of emotional connection. A baby works out her attachment to her parents based on how attuned and responsive they are to her needs and feelings. There are various degrees of attachment from insecure to ambivalent to secure—and babies figure out whether they'll get the support they need. Babies with severe attachment disorders fail to thrive, not just emotionally, but physically. And not just through infancy, but possibly for life.[5]

A child's first attachment is the basis for all the relationships in a lifetime.[6] Children learn to respond to people and situations based on how they are treated—to either love or hate, to trust or mistrust, to be kind or cruel.

If this attachment relationship has not been optimal for a child, Roots of Empathy gives the child another chance to witness a positive, loving relationship firsthand. There is no one right way to love. But by watching the loving interactions of the parent and the baby over the school year, children lay down tracks in their brains—biologically embedding what love looks like.[7]

If you take anything away from this chapter, take my well-used phrase: love grows brains.

The baby visits the classroom every three weeks. But the Roots of Empathy instructor is there every week basically through the school year, guiding the children through observations as they learn the "affective" or emotional aspect of empathy and the "cognitive" or thinking aspect of empathy, also known as perspective taking.

The children develop their emotional literacy as they learn to label the baby's feelings, reflect on their own feelings, and then bridge that understanding to the feelings of others.

Emotional literacy is the foundational literacy of life—but we tend to be an emotionally illiterate society. Without it, a person will struggle to be fully complete and often fail to build successful relationships; such a person will never have the full enjoyment of human connection and of being human.

Darren, or children like Darren, is why I created Roots of Empathy. Darren (not his real name) was in one of our early programs. He had a horrific early childhood. He witnessed his mother's murder when he was four. He'd been put in foster care and was passed from family to family. By the time he'd reached eighth grade, he was two grades behind. He was older, bigger, taller, even starting to grow facial hair. And yet he was smaller in invisible measures than the children in his class. His broken attachments put his empathy at severe risk.

One day our baby and parent were visiting Darren's class and they were talking about temperament. The mother explained how the baby liked to face outward in the baby carrier. She said she had hoped her six-month-old would be cuddlier. At the end of the class she asked if anyone wanted to try on the carrier—to see what it felt like. (This is an example of perspective taking.) To everyone's surprise, Darren volunteered. Once he had it strapped on, he asked if he could carry the baby in it. Although the mother was a little nervous, she gave the baby to him. Darren put the baby into the carrier facing him.

We've seen this over and over in every country where we have a program—little babies sense the children in most need, and Darren was no exception. This wise little baby snuggled right into Darren's chest. They went over to a quiet corner and Darren rocked the baby gently back and forth for a while. When he came back over to the mother, he said to her and the Roots of Empathy instructor, "If nobody has ever loved you, do you think you could still be a good father?"

And there it was. The seed of empathy. The power of attachment. It was still in Darren. He'd found the humanity in himself through this little baby. It just needed modeling, coaxing, and coaching.

I started as a kindergarten teacher, but early on I witnessed families suffering through domestic violence, child abuse, and neglect. The common denominator was the absence of empathy from the perpetrator.

I wanted to prove birth is not destiny. I started Roots of Empathy to give children, like Darren, the opportunity to spend a whole year with a deep connection to a neighborhood parent and infant who naturally demonstrate secure attachment and attunement, and are the best model of empathy. And to find out what difference it made, if any.

Our program is universal. It's not just for those who have had lives like Darren's. It's for everyone. All children need to develop an appreciation of their own uniqueness, find their voice, and, through developing empathy, learn how to make friends and be in relationships. They learn how to be connected. And to continue the lifeboat analogy—a rising tide lifts all boats.

We now know that loving relationships mitigate the huge levels of stress reported at alarming rates throughout North America.[8] Roots of Empathy helps children to understand their feelings and to learn to regulate their emotions, and it gives them a suit of armor allowing them to be able to communicate with others so that they are heard—and helped. Empathy has become a critical twenty-first-century necessity.

These aren't benefits that help the child just through school. A solid body of evidence shows a secure attachment bond from birth improves the well-being of a baby, not just through childhood but into adulthood. And it actually affects longevity.[9]

All this is to say, helping children like Darren, and the more than eight hundred thousand children who have been through our program, develop empathy has evolved from our core beliefs and the scientific pillars upon which the program is supported.

Nothing can better illustrate them than two minutes in one class, on one day, with one baby.

* * *

Baby Mei has been visiting a downtown Toronto school with her mother for six months. She isn't crawling yet. And on this day, in just two minutes, baby Mei teaches her fourth grade students a lifetime's worth of lessons—and demonstrates the depth of our program. There's a reason we talk about the power of the Tiny Teacher (they do, in fact, wear tiny T-shirts with the word "Teacher" across their chests).

Kathy, our instructor, brings out a toy that rattles and dings, is squishy and colorful. Mei, like all our babies, is intrigued immediately. Remember, Mei can't crawl. Yet.

This class of eight-year-olds, sitting around the green blanket watching her, come from all over the world. For many of them it is their first group experience of solidarity outside the home. They are deeply invested in how the little baby is doing. They are engaged. They are the team cheering for this little baby, whose Olympic challenge is to reach the toy. Kathy is following the baby's lead and guiding their observations.

These two minutes have become famous in our program because Kathy asks eighteen questions. (Kathy was a little shocked to find that out later—and little did she know it would become an iconic moment in our program.) I've highlighted some of them here.

Let's see what she can do. Do you want to play with this?
All the questions are experiential, 100 percent. All children have an opportunity to draw on their experience rather than their knowledge—to respond if they choose to, but no pressure. We train our instructors not

Figure 10.1. Kathy shakes the colorful toy to attract Baby Mei's attention. Video footage by Tim Chevrier, The Blend Media Group.

to ask the children who put their hand up first. They scan the class to see who hasn't contributed yet. The children stop competing for top spot. They're not judged on their participation or the quality of their contribution. No telling and yelling, just opening. Most of the questions aren't about facts and don't have an answer. They just help the children to develop their observational and reporting skills. The thinking about the question is more important than the answer. The way we help children understand and develop their empathic capacities, their emotional literacy, is by asking questions.

What does that sound like? What's that sound?
Kathy is asking the children to get inside Baby Mei's mind and read the cues she is communicating. We coach children in taking the perspective of the baby. This insight into the baby's mind is a powerful step in the development of empathy because perspective taking, as it's called, is the cognitive aspect of empathy. Understanding that others think, hold opinions, and have feelings is an important awareness referred to as Theory of Mind.[10] In Roots of Empathy, helping the children get into the mind

Figure 10.2. Kathy places the toy just out of reach of Baby Mei. Video footage by Tim Chevrier, The Blend Media Group.

Figure 10.3. Kathy solicits opinions and predictions on what Baby Mei is feeling and how she is communicating. Video footage by Tim Chevrier, The Blend Media Group.

of the baby builds their problem-solving abilities. Their ability to identify with others helps them to articulate their feelings, giving them abilities to build friendships. Perspective taking is the first step in *any* conflict resolution.

One student, very new to Canada, and just learning English, answers Kathy's question. "He's telling I want this toy, I want this toy." Baby Mei is a girl, but Kathy doesn't correct him; she repeats what he said, substituting the correct pronoun. We never embarrass a child. We know what that does to us as adults—we want to disengage, we want to hide, we feel humiliated. The children learn to help each other, rather than mocking each other. It's a safe place to take a risk. Just like Darren did when he volunteered to try on the baby carrier.

Mei is sitting and looking at the toy.

Do you think she'll be able to get this?
The bets start pouring in. Some feel compelled to answer, some don't. These questions are reflective questions that don't require a public answer. This respects a child's introverted or extroverted tendencies. We want children to become good thinkers, critical thinkers, problem solvers, and constructive collaborators.

That raises our core belief in authentic communication.

Authentic communication comes from a natural, unfettered interest in sharing what you're thinking and feeling with somebody. To be authentic, children have to listen or observe in order to have something hit them; they have to mull it around the blender of their minds, and then offer something. Whatever they offer is real, because they're not saying it with the goal of impressing or putting down. It's genuine. They feel part of this solidarity around the green blanket. Some of them may not ever have had that.

Or, maybe it's authentic communication, but it's internal. One little girl around the green blanket never speaks, but she is definitely watching. For children who are more introverted than extroverted, the conversations they have with themselves are important. The point in Roots of Empathy is that we care what a child thinks of herself.

Another core belief in the program is intrinsic pride and intrinsic motivation. The big thing about intrinsic motivation—where the children are focused and engaged around the green blanket—is that the children finally believe that we are listening to them and taking them seriously. School tends not to be about being listened to and taken seriously. When we ask children to describe their school experience they often say they don't feel respected. They feel like a herd. It's not a safe dialogue place. It's a place where children are judged daily. So for little ones of any age, to respond to a question based on what they think, without a lot of time to reflect on it, is probably the first time in their public lives they've done that. And it's hard for most of them. Roots of Empathy gives them a place to be safe. No judgment. No criticism. No one's wrong. No one's right. We're gathered around a space where our focus is on one little, vulnerable baby.

Roots of Empathy also helps children with metacognition—the capacity to think about what they think and to think about how they learn. It's rarely taught in school. It's not just insight into the little baby; it's insight into yourself, what you think, what you believe, what you feel. We're learning how baby Mei learns, so how do I learn? Who am I?

Now what is she going to do? Let's see if she keeps trying.
Baby Mei has the children completely gripped in the goal. She is sitting. She's eyeing the toy, and she starts leaning forward. The children gasp as she almost gets on her knees. The children urge her on. A boy pumps his fist whispering, "Go, go, go." The children are with her in the struggle as she moves forward. It's completely altruistic. It's fun.

And it's a key element of one of our pillars: executive function.[11]

Executive function skills are the higher order thinking skills. Focusing attention is one of the building blocks of executive function. Being able to pay attention and filter out distractions is vital for learning. From our very first breath, emotion drives attention. And while it's generally understood that attention drives learning, it's not so well appreciated how emotion drives deep learning. When we ask how the baby is feeling or what she is thinking, the children are focusing attention on the baby—and bringing together the cognitive (thinking) and affective (feeling) aspects of empathy.

Impulse control is another aspect of executive function—the ability to resist temptation. Perhaps not surprisingly, the ability of these children to control impulses is related to their ability to sustain their attention, to think before acting, to prioritize. Children who are developing empathy have a better understanding of the importance of words and

Figure 10.4. Baby Mei struggles almost to her knees to crawl; she is within reach. There's a collective intake of breath and silence. The children are starting to read Mei's emotional cues. Video footage by Tim Chevrier, The Blend Media Group.

behavior—they resist the impulse to speak or act in a hurtful way. That inhibition is driven by empathy.

What happened? So close.
Shall I pick you up? Do you need help?
Baby Mei suddenly loses her balance and lands on her back. "Awww," the children cry, and they deflate together. Kathy leans over her and asks if she'd like some help. Mei has her arms reaching up and is wriggling. All of our instructors deliberately ask a baby's permission to do something. A baby has ways to communicate if she wants or doesn't want something—vocal cues, facial cues (from her eyebrows to where she's looking), body language (rigid like a board, or floppy, hands open, hands closed). We ask the children where the baby is looking, what is her body doing, let's listen and hear if she makes any noise that tells us what she'd like us to do. The children always go silent and listen. As we like to say to the children, she may not be able to talk, but she can certainly communicate.

Figure 10.5. Kathy is asking Baby Mei if she needs help getting up, giving children a demonstration of respect for babies. Video footage by Tim Chevrier, The Blend Media Group.

There is another purpose—it sends a clear message that a baby can say no to an adult if she doesn't want to be touched or picked up. And this was born out of the experiences I witnessed of children suffering sexual abuse. The authority figures in their lives made children believe they didn't own their own bodies. They don't believe they can say no to an adult.

Our program gives children a voice, an opinion, and an ability to defend themselves and protect themselves. It acknowledges our human dignity. It protects human rights. So we're not just finding the humanity in the baby, we're finding her rights as a human.

After going through our program, children have frequently come forward to disclose to a teacher that they suffered from sexual abuse, witnessed domestic violence, experienced the death of a sibling or parent.

Kathy gently lifts Mei by her hands back to a sitting position and asks another key question:

Did she get upset when she tipped over?
They all shout "nooooo" in a chorus. Kathy points out that Mei, despite her setback, holds it together emotionally. She uses that moment to explore Baby Mei's temperament.

Is Mei easily frustrated?
Temperament is innate, but it can change over time. There are nine traits: mood, sensitivity, distractibility, intensity, rhythmicity, activity level, adaptability, first reaction, and persistence.[12]

We use the Baby Mei exercise in reaching for a toy in every program so the children can observe the baby's temperament traits. Is the baby really high in persistence, or does the baby have a really low frustration tolerance? When you help them understand the baby's temperament, they can reflect on their own. In this case, they were really frustrated because they couldn't stand her frustration—and that is empathic—so we need to be able to say, "You're feeling frustrated. You're feeling just like Baby Mei is—you're feeling with her."

And there it is: they've had a collective empathic experience.

The children can then reflect on others as well. It helps them behave appropriately in different situations and is a good way to help regulate their emotions.

When parents (and teachers) reflect on their own temperaments and on their children's—they often see what the scientists call "goodness of fit"[13]—how well they mesh or how different they are. If you're highly reactive and your child is highly reactive—that is a volatile mix. If you're calm and have an intense child, you might have a perfectly complementary temperament for bringing your child off the ceiling.

It is the alchemy of humanity. It offers insights to parents, teachers, and the children. The children see that a baby who cries a lot is not a bad baby. It's a baby who needs help. We can look at the world through different lenses.

Kathy helps Mei up to her feet and hands her over to her mother while she sets up the toy again. They all laugh as Mei starts dancing.

Let's try and put her back down again. A little bit closer.
Want to try again?
Kathy shakes the toy to make it jingle. Mei immediately turns her head to look at it while her mother holds her.

Figure 10.6. Mom puts Mei back on the blanket. Mei bends her knees, and reaches with her arms toward the toy. Video footage by Tim Chevrier, The Blend Media Group.

Want to try again?
What do you think? Do you think she wants to try again?
Some of the children say no. But for the second time, the little boy who was learning English pipes up, "He really wants to try again."
    Kathy repeated, *"You think she wants to try again?"*

Look. Look at her body reaching for it. Let's try and see what happens.
Does everyone remember when she was trying to roll over, how she kept
    trying?
"Remember when" is an important feature of executive function too—it is working memory. It's helping children develop the ability to hold and use information over short periods while dealing with new information. Kathy is asking the students to note the baby's development and think about her progress since she first came to class. It helps the children mine their experiences, informs how they think and feel, connecting cause and effect.
    Kathy is also pointing out Mei's persistence. Mei keeps trying because it is her temperament, but also because she feels safe and secure in her

attachment relationship with her mother. She can reach, she can risk, knowing her mom is there physically and psychologically.

Baby Mei goes right back at it. This time the toy is a little closer. But just as she comes within reach, she falls again, this time crashing her chin down on the blanket.

Mei is upset. She starts to cry. The children all fret.

This is a test of Mei's attachment to her mother. Her cortisol (stress hormone) has increased.[14]

Kathy offers to pick her up, and Mei turns to look for her mother. Her mother reaches out to her and rubs her head and her chin.

It's an instinctive reaction formed by a strong attachment relationship.

Her cortisol level lowers. Mei is immediately soothed and happy again. And . . . she's ready for another try.

This is another teachable moment for the children. Mei's mother is attuned to the baby's needs. She knows how to soothe her—with touch, with her voice. All the sensory stimulation from touch to sight to smell to hearing—all the loving interactions are helping the baby's brain grow. As the baby calms down, the children see self-regulation at work.[15]

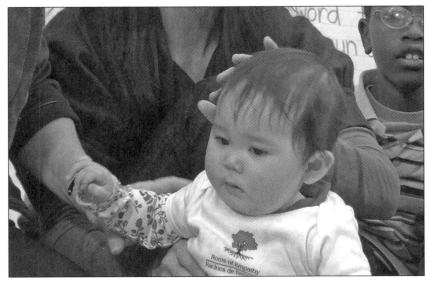

Figure 10.7. Mei falls again and immediately turns to her mother for comfort and reassurance. Video footage by Tim Chevrier, The Blend Media Group.

Children with secure attachment have a higher threshold for stress and can calm faster than children without it.

Emotional literacy is a key component of self-regulation. Recent research has shown that children who can self-regulate are more open to learning. Stressed children cannot learn.[16]

This moment in Mei's experience helps to reframe a huge problem in our society: that a crying baby is a bad baby. The students learn that a crying baby is a baby with a problem. We talk to them about shaken baby syndrome and other threats to the welfare of babies. The children remember them and take the messages home. In fact, they're our most effective public health advocates.

Children can reflect on Mei's experience and draft lessons about their own reactions to stressful situations, how they know they're stressed, what upsets them, and how they calm themselves. When children develop self-regulation, they're developing inner resilience.[17]

And resilience is one of the most important tools of life.

In our family visits, the children are experiencing multiple firing of neurons from different senses and the moments are being biologically embedded in their brains. It's a living example for the children of the saying "neurons that fire together, wire together." We're building the feelings of belonging. Of connection.

These crucial first years are when pathways are laid that determine how we will learn, regulate our emotions, respond to stress. And the research is now clear and replicated: how well those pathways are laid affects the well-being of the person not just through childhood but for life. The connection between the early years and disease in adulthood is now firmly established.[18]

If you want to know why Roots of Empathy works, Baby Mei shows you why. The children are unified in joy, unified in taking the perspective of the baby; their language is growing, their sense of self, and their sense of place in the whole. They're getting insights from Mei's frustration about their own temperaments. They're getting insights into how this little baby, whom they love, is failing.

Mei does not successfully get the toy. At least not in that visit. It is a "not yet" moment for her. It's important. We let children see that everyone develops uniquely—at their own pace. We've always said every baby has "not yet" moments. It's our way of saying to parents and teachers; sometimes you have to give the baby/the child/the adult a "not yet" break.

Mei has a stronger sense of self because of the attachment relationship. And this little baby, fueled by the power of that relationship knows in her mind and heart that she can try anything because her mother is just a step behind her. She can't walk, or talk, or even crawl, yet. But she is a high-powered machine for learning. And we can all learn from her.

So, in the end, Kathy moves the toy closer to Baby Mei. We want to challenge our children, but we want a reasonable challenge. It's unfair to expect that every child will be the same—it's unfair to expect universal outcomes for children when they are still developing at their own pace—at different and uneven levels. When it's a not yet . . . it's a not yet.

One of the things we did from the beginning of the program is to ask the classroom teacher to take photographs of their students around the green blanket. It served a couple of purposes. It helped record the program. But it also forced the teachers to literally focus on their students. Interestingly, they often focused on their most challenging students.

After the program, almost every teacher comments on how their view of their students changed. It gives them a positive experience to draw on and as they've reported to us, it's hard to catch the challenging students "being good."

Children wear their pain in their behavior. Challenging behavior should be met not with exclusion but with inclusion and understanding. A recent study out of Stanford University looked at whether a teacher's "empathic" response to misbehavior affected adolescent behavior. The study included almost seventeen hundred students and thirty-one teachers. Over one year the suspension rate dropped by 50 percent.[19]

Building connections between teachers and students is a positive step in building connection in society.

Imagine if teachers developed the capacity to understand their students' temperaments, to see their vulnerabilities, to see where they're coming from. Roots of Empathy gives teachers the chance to reflect on their students' temperaments, but also their own. Are they too sensitive? Do they respond intensely to certain things? Are they calm? It's good to know what they're sensitive about. It's good to know if they're very emotionally reactive, and it's good to know if they have difficulty down-regulating their reactions. They need to know how to handle themselves. They have to acknowledge themselves.

And it's nowhere in teacher preparation. Nowhere is there any sense of "Know Thyself." It's not the curriculum teachers bring to the children. It's themselves. A child starts first grade not with reading, writing, and math, but with her teacher. And how that teacher responds to that child is pretty much how that child will see herself.

I believe the classroom is a society. We build a community in that classroom. It's the second most influential community in a child's life. The ethic of care comes alive in that classroom, or not.

Emotions are a child's first language. Feeling and thinking are inextricably linked. Little children can't tease them apart. Our emotions direct our attention. If we're anxious, that's got our attention. We can't help it. Children can't regulate their emotions unless they know what they are. And when a child develops emotional literacy, academic literacy falls into place more readily. We try to open the whole child and help all the ingredients come together—understanding how to love well, how to label their feelings, understand who they are, how they learn, how others feel and think, find their voice, and how to stand up for themselves and for those who can't stand up for themselves.

If we've done that, we've helped them build their foundation: empathy.

So I encourage teachers to talk less and listen more, to start believing that every child has valuable experiences, every child has insights into her own capacity to learn, that every child has the ability to be empathic—even if she's pouring paint into the fish tank.

For students like Darren, for those who missed the boat early on, for those whose empathy was put at risk by a lack of steady, loving relationships, for all those children—can Roots of Empathy make a difference? I wanted to know. I knew the success and longevity of the program rested on being able to prove it.

Since 2000 we have had national and international evaluations of our program. We have randomized controlled trials. We have comparative studies. We have qualitative studies. We have quantitative studies. We have longitudinal studies. We have surveys of teachers and students from every year of the program.

And it all tells us that Roots of Empathy makes a difference.

Aggression and bullying go down. Interestingly, the decrease in bullying was a by-product of the program, not the intention. In some studies the measures were down as much as 88 percent and that was in the children who showed aggressive tendencies before the program.[20]

In control groups—the classrooms that didn't get the program—aggression and bullying increased over the school year.

Researchers have found an increase in prosocial behaviors (helping, caring, and including), an increase in social and emotional understanding, and an increased knowledge of responsive parenting.[21]

Our Scottish research found an interesting gender difference.[22] Boys, especially those who were the most vulnerable ("high deprivation") when the study started, improved their prosocial behavior more than the boys who were considered "low deprivation." Boys in the program also scored lower on anger management/aggression subscales. The boys in the control group increased their scores.

We also found in a study of our teacher reports conducted by the University of British Columbia that Roots of Empathy boys increased their prosocial behavior more than girls. However, there was no difference between girls and boys in the control group. This could suggest that Roots of Empathy has a greater impact on prosocial behaviors for boys. Although it is important to note that boys in this group initially reported lower levels of prosocial behaviors than girls and at posttest were still not at the same level as them. We haven't found gender differences in prosocial behavior in previous studies.[23]

Children had a better capacity to recognize emotions, and they showed a difference in their language around that. The children also had a greater understanding of infant development.[24]

One of the more unusual (but unpublished) studies was done with Steven Porges, of the University of North Carolina at Chapel Hill. He has done fascinating studies on how tone of voice itself, not words, communicates emotion.[25] He looks for variations of rhythm and pitch. If the person is using more variation in frequencies, the voice is more melodic and in a more positive emotional state. He conducted five-minute interviews with Roots of Empathy students and found a consistent pattern of greater prosody (which refers to intonation, stress pattern, loudness variations, pausing, and rhythm) in the students.

In 2011, Rob Santos published a randomized, accelerated longitudinal study with Roots of Empathy. The effects of the program on the children were evident three years after the program had finished.[26]

This finding was reinforced by researchers at Queen's University in Northern Ireland who recently finished a four-year randomized longitudinal study asking if the program was popular with teachers—did they want it? They also wanted to know if the program had high implementation fidelity and was cost-effective.[27]

The research showed that the program reduces what they called "disruptive behavior" both at school and at home—and the levels stayed down for the three years of the study. When the study started the children were eight years old. They're now twelve and the researchers will continue to follow these children for another three years to see if there is any impact on the rates of teenage pregnancy and school probation.

These researchers are looking at the program from a different perspective—they are considering the program as a national program to be implemented across Northern Ireland. So their focus is on whether it works, whether it will be implemented correctly, and if it will be cost-effective?

They've found it's very cost-effective.

The data told us and our funders what we needed to know from a scientific point of view. The children, teachers, and parents told us what they knew from the heart.

One boy who had been through Roots of Empathy in sixth grade had a sudden, lightning-bolt insight after one of the family visits. When he was an adult, he wrote us about it. He realized he was "nothing short of a bully. I was a straight up, pick-on-the-weaker-kids, bully."

He said he went home and cried the whole night. "That was a big turning point for me, . . . That night was an 'aha' moment."

He made a vow to himself—he would be kinder. And he lived up to it. He never said a word to the main victim of his bullying, "but I know my classmate in particular had a much better school experience from then on."

This boy is in a teachers college now. He wrote us about his childhood experience after a presentation from one of our Roots of Empathy team in his first-year teacher education class.

He said Roots of Empathy changed his life and that he didn't think he would be in the teacher program were it not for the program.

Empathy is simply the ability to understand how the other person feels, and to be able to feel with her. But it is the core of our humanity. It is essential to having peaceful, civil societies. And it is the base of all prosocial behavior.

We need to recognize the value of the upfront investment. It's so simple. If you're well loved, you learn to love well. And how a child surfaces from the earliest attachments has everything to do with her capacity to learn, her behavior, and her health. Nobel Laureate James Heckman won a Nobel Prize in economics for, among other things, developing methods to calculate the effects of labor and education programs. He has dedicated years to understanding the value of investing in early years programing for children. He calculated it at a $13 return for every $1 spent.[28] At the end of 2014 the President's Council of Economic Advisors looked at the return that would come from expanding early learning initiatives.[29] They calculated it at $8.60 for every $1. Half of that money comes from the increased earning potential of children as adults. They calculated an increase in incomes of 1.3 to 3.5 percent, which would more than pay the costs of implementing the programs.

Why isn't empathy considered an inoculation for a child's well-being? It makes economic sense. It makes cultural sense.

Supporting the development of empathy in children is one of our highest orders. It will build productive, playful children who know how to relate to one another and to the adults in their lives. It will build a base of citizenry responsible for one another.

It is essential that citizens know how to question. It is how we challenge injustice—it is how we protect human rights. Around the green blanket the children learn the art of questioning and receive support for their contributions—it can be an experience they take with them into their adult lives and help them shape the world they want to live in.

Since 1996, we have been telling children they are the "changers." They have the power to intervene, to stand up to injustice and cruelty, to protect, to change, to care. And that there is strength in kindness.

The children don't realize it, but in the Roots of Empathy class they are participating in a pluralistic society, a participatory democracy in a classroom, where every voice is equal. Where else do you ever find that—especially for children?

The quality of the education that we give our youngest citizens is a very good predictor of the developmental health and wealth of a nation.

We need to raise a generation of children who will have the capacity to see the other as themselves, to acknowledge our differences, but unite around our similarities. And our similarities are our feelings. They are the connective tissue of human kind. Empathy can be transformational to the child, the classroom, the school, the family, and the community. It *can* change the world, child by child.

Empathy cannot be taught. But, I promise you, it can be caught.

NOTES

1   Mary Gordon, *Roots of Empathy: Changing the World Child by Child* (New York: The Experiment, 2009).

2   Mario Mikulincer, Omri Gillath, Vered Halevy, Neta Avihou, Shelly Avidan, and Nitzan Eshkoli, "Attachment Theory and Reactions to Others' Needs: Evidence That Activation of the Sense of Attachment Security Promotes Empathic Responses," *Journal of Personality and Social Psychology* 81, no. 6 (December 2001): 1205–1224.

3   Vincent J. Felitti, Robert F. Anda, Dale Nordenberg, David F. Williamson, Alison M. Spitz, Valerie Edwards, Mary P. Koss, and James S. Marks, "Relationship of Childhood Abuse and Household Dysfunction to Many of the Leading Causes of Death in Adults: The Adverse Childhood Experiences (ACE) Study," *American Journal of Preventive Medicine* 14, no. 4 (1998): 245–258.

4   James J. Heckman, "The Economics of Inequality: The Value of Early Childhood Education," *American Educator* 35, no. 1 (2011): 31–35.

5   Bruce D. Perry, "Childhood Experience and the Expression of Genetic Potential: What Childhood Neglect Tells Us about Nature and Nurture," *Brain and Mind* 3, no. 1 (2002): 79–100.

6   Daniel N. Stern, *The First Relationship* (Cambridge, MA: Harvard University Press, 1977).

7   Allan N. Schore, "Attachment, Affect Regulation, and the Developing Right Brain: Linking Developmental Neuroscience to Paediatrics," *Pediatrics in Review* 26, no. 6 (2005): 204–217.

8   Center on the Developing Child, "InBrief: The Impact of Early Adversity on Child Development" (2007), www.developingchild.harvard.edu.

9   Center on the Developing Child, "The Foundations of Lifelong Health Are Built in Early Childhood" (2010), www.developingchild.harvard.edu.

10   Simon Baron-Cohen, "Precursors to a Theory of Mind: Understanding Attention in Others," in *Natural Theories of Mind: Evolution, Development and Simulation*

of Everyday Mindreading, ed. Andrew Whiten (Oxford: Basil Blackwell, 1991), 233–251.

11 Philip Zelazo, "Executive Function, Reflection, and Neuroplasticity: Implications for Promoting Empathy in Childhood" (presentation, Roots of Empathy Research Symposium Proceedings, 2014), www.rootsofempathy.org.

12 Alexander Thomas, *Temperament and Behavior Disorders in Children* (New York: New York University Press, 1968).

13 Sandra Graham McClowry, Eileen T. Rodriguez, and Robyn Koslowitz, "Temperament-Based Intervention: Re-examining Goodness of Fit," *International Journal of Developmental Science* 2, nos. 1–2 (2008): 120–135.

14 Jack P. Shonkoff, Andrew S. Garner, Benjamin S. Siegel, Mary I. Dobbins, Marian F. Earls, Laura McGuinn, John Pascoe, David L. Wood, Committee on Psychosocial Aspects of Child and Family Health, and Committee on Early Childhood, Adoption, and Dependent Care, "The Lifelong Effects of Early Childhood Adversity and Toxic Stress," *Pediatrics* 129, no. 1 (2012): e232–e246, doi:10.1542/peds.2011-2663.

15 Albert Bandura, "Social Cognitive Theory of Self-Regulation," *Organizational Behavior and Human Decision Processes* 50, no. 2 (1991): 248–287.

16 Shonkoff et al., "Lifelong Effects."

17 Allan N. Schore, *Affect Regulation and the Origin of Self: The Neurobiology of Emotional Development* (New York: Routledge, 2015).

18 Bernard Guyer, Sai Ma, Holly Grason, Kevin D. Frick, Deborah F. Perry, Alyssa Sharkey, and Jennifer McIntosh, "Early Childhood Health Promotion and Its Life-Course Health Consequences," *Academic Pediatrics* 9, no. 3 (2009): 142–149.

19 Jason A. Okonofua, David Paunesku, and Gregory M. Walton, "Brief Intervention to Encourage Empathic Discipline Cuts Suspension Rates in Half among Adolescents," *Proceedings of the National Academy of Sciences* 113, no. 19 (2016): 5221–5226.

20 Kimberly A. Schonert-Reichl, Veronica Smith, and Anat Zaidman-Zait, "Impact of the Roots of Empathy Program in Fostering the Social-Emotional Development of Primary Grade Children" (manuscript under review).

21 Kimberly A. Schonert-Reichl, Veronica Smith, Anat Zaidman-Zait, and Clyde Hertzman, "Promoting Children's Prosocial Behaviours in School: Impact of the Roots of Empathy Program on the Social and Emotional Competence of School-Aged Children," *School Mental Health* 4, no. 1 (2012): 1–12.

22 Alison MacDonald et al., "Evaluation of the Roots of Empathy Programme by North Lanarkshire Psychological Service" (North Lanarkshire Psychological Service Research, 2013).

23 Schonert-Reichl et al., "Promoting Children's Prosocial Behaviours in School."

24 MacDonald et al., "Evaluation of the Roots of Empathy Programme."

25 Adam Michael Stewart, Gregory F. Lewis, Keri J. Heilman, Maria I. Davila, Danielle D. Coleman, Stephanie A. Aylward, and Stephen W. Porges, "The Covariation

of Acoustic Features of Infant Cries and Autonomic State," *Psychology & Behavior* 120 (2013): 203–210.

26 Robert G. Santos, Mariette J. Chartier, Jeanne C. Whalen, Dan Chateau, and Leanne Boyd, "Effectiveness of School-Based Violence Prevention for Children and Youth: Cluster Randomized Field Trial of the Roots of Empathy Program with Replication and Three-Year Follow-Up," *Healthcare Quarterly* 14 (2011): 80–91.

27 Paul Connolly et al., "2011–2015: A Cluster Randomized Controlled Trial and Cost-Effectiveness Analysis of Roots of Empathy Program among 8–9 Year Olds in Northern Ireland" (manuscript under review).

28 Jorge Luis Garcia, James J. Heckman, Duncan Ermini Leaf, and María José Prados, "The Life-Cycle Benefits of an Influential Early Childhood Program" (Working Paper 22993, National Bureau of Economic Research, December 2016).

29 Council of Economic Advisers, "The Economics of Early Childhood Investments" (Executive Office of the President, 2014), www.obamawhitehouse.archives.gov.

11

The Listening Project

Fostering Curiosity and Connection in Middle Schools

NIOBE WAY AND JOSEPH D. NELSON

Middle schools in the United States exhibit some of the most egregious signs of a "crisis of connection." High rates of suspensions, detentions, stereotyping, bullying, and discrimination from peers and adults are typical, and have even become how American society characterizes the middle school years.[1] Students in middle schools are significantly more likely to be suspended for misconduct than high school students, and rates of bullying as well as physical and sexual assault peak during sixth through eighth grades.[2] A longitudinal study in New York City reveals that 55 percent of teachers who entered middle schools between 2002 and 2009 left these schools within three years.[3] The responses to this crisis have included blaming students for not being interested in learning, or having low levels of motivation and/or grit; parents for not valuing education or providing enough structure at home or being involved in school; and teachers for being ineffective, particularly at classroom management.[4] With its focus on changing individuals rather than contexts, educational reform has often overlooked the crisis of connection itself and thus, done little to address it.

As described in this volume, an emerging body of science provides vital insight into the roots of the crisis of connection, and underscores the importance of evidence-based efforts to address this crisis. Inclusive of a wide range of disciplines, the newly emerging science of human connection finds that humans are first and foremost social beings who need and want each other to thrive. Charles Darwin believed, in fact, that our social instincts were at the root of our survival as a species. Science has also underscored that we have extraordinary emotional and cognitive skills (e.g., empathy, curiosity) necessary for building relationships and community. Yet we live in a modern society that privileges the self over relationships, individual success over the common good, thinking over feeling, and asking and answering other people's questions rather than our own.[5] It is also a society that perpetuates dehumanizing stereotypes that divide humans into thinkers (e.g., Asian and White males) *or* feelers (e.g., females and people of color), but not thinkers *and* feelers.[6] What this means for middle school students and teachers is that while they want to be connected to each other, and have the skills to do so, they often find themselves in a context that discourages the very qualities that make it possible.[7] Similar to noted psychologist Jacquelynne Eccles's concept of *developmental mismatch*, there is often a mismatch between the needs of the people in middle schools and the culture of their schools.[8] It is this disconnect that lies at the root of the crisis of connection in middle schools and beyond.

When schools have focused on building more caring communities, learning and academic achievement have flourished.[9] The Harlem Children's Zone in New York City, and other "Promise Academies" in the United States, constitute remarkable examples of schools that have deliberately cultivated a caring climate in which building positive relationships across and among students, teachers, and parents, and challenging negative stereotypes, are critical parts of their efforts. Research has found that such caring schools effectively address the racial achievement gap.[10] Research has also found that in schools that explicitly nurture curiosity not only in academic topics but also in the people around them, students are more engaged and perform better than those in schools in which such qualities are not actively fostered.[11]

This chapter describes a project that we (Niobe Way and Joseph D. Nelson) have developed with middle school students at George Jackson Academy (GJA) and their English teacher, Ethan Podell, over the past three years. We sought explicitly to create a project that would be integrated into the language arts curriculum, and would address the crisis of connection evident in most middle schools. Rather than starting from the belief, evident in many middle schools, that education is about filling empty vessels (i.e., heads and/or brains) with information and then testing them to ascertain whether they have acquired or at least temporarily held knowledge or information deemed to be important by the teacher,[12] our project starts from a more expansive set of beliefs that education should nurture our human capacity to listen, learn, ask questions, explore, discover, and engage, not only between students and teachers, but also among students, teachers, and other adults.[13] The premise of our project is that education should aim to foster our human potential to thickly engage with, and ask and answer questions of, each other and the world, build strong communities, and contribute to it in meaningful ways. In order to achieve this goal, we have to move away from the empty vessel model and move toward the listen, ask and answer questions, learn, and engage model.

We know intuitively, as well as from decades of educational research, that we cannot educate through teaching to the test, disciplining students to foster compliance and conformity, and perpetuating divisive stereotypes that undermine individual growth and community building.[14] It is equally important to avoid blaming students, parents, or teachers for the problems that may plague their schools, as that also prevents thriving at the individual or community level. We also know that we *can* encourage listening, connection, exploration, curiosity, and engagement by valuing these qualities in the first place and embedding them into our academic curriculum. While such qualities and capacities have, at times, been downplayed in educational reform strategies, research suggests that they should, in fact, be key components.[15] Thus, the question becomes not who is to blame for the crisis of connection in middle schools, but how we can *effectively* nurture our human capacities to listen, ask and answer questions, and engage with each other to create more caring and connected, as well as more academically successful, middle schools.

As we have discovered in our research and partnerships in public and private schools, the first step in answering this question is to acknowledge, as we often do with teachers but not with students and their parents, how much students, teachers, and the parents of students can learn from one another. Teachers can teach students and each other about what they know about the topic that they teach, and the world, as well as about the joys of figuring out the answers to one's own questions or helping others answer their own questions. Teachers can teach students, parents, and other teachers about the importance of perspective taking and how it is linked to both individual and collective success. They can also partner with the parents of students to better nurture children's own curiosity and their social and emotional skills. Students can teach their teachers and their own parents the importance of listening to what they have to say even when it challenges mainstream ways of thinking and doing it. Students can also remind teachers and their parents of the critical questions that adults have yet to answer (e.g., "Why do we believe in things that we know are not true?") and what it means to have relationships that are grounded in genuine curiosity.[16] In addition, they can also answer questions that teachers and parents have about them and the larger world.[17] Parents of students can teach teachers what strategies of engagement work best for their children and how to support their children. They can also teach teachers about the worlds that they live in, which are often different from those of the teachers. Once students, teachers, and parents remember that they have much to learn from each other, they begin to see themselves in the other, recognize their common humanity, and question the stereotypes that led them to disconnect from each other in the first place. By focusing on what we can learn from each other, we implicitly and explicitly address the harmful stereotypes that get in the way of our ability to build healthy relationships and communities.

The science of human connection consistently reveals that it is our stereotypes of each other, and our lack of curiosity in each other, that lead us to believe that we have nothing to learn from one another.[18] According to research, stereotypes of children and adolescents across race, gender, class, sexuality, and religious identification are often not reflective of who they are or what they want and need to thrive.[19] These stereotypes lead schools to treat children as if their identities can be separated from their relationships, their minds from their hearts and bodies, and their learning from their contexts, cultures, and communities. When we see children and adolescents only through a stereotypic lens, and fail to ask real questions, we do not see the possibilities of learning *from* them and thus lose sight of their full humanity.

Our Listening Project approach entails training teachers and students in a method that we refer to as "transformative interviewing," in which students learn how to listen to each other and ask questions that reveal their capacities to think and feel and express what is most meaningful to them. As part of the training, students interview each other as well as their teachers and family members. They are asked to generate their own questions for their interview protocol. They are also asked to focus on one particular person, "whom they love but would like to know more about," and write a short biographical essay based on their multiple interviews with the person. Finally, the students present their biographies in public venues and/or spaces so that they share what they learned about another person when they followed their own curiosity in their transformative interviews.

Informed by the social science method of semi-structured interviewing and drawing explicitly from the science of human connection, transformative interviewing aims to disrupt stereotypes by fostering curiosity and connection.[20] Once we begin asking and answering questions with each other, stereotypes are exposed as false and connections are enhanced. Transformative interviewing asks the interviewer (e.g., the student) to start from the place that all human beings think and feel—regardless of gender, race, social class, and other social categories—and thus the task is to understand those thoughts and feelings and ways of seeing the world curated by the curiosity of the interviewer.

Listening in transformative interviewing is not a passive process but a responsive one in which the interviewer asks open-ended questions, offering a way into the hearts and minds of the interviewees rather than simply confirming what the interviewer assumes to be true of the interviewee. Instead of asking close-ended questions such as "Are you close to that friend?" open-ended questions and prompts are employed: "How would you describe your friendship?" "What do you like about him or her and why?" "Tell me about a time in which you trusted him." The aim here is not to simply gather information, but to understand how the interviewee experiences the world. The interviewer asks "thick" questions—rooted in Geertz's distinction between "thick" and "thin" interpretations[21]—that get at the nuances and details of an experience rather than a surface-level report of an experience. By focusing on open-ended questions and asking for stories, the interviewer begins to see the interviewee as more than simply a sum of stereotyped parts. They see themselves in the interviewees and thus experience a sense of shared humanity.[22] As a result of being closely listened to, interviewees are also transformed in this process as they begin to see themselves and the interviewer in new ways. The overarching goal of transformative interviewing is to tap into our natural capacity to listen, ask and answer questions, explore, understand, respond, and engage with each other so that we see beyond our gender, racial, and class stereotypes, and find the relationships and the community that we want and need to thrive in and out of school.

Our method of transformative interviewing initially grew out of learning about The Listening Guide—a relational method of analysis with narrative data created by the Harvard Project on Girls and Women.[23] We brought the method into our teaching of interviewing skills with doctoral students at New York University. Niobe Way has taught this doctoral class over the past two decades, and Joseph D. Nelson has taught it over the past five years. Teaching together for four years, we developed a technique of conducting semi-structured interviews that focuses on learning something new about one's own questions rather than simply testing hypotheses or gathering information. As a result of our method of interviewing, our doctoral students have reported that they see themselves and each other with more openness, empathy, and understanding. They also report being "better listeners" and "better thinkers" as they have learned to listen more closely to themselves (e.g., their own questions) and to each other. They also report being more aware of their own stereotypes and assumptions about themselves and others, and using their feelings to think more sharply and rigorously about the meaning of words and actions. As teachers, we have also seen through narrative essay writing that students' perspective taking and analytic skills improve from the beginning to the end of class, as does their ability to see themselves in others.

Following our experience teaching the interview method course together, we took our approach to a middle school for boys on the Lower East Side of New York City. Over the past four years, we have developed our transformative interviewing techniques with the seventh graders and their teacher. The boys have interviewed peers, teachers, and family members, produced biographical essays from their interviews, and presented these essays to their peers in school and at a conference held at New York University. Boys at the school reported an extraordinary transformation in how they see themselves and those around them. They disclosed, for example, feeling more connected to peers, teachers, and family members and becoming more interested in relationships and feelings. In addition, they described feeling more confident about how to make and maintain friendships as well as how to connect to others. Finally, they reported that their biographies and the public speaking events made them more confident in their writing and oral communication skills. Their English teacher also detailed to us that the Listening Project was highly effective in making a forceful life-to-literature connection. By focusing students' attention on the authentic, often vulnerable moments in the interviewee's life, the students are relearning from a different perspective what character and conflict mean and why these are such important elements of first-rate literature. Students, the teacher noted, often ask why they should read literature: "How is this book, and the story in it, going to be useful to me in life?" The Listening Project, according to the teacher, "is a compelling answer to this utilitarian question, as it subtly dismantles the wall that prevents some from seeing the strong, 'thick' connection between understanding literature and leading a rich and thoughtful life."

As a result of a generous grant from the Spencer Foundation, we have recently expanded our listening project to eight middle schools in New York City in order to more systematically assess its impact on students and teachers. Preliminary results from two additional middle schools suggest it has a transformative effect not only on students and teachers but also on others in the school and on those who are interviewed outside of the school. Participants (e.g., students, teachers, parents, principals, school staff) report that their relationships with their interviewers and interviewees have deepened and that they have begun to see themselves and others as having qualities of which they were unaware. In other words, stereotypes have been disrupted and relationships have been strengthened.

By sharing our experiences and approach in this chapter, we hope to inspire teachers and others who work with middle schools students and teachers to create their own versions of the Listening Project to nourish their natural curiosity and their capacity and desire to build stronger relationships and more inclusive and connected school communities.

The Listening Project at George Jackson Academy

We chose George Jackson Academy, an independent private school serving middle- and low-income boys in fourth through eighth grades, because it was already nourishing boys' curiosity and connection through various school-based initiatives. Thus it was an ideal school context in which to pilot our transformative interviewing strategies as part of our Listening Project.[24] We (Niobe Way and Joseph D. Nelson) partnered with the English teacher to develop and administer a fourteen-session training program with approximately thirty-five seventh graders each year. The training also involved two to three NYU students each year who had already been trained in the method. Founded in 2003, the school's stated mission centers on "helping boys recognize their abundant gifts within a learning environment designed to cultivate the widest sense of possibility in boys' lives."[25] Through its policies, practices, and traditions (e.g., advisory program, peer-to-peer mentoring, "gifted and talented" academics, and seventh and eighth grade retreats), the school embraces a fundamental commitment to providing boys with a rich intellectual life, infused with joy, gratitude, and love, where boys are instilled with a pride in who they are and a sense of brotherhood, and are encouraged to become community leaders. The institution's approach to educating boys is decidedly asset-based, or focused on promoting the strengths of the students, which makes it an ideal context for our project centered on transformative interviewing.

There are approximately one hundred and thirty boys enrolled, with twenty to thirty-six students per grade (i.e., two classes per grade). The overall student population is predominantly boys of color: Black (85 percent), Latino (10 percent), Asian (2 percent), Multicultural (e.g., Biracial; 2 percent), and White (1 percent), and 51 percent of boys are first-generation immigrants. The New York City boroughs of residence for boys are the Bronx (64 percent), Manhattan (17 percent), Brooklyn (10 percent), and Queens (9 percent). While the values of brotherhood, care, support, and respect make up the core values of GJA's learning community, boys in the school struggle at times with seeing themselves outside of racial and gender stereotypes.[26] Thus the Listening Project was welcomed by the school administration.

Transformative Interviewing in Fourteen Sessions

Within this school context, we (Niobe, Joseph, and Ethan) trained seventh grade boys in transformative interviewing, over fourteen sessions across four years, with four cohorts of seventh graders. Here, we describe session goals and guiding questions, and offer descriptions of each session with instructional strategies employed. The goal here is not to provide specific lesson plans but to offer ideas that can be adapted to meet the needs of a specific classroom or school environment.

Sessions 1 to 4: Learning about Interviewing

During the first two training sessions, we raise the following questions with the students: "Why conduct interviews?" "What could one learn from an interview?" We ask them to respond to our questions using their intuition and guide them with our follow-up questions (e.g., "Why do you think that is true?"). For example, we give the students the definition of semi-structured interviews and ask them to tell us why they think a semi-structured interview might be better than a structured interview for getting one's questions answered and understanding the interviewee's experiences.[27] With each question, we make sure to get at the students' views first before answering our own questions. We also discuss with the students how to create an environment in which their interviewees will openly share their experiences. From the very start of the training, the trainers are encouraging students to activate their natural curiosity and empathy as well as their capacity to ask and answer their own questions.

During the first and second sessions, the students collectively begin to use such skills by interviewing a trainer (e.g., someone unknown to them) or their teacher (e.g., someone known to them), both with the assistance of a trainer who is not being interviewed. These interviews are deliberate efforts to model engaged curiosity by an interviewer (e.g., asking for stories, examples, and other follow-up questions) and open and honest responses by an interviewee. The trainer or teacher being interviewed has been primed to be as forthright and open as possible so that the students can understand what type of responses they are seeking from their interviewees and the questions that will likely elicit such open responses (e.g., "Tell me a story about . . ."). While being interviewed by the students, the trainer guiding them in these interviews encourages the students to ask questions that allow for stories of both challenges and happiness in their lives. Telling stories only of challenges *or* happiness provides too limited an understanding of the interviewees' experiences. This component of the training is a conscious effort by the trainers to challenge stereotypes that pathologize groups of people (based on race, class, immigrant status, etc.) by suggesting that they have only suffered in life rather than also experienced joy.[28] Having the interviewees describe a wide range of experiences with the entire class encourages the students to seek such breadth in their own independent interviews.

The trainers make explicit to the students during the practice interviewing process that the goal is to get "gold nuggets" that reflect who the interviewees are and how they see the world. Gold nuggets are defined as stories that reveal emotional complexity, depth, and vivid detail so that the interviewer can visualize the experience. They also entail self-reflection and vulnerability by the interviewees and thus foster empathy for them. A story of being a bully, for example, would be a gold nugget only if the interviewees reflected on the reasons for their actions and what they learned from it about themselves. Such nuggets are distinguished from bronze or silver nuggets that may have potential for gold but don't have much detail, repeat stereotypes or clichés, or are generalized responses that don't give a sense of what the interviewee thought and felt in that particular moment. For example, if an interviewee reports that his or her mother died, that information by itself would only be a potential gold nugget. It would not become a gold nugget, however, until the interviewee describes the impact and meaning of the loss of his or her mother to the interviewer. The student trainees in the classroom often enjoy this process of trying to get the gold in their interviewees. They begin, after the first classroom-based practice interview, to offer tips to each other on how to ask questions that allow for people to express gold nugget stories.

When the students asked Joseph, for example, in a training session about a "challenging" and a "favorite" childhood memory, he first told them the story of feeling lonely and isolated as a child because he wore "thick glasses" that prevented him from playing with his older brother and friends in his neighborhood growing up. As a result of the students' repeated questions, Joseph provided much vivid detail to the story so they and the adults in the room could visualize his story. Answering their second question about a favorite childhood memory, Joseph then told a joyful story of the strong relationships he developed with the other boys of color at a predominantly White high school he attended in his hometown in the Midwest. As part of his story, Joseph described his feelings of social anxiety in such a context and the relief provided by the other boys of color in his school. When the boys of color in the classroom heard such stories, they learned not only about the effectiveness of their own questions but also something meaningful about another person that had resonance to their own self-understanding. These practice interviews not only help the students with their listening skills, but also model the ways in which open-ended questions and the expression of vulnerability lead to greater understanding of oneself and others. When Ethan, the teacher, was asked by one of the students about a meaningful childhood memory and responded by describing being bullied, one of the students said: "I understand you; I see where you are coming from. I've been there." In response to a question about friendships, Niobe revealed in her interview feeling insecure with her friends; a boy in the classroom piped up and said, "Me too!" These moments in the classroom underscore a common humanity between and among the students, teacher, and trainers and are a critical part of the training of transformative interviewing.

In the third and fourth sessions, students are asked to pick two people in the school with whom to conduct their own independent interviews to practice their interviewing skills. Specifically, they are asked to pick someone they don't know very well in the school and someone they know pretty well but would like to know more about. The objective of these interviews is to help the students not only practice their skills but also use their curiosity about other people in the school to connect more deeply with them and thus feel more connected to school. The adults who get interviewed as part of these practice interviews are happy for the chance to share their stories with the students. The students also report enjoying this process that is often the first time they have been in this position of directing the topic of an interview, and they report feeling a newfound sense of independence and confidence.

Following each of these practice interviews, the students discuss in class how their first interviews went and get feedback from the trainer, the teacher, and the other students. The feedback is focused on their notes from the practice interviews and discussing whether they got gold nuggets. The students typically come back to the classroom feeling like they didn't do as good a job as they had hoped, and are eager to try again. Students also report genuinely liking this part of the training as they get to ask their own questions of people whom they never had a chance to talk to but have an interest in learning more about.

In these first sessions, a reciprocal process of learning is occurring, where the trainers and teacher are teaching and learning from the students, and the students are learning and teaching the trainers and the teachers about what they know about how to get their own questions answered, and understand another person's experience.

Sessions 5 to 9: Preparing for the Interview

The fifth and sixth training sessions are devoted to helping the students select whom they want to interview for their biographical essay and to develop their interview protocols—the actual list of questions that students will ask during their interview. The process of selecting their interviewees for their biographical essay is carefully considered, where the students are asked to interview a person with whom they have a close relationship, but whose life story is at least partially unfamiliar to them. Most students choose family members such as "my mom," "my grandma," "my cousin," "my dad," or "my uncle," but others choose teachers or administrators in the school building. The students are asked to focus on questions that might promote deep reflection by the interviewees about the significant events and experiences in their lives. The trainers and teacher also discuss at length the kinds of questions that may limit the possibilities of responses. For example, close-ended questions such as yes/no questions (e.g., "Are you close with your best friend?") provide a more limited type of response than open-ended questions or prompts (e.g., "Tell me about your friendship with your best friend." or "What do you like about your friendship and why?"). The different types of responses one may get when asking an open-ended versus a close-ended question are discussed by the trainers. The students generate their own list of open-ended questions they have for their interviewees and give each other feedback, assessing the usefulness of different questions in light of the focus of their interview. The students are encouraged to focus on areas of interest for them, such as childhood memories, fears and desires, immigration experiences, and friendships and romantic relationships, so that the focus can be on depth rather than breadth. They are told to try to get at least two gold nuggets in their interviews.

While students may generate fairly superficial questions initially ("What is your favorite food?"), by the end of these sessions focused on their interview protocol they are generating deeper and more meaningful questions (e.g., "Why did you break up with that friend?"). Students are encouraged to ask for detailed stories from their interviewees so that they can understand more fully the meaning of the story for the interviewee himself or herself. They are also encouraged to ask questions that will allow them to learn something that they didn't know before from their interviewee and not just focus on stories that they already know as confirming stereotypes or expectations. Middle school students possess a remarkable ability to follow their curiosity and ask questions that foster self-reflection on the part of the interviewee. The overarching goal of these sessions is to make sure the students focus on a set of questions that they are interested in and that allows them to come to know their interviewees on a deeper level.

The seventh, eighth, and ninth sessions are focused on processing the students' interviews with their selected interviewees that have been conducted outside of class time, tape-recorded, and transcribed verbatim by the student interviewer. With each interview they conduct, they receive extensive feedback from each other and from the trainer or teacher by sitting in small groups of three or four students with one trainer or teacher and listening to each other's interviews on their phone or tape recorder (we provide tape recorders for those who don't have smart phones). The purpose of these feedback groups is to find out if there is information that they missed in the first and second rounds of their interviews that is necessary for them to have gold nuggets to include in their biographical essays. Usually missing from these initial interviews are details about the event or experience that allow the interviewer to visualize what the interviewees are saying and self-reflective comments by the interviewees that reveal why this memory or story is important to them. Rather than simply, for example, knowing that the interviewee immigrated to the United States from the Dominican Republic, students get details about how she immigrated, whom she was with, what her experience was leaving home, what it was like when she first arrived, how she found work, and other questions that allow the reader to understand the interviewee's experience. Students conduct their second and third interviews with their primary interviewees using the feedback from these small groups. This process of repeated interviews and feedback after each interview fosters the students' perspective taking, critical thinking, and curiosity, as well as their empathy and understanding.

Sessions 10 to 14: Biographical Essays and Public Presentations

The remaining sessions are dedicated to helping students review their transcripts of their interviewee to identify gold nugget stories to include in their biographical essay. During these sessions, the students have lively discussions with their classmates about what does and does not constitute a golden nugget in their interviews. Following the identification of such gold stories, the students focus on writing and rewriting their essay outside of class and getting detailed feedback on the quality of their writing from their peers, the trainers, and the teacher during class. They read the drafts of their essays aloud during class, and their classmates and teacher provide feedback on the quality of their thinking and writing. This component of the training is similar to a typical English class where they are being taught the skills of high-quality writing. It is in response, however, to the stories that they have collected from a person whom they know and wanted to know better.

In the final session, the students formally present their essays to the class and provide each other with feedback on the final product. Putting the students in the position of giving each other feedback, in large and small groups, not only allows them to learn the skills of interviewing and writing and presenting their essays, but also enhances their listening capacities. At George Jackson Academy, samples of these essays have been published in the school's literary magazine and presented at a youth conference at New York University.[29]

The transformative interviewing achieves its goal of nurturing curiosity, empathy, trust, perspective taking, and critical thinking skills by teaching the students how to listen closely and ask meaningful questions. The goal is to gain insight into another person and see her or him outside of the constraints of a stereotype. The students and teachers who have participated in our Listening Project report learning new things about themselves and each other that enhance their sense of connection to those in and outside of school.

The Listening Project in Middle Schools

Transformative interviewing is a democratic approach informed by methods of emancipatory inquiry that encourage both the listener (interviewer) and the speaker (interviewee) to transcend traditional divides in order to listen and connect from a place of openness and curiosity.[30] The direct engagement with each other, the disruption of stereotypes, and the recognition of both similarities and differences between interviewer and interviewee foster the necessary humility, empathy, curiosity, and mutual understanding that are critical for building trusting and supportive communities and for learning.[31] Training students and teachers in the skills of transformative interviewing disrupts the dehumanization and stereotypes that lie at the root of the crisis of connection and fosters the types of community that we want for our children, for our students, and for ourselves.

The Listening Project reimagines both students and teachers in middle schools as humans who can contribute in significant ways to our understanding of the world. It also reimagines middle schools and education more generally. Rather than being a place simply of test taking and disciplinary action, it creates a place of active curiosity, exploration, understanding, and connection—a place in which students and adults are better equipped to build supportive communities and make the world a better place. Noted educators Michael Dumas and Joseph D. Nelson call for a *reimagining of Black boyhood*:

> Schools, community centers, neighborhoods, and families [become] places that are less concerned with, for instance, the discipline and control of Black male bodies, and more concerned with being places where Black boys can giggle, play, cry, pout, and be just as silly and frivolous as other children without these activities being perceived as an impediment to their educational attainment or a threat to the well-being of others.[32]

Their vision is equally applicable to all students who suffer the consequences of living in a culture and a context that blames them, their parents, and their teachers for their woes and tells them to fix them without recognizing the impossibility of doing so in a context that doesn't recognize their shared humanity. Yet the implication of the call for a reimagining is more than simply about children, their parents, or their teachers. It is reimagining what we are doing as educators and what we should be doing to promote a more just and humane world. Our project asks us to start from a new place in our discussions of educational reform by moving away from an individually focused solution to one that focuses on the context and the human capacity to reach across the divides in a way that nourishes the souls of our students as well as ourselves.

Training students and teachers in the method of transformative interviewing, in particular, addresses the crisis of connection by reframing teaching and learning as a process of elucidating and enhancing our drive to listen, connect, know, and learn. The premise is that active listening and engagement around questions that underscore and evoke our common humanity are themselves an intervention that positively transforms individuals, relationships, and schools. With the Listening Project, we aim to create a paradigm shift in education, transferring the focus from interventions that supposedly address individual behaviors and learning deficits to curiosity and relationship building. And from disparities, bullying, and discrimination to a focus on listening, exploration, discovery, and, of course, connection across "difference" in America. This shift bridges cognitive, social, and emotional capacities and needs; it enables us to make an impact on educational transactions by transforming the context in which they take place. The newly emerging science of human connection points to our common need for caring communities and to the integration of our cognitive, social, and emotional capacities and needs: teachers and students are more motivated, successful, and fulfilled when they feel listened to, when their natural curiosity about each other and their desires to learn are nourished, and when they are connected to each other and to their communities.[33] The Listening Project applies what we have learned from the science of human connection to transform our goals during the middle school years so that we underscore and nourish our common humanity, and thus foster our individual and collective potential to help make the world a more just and humane place.

Appendix: Biographical Essays

The Story of My Mother

My mother was born in Harlem of New York City in 1966. She went to Pre-K at the age of five at Public School Thirty-Six on 123rd Street and Amsterdam Avenue. She was shy and didn't say much when she was young which meant that she didn't have many friends. "I just didn't know how to talk to people. I was afraid to say the wrong thing to people." Yet in September about two weeks after the first day of 1st grade, a girl approached her and they made small talk. The girl's name was Brenda. My mom liked how Brenda was "simple in personality" and someone that she could trust with things such as gossip or secrets. Their relationship continued to grow throughout their school years. They ended up going to the same middle school, the Ascension School, and talked on the phone and played games such as jacks as they lived on the same street and could easily go to each other's houses. My mother and Brenda still live on the same street and Brenda is my godmother.

My mother grew up in a three-person household that included her mother, her father, and her sister, who is three years older than her. The relationship with her sister was not always as loving as it is now. They used to fight over silly things such as the possession of candy or whose bed someone was going to sleep on. After years of tormenting each other, they learned to protect each other as they started to understand that the fighting was taking a toll on them physically and they were really tired of it. My mother said:

> It took time for the fighting to diminish and the healing process to occur. We started giving each other time to let our emotions out and hear each other out if we were angry. Counting to ten also helped. We were getting into a lot of trouble with our parents and they were telling us to stop. So we took the time to look at each other as human beings with emotions instead of as annoying pests. When we took this new approach during the end of middle school and the transition to high school, we learned new things about each other, like what our favorite thing to do on the weekend was or what books we enjoyed, and we slowly began to heal.

They became quite close to each other and remain close to this day. My mom's experience with her sister affects the way she parents her children. When she sees her children (my brother and me) fighting it reminds her of her relationship with her sister. She knows that in the future her children will need each other and thus she wants them to build a close relationship now: "I see it now, you and your brother were just like my sister and I growing up when we fought. You will need each other one day."

My mother knows all about the extent to which sisters and brothers need each other because recently her sister got liver cancer at the age of 50 and she is spending her time now taking care of her. She was terrified when she heard the news about her sister because their own mother, my grandmother, had died from breast cancer at the age of fifty-two: "The reason why I stress so much about my sister is because it scares me that the situation is playing out in the same way it did for our mother." My mother's sister helps her every day with cleaning her apartment, getting her medicine, or preparing the food that she is allowed to eat. In addition, on every other Saturday, she helps her sister go regularly to appointments at the hospital on 101st Street and Fifth Avenue. She is relieved that her sister is strong and is actively fighting cancer and surviving.

In addition to her sister, my mother also had a supportive relationship with her own mother before she died. Her mother was an English and Theater major at Hunter College in the early and mid 1950s. She said:

Whether it was with my homework or with dating advice, my mother was always there to help me whenever I needed it most. . . . I would ask if I did the right thing in that situation. For example, when I was seventeen and I had just finished my shift at Woolworths on 116th street and Broadway, a twenty-five-year-old man approached and asked me for my phone number. I declined his request and asked for his phone number because I never liked giving my phone number to people. It felt that a person who had my phone number knew something about me and that seemed weird to me. It turned out that he didn't have a phone and I knew that I didn't want to get involved with him, so I left the scene. When I got home, I talked to my mother about this situation and she said that I made the right move and what twenty-five-year-old doesn't have a phone at such a low price as they were back then. I became less naive as a result of this experience and I realized how valuable my mother's lessons were to me.

Only five years later, however, when my mom was only twenty-two years old in her sophomore year of college at Baruch College studying law, her mother died from breast cancer. Her mother's death was devastating as she lost an open and loving relationship: "My mom had cancer for about a year before she died and it ate me up inside to know that she was suffering. The rest of my family was struggling as well. We supported each other throughout, however, as we saw that each of us was struggling to keep our emotions intact." My mother was depressed for about a year after her own mother's death. It even affected her thoughts about having children: "For a long time I didn't want children because I was fearful of dying and my children feeling that loss of love and support. When you were a baby, I always wanted you to get close to your father so if I died you would have someone."

While she is still fearful of dying, my mother is now happy she had children and spends a lot of time with her children, or me and my brother, and "appreciates and loves [us] with all [her] heart."

Inside Out

My mother was born on July 14, 1978 in Venezuela. Her dad was a farmer and her mom was a nurse and there were six children in the household.

She is currently married, has two children, and is working as a maid throughout the five boroughs. She had a hard time growing up because in her country the military patrolled the streets.

Her family was not poor, but they couldn't buy many things. One time, her father wanted to buy a doll for each of his five daughters, but my mother knew that he couldn't afford it. She told him, "no, give it to the youngest first and then I can wait." Her father was impressed: "I am very proud of you. It is very hard for a nine-year-old to make such a mature decision, since most young children are always complaining about wanting more toys, but you were an exception." When her father said that to her, my mother felt very happy since, coming from such a big family, she was rarely recognized individually. My mother remembers feeling unstoppable and that nothing could bring her down. To this day, she has the same doll that she eventually received from her father and can still remember exactly what her father said to her when she was nine.

Not long after the doll incident, my mother was bitten by a rattlesnake and had to stay in the hospital for three days. When it happened, it was morning and she was in the backyard which were often "mini jungles" in Venezuela. The rattlesnake came out of the jungle and was hissing when she turned around and was bitten. She yelled so loud you could hear it from the moon. No one came. She thought she was going to die because of the poison she assumed was in its fangs. Eventually, her parents came running into the backyard and scared it away. To this day she is scared of snakes: "It sends shivers down my spine every time I think of snakes."

When my mother was 15 years old, another incident occurred that would affect her the rest of her life. It was a day in which the ground, sky, and sun were at peace with one another. It was a day like any other day. Nothing seemed wrong until my grandfather crashed into a huge truck and broke his vertebrae. Now without the ability to turn his head, life became very difficult for him. It also became difficult for my mother who could no longer go places with him or play with him. Her father was in a hospital for year and then in physical therapy for six months using a wheelchair for two or three months. He finally used a cane to walk. My mom was very sad about her father and said, "I felt as if at that moment [when the accident occurred] I could not continue on with my life. But then I realized I must do as much as possible to make sure that he is taken care of and well nourished." It was at that point in time that she decided to go to America to make money and send it home so she could help out financially.

Her father and her mom agreed that she could go to the U.S., but told her that she had to come back as soon as possible. When she finally arrived in America, she immediately received a grave message from her parents. Her grandfather on her mother's side had died. My mother cried for "what seemed like forever." She was crying mostly for her mom as she knew how important he was to her. It took her about ten years before she could return to Venezuela. Now my mother visits them in Venezuela more often and has never stopped loving them.

When she first arrived in America, my mom went to look for a job. Since she could not speak English very well, it was hard to find one. She finally found one as a waitress in a restaurant. When she was at the end of her shift one day and everyone else had left, the cops showed up and arrested her because there were illegal casino machines in the restaurant. She happened to be in the wrong place at the wrong time. Going to jail in her first year in America made her feel "like killing myself with all this negativity in my life." But when she had children, they made her feel recognized and happy again so she brushed away the dark memories.

My mother is currently living in Queens with her two children and a husband. She remembers these memories the most because they are the ones that touched her emotionally inside and physically outside. That is why my biography of my mother is called inside out.

NOTES

1 National Center for Education Statistics, "Nation's Report Card" (2015), www.nces.ed.gov; Center for American Progress, "2016 Report" (2016), www.americanprogress.org; Diane Ravitch, *The Death and Life of the Great American School System: How Testing and Choice Are Undermining Education* (New York: Basic Books, 2010); Heinz-Dieter Meyer and Brian Rowan, eds., *The New Institutionalism in Education* (Albany: State University of New York Press, 2012).

2 John C. Liu, "The Suspension Spike: Changing the Discipline Culture in NYC's Middle Schools" (New York City Comptroller's Office, 2013), 1–65; Michael J. Kieffer, William H. Marinell, and Nicky S. Stephenson, "The Middle Grades Student Transitions Study" (Research Alliance for New York City

Schools, 2011), www.steinhardt.nyu.edu; "Children's Exposure to Violence" (Child Trends, 2016), www.childtrends.org; "Bullying" (Child Trends, 2016), www.childtrends.org.

3 William H. Marinell, "The Middle School Teacher Turnover Project: A Descriptive Analysis of Teacher Turnover in New York City's Middle Schools" (Research Alliance for New York City Schools, 2011), www.steinhardt.nyu.edu.

4 Arrastia, this volume; Jean Anyon, *Ghetto Schooling: A Political Economy of Urban Educational Reform* (New York: Teachers College Press, 1997); Angela Duckworth, *Grit: The Power of Passion and Perseverance* (New York: Simon & Schuster, 2016); Pedro Noguera, *City Schools and the American Dream: Reclaiming the Promise of Public Education* (New York: Teachers College Press, 2003); Noguera, this volume; Michael J. Nakkula and Eric Toshalis, *Understanding Youth: Adolescent Development for Educators* (Cambridge, MA: Harvard Education Press, 2010); Michael Sadowski, *Adolescents at School: Perspectives on Identity, Youth, and Education* (Cambridge, MA: Harvard Education Press, 2008); Kevin Kumashiro, *Bad Teacher! How Blaming Teachers Distorts the Bigger Picture* (New York: Teachers College Press, 2012).

5 David Brooks, *The Social Animal: The Hidden Sources of Love, Character, and Achievement* (New York: Random House, 2012); Sarah Blaffer Hrdy, *Mothers and Others: The Evolutionary Origins of Mutual Understanding* (Cambridge, MA: Harvard University Press, 2009); Carol Gilligan, *In a Different Voice: Psychological Theory and Women's Development* (Cambridge, MA: Harvard University Press, 1982); Noguera, this volume.

6 Niobe Way and Leoandra Rogers, "Resistance to Dehumanization during Childhood and Adolescence: A Developmental and Contextual Process," in *New Perspectives on Human Development*, ed. Nancy Budwig, Elliot Turiel, and Philip David Zelazo (Cambridge: Cambridge University Press, 2017), 209–228.

7 Noguera, this volume; Arrastia, this volume; Leoandra Onnie Rogers and Niobe Way, "Stereotypes as a Context for the Social and Emotional Development of Marginalized Youth" (invited manuscript for *American Psychologist*, under review).

8 Jacquelynne S. Eccles, Carol Midgley, Allan Wigfield, Christy Miller Buchanan, David Reuman, Constance Flanagan, and Douglas Mac Iver, "Development during Adolescence: The Impact of Stage-Environment Fit on Young Adolescents' Experiences in Schools and in Families," *American Psychologist* 48, no. 2 (1993): 90–101.

9 Anthony Bryk and Barbara Schneider, *Trust in Schools: A Core Resource for Improvement* (New York: Russell Sage Foundation, 2002); Lyndal Bond, Helen Butler, Lyndal Thomas, John Carlin, Sara Glover, Glenn Bowes, and George Patton, "Social and School Connectedness in Early Secondary School as Predictors of Late Teenage Substance Use, Mental Health, and Academic Outcomes," *Journal of Adolescent Health* 40, no. 4 (2007): 357e9–357e18; Julie M. Bower and Annemaree Carroll, "Benefits of Getting Hooked on Sports or the Arts: Examining the Connectedness of Youth Who Participate in Sport and Creative

Arts Activities," *International Journal of Child and Adolescent Health* 8, no. 2 (2015): 169–178; Bridget K. Hamre and Robert C. Pianta, "Early Teacher–Child Relationships and the Trajectory of Children's School Outcomes through Eighth Grade," *Child Development* 72, no. 2 (2001): 625–638; Bridget K. Hamre, Robert C. Pianta, Jason T. Downer, Jamie DeCoster, Andrew J. Mashburn, Stephanie M. Jones, Joshua L. Brown, et al., "Teaching through Interactions: Testing a Developmental Framework of Teacher Effectiveness in over 4,000 Classrooms," *The Elementary School Journal* 113, no. 4 (2013): 461–487; Nel Noddings, "Care, Justice, and Equity," in *Justice and Caring: The Search for Common Ground in Education*, ed. Michael S. Katz, Nel Noddings, and Kenneth A. Strike (New York: Teachers College Press, 1999), 7–20; Robert C. Pianta, Michael S. Steinberg, and Kristin B. Rollins, "The First Two Years of School: Teacher-Child Relationships and Deflections in Children's Classroom Adjustment," *Development and Psychopathology* 7, no. 2 (1995): 295–312; Miriam Raider-Roth, *Trusting What You Know: The High Stakes of Classroom Relationships* (San Francisco: Jossey-Bass, 2005); Michael Reichert and Richard Hawley, *I Can Learn from You: Boys as Relational Learners* (Cambridge, MA: Harvard Education Press, 2014); Kathleen Mortiz Rudasill, Kathleen Cranley Gallagher, and Jamie M. White, "Temperamental Attention and Activity, Classroom Emotional Support, and Academic Achievement in Third Grade," *Journal of School Psychology* 48, no. 2 (2010): 113–134; Huiyoung Shin and Allison M. Ryan, "Friend Influence on Early Adolescent Disruptive Behavior in the Classroom: Teacher Emotional Support Matters," *Developmental Psychology* 53, no. 1 (2017): 114–125.

10 Roland Fryer and Will Dobbie, "Are High-Quality Schools Enough to Increase Achievement among the Poor? Evidence from the Harlem Children's Zone," *American Economic Journal: Applied Economics* 3, no. 3 (2011): 158–187.

11 See Marianne Stenger, "Why Curiosity Enhances Learning," *Edutopia*, December 17, 2014, www.edutopia.org.

12 Paolo Freire, *Pedagogy of the Oppressed*, trans. Myra Bergman Ramos (New York: Herder & Herder, 1968).

13 Kirkland, this volume; Noguera, this volume.

14 Noguera, *City Schools and the American Dream*; Noguera, this volume.

15 Robert C. Pianta and Megan W. Stuhlman, "Teacher-Child Relationships and Children's Success in the First Years of School," *School Psychology Review* 33, no. 3 (2004): 444.

16 Niobe Way, "Thick Love: What the Science of Human Connection Tells Us about How to Fix the World" (manuscript in progress).

17 Niobe Way, *Deep Secrets: Boys' Friendships and the Crisis of Connection* (Cambridge, MA: Harvard University Press, 2011); Gilligan, Rogers, and Noel, this volume; Chu, this volume; Ward, this volume; Rogers, this volume.

18 Rogers and Way, "Stereotypes."

19 Lyn Mikel Brown and Carol Gilligan, *Meeting at the Crossroads: Women's Psychology and Girls' Development* (Cambridge, MA: Harvard University Press,

1992); Judy Y. Chu, "A Relational Perspective on Adolescent Boys' Identity Development," in *Adolescent Boys: Exploring Diverse Cultures of Boyhood*, ed. Niobe Way and Judy Y. Chu (New York: New York University Press, 2004), 78–104; David Kirkland, *A Search Past Silence: The Literacy of Young Black Men* (New York: Teachers College Press, 2013); Pedro Noguera, *The Trouble with Black Boys: And Other Reflections on Race, Equity, and the Future of Public Education* (San Francisco: Jossey-Bass, 2008); Niobe Way, *Everyday Courage: The Lives and Stories of Urban Teenagers* (New York: New York University Press, 1998); Way, *Deep Secrets*; Gilligan, Rogers, and Noel, this volume; Chu, this volume; Ward, this volume; Rogers, this volume.

20 Irving Seidman, *Interviewing as Qualitative Research: A Guide for Researchers in Education and the Social Sciences*, 4th ed. (New York: Teachers College Press, 2013); Herbert J. Rubin and Irene S. Rubin, *Qualitative Interviewing: The Art of Hearing Data*, 2nd ed. (London: SAGE, 2005).

21 Clifford Geertz, *The Interpretation of Cultures* (New York: Basic Books, 1977); Way, *Deep Secrets*.

22 Way, *Deep Secrets*.

23 Brown and Gilligan, *Meeting at the Crossroads*; Carol Gilligan, *Joining the Resistance: Psychology, Politics, Girls and Women* (Cambridge: Polity Press, 1991).

24 "NYU Steinhardt Receives Spencer Foundation Grant to Address Societal Divisions in NYC Middle Schools," *At a Glance*, November 2, 2017, https://steinhardt.nyu.edu.

25 Head of School, "George Jackson Academy School Proposal" (2003), 12.

26 Joseph D. Nelson, "'I Want to Be a Soccer Player or a Mathematician': Fifth-Grade Black Boys' Aspirations at a 'Neoliberal' Single-Sex School," in *Masculinity and Aspiration in the Era of Neoliberal Education: International Perspectives*, ed. Garth Stahl, Joseph D. Nelson, and Derron Wallace (New York: Routledge, 2017).

27 Eliot Mishler, *Research Interviewing: Context and Narrative* (Cambridge, MA: Harvard University Press, 1985); Rubin and Rubin, *Qualitative Interviewing*; Seidman, *Interviewing as Qualitative Research*.

28 Michael Dumas and Joseph D. Nelson, "(Re)imagining Black Boyhood: Toward a Critical Framework for Educational Research," *Harvard Educational Review* 86, no. 1 (2016): 27–47.

29 See the appendix for two examples of biographical essays written by seventh graders.

30 Carol Gilligan, "The Listening Guide Method of Psychological Inquiry," *Qualitative Psychology* 2, no. 1 (2015): 69–77; Brown and Gilligan, *Meeting at the Crossroads*; Carol Gilligan, *Joining the Resistance* (Cambridge: Polity Press, 2011); Alisha Ali, "The Convergence of Foucault and Feminist Psychiatry: Exploring Emancipatory Knowledge-Building," *Journal of Gender Studies* 11, no. 2 (2002): 233–242; Alisha Ali, "A Framework for Emancipatory Inquiry in Psychology: Lessons from Feminist Methodology," *Race, Gender, and Class* 13, nos. 1–2 (2006): 1–14; Niobe

Way, Dana Edell, and Joseph D. Nelson, "Transformative Interviewing: A New Method of Semi-structured Interviewing" (manuscript in progress).

31 María Elena Torre, Michelle Fine, Brett G. Stoudt, and Madeline Fox, "Critical Participatory Action Research as Public Science," in *APA Handbook of Research Methods in Psychology. Research Designs: Quantitative, Qualitative, Neuropsychological, and Biological*, vol. 2, ed. Harris Cooper et al. (Washington, DC: American Psychological Association, 2012), 171–184; Way, *Deep Secrets*.

32 Dumas and Nelson, "(Re)imagining Black Boyhood."

33 Reichert and Hawley, *I Can Learn from You*; Raider-Roth, *Trusting What You Know*.

12

The Courage to Care

Building Connection between Young Women and Men with Shakespeare

VICTORIA RHOADES

Relationship seems to be the lesson of our time in culture. We are charged to learn about how to relate to ourselves and to other human beings. Our ability to do so makes the difference in couples connecting, a family that is lively together, a dance company that can continue to perform, a corporation that flourishes, or a world that survives.
—Peggy Hackney, *Making Connections*

Things done well, and with a care, exempt themselves from fear.
—William Shakespeare, *The Tempest*

The Threat of Gender

The smell of freshly cut grass pours in through the open windows. The sound of the mower pounds in the distance. I sit in a small basement classroom with Maura. She is nineteen, and from Oklahoma. She could be described as a young white woman, but I know from her stories about herself that she is of Native American and European heritage. Her extended family, she tells me, went to great efforts to hide and destroy evidence of their indigenous ancestors. As we talk, laughter flows freely in our conversation, while at other moments, Maura speaks with a pointed seriousness and emotional weight. The girl in her pops in—mischievous, fragile, warm—transforming her previous bound anger to newfound courage.

I have gotten to know Maura as her acting and movement teacher over a five-week intensive Shakespeare workshop for young actors.[1] At the end of the workshop, she volunteers to share her insights into my teaching and how it has affected her. I ask a simple question: "How did my teaching affect you?" She begins, "You were so good with the boys," as if this is a relief to her, and continues, "but you were SOOOO good with the girls." I am surprised, and curious. "What did you see?" I ask. She replies:

> With the girls it was—with the boys—[pause]. You know, there's this thing in men that I've observed—I've talked about it—there's this *thing* [her emphasis] in men that's threatening.

I stop. I am listening to the recording of our interview. I rewind and listen to her statements again, pausing at the word, "threatening." I realize that in asking a question about teaching, Maura has brought me to the intersection of teaching and learning and gender. She reminds me that in teaching we cannot pretend that cultural messages of gender do not matter, or that entering a classroom means beginning anew with relationships; for when we enter any new group we carry the experience of our past relationships with us, whether it is in our awareness or not.[2]

I return to Maura's first statements, and notice that she distinguishes between the way I worked with the young men and the young women. She calls those ways "so good" for the boys and "SOOOO good" for the girls, implying that I had a deeper effect on the young women in the room. Her classmate, Luke, tells me, "there was something *different* [his emphasis] in the way you were teaching." The difference, I have learned, is an attention to the way that gendered assumptions can influence the way we listen and respond to one another, the language we choose or the potential we imagine in ourselves or others. Maura's statements, and those of other students, reinforce what I had come to know: I needed to find another way of reaching the young men that I had instinctively found with young women. Because cultural messages of gender impact girls and boys differently, and at different points in their developmental process, the young women and men had adopted protections that suited those ways of relating at different points in their developmental process. I needed to gain a better sense of their protective habits, and in doing so, I might catch a glimpse of what was hiding underneath.

I interview Maura's classmate, Luke, a young white man of twenty-two. He is in college in Boston, but grew up in Maine. Tall and stoic, he moves steadily and with gentle energy. The son of two social workers, Luke attended a Waldorf school for his early and elementary education.[3] We share this experience, and make a connection, as I tell Luke that my young daughter attends a Waldorf school in Pennsylvania. We talk about the way the pedagogy invites children to awaken their imaginations, to express and work through feelings. He tells me that the school allowed him to be the "sensitive boy" that he was—different from his experience when he moved to another school. I note this. Like Maura, I ask him how my teaching affected him. He replies:

> I think it has to be really safe. I don't know—maybe it's just judgment or something more—because it's so deep in the culture—I don't know—I think at this point I've gotten to know most of the men here on a deeper level so it's not such a huge threat.

Again, I stop. Two phrases catch my ear: "really safe" and "huge threat." By "really safe" he means "judgment or something more" is kept out of the room. Later in his interview he tells me, "We really did seem to have the space that was free of judgment . . . which was pretty cool and pretty rare." Luke names what Maura finds threatening, and chooses the same word ("threat") to describe his experience of being in a learning environment with other men. Luke clarifies that what he finds threatening is the judgment brought into the room by other men. I am surprised. My false assumption, as a woman, who was a girl, was that men would not feel threatened by other men. Luke explains that without that feeling of safety in a learning environment, he will not let down his guard. His experience is that this threat of judgment is "so deep in the culture," it is such an ingrained pattern of behavior that it is passed on without question from father to son, from brother to brother, from media images and cultural messages. It is an initiation rite gone awry.

I listen further to Luke's response:

> But I notice myself bristling in this world, like when new men come in . . . from the outside world . . . it's like—you know—I don't talk to people 'cause—ya know—it's just it's just really not worth it, and it hasn't been for a

long time. But, um, like one guy in the seats today had sunglasses on and sat in the front to watch us work—What is *that?! What is that?!* [his emphasis].

Luke is made physically uncomfortable by "new men [who] come in" to the environment created at this Shakespeare workshop, implying that they are behaving differently from the men in the workshop. It is a feeling that reverberates through his whole body. As a result, he senses this different energy, and he stops talking because "it's just really not worth it," implying that he has known and experienced this before. He reacts in disbelief and anger as he relays that one man came in to his rehearsal with his scene partner, and sat in the front row wearing sunglasses. He shouts, "What is *that?! What is that?!*" I feel him "bristle" as I listen to the rhythm, pattern, and inflection of his words, reacting to the physical and emotional mask this man puts on in front of them. Luke's sensitivity and keen observation allow him to pick up these unspoken messages from others, in turn forming the armor he creates for himself.

Later in the interview, Luke explains that when his feelings are large, his voice gets trapped in his chest: "There's a lot of tension, just this shield on my chest." I sense that shield, the energy he expends to cover his heart; it is so strong that when I work with him, I have to listen more attentively to remain fully present, and then, I consciously move slightly aside to give him space to respond. He does respond: he breathes, his muscles release, letting his "shield" fall away, allowing his heart to be open and in relationship. He is present with his scene partner, and alive in his creative work, but the moment someone enters guarded or with threatening energy, his shield rises and he is on the defense.

Building Connections as People, Not Just Women and Men

I wonder if it is Luke's defensive shield that Maura senses to be the "threat" she feels in our small acting class of eight, with two men and six women. Or possibly, the "intellectual superiority" Luke tells me that he puts on for others, or the constant joking and high energy attention-getting behavior that twenty-year-old Kai projects. Neither of these men harmed her or said anything meant to threaten her. Yet, the behavior they have learned in order to negotiate what it means to be men in the

culture has caused them to develop mannerisms and coverings to protect themselves that in turn affect her. Yet, despite her discomfort, Maura
sees beneath their masks to something more:

> And it's not that they're meaning to be, they just feel like they have to
> have it [next words, inaudible]. And, I mean, if they ever tried to pull
> it—I mean, it just went by the wayside with you, and it didn't exist in the
> room. Which made us feel like *people* [her emphasis]—not just men and
> women—and that was really nice.

I attune my ear to the words she chooses, to the pitch and cadence
of her speech.[4] She moves from her observations of the teacher in
relationship with the young men and women to naming a threat she
feels when in groups with men. And then, she shows empathy for the
young men ("and it's not that they're meaning to be, they just feel like
they have to have it"). She reveals her deep perception, seeing beyond
what the young men present to the group to what they really think or
feel within.

And yet, their behavior does affect her—as she explains later in the
interview—and she is affected by the way in which their behavior impacts
the other women in the room. I notice that once I acknowledge aloud
the women's experiences as real and their feelings justified, the women
in the group begin to look out for and quietly support one another. It is a
thought, a feeling, a glance, a whisper, or a direct address. As the young
women join with each other, they make space for the young men to join
in. Eventually, the threat "just went by the wayside . . . and it didn't exist
in the room." The façades fall away. With fewer barriers, it becomes easier to listen, and they respond with empathy. They feel connected, they
laugh. They are touched by each other—through joy, sadness, surprise, or
disagreement—and they want more.

The Roots of My Teaching

I am an educator and a theater artist with a deep understanding of relational psychology; I teach and direct Shakespeare and movement for
professional actors, actors-in-training, and adolescents in schools. My
work centers around the nuances of human relationship and is held

through a lens of gender, particularly the impact of cultural messages upon girls and boys at different points in development. In my research with some of my students—young women and men aged nineteen into their mid-twenties—I asked a question reflecting upon my practice: "How did my teaching affect you?"

In response, I hear stories of sadness and fear—sadness from loss in their lives, and the fear of being shamed or judged for not being the "right" kind of man, or a "nice" enough woman when entering a classroom with others. I first listened to these students at a time when leadership and movements in the country were pushing hierarchical and gender boundaries. We had our first African American president, who modeled a deeply held respect for women and girls through his relationships with his wife and daughters, and barriers around gender were shifting. Then we arrived at a different moment in history, with a president who modeled judgment and shame, promoted divisions and barriers, and reestablished an imposing and overt patriarchal hierarchy. In such an environment, the students' words still held true, yet they rang with a resound louder than I had imagined. I became more aware of the profound impact cultural messages of gender have on the way young women and men think about themselves, and the subsequent effect on their bodies and voices. Divided within themselves, young women and young men (whatever the ethnicity or race) struggle, then, to stay in relationship with one another. Bridging the divide and creating environments where all young people can rediscover ways of connecting to themselves feel more pressing than before.

The female students I work with speak of feeling fear coupled with deep anger, and a desire to resist such changes, while other young women are unsure or lost, severed from the vibrant, intuitive knowing they may have felt as a girl of nine or ten. For, as they enter adolescence, girls want to be accepted. Exclusion becomes the most painful relational possibility. Thus, they pick up messages that tell them that in order to be liked, they may need to bury their honest thoughts, ignore their impulses, and cover feelings like hurt or anger with a façade of "niceness," or false confidence. They learn that "speaking out" and "speaking up" can get them into trouble. In turn, they show signs of dissociation: that is, they begin to separate their real feelings, or what they know in their bodies, from their intellect, demonstrating constrained silence, an inauthentic voice, or habitual mannerisms that become a permanent mask. Still, they long to be connected, even if it means sacrificing parts of themselves.[5]

Boys first encounter the cultural "boy rules" in early childhood. As Judy Chu discusses in this volume, between the ages of four and six, boys take in messages from their peers at play, from adults around them, and from media images telling them that being a "boy" means *not* being like a "girl." Through words and nonverbal messages, they may learn to cover their feelings or sensitivity toward others.[6] As they develop, boys hold on to strong relationships, often with great affection, but there are rules that dictate the norms of boys' relationships. In later adolescence, boys may separate even further from others and from themselves, because the threat of revealing their desire for connection or any vulnerability is to be openly shamed and labeled "homo," "sissy," or a "girl."[7] Erecting a "shield" becomes a useful means of protection.

As the teacher, my job is to listen for the story—the story Shakespeare writes, and the story I hear in what is unspoken. Through the actor's body, voice, and emotional connection, I hear real-life events awakened by Shakespeare's imagery. I see young women needing to be heard, to be recognized as worth our time and our energy, young women who can no longer distinguish what they know in their "gut" from what others tell them they "should" know, for the words "I don't know" pepper the land-scape of their stories like bubbles in the stream of their thoughts. I hear young men not knowing if they can look us in the eye as they speak, or if they do, wondering if the words that come from within them are real. The young men often tell me that they do not know if they can even feel anymore, as the phrase "I don't care" has washed over their sense of themselves like thick paint brushed over the canvas of secrets, encasing the broken relationships that lie hidden in their hearts.

Young women speak of a struggle to believe in themselves because the people around them have stopped believing in them—in the words that they speak, in the events they relate—*because* they are young and they are women. They spend so much energy worrying about the ways in which their bodies are seen or their voices are interpreted that they no longer have a sense of what it feels like to be connected in body and voice. Some speak of feeling invisible, others wear a wall masked with what they imagine others want them to be. I hear young men strug-gling to admit that they have the capacity to love, to care—even if they know deep down that they do. Their bodies have become armored with a wide range of defenses, their voices sit in a few notes of their lower registers, placed like china on an earthquake-prone shelf, carefully near the back of the throat so that the chords will only vibrate with a certain feeling that reveals authority, or "don't mess with me," or it hardly vibrates at all. I feel the absence, or sadness, or rage-in-hiding in my own body. It is as though I feel on their behalf what they will not admit they feel within. My job then, is to take this information, and help them express it through their own bodies and voices and consciousness; to help them reconnect to what they have buried inside them so they can sense what it is like to be whole again—that is, to embody their thoughts, to feel their range of authentic feelings, and to remove the masks they wear that keep them from connecting to others and to themselves.

An Approach Centered on Care

I strive to create an environment where the language we use is chosen with "mindfulness and care," as Luke described it to me. I strive to speak from an honest place, and I encourage and help students to practice speaking honestly as they share their experiences in class. I also ask for specificity and accuracy of language, as well as a respect for others in the room, and I expect the same of myself. If I really *see* into the eyes of each student, beneath a tightly held expression of the face, or listen beneath the surface talk to the language that is used, or take in what is *not* being spoken, but screams aloud in the body and in the weight of silence, I know these young people need a place where they can express themselves within the safety of a form and a structure that can capture their experience, hold their feelings and the complexity of relationship. Shakespeare's plays both provide a structure for the text and give story a form.

I, too, rely on balance and form. I remind my students—and myself— that we cannot really know joy if we have not known sadness. We cannot appreciate love if we have not lived through loss. We cannot live fully if we do not let ourselves experience the range of human feelings. The structure and clarity of thought in Shakespeare's text and the form of exercises I use in the classroom provide a container to help hold the students' stories. These stories and the universal emotions they touch provide the foundation for connection. The connections we make in challenging or joyful times become the foundation of relationships that buoy us through inevitable struggles and come out on the other side.

But, how do we help students to reach across unspoken barriers of gender? How do we remove the "threat" from the classroom? This chapter shares key elements of an integrated method I have created to support young women and men so they may reconnect with themselves, find the courage to reveal their humanity, and, in doing so, build connections across any gender divide. I will note here that I do not address the experiences of transgender students because there were none in my research group. Yet I recognize that these experiences are both valid and likely different from what I share here, and worthy of future research.

I learned through my teaching and listening that the shift in the room begins with the young women. As they find permission to fill the space with their experience, they describe feeling "huge and beautiful" and, as a result, unleash a "voice that was ringing out across the whole room . . . I sounded like the woman that I know I am, but have not yet known how to share." In order for this to happen, I, as the teacher, must be grounded in myself, physically and energetically, and able to shift into lightness and playful energy. I know my subject, I have prepared, yet I am spontaneous, I hold respect and curiosity for the students. I set boundaries, but most importantly, I bring love. All of the students I interviewed told me that what they valued most in the environment we created was love and care. Twenty-year-old Kai tells me,

KAI: Our relationship was very special to me.
T: Why was that?
KAI: Umm. [pause] I guess it was just because of how much you cared. I think it really was. You know, I always felt so loved around you and—yeah. That's all it was.

The young men taught me that as the young women's voices and energy filled the room, as their wit and joy and anger spoke out loud, the young men could reveal their vulnerability. I had to shift my way of thinking from an assumed expectation of boys' and men's behavior to a genuine curiosity to understand what it was like for them to be boys or men. "I don't know," I tell them, "because I was a girl." Little by little they removed their guard, held by the young women's encouragement, and shared moments of laughter and an ethic of love and care.

Carol Gilligan built her work grounded in the idea that care is an innate *human* quality, not a gendered "female" quality.[8] I build upon the work in girls' development of Gilligan and her collaborators, as well as Judy Chu and Niobe Way's research with boys. Further scholarship by Gilligan, Chu, and Way appears earlier in this book. I, then, integrate an approach to teaching and directing Shakespeare for performance developed by artists of Shakespeare & Company in Lenox, Massachusetts (I am one of these artists). I support this integration with my training as an actor and dancer, with the study of trauma, group dynamics, and theater as a tool for change, healing, and well-being.[9] I use aspects of the Linklater Voice Method and influences of yoga, dance, and the movement work of Susan Dibble, Trish Arnold, Irmgard Bartenieff, Peggy Hackney, Rudolf Laban, and F. M. Alexander. Finally, I rely upon the plays of William Shakespeare. His plays are the guide on our journey, and an invaluable tool. His stories offer a window into human experience, the structure of his verse provides a clear form akin to musical composition, and the poetic imagery, when performed, demands that the performer bring her full self in body, voice, emotion, imagination, and intellect to the story and the text. Committing to the language, while in relationship with an audience, begins a process of reconnection. What had been buried and out of relationship is slowly unearthed while supported through relationship. It is a complex web of connection, but it begins with the teacher as the guide and guardian of the learning space.

Setting the Stage for Relationship

More than the skills or information we are asked to teach, I believe it is the *manner* in which we communicate and pass on that information or those skills that leaves a lasting mark upon the students. The way in which we set up our physical and relational space, and how we lead our way through that arena, sets the tone upon first entrance, and establishes norms for discussion, genuine communication, expression, and creative thinking. The students are learning not only by what we say but also by *how* we say it, by watching our every move, listening to our every word. Students learn as much through our model of behavior and language as they do through the information we choose to share with them. Thus, as a teacher, attending to myself, remembering my experience, and listening for my own unresolved stories are as important as preparing a lesson plan for the class. I take the time to notice when my own untold or unfinished story of relationship and my own biases of gender are interfering with the way I see or hear the student in front of me. In the following sections, I point to three key elements I rely upon, and five basic tools I use for any class or rehearsal I lead. I believe these elements and tools can be transferred across disciplines, and so I share them with you.

The Teacher as Model: Attending to Myself

Human beings seek role models, and inherently learn through imitation.[10] Thus, before I step into the room to teach, I take at least a few minutes to breathe, to focus, to stretch, to do what I need to attend to myself. How do I feel today? How does my body feel? What is happening to the patterns of my breath? Are there parts of my life at the moment that need my attention? I do not need to solve the problem in that moment, but acknowledging it to myself allows me to know it is there. When I hold the awareness of what is present in me, my psyche is not working to keep it hidden. I then focus upon the goal or theme of my class for that day, and step into the room. Sometimes, of course, there are times when the struggle I am facing may be big enough that outside assistance is needed to work through it. In these cases, I believe it is my responsibility as a teacher who works to guide other human beings to take the appropriate time to attend to myself.

Setting the Physical Space

Ideally, I have had the opportunity to see the space I will be working in before I have the first class or rehearsal. If not, I like to at least have the chance to be in the room before the students enter so that I can take in the physical space, get a sense of what it is like, what the challenges might be, and how we might make the space work in our favor rather than be a continual obstacle. For example, I make sure the room is orderly and clean to the best of my ability. I like to have very little furniture in the room other than chairs stacked or pushed to the periphery that can easily be brought in and out of the center of the space as needed. I usually have one simple table at the edge of the room to hold the objects I might need for class. I want obstacles to be removed and barriers to be nonexistent. If they are there, I want to be able to move them easily aside. If they cannot be moved, I will ask for another room. I am teaching acting and movement, so an open space is important. If I were teaching English or math, desks would be standard and needed for students to write, yet I still want to have desks and chairs that are easily moveable. I want to be able to create different physical shapes to invite different physical relationships for the group as needed. I find that rows of seats create an inevitable hierarchy, especially when it is never shifted; and my experience is that this formation is an obstacle to creating a healthy group dynamic. Finally, I find it to be extremely disruptive to hold class in a public space. It becomes difficult to build a sense of trust in the group. The work space is "sacred," as one of my students told me. The space we create together requires the teacher to serve as the leader in holding the space, but it actually needs each individual to play a part in maintaining the integrity of the working environment without chaotic disruption.

Building the Group Dynamic, the Energetic Space

As students filter into the classroom, I want them to feel welcomed. I speak casually but with resonance in order to create a sense of ease in the room as well as authority. I ask them each to grab a chair and form it into a circle. I could have had this prepared for them—and depending on the goal or timing of the class, I may. But, with a more intimate group, the action gives them a task. And, because this is our first class together, it allows them to have some authority over their place in the room—by taking a small action to contribute to the setup of the space. They can choose their place in the circle, and how the circle is shaped. The simple task of forming a circle with chairs allows the group itself to begin to interact and solve a problem together. They have to communicate with each other; they have to collaborate to form a circle.

When that is done, they are ready. And, their first introduction has begun. At our first class, I always take time for the students to share something about themselves. I ask them to say their name, where they are from, and why they are here. Or what are they hoping for from our class. I also ask them a question that invites them to go a bit deeper but does not trap them in *having* to go there, such as "What was a significant event in your life?" or "What relationship is most important to you right now and why?" How they answer the questions becomes as revealing as what they actually say. When someone in the group takes a step out to speak honestly, others follow. These questions are an icebreaker, a way for each person in the group to have their voice heard, and to share something about themselves with us. I participate too. Yet, I am aware when I participate that I am modeling for them. I may or may not choose to go first; it depends on the group. I usually allow someone else to begin. But, when it is my turn, I am honest; I share something that reveals a part of me, and yet, I am still holding the space, I am still the leader of the group, and I know that as I speak. I am conscious—not calculated—of the words I choose. I am authentic with my feelings and thoughts, but this is not a place for me to "spill my guts." My goal in the first class, and at the beginning of every class, is to set up a norm that each person's voice is valued, each of us is vulnerable, and by listening to each other, we find ourselves affected, touched by humanity.

Next we set the "ground rules" for the work space. These are my basic rules: (1) do not hurt yourself; (2) do not hurt each other; (3) do not hurt the furniture or the room; (4) you are the author of your own experience, and I will ask you questions or cheer you on, or ask you to participate, but *you* can tell me you need to stop at any time if you need to, and I will listen. I then give all students the opportunity to contribute any norms or expectations that they request from the group. We agree upon it, and often we write it down. Sometimes we formalize it, and we all sign it. This gives weight to what we have said, and is a reference point for those moments when someone has broken the norms of the agreement. And I do not hesitate to use it.

Engaging with Play

Then, we begin to work as actors. I invite students to play in a variety of ways, and to tell their stories. We usually begin with games or group exercises that awaken the imagination, set the tone for a sense of ease and permission, and the freedom to make mistakes and work through them. Yet with clear boundaries. I consciously move between playful or silly, then delving deeper into emotional authenticity, thoughtful discussion, or useful skills or facts. In a variety of ways, I encourage them repeatedly to practice listening to the impulses that arise in their bodies as they engage in relationship, and I ask them what action they choose in response to this impulse. I lead exercises to help them practice listening to their bodies, and then give them the space to find language to capture what it is they feel. If they "don't know," as is a common answer among young women and men who have grown disconnected from their bodies, I invite them to "make it up!" And, I may begin to ask some questions. When I enquire, I always do so with a genuine desire to learn from them. And I often engage the imagination. I may ask, "Is there a shape that captures what it is? A color? An image? A metaphor of some kind?" As they begin with the abstract or use a metaphor to name what they feel or know, gradually they begin to rebuild the pathways of communication between body and mind.

Engaging with Rhetoric, Rhythm, and Form—Shakespeare's Text

In acting class, we use the language of plays by William Shakespeare, as well as their own stories, told in their own words. Through this telling, heard by their fellow artists or peers, they find connection with one another and with themselves. I encourage them to articulate what they find. Then, we move back to Shakespeare's words, while holding onto the feelings and thoughts they experienced in telling their own story. We rely upon the structure and rhythm of Shakespeare's text—the shifts and breaks in patterns—to guide us, and inform us about the character. By asking how a word affected me, or what image comes to mind, or how the rhythm of the text feels in my body, and so on, the actor awakens to a physical and emotional freedom within the reliable framework of the structure of the text.

The Elizabethans sought to bring chaos into harmony, to find balance and restore order. But they were not afraid of the chaos. The chaos that we might fear by allowing students the freedom to express themselves is calmed into harmony, held by the rhythm and structure of the text, and the norms and rituals of the class.

Finding Expression through the Body

Dance and music were ways of restoring order and harmony for the Elizabethans. In movement class, I give simple choreography—a form—to carefully chosen music in order to give students the experience of finding subtle expressions of character within the simple form of the dance. They are telling a story through the way they execute the choreography. Students find expression for personal experience through movement exercises using gesture as our language, discovering that through simple movement it is possible for memories to be unlocked because memories are held in the body.[11] In witnessing the creative work that evolves out of their experience, they speak about finding joy and pleasure in moving their bodies in a way they have not felt since they were very young. Giving opportunities for creating metaphor through movement and gesture—through living "statues," or simple gestures that when put together become a dance—offers a means of taking a simple task or idea and creating something larger than themselves, and often with surprising meaning.

Simple Pleasures

There are times when it is necessary to bring out a box of crayons or paint. I give an instruction that guides students through a creative exploration, continually encouraging them to just follow where it takes them. I find that these moments of easygoing expression with words and imagery help to bridge pathways of mind and body, intellect and heart. Other times I will give a prompt inviting reflection, to build an awareness of one's habits or hopes, or a time to remember a fading memory. Sometimes I will build an exercise in class that comes out of these colorings or journal writing assignments so that they have the experience of taking something personal and transforming it through creativity and collaboration to something universal. Sometimes I make space for them to share their writing by setting up an informal "café" space around the room that is relaxed and yet respected, that allows everyone to be seen and no one to hide, that supports listening to the person who is speaking.

Rituals of Opening and Closing

In every class I teach, in every rehearsal I lead, I *always* begin with a version of Check-In. It may be formal or informal, brief or longer, voiced or performed through movement, but I always do it. Check-In is a time when each member of the group, gathered in a circle, takes a turn to say how he or she feels at that moment. The goal of Check-In is to allow everyone's voice to be heard, even if it is to say "I don't know" or "I need to pass today." It is also another moment when members of the group build connections and develop empathy for one another because they hear others express feelings they may feel, or are simply touched by something that is happening in their classmate's life. Learning about what others cope with every day allows most students to shift their assumptions about their peers, and about themselves.

Check-In is also about specificity of language and speaking from one's personal experience. There is a form, and I help them stick to it. The physical form is the circle. The verbal form is "I feel [and they name a feeling]" or "I'm sad today . . . we had to put my cat to sleep." Ideally I strive for efficiency of language, but there are times when I find it is beneficial to let someone speak what's going on; I find it pays off—later that day, or sometime that term. I provide gentle guidance or reminders or direct questions, if that student needs it. I do find that I have to remind the students that there are only five or six basic feelings in our human experience. We name them, and we name versions of them. "Good" and "bad" are judgments—not feelings. Physical sensations are just that, and they can be a part of Check-In, but then I ask (or wait) for them to articulate the emotion beneath it. At first, I may invite students to Check-In with a metaphor: "If you were a weather pattern, what would you be?" or "If you were a main course at a fancy restaurant, what would you be?" They enjoy the playfulness in this, and the distance of a metaphor gives freedom to those who may be hesitant to reveal more about themselves. We work to eliminate habits of language such as the phrase "I feel like," which typically leads to a judgment. Practicing specificity transfers to our own lives and is critical to embodying Shakespeare's writing.

I always end the class with Reinforcement, or some form of closure for the work we have done. In Movement class, I use an easy-to-follow reverence I have created to a classic 1930s song by Ivor Novello. This simple closure allows us to honor and let go of the work we have done. In acting class, I use Reinforcement, a verbal way of bringing closure to the work. We gather in a circle and name one positive thing from the work we did, or the work someone else did, or something that happened in the midst of class, and we highlight it, or "reinforce" it. The language I use comes from Shakespeare & Company's Education Program: "I want to reinforce. . . ." And then each person has a chance to name something. But it cannot be negative. If students delve into negativity, I guide them through reframing it or help them to choose something else, like "the piece of chocolate in my pocket," something that leaves them in a positive place. Again, taking the time to close the class, rather than just getting up and dispersing, helps to give integrity to the work done: "It makes us feel like the work is sacred" one young woman told me. And it is. But within the group, how do I encourage the nuances of connections to form between young men and young women as they work together? In broad terms, I hold in my teaching framework the points of intersection between cultural messages and human development that affect girls and boys differently, I listen and validate their individual experiences, and I uncover and reinforce those moments of shared humanity.

Bridging the Gender Divide

I am in the studio with two young actors—both in their mid-twenties—working on a scene from Shakespeare's *The Tempest*. Liz, playing Miranda, struggles to ask Miranda's questions about the world, and about love. Her partner, Thomas, listens patiently and quietly. I hear cynicism and hurt in her voice as she speaks the words of the joy and confusion of young love, and so I ask Liz about her own relationship to young love. She tells me a story that resonates across the women I teach—a story of repeated sexual abuse by older men from the time she was twelve through her adolescence. It is no wonder she struggles to be vulnerable in the face of love. Liz's Miranda carries this betrayal and loss, yet Shakespeare's Miranda has grown up as the only young woman on the island; she is a young adolescent, vibrant, courageous, agile, and able to openly disagree with her father, but very new at love. At some point in our conversation, I ask Liz, "What happened to your twelve-year-old?"

I notice her body: there is tremendous tension in her shoulders. I ask what lives back in the shoulder area, where I see all of this tension. She tells me that's where her twelve-year-old is hiding. Liz has told me that she has worked through her experience of abuse with a therapist. But, sitting and talking about an event one-on-one is not the same as telling one's story to an audience, moving the held physical or emotional energy through the body with creative energy. The story still lives in her, and it continues to hinder her emotional flexibility as an actor, and her ability to be fully present as a human being. As she tells her very moving story, I stay with her, my hand on her back. I feel her entire body release the tension it held. What she really wanted was to be loved, she tells us, not to be a body upon which sexual acts were done. I hear her vocal range open as she moves from a voice held in her chest—a place of authority—to one that flows into the upper vocal registers—the more vulnerable and youthful places in the human voice.

When she finishes, I ask Thomas, her partner, if he wants to say anything to her. He does. He reassures her and lets her know that he is there for her. It is clear in his face that he is present, and strikingly, it is evident that he understands her struggle. She acknowledges this, but I see that she is afraid. They stand in front of each other. I ask her gently, "Can you recognize that this man in front of you is not the same man who hurt you?" She does. I acknowledge that her body's habit may signal one thing, but her mind can help her body to understand this person is different. I ask her to notice his face, to name what she actually sees there. Gentleness and care, she says, kindness and wit. I ask her if she can see Thomas before they start, to help her know that he is not any of the men who have hurt her. She does. I ask her to jump back in to the text of her scene. When she does, she comes alive with joy, vulnerability, and a sense of play that I hadn't seen before. Thomas responds as Ferdinand; he stays with her. I am surprised by his openness, his sensitivity, and his willingness to stay.

A week later, Thomas, as Ferdinand, is forcing his voice as he speaks, as if he is trying to *make* joy happen. I stop them. I kneel on the floor beneath them, and I tell him what I see. Thomas tells me that he struggles to express his vulnerability and often feels numb. Gently, I ask why he thinks it might be difficult for him to be vulnerable. I notice him resist. I stay with him. I wait and I breathe. He breathes, and tells me about words that have hurt him. I ask whose words. It is the other boys at school and his dad. I ask if he recalls any of these words. Again, he speaks dryly, as if he were reciting a recipe. Through the lack of resonance in his voice, the holding in the back of his throat, I know that he is actively disconnecting from what he tells me. I stay with him, listening, putting the pieces together in my mind.

Finally, he pauses, sits down, breathes a vocal sigh. I stay sitting on the floor, but I move a bit closer, and I listen. He begins to tell me about the nights when he was six years old. His mom had taken a night job and his father was his caretaker. His father would drink to intoxication and tell the boy about wanting to kill himself, and soon, the nights grew worse as he began beating the child. The boys at school made fun of Thomas for being different because his culture was different from theirs. The games, the songs, the stories he knew were different. For ten years his father beat him in his drunken nighttime stupors, and then he would buy him gifts to make up for the pain he had caused him—inflicting his own inner pain on the young boy that stood before him. At age sixteen, Thomas was finally big enough to stop him.

What I know, from talking with Thomas, is that this is not the first time he has spoken about being abused by his father. But it is new to speak about it with someone who is his teacher and in front of an acting partner, a young woman and his peer. Knowing he has processed this relationship earlier in his life, I ask him if it would be useful to tell his story out loud to our small audience of four. The point of doing so is that when we are stuck in a repeated pattern of stories in our life, or a limited emotional range, it is difficult to just "pull ourselves out of it." But if the traumatic impact of the event—the initial remembering and making sense of what happened—has been worked through in counseling, it is possible to bring the story to our creative work, using creative tools to invite the body and the imagination, to a new experience of a story of relationship.[12] Thus, his inability to access his delight and genuine joy was related to the fact that his body was accustomed to living in a pattern. But, in order to play the scene as Shakespeare wrote it, he *must* feel joy—because it is written in the language of the text.

I hold in my mind the knowledge that as children we instinctively turn to play to work through our difficulties—through the roles we take on and the plots we invent.[13] It is the child's way of making sense of the world around her. Thus in the context of play, I ask if he were the six-year-old boy, what he might say to his father. Different from being with Liz, I give him physical space and I stay kneeling in front of him. As he chooses a simple phrase, anger fills his body, and then it releases into tears. I reassure him, and remind him to allow his breath to move through him. I remind him they are just feelings, they will move through him and then shift. I watch the shield of held anger let go and I see the heartbreak now has space to release its hidden sadness. After a few moments of giving him time to say what he needs to say, we pause. And now I ask him what gives him joy, what gives him hope—because I see such hope in his face. He tells me of the joy he felt creating as a child— artwork and music. He is a musician. Playing music on the violin allowed him to find calm, to find beauty, and to release his heart and soul into the music. "I came here to feel again," he tells me. "And now I can." His scene partner, Liz, turns to him and offers an embrace of support. He accepts. We return to the text of the scene and begin again, bringing his new experience of his story to Shakespeare's.

On a final occasion, we work again. This time, I see a give-and-take of relationship—an ease, a sense of play, and a fluidity, allowing a range of emotions to live in the text and between them. But, there is one moment when things get muddled. I want to invite them to bring what they know of the multitudinous feelings that come with pledging oneself to another into the language and the physical gestures of relationship. They go to this place in the scene:

MIRANDA: My husband, then?
FERDINAND: Ay, with a heart as willing
   As bondage e'er of freedom: here's my hand.

Thomas kneels down and offers her his hand.

MIRANDA: And mine, with my heart in't . . .[14]

Liz shows him her hand, and places it in the palm of his as if giving him the gift of her heart. On impulse, then, she brings their joined hands to her heart. In that simple gesture, I am struck by what I see: it is Ferdinand and Miranda, a young man and a young woman who love one another equally, in the freedom of an island, without the cultural weight of social rules or hierarchy or a monarchy. There is a dominant father, Prospero, but they have succeeded in changing him. Miranda's ability to listen to her intuitive knowing, to speak honestly, even when it is uncomfortable, shifts Prospero's own familial conflicts. The two actors show that revealing one's fear can allow another to listen with care, and then, find the courage to do the same. They discover that the boy at six and the girl at twelve, though very different developmental periods, hit up against cultural expectations of gender that bring about a loss, and a desire to resist that loss in oneself. Turning to creative outlets, they notice the similarities in their differences. Instead of entering relationship with a presumption of fear, they remove their habitual barriers, and offer each other a hand. In that moment of connection between two human hands, they find strength in the human heart, and create a new model of relationship.

When a young woman is given space and encouragement to face her fear, to voice what has been hidden within her mind and body, to have permission to be the complex, imperfect being that she is, she can return to an experience of courage in spite of fear, and the complexity of emotions that she knew as a girl. If space is created so a young man can stay with her, and listen, without fear of being shamed by others, then he has room to trust in what he knows and with guidance and care, trust can develop between them. Being heard and seen in her messiness as well as her strengths, the young woman settles, and makes space for the young man to tell his own story. Sometimes, she needs to stay with him patiently, for it may be difficult for him to find the words. But when he does, she sees a part of him that shines with delight in having permission to be imperfect, to reveal his vulnerability, which becomes the strength of relationship. Liz had shielded her voice, disconnected from her body, hiding a story of loss that began when she was twelve, at the cusp of adolescence. Thomas had armored his heart, broken by betrayal and shame, a story that began at the age of six, at the transition from early childhood to elementary school. Yet, as they recognized themselves in one another, in spite of their differences, they opened their hearts, and found the strength of connection in relationship.

My hope is to invite teachers and students to step back, and to notice if there might be another way of seeing the challenges before us. Can we create a space where young women and men may celebrate their shared humanity by developing skills of relationship, inquiry, creativity, and communication, and inspire others to do the same? I imagine not a hierarchal ladder, but a web of interconnection. I may never solve this task, but I will continue to ask real questions, to listen, to invite playful intuitive expression, and to provide space for young adults and teachers to tell a story. A story where care gives us the courage to remove a wall or a shield, and a touch of the hand can open a heart.

NOTES

1 The workshop called the Summer Training Institute was held at Shakespeare & Company in Lenox, Massachusetts.

2 Irvin D. Yalom and Molyn Leszcz, *The Theory and Practice of Group Psychotherapy*, 5th ed. (New York: Basic Books, 2008).

3 Waldorf is a form of education developed by philosopher Rudolf Steiner that exists today around the world. The underlying goal is to bring peace to the world by educating the whole child in "heart, hand, head," using creative methods and storytelling.

4 For my research, I use the Listening Guide Method developed by Carol Gilligan and her colleagues working at the Harvard Project on Women's Psychology and Girls' Development.

5 Lyn Mikel Brown and Carol Gilligan, *Meeting at the Crossroads: Women's Psychology and Girls' Development* (Cambridge, MA: Harvard University Press, 1992); Lyn Mikel Brown, *Girlfighting: Betrayal and Rejection among Girls* (New York: New York University Press, 2003); Carol Gilligan, *The Birth of Pleasure: A New Map of Love* (New York: Knopf, 2003).

6 Gilligan, *Birth of Pleasure*; Judy Y. Chu, *When Boys Become Boys: Development, Relationships, and Masculinity* (New York: New York University Press, 2014).

7 Niobe Way, *Deep Secrets: Boys' Friendships and the Crisis of Connection* (Cambridge, MA: Harvard University Press, 2011).

8 Carol Gilligan, *In a Different Voice: Psychological Theory and Women's Development* (Cambridge, MA: Harvard University Press, 1982); Carol Gilligan, *Joining the Resistance* (Cambridge: Polity Press, 2011).

9 Robert Landy and David Montgomery, *Theatre for Change: Education, Social Action and Therapy* (New York: Palgrave Macmillan, 2012).

10 Sharifa Oppenheimer, *Heaven on Earth: A Handbook for Parents of Young Children* (Great Barrington, MA: Steiner Books, 2006).

11 Bessel van der Kolk, *The Body Keeps Score: Brain, Mind and Body in the Healing of Trauma* (New York: Penguin, 2014).

12 Robert Landy, *Persona and Performance: The Meaning of Role in Drama, Therapy and Everyday Life* (New York: Guilford, 1993); Robert Landy, *The Couch and the*

Stage: Integrating Worlds and Acton in Psychotherapy (Lanham, MD: Jason Aronson, 2008); Gilligan, *Birth of Pleasure*; Gilligan, *In a Different Voice.*

13 Landy, *Persona and Performance*; Oppenheimer, *Heaven on Earth.*

14 William Shakespeare, *The Tempest* (1623), in *The RSC Shakespeare: William Shakespeare Complete Works*, ed. Jonathan Bate and Eric Rasmussen (New York: Modern Library, 1995), 31.

13

Splitting the World Open

Connection and Disconnection among Women Teaching Girls

JUDITH A. DORNEY

Following a faculty meeting at which Carol Gilligan and Lyn Brown presented information about what researchers were hearing from the girls at a private school, a seventh grade teacher, Sharon Miller, approached Carol to tell her about a conversation she had with her eleven-year-old daughter. "I'm angry with you," her daughter had said, "because when you and Daddy fight, you always give in." Reflecting on this experience, Sharon said, "I was so humiliated, so ashamed." Later, as Sharon worked with other women teachers to explore their experiences as women teaching girls, she described a similar incident that had occurred with the homeroom students she shared with a charismatic male teacher. One day he had announced that there was a new rule—no one could leave lunch until everyone had finished. Sharon Miller didn't agree with this rule, but she had not said anything to dispute it. "I related to him as I relate to my husband," she explained. But later that week, when some girls from orchestra came late to lunch, she turned to the others who had finished and said, "You may be excused." On their way out of the dining room, one of the girls turned and said, "Good for you, Mrs. Miller. We're proud of you." It was clear that the girls had observed everything, and also that Sharon had become more cognizant about what she was and what she wanted to be teaching them.

This chapter presents a curriculum I developed to directly address the dissonant moments Sharon experienced as well as a larger crisis of connection between women and girls, women's relationships with one another, and women's relationship with themselves. It draws on the astute steps outlined by Maria Harris in her book *Women and Teaching*, and was designed initially for a pair of retreats with women teachers, administrators, and researchers at the Laurel School for Girls in Ohio, a school that educates girls from early childhood through twelfth grade.[1] I wove the voices of girls, many of whom participated in the five-year research project on girls' development, into the steps identified by Harris. I was a member of the research team and constructed this curriculum in response to a request by several women teachers at the school who wanted to explore what it meant to be women teaching girls, with special attention to their relationship as women to the traditions we either pass on or challenge. The curriculum enabled the participants to uncover and name long-standing disconnections within themselves as well as within their practice and relationships as educators. These revelations came as a result of the retreat process, and central to these disclosures was the development of a profound sense of community among the female participants. But the community faced its own crisis of connection. This chapter offers an opportunity for reflection on the power of this work, the deep connection, and the disconnection we confronted, and it raises questions about the challenge of creating and sustaining community in order to continue the work of change. But first a bit more background.

Context

At the schoolwide faculty meeting mentioned in the introduction, early in the five-year research project on girls' development at the Laurel School for Girls, the two principal researchers, Carol Gilligan and Lyn Brown, shared with the faculty some of what researchers' interviews had revealed about their female students. The researchers heard strength and directness in the younger girls, as well as a comfort with conflict. Interviews with the older girls illustrated more muting of voice, a lack of directness, and a discomfort with conflict so that the girls would oftentimes keep silent rather than speak their feelings and cause what they felt was a disruption in relationships. This shift began when the girls were in seventh grade, right at the cusp of adolescence. As Carol and Lyn shared these insights, some of the faculty women commented that what they were hearing was resonating with them and identified moments of self-silencing and being silenced in their work and family lives. Some named an inability to bring their genuine thoughts and feelings into the school, both at meetings and in other venues. A few of the women noted that they experienced headaches and stomach problems. One said she felt she was working "under a great weight." Following the faculty meeting, a number of these women spoke about wanting opportunities to explore what it meant to be women teaching girls at this time, in this place. Was their development as women linked to the girls' development? How did schooling, even in an all-girls school, contribute to this change in voice and diminished sense of self for many of the girls as they moved into their teen years?

The head of the school, Leah Rhys, was most supportive in securing funding and creating the opportunity for teachers to investigate such questions. In October 1988, thirteen women from Laurel (who came to be identified as the research affiliates) and three women from the Harvard Graduate School of Education (Carol, Lyn, and me) joined together for the first of what would become a series of three retreat weekends.

The retreats took place in an elite setting with women who were white, middle- to upper-middle-class, and well-educated. There was diversity in age, the women being in their early thirties to their sixties, and the educators encompassed those in early education, middle school, and secondary school. There were also at least three administrators who were members of the group, although the head of school was not a participant. It was, in fact, the mix of teachers and administrators that created some of the most profound moments of the retreats. While this particular set of retreats took place many years ago and with private school faculty, the concerns propelling the retreats remain current and the process has constructive implications for all girls and women. Indeed, this retreat process was conducted, with some modifications in the curriculum, with racially and ethnically diverse teachers and administrators from the Boston public schools, public school teachers in Upstate New York, and private school teachers in El Paso, Texas, and in one-day workshops with educators across the country from Boston, Chicago, St. Louis, and San Francisco. For the purpose of this chapter, however, I focus on the retreats with the Laurel School educators as this is the process I have documented through tape recordings and interviews.

Using the text of *Women and Teaching*, I developed the retreat curriculum in consultation with Pat Flanders Hall, who was the head of the upper school at Laurel. In her text, Harris identifies and describes steps in a pedagogy that takes women as teachers and women and girls as students seriously. The steps are *Silence, Remembering, Mourning, Artistry,* and *Birthing,* so named because Harris believes these are central and generative themes in the lives of women. On the first retreat we proceeded through Silence and Remembering. On the second retreat, one year after our first gathering, we moved through Mourning, Artistry, and Birthing. Each retreat weekend was introduced with a paired conversation between the women, and the questions for these dialogues were created by Pat. Following lunch we entered into the retreat themes. A third retreat took place the January following the second retreat. The movement through that weekend was organic and focused on issues and struggles raised by the teachers.

I interviewed all the participants individually several months after the final retreat. The women described changes in themselves, in their relationships with each other, and with their female students. For example, some spoke of allowing their students to explore conflict. Some of the women made life-changing decisions following the retreats. Three women resigned from the school. The process of communicating honestly and directly with their peers and with the administrators who attended enabled the development of courageous connections among the affiliates as well as some courageous action.

First Retreat

We began the first afternoon with the story of Eva Wolff, a first grade student, and Miss Williams, her teacher. This is the story that opens Harris's book. On her first day of school, Eva enters her classroom and sees the sentence "The cat is black." on the board. She sits down and with her left hand begins to write the sentence out, starting with the letter "k" and working backward. Miss Williams positively acknowledges Eva's work but then suggests that she put her pencil in the right hand and begin at the other end of the sentence. Harris notes that this simple story captures the experience of many women who have had to "recast our forms of learning into molds which were not initially designed for us, into shapes and styles and sentences which often feel quite foreign."[2] Harris also acknowledges that Miss Williams may know that something is being lost here but feels compelled to follow the rules, in this case, of the acceptable handwriting method.

I opened with this story from Harris's text because it captures so well that disequilibrium shared by both the female teacher and her female student. One feels the need to play by the rules. The other is being initiated into the rules. This story has been repeated in schools for as long as women and girls have inhabited this space together. The wisdom of the pedagogy Harris articulates is in its power to disrupt this story. Following this example I briefly explained the steps from Silence to Birthing and told the women that for the next day and a half we would be moving through Silence and Remembering.

We began with *Silence* because it has been a pervasive theme in the contemporary study of women and because there has been much silence in the history and life experience of girls and women. To help us consider what silence might mean for us as women teaching girls and women, we examined two aspects of silence: silence in the curriculum and silence as a method for listening to one's own voice and the voice of other silenced beings.

In order to look at Silence in the curriculum, Harris calls upon the categories of Explicit, Implicit, and Null curricula identified by Elliott Eisner in *The Educational Imagination*.[3] The Explicit curriculum is what is "consciously taught, what is overtly and verbally addressed, what is printed and presented as the subject matter to be studied." The Implicit curriculum is "less obvious but still intentional, and found in the atmosphere: patterns of direct address, or of decision making or of designating positions of influence . . . what REALLY gets said . . . what REALLY goes on subtly and at the margins . . . not only who speaks but who gets heard." The Null curriculum "refers to areas left out, ideas not addressed, concepts not offered . . . also processes and procedures which are rarely, if ever, employed."[4]

I explained these categories and broke into two groups for discussion about our own experiences as students and now as educators. When this discussion seemed to be drawing to a close, one woman from each group read to her group an excerpt by the poet and essayist Adrienne Rich about silences in the classroom.[5]

After our small group discussion we returned to the large group to report back on the discussions and then moved to an examination of

Silence as a healing power. Prefacing our silent time with passages from Virginia Woolf as well as Beck, Walters, and Francisco's book, *Sacred Ways of Knowing*, we took time alone to consider the ways in which silence can inform and heal us, connect us to the stories of others, and lead to a reconnection with our own voices.[6]

During the small group exploration of the silences identified by Eisner, one woman spoke of learning to "correct" her words and her writing so they would be more acceptable to a larger culture. Another told of a time when she volunteered to do a math problem on the board in her sixth grade math class. The male teacher told her to step aside because the class couldn't "see through your breasts." In the second group there was discussion of how conflict was handled in the school, a theme that would emerge in a variety of discussions throughout the retreats. In the large group session the women's sense of being overwhelmed by their work surfaced as they acknowledged that the students could well see them as "frantic" because of their workloads and the pressure to educate so that the girls would be admitted to top schools. Following this discussion one of the administrators burst into tears as she voiced her discomfort with her role as an administrator. She was seeing the stress of the teachers and contemplating her role in maintaining the pressure they felt. The examination of silence as both problem and possibility had opened up the past and present pain of the women's educational lives. In the next portion of the retreat, after dinner and the following morning, we would remember more broadly the stories of women and our place in them.

We gathered after dinner to continue our work and were joined for the evening by the head of school, Leah Rhys, and also by the head of development. I did not pick up on any tension in the room due to their presence. In hindsight, and given the evolution of the group's concerns, the tension must have been there. But at the time it seemed more than appropriate that they join us as Leah had been so instrumental in securing resources and time for the retreats.

There are four forms of *Remembering* explored by Maria Harris: Mythic, Dangerous, Communal, and Ritual (a form she refers to as Liturgical). We began with Mythic Remembering, which recalls and examines myths through a critical feminist lens. I introduced the myths of Medusa and Lilith, and we considered the disconnection of head from body and head from emotions in educational practice. Individual women shared moments when they felt a need to protect students from feelings that are both deep and considered disruptive, especially anger and sadness. We moved into Dangerous Remembering, which proved to be a significant step for the women. Five women mentioned this step directly in the interviews I conducted with them. Dangerous Remembering is a term used by theologian Johannes Baptiste Metz.[7] This form of remembering conjures stories of suffering and freedom, courage and resistance, thus bringing the work at hand into the realm of the political. After explaining this form of remembering I played two pieces of music for the women. One of these songs identified the struggles of challenging dictatorship and political repression in Chile, naming eight of the women who were "disappeared."[8] The second song told the story of Bridget Evans, a peace worker at Greenham Common Women's Peace Encampment.[9] The camp was created by women to oppose the storage of cruise missiles from the United States at Greenham Common. It was closed in 2000, after being a site of resistance for nineteen years.

Following the songs we discussed their impact on us. One teacher who had earlier asserted that we had to protect the girls especially from anger stated, "We are not angry enough." Later on, in her interview, she would say, "We have to teach girls to be angry about sacred things." To some extent her first comment foreshadowed work we would do in the second retreat as we pinpointed anger as an emotion that had to be scrutinized and reclaimed.

On Saturday morning we met to conclude the step of Remembering with an exploration of Communal Remembering and Ritual Remembering. The task in Communal Remembering is to detect and listen to voices of those who are absent or underrepresented in our teaching and learning communities or whose approaches to knowledge are unorthodox. They may be voices that exemplify ways of knowing that are not often called upon in traditional schooling, or they may be those who are present but ignored or disdained. I chose four voices for this exercise, two adult women, scientist Barbara McClintock and artist Georgia O'Keeffe, a fictional female adolescent, Agnes Angst, and a young girl, Ruby Bridges, who was one of the first children to desegregate the William Frantz Elementary School in Louisiana in 1960.[10] I asked the women to consider these readings and see what emerged for them in the next twenty minutes of silence. Using Agnes Angst as her template, Pat went to her room and made a list of all the things she minded, thus giving herself permission to voice her dissatisfaction. Another teacher recounted that she was thinking of a young girl whose life was so rigidly structured at home, she could not make simple decisions, like where to sit, on her own. This teacher wondered if she was helping her student by encouraging her to choose. I suggested that in allowing the girl this opportunity she might be providing her with a small but real dangerous memory, of choosing based on her own desire.

We ended the morning with Ritual Remembering. Maria Harris identifies this final form of remembering as Liturgical Remembering and explains, in part, how this form of remembering involves the creation of rituals of commemoration. I chose to highlight the dimension of ritual by celebrating teachers who had inspired the women in the room and began with a dramatic reading from *The Small Room* by May Sarton.[11] When the reading was done the women in the room were asked to reflect on who was brought to mind by that excerpt. Who was the teacher (in or out of formal schooling) whose head and heart were on fire, like Caryl, the educator in the reading? At the close of the reflection the women were invited to name their teachers and identify the passion they "caught" from them.

In both Communal and Ritual Remembering the women cried more than I had expected. The tears came with sad or poignant stories. We were ending this retreat at the edge of Mourning, the next step in Harris's pedagogy. I wondered at the wisdom of ending at this point. But the women took the retreat experience back to the school and began to speak with each other about the stresses they were feeling. Something had broken open.

Second Retreat

As with the first retreat weekend, we began in discussion pairs. In the general discussion following the paired conversations, Renee and Pat shared that their conversation focused on two issues: learning to be a "good girl" who develops into the "good woman," one who does not express disruptive thoughts and feelings, and the consequential difficulty in being angry and having anger heard. The good girl/woman is confined to a relational role lacking agency and thus assumes a childlike position in reference to authority. Indeed, at different points in the retreat transcripts the head of school was mentioned as "mother" and "matriarch." This led to some exploration of the kind of relationships that are possible in schools—between women and the traditions we teach as well as with each other and with students, in this case female students. At this point in the discussion Carol interjected, "You're saying, 'I maintain relationship by not having strong feelings.' And then I say, which is always my question to myself, 'What relationship?' I mean, who's in relationship? And to that sense in the name of relationship I keep myself out of relationship and the bizarreness of that." This issue of silencing certain feelings grew more complex as more people spoke. Fear of fracturing relationships, self-silencing, and fear of retribution from administration came up. Skip, a woman who had lived through the terms of five different heads of school, relayed that when she had sat down and talked with Leah, she had been very honest with Skip. Their conversation felt mutual. Renee asserted that when she had chosen her "forum carefully," the response from Leah had not been the negative one she anticipated. Renee claimed she had to take responsibility for her self-silencing at times. Terri acknowledged that the power differential was real and served to intimidate her as she was mindful that if she appeared to be a problem or a troublemaker she could lose her job. JoAnn, who was head of the lower school, noted that she had felt humiliated by Leah at faculty meetings and so was wary of speaking up. I asked, at this point, "Where are all of you when JoAnn needs to speak and is silenced? How can you help each other to speak?" We had not yet begun Harris's steps for this second weekend, but we were well into the heart of our ongoing work together.

Harris names *Mourning* as the third step because it emerges, rather organically, from the work of Silence and Remembering. She writes, "If we believe that teaching is the work of taking seriously the experience of all of us and being critical of how and when it does or does not; and if we believe we must develop a pedagogy which incorporates the fullness of women's lives, then much of our present limited concentration on only a part of human history, and many of the procedures presently included and excluded, will have to be examined."[12] This statement underscores the requirement of naming who and what have been missing or lost, a process the women had already begun in their partnered conversations.

For this session of Mourning, in an effort to uncover voices that had been absent or unheard due to cultural and/or institutional silencing, Lyn Brown and I had prepared portions of interviews from the girls at the school. Lyn's comments were drawn from her dissertation and reflected both strength of voice and loss of it in the girls' development and schooling.[13] The statements I chose were from a paper I had written focusing on interviews with African American students about some of the dissonance the girls experienced at a predominantly white, upper-middle-class private school. Pat, Carol, Lyn, and I read their words and followed up with group discussion questions.

This led to pinpointing how the losses we identified might result from a lack of awareness of our limited perspective, our learned racism, and our efforts to conform to the good girl/woman ideal as well as a tendency to disengage from difference. Peggy McIntosh's essay on white privilege assisted our dialogue.[14]

I then shared a portion from the book *Beloved* by Toni Morrison.[15] In the scene I chose, Sethe, a pregnant slave, has finally managed to run away from her owner. But she is severely injured from a brutal beating and collapses before she arrives at the river she must cross to reach Ohio and freedom. Amy, a white woman who is also fleeing a desperate situation, comes upon Sethe and tends to her wounds. As Sethe is about to get into a rowboat to cross the river, she goes into labor and Amy and Sethe participate together in birthing a baby girl. Then the women separate and Sethe crosses the river with her daughter. Following this excerpt I asked, "What is it we want to give birth to? How can we stay with each other?" Both questions carried the threads of the earlier discussion forward and were woven into our exchanges for the remainder of the retreat.

Artistry is about creation. It is about identifying the knowledge and tools we have to work with once we have explored the silences and losses of the previous steps. We dealt with two of the forms of artistry named by Harris, Embodiment and Revelation. For Embodiment I read a few pieces of writing by Marge Piercy, Audre Lorde, and Madeleine Grumet and then invited the women to disclose some of their embodied knowledge. After the women's examples of what seemed like sacred knowledge, Carol asked what it would mean to teach this to girls. She challenged that leaving this knowledge out perpetuates the absence of women's knowledge in education.

We broke for exercise and dinner, and I recall feeling somewhat frustrated that for all our individual and collective insights there was still very much a tendency to blame the person in charge for what felt problematic in the school and to assume that she should know things without people communicating with her. These are not uncommon relational expectations. We often feel friends or partners, for example, should just know how we feel or what we want. But these expectations come with relationships that may be somewhat idealized—where people don't communicate clearly and directly bringing their real thoughts and feelings into their affiliations. And they come with connections where there is a power differential, where those with less power learn to fear speaking their truth. This was some of the work that lay ahead of us in our last two retreat sessions. But in the meantime we had dinner. It was relaxed and full of laughter, and with the laughter came a feeling of freedom. The feminist humorist Kate Clinton claims that humor is an essential tool in the process of change. "Humor helps us see that there is a possibility of going through it . . . laughter is, in so many ways a healing tool."[16] This night laughter seemed to create a bridge to some of our hardest dialogue.

Revelation is a liberating movement as Maria Harris describes it. It is about "self-discovery; self-understanding; self-possession in a community of free and authentic selves. Revelation is the realization of deliverance of ourselves, to ourselves in communion with all that is."[17] This is the work we moved into following our dinner.

The reading I chose to begin the evening was one of the letters Celie wrote to her sister, Nettie, in *The Color Purple*. Celie tells about a conversation she had about God with her lover, Shug Avery. Shug states that in order to view God differently you have to "get man off your eyeballs," and Celie notes that this is hard work.[18] I chose this piece because it places much responsibility for changing the relationship with God in the hands of Celie. I wanted the women to think about who or what was on their eyeballs and what it would take to change that. Four women revealed that cultural images of the "perfect family" and "the perfect woman" were on their eyeballs.

This step of Artistry and the discussion about claiming one's authority proved to be pivotal for the group. Issues of power clearly surfaced. There were three administrators who were a part of the affiliate group:

Pat, who was the head of the upper school, JoAnn, who was head of the lower school, and Linda, associate director of the Early Childhood Division. As the teachers deliberated about their concerns around the head of the school, one of them courageously addressed Pat. She claimed that there was less than honest communication from Pat about policies and decisions made at the school. With some passion she said, "And regardless of how you might see yourself, when you are in an administrative position it puts you also in the hierarchal position to us at times. . . . And I would love more, I would like more honesty!" A second issue was raised around the need for group solidarity in meetings where, because of fear, people tend not to disagree or challenge the head of school and group silence is the collective response. Renee, the school psychologist, asserted, "The women in this room can be a force . . . I think that we can support each other." Pat stressed that this effort had to be a "group thing and . . . we have to expect the rejection feelings and you have to expect the pain that can create." I asked how they would survive this, and Terri replied, "With our beepers." Skip added, "Be united." The women continued to strategize about how they might be there for each other and what specifically they would have to do differently at meetings. They outlined some of the ways they might approach Leah with ideas. There was a palpable sense of agency and the potential for change in their behavior as well as their expectations of the head of school. Earlier in the day I had asked the question, "Where are you all when JoAnn is being silenced?"

The theme of Artistry led us to the answer and to a group of women beginning to put themselves, each other, and girls on their eyeballs. As I reread Renee's statement, "I think we can support each other," I am struck with the disconnection, the isolation that existed among these women. The idea that they could indeed support each other was radical and daring. And from subsequent work with women educators as well as my own experience in educational institutions, I know that this is not an unusual sensibility. Hierarchical institutions are designed to perpetuate themselves and to maintain current power structures, and they do that, in part, by silencing their members with threats of punishment and/or exclusion. The construction of a network of support among the members with the least clout is one tried and true way to speak back to power. Unions know this. These women were coming to this awareness and were taking the risk to do some of that speaking within the group. One of the brilliant notes in Maria Harris's steps is that the next dimension of Artistry is Receptivity to Power. By the end of our evening's work on Artistry, we were already there.

The next morning we were to meet for what we thought would be our final step in this retreat process. On my way to the meeting room I passed Pat's room and the door was open. I saw her sitting on a chair propped next to a window. She was smoking and appeared to be deep in thought as she looked out onto the city street. I asked how she was and she replied, "I'm thinking about collusion." She did not add more to that comment. A short time later I learned that at least half of the affiliates stayed up talking into the early morning hours. Pat was among them. While I did not have access to that conversation, it is possible that it became evident to those who stayed up talking how the power and communication dynamics within the school were something to which they all contributed.

The ultimate step in this pedagogy is *Birthing*. In opening I drew on the writing of Madeleine Grumet, who challenges women teachers to stop leading the "great escape" from the maternal order to the patriarchy. She charges women teachers with the task of uncovering what we know and/or developing a critical understanding of how schooling has perpetuated the "asymmetrical patterns of class, race, and gender."[19] In *Maternal Thinking*, Sara Ruddick speaks about the need for an "imaginative collective" of women.[20] Like the Madres in Argentina who met weekly from 1977 to 1983 in order to challenge the government to release their disappeared children and grandchildren, Ruddick sees such collectives drawing their strength and vision from the act of birthing, which incarnates bodily knowing, pleasure and pain, intimacy and distinctiveness.

The cumulative labor of the women during all of the retreat process bore fruition in this step. Several topics were raised and questions were posed. One was the tendency to blame one person for the problems in the school and the need to reach out to women faculty who had not attended the retreats. Picking up on Grumet's statements, four of the women advanced the discussion on how we bring ourselves and our knowledge into our work. One woman said she just "pulls away" at meetings where a difficult topic comes up and added, "I'm not there." She equated this with trying to be a "good person" who listens but has no strong feelings herself. Terri added that she could take the risk of speaking up at meetings, but this could be seen as "too much disruption" and she would be out there alone. Mindful of previous conversations, I asked, "Why do you put yourself out there alone? You are not alone in this room right now. What would have to happen for you to not be [alone out there]?" She answered with a strategy for speaking and acting that included preparation and the gathering of allies.

Carol reminded us of the research with girls asserting that when girls withhold or lose their voices they enter into relationships in which the possibilities for connection are lessened. Noting that in school the girls were around and observing the women, Sharon recalled the story of Jesse, a second grader, who was able to leave a group of friends because she was not having fun. Sharon noted that Jesse could leave because she knew there was someone to leave with, herself. She asserted that for middle school girls it is much harder. "They have let go of themselves . . . there's no one there." Carol asked why this was the case, and Sharon replied that this is when they begin to identify with adult women. "My god," she said. "And there's nothing there." As this last statement left her mouth she covered her mouth with her hand and cried. There was an audible reaction from the women in the room, perhaps a deepened knowledge of the connection between girls and women and how we depend upon each other for courage.

Third Retreat

The third and final retreat took place the following January. There was no curriculum, but there was a task. We needed to explore whether and how we would continue our work together and to organize a Women Teaching Girls workshop scheduled for the day after a national conference in Cleveland at which the larger five-year research project with the girls would be presented to a national audience. At the time we met for this retreat the Laurel faculty were not scheduled to be in attendance at the conference itself, although the affiliate teachers would be present for the Women Teaching Girls workshop. The women felt strongly that the entire Laurel faculty should be present at the conference, at which the voices of their students would be central. They believed the absence of the faculty would be undermining and disrespectful. After much conversation during the day-and-a-half retreat, the women came up with an alternative plan to present to the head of school.

The most essential element was their commitment to work together to bring this plan about, and they lived this commitment in their strategizing and in their action. The tactic was to use their one remaining professional day for faculty to attend the conference so they would learn the research findings when they were first announced to the larger educational community. Their plan was to have the affiliates meet with the head of the school one morning before school in the room of one of the teacher affiliates. All were present, and each woman spoke about why she felt it critical for faculty to be in attendance for the conference. They laid out their proposal and had ensured that the venue could sustain seventy-five more attendees. To their surprise, Leah thought this was a wonderful plan. In a phone conversation with Carol later that day, Leah noted that implementing their idea would be a way of "honoring the work" as well as the faculty. She added, "The power of that group has emerged . . . [it was] a very exciting conversation." Her response could not have been more positive and suggests that Leah might have been open to more such efforts by the women. This was indeed an encouraging step. In this instance their commitment to each other and their planning and willingness to speak brought change that served the entire faculty. But, in my experience, sustained change comes through the daily work of continuing to speak and act in ways that challenge old relational patterns.

Changes for the Women and Girls

I interviewed all the participants in the summer and fall following the third retreat and the national conference. All of the affiliates spoke about a renewed appreciation for and ability to connect with their feelings and listen to their own voices. Terri, using a dated but apt analogy, compared it to popping the buttons off a girdle. The women were also able to discern the ways in which they were complicit in the silencing of girls, and each one had to find her way into how she would interrupt that relational pattern and alter her approach to the teaching of girls. The voices of female students reminded them of the importance of attending to what is needed in the moment and to honoring the truth and knowledge located in emotion.

I offer just two examples of how the women related differently with the girls. Claudia narrated an incident where three female students from the upper school were verbally fighting in a hall. While the argument was verbal, it was very emotional, loud, and "very close to being physical." Witnessing this, she had two competing instincts. One was the "nice girl" instinct that says girls don't fight or attack their friends. The other was "the realization that these emotions had to come out just as they have come out among the women who worked together." Claudia brought the girls into her empty classroom and allowed them to work out the feelings while she stood down the hall. When the period ended, the girls emerged with puffy faces, but were smiling and told her they were okay. I'm not certain what the girls absorbed from this moment in school, but they might have learned that difficult feelings like anger and jealousy can be worked through, that relationships can survive and grow from conflict, and that an adult woman did not try to silence them but gave them the space to do that work.

Susie, who reported that her knowledge from the retreat work involved the awareness that she was not alone, also relayed a story of a fight. This time it involved a fourth grader who got angry at a classmate who would not share her computer time. After asking her classmate a number of times to share the computer with her, Katie removed the disk from the computer and also scratched the girl who was using it. Katie was sent to Susie for disciplinary action, and Susie asked Katie to explain what had happened. They discussed the incident. Susie acknowledged Katie's anger and frustration, considered with her other alternatives to taking the disk and scratching, and learned during the conversation that the other girl was Katie's friend. Katie began to cry when she said she hoped for forgiveness from this friend. Susie felt that she was able to allow Katie to hold on to her experience of anger and sadness while also helping her to see the inappropriateness and danger of her physical response to that anger. The woman who realized in the retreat process that she was no longer alone sat with a girl, allowing her to feel her sadness and her desire to reunite with her friend. Susie acknowledged that the retreat work had "enabled her to get what is going on, what matters to these kids, what it is they really care about."[21]

Three of the women affiliates also resigned. One was moving to another city because her husband had been transferred, but she noted that her knowledge coming out of the retreats involved listening to what she truly felt, something she had not done for a very long time. She was now aware of the price she paid when she did not do that. The other two women also noted that reconnection within themselves and felt it would be in jeopardy if they remained at the school. As Pat said, "I'm happy to report to you . . . that there's a greater congruence between what I've carried around inside of me all this time and what I do and say and act in public."[22] At the end of the year all three women had exit interviews with the school's Board of Directors. In July of that year, the head of school, Leah Rhys, also resigned from her position. This news was startling, and following the announcement I asked the school's head of development if there was any sense that our work with the affiliates contributed to Leah's decision. She replied that there was no sense of a connection between the two. But the time frame and the fact that the three affiliates who resigned gave exit interviews to the board of directors called this into question for at least some of us.

Questions and Reflections

There is no question that this work led to potent connections for the women who participated. When Carol returned to the school a year ago on the twenty-fifth anniversary of the larger research project, several of the women affiliates returned to hear her speak. They told her that this retreat work was the most meaningful experience of their teaching careers. But, while noting the successes, there are also critical questions about connection, process, and institutions that bear exploration.

The first question emerges from the fact that this community did not include all the women in the school, and this was perhaps most relevant in the absence of the head of the school. Initially this did not appear to be a problem. There were other administrators present, and issues of inequality of power surfaced. Her presence would undoubtedly have changed the dynamic considerably, but in her absence she was the target of much attention from the group. There were clearly several women who felt silenced by her and who felt she conducted herself in an autocratic way. Her absence may have fueled those feelings or may have simply provided a space where they could be articulated in a community of support. However, there were also a few women who felt she could be approached and found her to be responsive. As noted earlier, Leah secured the funding for the retreat work, gave the women the time off to attend the retreats on three Fridays, appreciated their initiative in proposing that all faculty attend the conference day, and altered the arrangements to make that happen. So, as is the case with the rest of us, she was a complex figure. I have noted that she was occasionally referred to as "mother" and "matriarch." As I recall the affiliates' struggle to free themselves from captivity to the notion of the ideal or perfect woman, these maternal references make me wonder if there was some idealization of female leadership at play, some underlying sense that a female leader should be "perfect" and should know when something was wrong without anyone communicating the problem to her. Perhaps we were not so successful in throwing off the yoke of the ideal mother and recognizing that Leah, too, was located in the patriarchal context of a traditional private, independent, all-girls school. This is something I wish we had examined at the time.

Of course a contributing factor to the difficulty with Leah is the factor that exists wherever there are differences of power, especially the power to terminate an employee's position. But, as one of the women expressed during the second retreat, one person alone is not responsible for this problem. I want to be able to say that truthful community is possible even when such differences exist. I also understand the vulnerability of the worker who does not know if she can trust the leader not to retaliate or the student who doesn't feel she can count on the teacher not to grade her poorly. One possible response is for the leader to make herself vulnerable as well. Elizabeth Spelman proposes that women who are in privileged positions adopt the relational qualities of an apprentice.[23] This standpoint is one of a learner. The goal is to try to understand from the less privileged position what that experience is. It requires humility and a commitment and, I think, some courage. Having said that, I now think some sort of meeting or intervention with Leah could have been fruitful. I don't know if it would have stemmed the resignations, but with the women able to speak when they felt the support of others, a gathering of the affiliates with Leah could have perhaps led to even more radical change.

A second question that troubles me is why we did not talk as a group about our thoughts and feelings around the resignations. So in a certain way, in the face of some radical change, we as a whole group, and the women affiliates in particular, did not sustain the connection of the group. On the third retreat, when Pat announced her decision to resign, there was observable pain in some of the women. We addressed the discomfort but not in any depth, partially because the affiliates wanted/needed to strategize about the faculty conference attendance. Again, I think we should have attended to this with more complexity. This would have required that those of us involved in facilitating the group recognized Pat's resignation as highly significant for the group. We were all given the news at the same time during one of the sessions and thus were not prepared ahead of time to assist the group in processing this significant information. Also, we never, as a group, discussed Leah's resignation during the following summer. I learned in the interviews I did following the retreats that her leaving left some of the women very disturbed, but those were individual and confidential conversations. I'm not aware of whether and/or how the affiliates talked with each other about this startling news. And I think it may have caused them to wonder how our work might have been linked to her resignation.

A third concern is that there was no structure of support for the affiliates and researchers to continue to work together after the larger research project ended. While the two previous questions center more on relationship and unanticipated change, this problem may be a more practical issue as well as a commonly recognized shortcoming in teacher professional development. Most typically "experts" appear, work with faculty for a time, and then leave. There is little if any sense or understanding that change work with teachers is relational and requires sustaining connection. Faculty members are left without the needed supports to continue the development work that was initiated by others. I know from my teaching experience in high schools as well as my work with many educators around the country that teachers generally do not have time to generate and continue these structures for themselves. As one of the teachers remarked during the retreats, she had ten minutes for lunch. No one of us had anticipated the intense power of these retreats and did not see a need to build supports for maintaining and renewing connections into the work. In the absence of these larger supports each woman was left on her own to seek ways to bring her reconnected knowledge to her work. The gain should not be underestimated, but it was a far cry from the power and collaboration of the group.

The final question is perhaps the most challenging. What does it mean when women educators connect with something very deep, what Audre Lorde would call "the erotic," within themselves?[24] What does it mean for their relationships and their workplaces? What we touched in this work was formidable. Women resigned from their jobs, and teaching relationships among colleagues and students were changed radically, even between affiliates and faculty who had not participated in the retreats. Women identified their embodied knowledge and began to speak and act from that place. In her oft-quoted poem about the artist Kathe Kollwitz, Muriel Rukeyser asks, "What would happen if one woman told the truth about her life? The world would split open."[25] These lines denote the radical change that would come if even one woman's embodied knowledge and truth were released into the world. In this case, the knowledge released changed the individuals, but it also, to a certain extent, changed the institution and causes me to wonder what part these unanticipated changes played in the breakdown of the group. At one point during the retreats one of the upper school teachers asked if we were ready for a classroom where girls really spoke and acted from their minds and hearts, suggesting that we were moving into uncharted and perhaps uncomfortable territory. This is exactly where the retreats took us as individuals and as a group, and it seems, in certain ways, we were not ready for it. I now see naming and preparing for such unexpected results as part of the retreat process.

I opened this chapter asserting that the retreat curriculum directly addressed the crisis of connection. As we began our work together, the women were disconnected from their work, from themselves, from each other, and from their female students. This curriculum charts a way to create connection and to sustain it for a time. It gives us some clues. So in certain ways it is a good story. But it also uncovers some of the challenges of connection. Perhaps that saves us from idealization and checks any possible hubris. It seems to me that a central part of the work of connection is in dealing with the crises that emerge as we move forward. And when working with connections within institutions those crises will be shaped by individual and interpersonal forces but perhaps more significantly by institutional forces, which will generally work to maintain the status quo and disrupt the connections that threaten it. Certainly traditional schooling is not currently designed to hold these kinds of intense connections or to challenge the traditions and conventional power relationships. If we all had been more aware of these patterns and forces, I believe this could have been not just a good story, but a revolutionary one.

NOTES

1 Maria Harris, *Women and Teaching: Themes for a Spirituality of Pedagogy* (Mahwah, NJ: Paulist Press, 1988).

2 Ibid., 1.

3 Elliott Eisner, *The Educational Imagination* (New York: Macmillan, 1979).

4 Harris, *Women and Teaching*, 19–21.

5 Adrienne Rich, *On Lies, Secrets, and Silences* (New York: Norton, 1979), 243.

6 Virginia Woolf, *A Room of One's Own* (New York: Harcourt, Brace & World, 1957); Peggy V. Beck, Anna L. Walters, and Nia Francisco, *Sacred Ways of Knowing: Ways of Knowledge, Sources of Life* (Tsaile, AZ: Navajo Community College Press, 1977).

7 Johannes Baptiste Metz, *Faith in History and Society: Toward a Practical Fundamental Theology* (New York: Seabury Press, 1980).

8 Holly Near, "Hay Una Mujer," on *And Still We Sing*, cassette (Fullerton, CA: Redwood Records, 1978).

9 Judy Small, "Bridget Evans," on *Mothers, Daughters, Wives*, vinyl (Fullerton, CA: Redwood Records, 1984).

10 Jane Wagner, *The Search for Signs of Intelligent Life in the Universe* (New York: Harper & Row, 1986); Robert Coles, *The Moral Life of Children* (Boston: Houghton Mifflin, 1986).

11 May Sarton, *The Small Room* (New York: Norton, 1961).

12 Harris, *Women and Teaching*, 48.

13 Lyn Mikel Brown, "Narratives of Relationship and the Development of a Care Voice in Girls Ages 7 to 16" (PhD diss., Harvard University, 1989).

14 Peggy McIntosh, "White Privilege: Unpacking the Invisible Knapsack," *Peace and Freedom Magazine*, July–August 1989, 10–12.

15 Toni Morrison, *Beloved* (New York: Knopf, 1987).

16 Carolann Barrett, "Be Bold and Bad: An Interview with the Lovely Kate Clinton," *Woman of Power* 17 (1990): 60–63.

17 Harris, *Women and Teaching*, 69.

18 Alice Walker, *The Color Purple* (New York: Harcourt Brace Jovanovich, 1982), 168.

19 Madeleine Grumet, *Bitter Milk: Women and Teaching* (Amherst: University of Massachusetts Press, 1988), 28, 58.

20 Sara Ruddick, *Maternal Thinking* (Boston: Beacon, 1989).

21 Judith A. Dorney, "'Courage to Act in a Small Way': Clues toward Community and Change among Women Teaching Girls" (PhD diss., Harvard University, 1991), 169.

22 Ibid., 152.

23 Elizabeth Spelman, *Inessential Woman: Problems of Exclusion in Feminist Thought* (Boston: Beacon, 1988).

24 Audre Lorde, "Uses of the Erotic," in *Sister Outsider: Essays and Speeches* (Trumansburg, NY: Crossing Press, 1984), 53–59.

25 Muriel Rukeyser, "Kathe Kollwitz," in *The Collected Poems of Muriel Rukeyser* (New York: McGraw-Hill, 1978), 479–484.

14

I Want to Learn from You

Relational Strategies to Engage Boys in School

MICHAEL C. REICHERT AND JOSEPH D. NELSON

Educational Sacrifices of Boyhood

Both the promise and the problems of the new era of gender equality are more visible today. The rise of women has incidentally cast light on a masculine code that benefits neither boys nor our society. But there are two problems with talk of a "boy crisis." First, underperforming boys and their troubling, sometimes tragic, outcomes are nothing new. Noted educational researchers Thomas DiPrete and Claudia Buchmann have shown that a gender achievement gap has existed in the United States for over a century.[1] Even before they enter kindergarten, many boys have fallen behind in the development of "soft" skills essential for success.

But while the costs of boyhood begin early and seep deeply into all boys' self-concepts, ambitions, and accomplishments, the most troubling aspect of the educational gap is that, while observable across virtually all socioeconomic, cultural, and geographic conditions, it is most pronounced when the impact of masculine conditioning is compounded by other social stresses, like racism and poverty. In a recent study examining outcomes for children from low-SES households, a research team matched birth certificates and health, disciplinary, academic, and high school graduation records for more than one million children born in Florida between 1992 and 2002, and found that, compared to girls, boys born to low-education and unmarried mothers, raised in low-income neighborhoods, and enrolled at poor-quality public schools have a higher incidence of truancy and behavioral problems throughout elementary and middle school, exhibit higher rates of behavioral and cognitive disability, perform worse on standardized tests, are less likely to graduate high school, and are more likely to commit serious crimes as juveniles.[2]

The authors ruled out two common explanations for this gap—biological vulnerabilities and SES-related disadvantages—to show that family disadvantage more adversely affects boys as a result of their experience as males: "Not because boys are more affected by family environment per se, but because the neighborhoods and schools in which disadvantaged children are raised are particularly adverse for boys."[3]

The second problem with talk of a crisis is that there is nothing surprising about this story. The science of human development points to a fatal contradiction at the heart of how boys are raised. Boyhood was never intended to serve boys themselves, and has never worked very well for them.[4] Losses and casualties have always been an inconvenient truth built into its design. Instead of a focus on "what people are actually able to do and to be" as the proper measure of boyhood's success, masculine socialization makes sure boys "man up."[5] As boys of all kinds fit themselves to masculine identities that are restrictive, are coercive, and violate their human natures, educators and developmentalists might ask how to create conditions—resources and relationships—that allow all boys to translate their innate capabilities into actual abilities.

In the past twenty years, there has been an explosion of new research on "interpersonal neuroscience."[6] Psychiatrist Amy Banks argues that how independence and individuality are conceived, at the heart of boyhood's value system, works against the very design of human anatomy. She identifies four separate neurobiological systems, from brain structures to adrenal-cortical interactions, ensuring that each individual is in sync with others. Every person, male as well as female, is "built to operate within a network of caring human relationships," she argues. Health and happiness, in her view, are a function of the vitality of these relational connections.[7]

Attachment experience has been studied with particular attention. Challenging the traditional view that biology sets a frame for behavior and personality—that boys develop as "boys" because of their biological inheritance—psychiatrist Daniel Siegel and developmental psychologist Mary Hartzell argue, "Experience *is* biology. How we treat our children changes who they are and how they will develop."[8] Children's mental models, the basis for how they relate to others, develop directly and continuously from experience and have little to do with "boys will be boys" clichés:

"Recent findings of neural science in fact point to just the opposite: Interactions with the environment, especially relationships with other people, directly shape the development of the brain's structure and function."[9]

These child development findings have been extended to the field of education. In response to the global "crisis" of boys' underachievement, there have been a host of reforms: more male teachers, more kinesthetic movement, longer recess times, and boy-friendly curricula and pedagogies. One country, Australia, issued a parliamentary-level set of recommendations that established special single-sex schools for boys, something that is also being tried in the United States, especially for boys of color from low-income backgrounds. But there has been a basic problem with these reforms: the understanding of boys underlying them represents what developmental psychologist Niobe Way has called "false stories."[10] Doing things the same way, only with more fervor, is unlikely to produce better results. A better approach is to build a model of how boys learn that does not begin with assumptions steeped in mistaken stereotypes.

A Relational Approach to Boys' Learning

In 2008–2010 and again in 2010–2012, the International Boys' School Coalition, a collection of over three hundred schools of all kinds, from fully fee-based to fully government-funded, elite to urban, partnered with the Center for the Study of Boys' and Girls' Lives, a research collaborative at the University of Pennsylvania, to develop an empirical understanding of boys' education by studying what was *working* in real classrooms. From surveys and interviews with twenty-five hundred adolescent boys and two thousand of their teachers from over forty schools of all types, we found that underlying successful learning was a phenomenon we termed "eliciting": attentive teachers, committed to getting it right with their students, refined their lessons until they succeeded in engaging boys.[11] In a reciprocal, "serve and volley," communication process, boys provide teachers with constant feedback in their levels of attentiveness, their posture, their on-task and off-task behavior, their test marks, and the quality of their homework assignments; in response, conscientious teachers modify their lessons until they reliably work. Their pedagogy, in this sense, is elicited from their students.

We found great convergence between how boys and teachers described the successful lessons that result, which usually represented general teaching practices but might also be specifically tailored to boys' interests, needs, or relational styles. Good teachers, we found, were both flexible and willing to employ whatever they could to connect with their students and lead them to the lesson.

But there was a large—and important—divergence between teachers' and students' descriptions of what worked. While teachers focused on the craft of their lessons and spoke in technical language about them, boys spoke in equal detail—but about the qualities and personalities of the teachers themselves. We were led to the primacy of the student-teacher relationship by the boys. In their resounding validation of teachers who inspired, helped, and uplifted them, we had concluded that, for boys, "relationship is the very *medium* through which successful teaching and learning is performed."[12]

Surprising for the clarity of their relational embrace, boys' stories of successful student-teacher partnerships validated converging lines of inquiry settling on the efficacy of relational approaches to stem educational casualties. "Positive student-teacher relationships" were found to explain the success of students in the Programme for International Student Assessment.[13] Meanwhile, in a meta-analysis of nearly one hundred studies, a Dutch research team demonstrated that both positive and negative teacher-student relationships have a significant effect on scholastic achievement. Even hard-to-engage students respond to relational strategies, they found; positive learning relationships may be especially beneficial in reaching those—mainly boys—at the bottom of the achievement gap.[14]

Despite these recent investigations, when we searched educational literature for research detailing the role of relationship in teaching boys, we discovered very little. The paucity of research-based recommendations until this most recent period matched what we had found in the field: teachers all *knew* that boys required connection in order to engage with their lessons but had given little systematic thought to what that meant. Asked to talk about why they did what they had done, what they were thinking, it was often hard for teachers to find words. Their relational pedagogy occurred on the level of intuition, as if crafted in a black box.

It seems that many working in schools, steeped in cultural stereotypes of boys as arelational, have trouble knowing what we really should know. This was the conclusion of the consortium of writers and researchers behind the Manifesto of Relational Pedagogy, which cautioned:

> A fog of forgetfulness is looming over education. Forgotten in the fog is that education is about human beings. And as schools are places where human beings get together, we have also forgotten that education is primarily about human beings who are in relation with one another.[15]

But boys themselves are quite clear and articulate about the relational dimension of their learning. In one focus group, in response to our question about a teacher they had gotten on well with, one boy began to talk animatedly about how the teacher had "ignited" him. Other boys in the group chimed in, speaking of this teacher with something like reverence and describing the atmosphere of his classroom as though it were a church or a sacred space. "It's a class," they said, "where you wouldn't *think* of acting out." The teacher's presence was not strict or commanding. The seriousness of purpose they felt stemmed from the teacher's own seriousness about his subject—the boys spoke of his "passion"— and the care he took with them. Patient, committed, concerned, and helpful: this was how he was described. "There is just something *about* him," one of the boys said. "You would be ashamed not to do your work, your best work."

The qualities of successful teachers listed by the teenage boys in our study were consistent across all the different cultures, countries, and types of schools. Reviewing their stories in the aggregate, we could deduce the common features of successful relationships. First and foremost, because it is an instrumental relationship from which boys are looking to learn, the mastery of the teacher was fundamentally important for the establishment of a working alliance: teachers must be seen as competent, as invested in their subjects and their pedagogy, and as reliable guides for the learning journey. Then, they must also be approachable, attentive, and responsive to boys' needs, as well as interested in knowing them beyond their performance in their particular classrooms. Both boys and teachers agreed to a remarkable extent on the list of relational gestures offered by teachers that promoted successful learning partnerships:

- Demonstrating an attractive *mastery of their subjects.* Perhaps counterin-tuitively, positive teacher-student relationships were not simply a matter of establishing mutually warm affect. Instead, clear mastery of teachers' fields was the relational sine qua non in many of the stories of success, underscoring that these are *working* alliances in which boys hope to advance their educational goals.

- Maintaining *high standards.* Likewise, boys often cited teachers who maintained clear and even demanding standards of classroom conduct and quality of work as those with whom they had the most trust and, overall, the best relationships.

- Responding to a student's *personal interest or talent.* Another strong theme running through both boys' and teachers' relational accounts was the enabling effect of a boy's realization that his teacher knew him beyond his status as, say, a seventh grade math or English student.

- Sharing *a common interest* with a student. For the reasons discussed above, teachers and boys sharing a personal interest—whether athletic, musical, mechanical—is a reliable relationship builder with similar posi-tive effects on scholastic performance.

- Sharing *a common characteristic* with a student. The fact that the boy and the teacher share and acknowledge a common characteristic—a defining physical feature, background, ethnicity, wound, problem overcome—can be a reliable, if serendipitous, relationship builder.

- Accommodating *a measure of opposition.* Teachers and boys alike report-ed that teachers who can resist personalizing boys' oppositional behavior and respond to it with restraint and civility, not only succeed in building relationships with difficult students but also create a promising climate for relationship building class-wide.

- A willingness *to reveal vulnerability.* While the gesture was least frequent-ly reported in the positive narratives, those that did discuss it—from both the boys' and the teachers' perspectives—may indicate an important ele-ment in relationship making.

When these relational gestures are offered and a learning relationship is struck, teachers make a tremendous difference for boys, even beyond their learning. Certainly, there is the practical benefit of acquiring skills or mastering subject matter well enough to pass required tests. But there are also transformational and even existential benefits from these learning partnerships. When they develop new abilities, boys' self-concepts grow as they come to see possibilities they could not imagine previously. Even more profoundly, the life-altering lesson boys absorb from teachers who care for them, and who demonstrate a willingness to go an extra mile on their behalf, influences their orientation to the world: they discover that there is help, that they can expect their needs to be met, that they are cared for. Educational philosopher David Hawkins, in his famous essay "I, Thou, and It," described what students feel about teachers who help them to mastery and success:

> What is the feeling you have toward a person who does this for you? It needn't be what we call love, but it certainly *is* what we call respect. You value the other person because he is uniquely useful to you in helping you on with your life.[16]

Disconnection in Learning Relationships

Absent such connections, boys are quite willing to check out and thence to act out. Their stance as learners assumes a teacher willing and able to guide them; in relationships with teachers where there is a relational rupture, boys described the teacher as unresponsive, inattentive, and disrespectful, as poor pedagogues, or as downright mean. For a variety of revealing reasons, reflecting the power asymmetry of teacher-student relationships, it is rare that a student takes any responsibility to repair a breakdown in a relationship with his teacher or coach. Instead of trying to fix the relationship, boys vote with their feet. As a boy at a Catholic school explained about a teacher he felt mistreated by: "I *hate* him. I'm not doing anything in that class. He can flunk me, they can kick me out—I'm not doing anything." When asked why, despite the obvious fact that this stance hurt him more than the teacher, he remained adamant: "I won't do *anything* for him." Such hardened attitudes were the norm in boys' stories of relational breakdowns; feeling violated, boys disconnect righteously and readily.

The following seven features represented boys' views of why things had not gone well with teachers. The list is virtually opposite to the previous list of successful relational gestures:

- *Teachers who were disrespectful or disparaging.* Respect was the sine qua non for relational partnership in boys' views; its absence was the most common explanation offered by boys for relationship failure. Teachers who displayed negative or critical attitudes risked boys' absolute refusal to relate, no matter the consequences.
- *Teachers who showed little personal enthusiasm.* Boys expected teachers who not only had mastered their subjects but also cared deeply about them; they hoped to be guided by teachers' personal passion in ways that elevated the class above the mundane.
- *Teachers who were inattentive or indifferent.* Boys expected not only good teaching but also teachers who were capable of *noticing them* and *responding with care.* They could be quite disdainful of teachers they perceived as somehow out of it.
- *Teachers who were unresponsive.* Similarly, boys expected—needed— teachers who would respond to their struggles in the triadic context with their own commitment to help, including a willingness to revisit their present approach in search of a better match for a boy's learning style.
- *Teachers who were unable to control their classes.* In many ways the frequency of this reported theme reinforced our hopeful finding that boys do, indeed, hope for classes managed by competent teachers in which they can focus and learn.
- *Teachers who were uninspiring or boring.* Distinct from teachers' level of passion and involvement with their subject, *how* teachers taught their lessons mattered a great deal to boys who, again, hoped to be lifted by their teachers out of the tedium of school routines.
- *Teachers who communicated poorly.* Sometimes boys may not have felt any particular animus toward teachers they named in their negative relational example; rather, they simply could not understand them or their lessons.

In their own accounts of relational breakdowns, teachers did acknowledge responsibility for relational failure, as well as considerable regret when a working relationship could not be restored. In fact, both in survey responses and in workshops, their accounts of these breakdowns were poignant and often quite painful. But like the boys, they tended not to blame themselves. In the end, teachers attributed relational impasse and failure to intractable personal or family circumstances, psychological problems, severe learning deficits, or, in some cases, larger cultural stresses bearing upon the boy. In fact, many teachers took pains to convey that they had done everything that could be professionally expected of them to reach the boy, whereas in their positive accounts they celebrated the serial attempts and sustained effort they made to overcome these same circumstances.

From these observations about what distinguishes successful from unsuccessful teaching relationships, we concluded that there are relational responsibilities that belong to the teacher, as the adult and the professional, and not to the boy regardless of his age. Clinical psychologist Daniel Rogers has described three responsibilities of the teacher, as relationship manager, that are not shared by students: (1) to serve as the expert facilitating the student's learning, (2) to maintain an overall awareness of the alliance, and (3) to monitor and mend strains in the alliance.[17] In our study, relationally successful teachers did not *expect* students to assume mutual responsibility for an improved working alliance in the classroom.

That there are frequent breakdowns in learning relationships should surprise no one. After all, both boys and their teachers have full lives, with various stresses and challenges that impact their ability to be present in the partnership. As psychologist Linda Hartling and colleagues in the relational-cultural school have described, every human relationship cycles through periods of connection-disconnection-reconnection.[18] Given the ubiquity of disconnections, small and large, in all kinds of relationships, we wondered whether boys might be expected to take more responsibility when a breakdown occurs in their relationships with teachers and coaches, as a way to build their relational repair repertoire. Exploring this question in a focus group with top student leaders at a Canadian high school, we learned that even the most empowered and endorsed students are largely paralyzed when a school relationship goes awry; they typically write the course or the teacher off, resolving to endure until the end of the term and sometimes developing a negative attitude that can seep into their behavior. Power asymmetry in these relationships and most boys' experience with arbitrary consequences when they have challenged teachers' power inhibit boys' initiative.

Unfortunately, in ways that may be particularly problematic for teachers of boys, the resistance of male students when they are offended, frightened, or overwhelmed often manifests in ways that put teachers off.[19] When confronted by a belligerent, disruptive, or disrespectful attitude, many teachers defensively conclude that they have done all they can and that it is up to the boy—despite his disadvantages—to take the next step. Thus, underlying most relational breakdowns is a teacher who has reached the end of the proverbial rope, and has reverted from relationship management to self-management.

Relational Teaching with Boys of Color

Exploring how well this relational teaching framework applies to boys of color from low-income communities, educational sociologist Joseph D. Nelson conducted interviews, observations, and open-ended surveys with fifty Black and Latino boys attending a single-sex middle school for boys of color in New York City.[20] His research found several themes that addressed how boys related to their teachers, particularly in light of how race and gender stereotypes, as well as class background, both shape and inform teacher perceptions of Black boys in the United States:

- *Subject and pedagogical mastery.* Similar to boys in the global study, boys of color at this NYC school also held an expectation that teachers would be knowledgeable in their subject areas and would demonstrate the ability to communicate the material in a clear and compelling manner, while effectively managing their classes and maintaining a learning environment. In fact, it was a "given."
- But *care* was more important to them, especially when it was expressed in their "being seen" in ways that were outside of the negative stereotypes associated with Black masculinity (e.g., hyperaggressive, anti-intellectual, and hypersexual).[21] In this view, care was expressed by holding high expectations of these boys' academic ability and performance, as well as of their ability to "stay out of trouble." They wanted to be held accountable for their actions in class or related to schoolwork, but they also wanted to "be" and "feel" supported to meet these high expectations.

- *Care* was also expressed by demonstrating a clear understanding of specifics associated with a boy's life circumstances. In situations where difficult and stressful circumstances were a reality of their everyday lives, maintaining high expectations while offering accommodations (e.g., extensions in assignments) effectively communicated the teacher's caring.
- *Reaching out and going beyond.* There were many examples cited by boys that registered the commitment of the teacher or advisor to their success, including picking up and dropping boys off at home and school; taking students on a range of field trips to experience "new things" (e.g., opera, Julliard performance, museums, music camps, science camps, "famous" guest speakers); allowing boys to share "their side of the story" when they misbehave; remembering boys' birthdays and celebrating them.
- *Being relaxed about misbehavior.* Boys appreciated and felt cared for by teachers who, rather than issuing knee-jerk, formulaic consequences, took their circumstances into consideration as they responded to misbehavior or poor performance. Boys overwhelmingly felt that more rigid responses were flat-out "unfair," but agreed that special accommodations should be made "in private" and with the general understanding that they are intended to support school success. Boys appreciated teachers who made adjustments to policies or classroom practices when they learned of challenges in a boy's personal life that affect his schoolwork: examples included setting flexible due dates for assignments when there was no computer at home; allowing the student to be a little late to first period because of a long commute to school; letting the student slide with grammar/punctuation issues if the boy generally struggles with communicating his ideas, and so on.
- *Personal advocacy.* Making a special commitment to a boy was another frequently cited theme. With boys who experienced more pronounced social stresses, including domestic and/or child abuse, father absenteeism, incarceration or deportation, housing instability, or caregiver substance abuse, teachers sometimes helped families find housing, legal representation, or even substance abuse rehabilitation. Facilitating on-site social services (e.g., counseling) also communicated a personal commitment.
- *Establishing common ground* was the most prominent relational teaching strategy mentioned in these interviews. Boys stated that it "felt good" for them to know that their teachers shared some of their life experiences related to poverty and still managed to be successful, especially when

the teacher was a male of color. There was a "closeness" that came from knowing about this shared experience, and in the bond established with their teacher, boys were less inclined to feel "less than" or "messed up." Boys also stated that this relational gesture relieved pressures they often felt to "be perfect"; instead, they felt that they were in a "safe environment," able to make mistakes, to learn, and to grow. In addition to sharing the "common ground" of poverty, teachers could establish a connection through a shared interest in sports (e.g., basketball and football), music (e.g., nontraditional music choices, classical or "Indie"), and theater (e.g., Broadway musicals or plays).

Becoming a Relational School

The professional responsibilities of relationship manager raise the stakes for schools hoping to do better with boys. Unless teachers can reflect on their relational pedagogy and persist in their efforts to reach for struggling and resistant boys, they are more likely to disconnect from them, pointing to "laziness," families' lack of support, learning or psychological handicaps, or overwhelming stresses stemming from poverty or racial marginalization. Both stories of success and tales of breakdown tended to begin with relational challenges to be overcome—boys whose resistance required special attention and teachers' willingness to adjust present practice. But despite the steep challenges faced by some of the boys whose learning differences, family circumstances, or social stresses created real barriers to engagement in schooling, relationally successful teachers reported positive transformations with boys beset by the *same—or worse—circumstances*. This finding was critically important: it was not a boy's circumstances that differentiated successful and less successful teaching relationships.

Strong teaching alliances can overcome a host of difficulties carried to school by boys of all races, ethnicities, and class backgrounds—and do so every day, including with boys who live in neighborhoods with concentrated poverty. As sociologist Pedro Noguera has written, "The research never suggests that poor children are incapable of learning or that poverty itself should be regarded as a learning disability."[22] In fact, in the stories that the boys shared with us, it was the teacher's perception of the boy that most affected the relationship's trajectory.

Too commonly, as University of Pennsylvania psychologists Michael Nakkula and Sharon Ravitch have cautioned, such assessments create a "forestructure of understanding" that prompts and guides a teacher's subsequent responses to a student.[23]

Negative or pessimistic interpretations arose in teachers' stories of breakdown most often when they were under particular stress themselves, facing challenges to their sense of professional competence and general self-worth. In these circumstances teachers tended to abdicate their role as relationship manager and reverted to more defensive management *of themselves*. Boston College's Andy Hargreaves has detailed the "emotional practice of teaching," in which feelings of powerlessness can be especially unsettling for teachers whose professional identities depend on being liked or welcomed by their students.[24] When stressed, depleted, or confronted with intractable resistance, teachers are vulnerable to "flooding," and can respond with defensiveness and self-protectiveness.

Relationally successful teachers described a repertoire of specific relational gestures to invite their students to join them in a working partnership; if a particular strategy failed to achieve the desired connection, these teachers would simply try another. A defining difference between the positive and negative accounts was the teacher's honest appraisal of the success of the relational strategy and an acknowledgment of the need to change the approach if it was not working. By contrast with the successful accounts, stories of breakdown reflected more rigid stances taken by teachers who had run out of ideas, likely becoming frustrated and upset, and were unable to reinvent their relational strategy.

Creating a professional growth climate in which teachers can review their relational difficulties and be open about them requires that they be *supervised relationally*: guided by department chairs, curriculum specialists, and other administrators who establish trust and build collaboration, inspiration, and encouragement. The emphasis on sorting and measuring that has filtered into professional evaluation systems may mitigate the safety and openness that is the sine qua non of relational reflexivity. In fact, educational researcher Eleanor Drago-Severson recommends a professional development approach characterized by observant *peer* relationships, in which performance can be assessed in mutually supportive ways: "I noted that when teachers, myself included, felt *well held* by administrators in a psychological sense—listened to, heard, and cared about—it seemed to have a direct and positive effect on the children."[25]

In continuing work with schools to implement the findings of this research—the action phase of the research cycle—we have learned that school cultures in which teachers may be well held while struggling with difficult students display three features. Establishing that the relationship manager role belongs to the teacher, not the student, is the first, essential condition. In the economy of teachers' limited personal resource—time, attention, patience—calculations are often made about where and how to distribute relational efforts. With boys who are resistant to a teacher's preferred relational strategies, bargaining for more mutuality as a precondition for further investment is common. But as we found, waiting for a boy to put up more effort can be fruitless, and is generally not a prudent response to a relational breakdown. Teachers must assume that they are the ones to solve the relational puzzle.

To do so, when they reach the edge of their relational skills, teachers also must recognize that they are stuck and yet believe that it is still possible, at least theoretically, for the boy to be reached—somehow, sometime, by someone. The successful relationships narrated by the teachers in our study were broadly characterized by (1) a willingness to be *flexible* and to improvise alternate approaches and (2) a capacity to step back and *reflect* on what was working and not working in their relational efforts. Instead of defensively digging their own heels in and requiring some change on the boy's part, these teachers took the relational impasse less personally and saw it more as an indication that they had not yet hit upon a workable approach.

Even with a commitment to personal reflection, in emotionally charged relationships and under considerable stress as the boy, his parents, and school managers all bear down, it may be difficult for teachers to find new, creative solutions to these relational puzzles. While an imperative to see beyond one's blind spots may seem oxymoronic, University of Cincinnati psychologist Miriam Raider-Roth reminds teachers that assistance in transcending limiting perspectives lies very near at hand:

> We cannot see our blind spots without our colleagues' gentle and persistent feedback. We cannot see the complexity of children without viewing their worlds from multiple perspectives.[26]

The third feature found in faculty cultures that supports a reflective relational practice is sufficient opportunity for peer coaching and collaboration. To uphold the relationship manager role and to provide opportunities for peer collaboration, it is necessary to structure relational reflection into school schedules. To this end, a hybrid model for structured reflective practice has been helpful. A model that melds the approach developed by learning theorist Graham Gibbs with a critical friends framework offered by the National School Reform Faculty has been employed with some success at a number of schools.[27] In following this protocol, participants meet monthly in small professional learning groups to share specific relational stalemates and to collaborate with each other in fashioning a way forward. The point of the exercise is a mutual exploration of relational challenges and problem solving in a supportive and coaching context.

Ultimately, we hope that the experiences of these schools will stand as practical examples of how reflective relational practice can be built into the fabric of busy school schedules. It is worth saying that the central role of relationships in engaging boys in learning is not new. To help children in caring, mentoring, coaching, and teaching relationships is the main reason most teachers enter the profession. But how boys are affected by cultural norms and how challenging they can become is the subtext for the current gender achievement gap. Fortunately, committed teachers, well supported by their schools, can work relational magic with such boys—and do so every day, in every school, everywhere.

NOTES

1 Thomas DiPrete and Claudia Buchmann, *The Rise of Women: The Growing Gender Gap in Education and What It Means for American Schools* (New York: Russell Sage Foundation, 2013).

2 David Autor, David Figlio, Krzysztof Karbownik, Jeffrey Roth, and Melanie Wasserman, "Family Disadvantage and the Gender Gap in Behavioral and Educational Outcomes" (Chicago: Institute for Policy Research, 2015), 2.

3 Ibid., 30.

4 Judy Y. Chu, *When Boys Become Boys: Development, Relationships, and Masculinity* (New York: New York University Press, 2014); Michael Kimmel, *Manhood in America: A Cultural History* (New York: Free Press, 1996); Niobe Way, *Deep Secrets: Boys' Friendships and the Crisis of Connection* (Cambridge, MA: Harvard University Press, 2011).

5 Martha C. Nussbaum, *Creating Capabilities: The Human Development Approach* (Cambridge, MA: Belknap, 2011), 18.

6 Daniel J. Siegel, *The Developing Mind: How Relationships and the Brain Interact to Shape Who We Are* (New York: Guilford, 1999).

7 Amy Banks, *Wired to Connect: The Surprising Link between Brain Science and Strong, Healthy Relationships* (New York: Tarcher/Penguin, 2015), 3.

8 Daniel Siegel and Mary Hartzell, *Parenting from the Inside Out: How a Deeper Self-Understanding Can Help You Raise Children Who Thrive* (New York: Tarcher/Penguin, 2003), 34.

9 Ibid., 36.

10 Way, *Deep Secrets*, 10.

11 Michael Reichert and Richard Hawley, *Reaching Boys, Teaching Boys* (San Francisco: Jossey-Bass, 2010); Michael Reichert and Richard Hawley, *I Can Learn from You: Boys as Relational Learners* (Cambridge, MA: Harvard Education Press, 2014).

12 Reichert and Hawley, *Reaching Boys, Teaching Boys*, 191.

13 Organisation for Economic Co-operation and Development (OECD), "PISA 2009 Results: What Makes a School Successful? Resources, Policies and Practices" (Vol. 4, 2010), doi:10.1787/9789264091559.

14 Debora L. Roorda, "The Influence of Affective Teacher-Student Relationships on Students' School Engagement and Achievement," *Review of Educational Research* 81, no. 4 (2011): 493–529.

15 Charles W. Bingham and Alexander M. Sidorkin, *No Education without Relation* (New York: Peter Lang, 2004), 4.

16 David Hawkins, *The Informed Vision: Essays on Learning and Human Nature* (New York: Agathon Press, 1974), 58.

17 Daniel Rogers, "The Working Alliance in Teaching and Learning: Theoretical Clarity and Research Implications," *International Journal for the Scholarship of Teaching and Learning* 3, no. 2 (2009): article 28.

18 Linda M. Hartling, Wendy Rosen, Maureen Walker, and Judith V. Jordan, *Shame and Humiliation: From Isolation to Relational Transformation* (Wellesley, MA: Wellesley Center for Women, 2004).

19 Miriam Raider-Roth, Marta Albert, Ingrid Bircann-Barkey, Eric Gidseg, and Terry Murray, "Resisting Boys, Resisting Teachers," *Journal of Boyhood Studies* 9, no. 1 (2012): 34–54.

20 Joseph Derrick Nelson, "Transformative Brotherhood: Black Boys' Identity in a Single-Sex School for Boys of Color" (PhD diss., Graduate Center of the City University of New York, 2013); Joseph Derrick Nelson, "Relational Teaching with Black Boys: Strategies for Learning at a Single-Sex Middle School for Boys of Color," *Teachers College Record* 118, no. 6 (2016): 1–30.

21 Richard Majors and Janet Manici Billson, *Cool Pose: The Dilemma of Black Manhood in America* (New York: Simon & Schuster, 1993); Ellis Cose, *The Envy of the World: On Being A Black Man in America* (New York: Simon & Schuster, 2002).

22 Pedro A. Noguera, "Saving Black and Latino Boys," *Phi Delta Kappan* 93, no. 5 (2011): 9–12.

23 Michael Nakkula and Sharon Ravitch, *Matters of Interpretation* (San Francisco: Jossey-Bass, 1998), 5.

24 Andy Hargreaves, "The Emotional Practice of Teaching," *Teaching and Teacher Education* 14 (1998): 835–854.

25 Eleanor Drago-Severson, *Helping Educators Grow* (Cambridge, MA: Harvard Education Press, 2012), 5.

26 Miriam Raider-Roth, *Trusting What You Know: The High Stakes of Classroom Relationships* (San Francisco: Jossey-Bass, 2005), 157.

27 Graham Gibbs, *Learning by Doing: A Guide to Teaching and Learning Methods* (Oxford: Further Education Unit, 1998).

Community-Based Solutions

15

"We Don't Come from the Same Background . . . but I Get You"

Performing Our Common Humanity by Creating Original Theater with Girls

DANA EDELL

We are human
The smooth sound of vocal chords scraping
Together to form the sweetest of sounds
Laughter about a slip, spilt milk, family
A wafting sense of smell
BBQ chicken with rice and beans
Fresh apples, ripe enough to bite with baby teeth
The playful contact of arms and shoulders or hand and head
We talk, we fight, we joke
We build one another up
And care for the other
We care for the person smiling in front of us
Not the phone or tv screen that separates us
Because
We are human
—Briana and Nzingha

Briana and Nzingha, two teenage girls, cross back and forth across the stage, speaking these lines they wrote as they clasp their hands together, spin in spirals, shout and whisper into the audience. They are using the power of performance to express their beliefs and feelings, their stories and desires, their struggles and dreams. Through collaborative performance programs for girls, we are directly challenging the culture of disconnection that perpetuates false narratives that girls can't work together, that the arts are frivolous, that young people can't change the world. This chapter offers a strategy to combat the crisis of connection plaguing our communities and outlined earlier in this book. Over the past twenty years that I have been directing and producing original theater, written and performed by teenage girls, I have witnessed and directly experienced hundreds of examples of girls using theater to deepen their relationships and forge intimate connections.

Girlfighting

Click through the latest reality television hit and you will drown in waves of women screaming at women, jutting out hips, pointing gel-manicured fingers, and clacking heels strutting in and out of conflict. Drama sells. The media loves the stories of women fighting with women and perpetuates this false narrative that women don't get along with each other, that there is always competition over some man's attention.[1] Of course, women wasting time believing that our antagonists are other women prevents us from the true reality that it is not other women keeping us down, but patriarchy.[2] Within this gender-based hierarchy, women (and girls who learn how to live by watching women) are trained and groomed to see each other as competition, not as allies and friends. And the popularity of *America's Next Top Model*, *The Bachelor*, and every year's teen movie version of *Mean Girls* normalizes the idea that girls hating girls is completely "natural."[3] Patriarchy tricks us into assuming greed, competition, and violence are natural parts of human nature. Yet, current research, described in detail throughout this book, is showing us, unequivocally, that they are not.[4]

This endless, lucrative, and sexy story of girlfighting provides a thick enough fog to prevent us from seeing that we actually have a real crisis, a "crisis of connection." Luckily, we have some excellent strategies to tackle this crisis by providing spaces for girls to deconstruct these cultural narratives that tell them they are "supposed to" fight with other girls, hate their bodies, compete for the attention of boys, and silence themselves— all feats that require them to dissociate themselves from their humanity.

This chapter outlines a three-pronged strategy for using theater as a space for girls to thrive: self-expression, collaboration, and activism. To that end, I interviewed more than thirty girls and young women, current and past participants in the viBe Theater Experience (viBe), a community-based performing arts/education organization whose mission is "to empower under-served teenage girls by engaging and inspiring them to write, design, publish, create, and perform personal and truthful collaborative theater pieces."[5] "ViBeGirls" are primarily girls of color (65 percent of African descent, 30 percent Latina, 3 percent European American, and 2 percent Asian American) from low- to middle-income communities in all five boroughs of New York City. They are "under-served" because they have limited access to creative opportunities, "all-girls" groups, or positive adult mentorship. Most attend overcrowded public high schools with insufficient resources and a dearth of curricular or extracurricular after-school arts opportunities. I am the co-founder of viBe and served as the Executive Director from 2002 to 2012.

Over the past few decades, research has shown the benefits of creating theater with young people.[6] Theater provides a "safe" space for teenagers to take risks and express themselves and offers a ready-made community of collaborators who work closely together throughout the intimate process of sharing stories and creating a performance.[7] According to a ten-year study that tracked more than twenty-five thousand teens, researchers found that young people who participated in theater arts activities showed "higher levels of empathy and tolerance for peers," among many other benefits.[8] This chapter examines the ways in which a theater process with teenage girls can provide the nurturing space where girls directly challenge the assumptions that when placed in a room together, they will release their "cat claws" to scratch each other's feelings. In fact, we have found the absolute opposite to be true.

"We're Gonna Be Sisters for Life, Now": Fostering Love and Trust through Collaboration in the Theater

Echoing the cultural narratives related to girlfighting articulated above, Izzy, a young Haitian American woman who participated in viBe throughout high school, tells me in an interview:[9]

> We hear from the time that we're small, girls don't get along. Ladies will walk in the room, look her up and down and be like, "her shoes are ugly, I don't like her." So we're fed that jargon since we're small, so when you

choose the option of being in an all girls' after school program, everyone's looking at you like, "what are you doing, why are you creating theater with a bunch of other girls?" It doesn't really make sense at first. . . . And it was in that hub, the first time I was just like, "you know what? Maybe that's really not all true."

When girls hear again and again that they're "not supposed to" be able to work together, they begin to believe it. Rejecting this self-fulfilling prophecy, Izzy and her peers expose its danger and advocate for encouraging girls to move past their assumptions. We need to move past these stereotypes and demand that girls resist this dangerous narrative, demand that they deconstruct it, expose its falsehood, and then choose love. We need to flip the script to tell a new and truer story where the norm is not conflict and aggression, but girls' collaboration and deep friendship. Theater spaces for girls help us get there.

Collaboration is embedded in the DNA of theater. Actors work with writers who rely on directors who need designers who then dress and light actors. Theater artists are all spokes on the same wheel, and we need each other to keep spinning and moving forward. In a culture that sadly and recklessly places excessive focus on independence and autonomy, particularly for adolescents as they grow up and are encouraged to separate from their parents, collaboratively devised theater is a space where dependence on each other is vital. When we are all working toward the same end goal—the performance—girls have to quickly learn to trust and support each other. Izzy articulates it:

> We got along and I think it's also because you see the end result. You put together something that you didn't think you could do . . . because you're told that you're not supposed to do it . . . but it doesn't make sense during the process, nothing ever makes sense during the process. It's at the end, after the first show when everyone's crying that you start to feel like . . . I made this with all of you, and we might not talk after this ever again. But I did this with you . . . so that bond never really ever goes away.

Fourteen-year-old Maddie, round black eyes shimmering from dried tears in the dressing room, describes her feeling after the performance:

"You know, we're gonna be sisters for life now." And fifteen-year-old Michelle says, "We spent a lot of time with each other and a lot of time sharing stuff with each other. So . . . the bond was so thick. It felt like nobody could penetrate it." Going through a shared, intensive experience together allows girls the space to connect with other girls and live a new reality that girls can love and trust each other deeply.

How does this happen? Do the hearts inside the young people in every theater process spontaneously explode and sprinkle love glitter over each other that sticks for eternity? Obviously not. But there are techniques and creative strategies that can help lead girls toward stronger and thicker connections. Over the past two decades making theater collaboratively with teenage girls, I have developed an arts-based, love-fueled pedagogy for facilitating girls' theater projects. As an example for a strategy to combat the crisis the connection we have exposed throughout this book, I offer theater as one potential solution.

Setting the Vibe: Love and Ritual in Fostering Community

Imagine the first day of rehearsal. Girls stumble into the practice space, looking around, noticing that they do not recognize any of the other girls. Jackets zipped tight to their necks, hands shoved into pockets even though the heat is blasting from the radiator. Their backpacks are slung against the arch at the base of their spines dangling from the expanded, worn straps. In these awkward first minutes, they assess the other girls, the staff, and the space, make decisions, harness assumptions, doubt whether this is the right program for them, feel excitement and nervousness and fear. Within seconds of her arrival, my co-director and I embrace each girl, remembering her name and attempting to reflect on something positive we remembered from her tryout or her application. These first moments are crucial in setting up an atmosphere where affectionate, physical contact is normative and praise and effusive support is constant.

We have stacks of empty binders and piles of Skittles-colored papers in columns on a table next to a bag of pretzels and bowl of berries. We ask the girls who have arrived early to help collate the papers and secure them in the binders. These tasks, seemingly meaningless or easily completed by the staff ahead of time, are part of the strategy of building our community. The girls learn on this first day that responsibilities are shared, and that they are useful, helpful, and trusted to complete random jobs.

* * *

Every viBe Theater rehearsal begins with a ritual and ends with a ritual. Rituals seal the space and time of the rehearsal period and contain its structure within these boundaries.[10] The consistent repetition of shared activities and experiences helps the group of girls to bond tighter as they learn a shared language. A "viBe culture" is created that every current participant and past alumna recognizes. These rituals, specific to viBe's programs, provide the alumnae with an access key to a "secret club," with limited membership. Girls, in particular, connect with the process of creating and maintaining rituals.[11] In adolescence, there is a fierce tug toward wanting to fit in with groups and striving to be independent and unique.[12] The viBe rituals celebrate and provide space for both impulses. As anthropologist Bobby Alexander writes: "Ritual is a planned or improvised performance that effects a transition from everyday life to an alternative framework within which the everyday is transformed."[13] Through viBe's rituals, the girls co-construct and transform the rehearsal space into a space more special than the "everyday," a space where they can say and write and do things that they might not do in other spaces.

At the beginning of every rehearsal, the girls reflect upon their days and check-in with the group about how they are feeling, what issues are weighing them down, and what is keeping them going. We use the popular summer camp activity, "Roses and Thorns." The girls, along with the staff, form a circle and the girl who was the first to arrive at rehearsal will begin and tell the group her "Rose," or positive and happy event or situation in her life, of the day and her "Thorn," her challenge or struggle or negative event that might be prickling her that day. We introduce the activity at the first rehearsal with a real rose and pass the flower around the circle, inviting everyone to smell the sweet pungency and feel the prick of the thorn. Like Proust's Madeleine cookie, the sensual, olfactory, and tactile engagement with the flower instills the experience more forcefully into the girls' memories.[14] We talk about how every rose has both the beauty of the flower and the sharpness of the thorn. We deconstruct how both parts are necessary for the flower's survival. The beauty attracts the bees and makes others happy and the thorns give it strength and structure and protect it from predators. The girls analyze how the situations in their lives are often filled with both roses and thorns. The staff encourages the girls to speak about both every day. Nothing is ever 100 percent "rosy." There is still suffering somewhere or stresses on the horizon. Also, no day is ever entirely "thorny" with nothing to be thankful for or to live for.

This ritual is useful in multiple ways and provides a core curriculum element to all viBe's programs. This opening "check-in" helps the adult director understand the girls' lives at a deeper and more personal level and creates a community space that acknowledges that part of building trust and learning how to collaborate involves first understanding others' unique struggles, strengths, and desires. By listening to each other, the girls begin to recognize that their challenges are not isolated, that they share similar struggles, and that they often celebrate similar achievements. This collectivity reminds them that they are not isolated or as alone as teenagers sometimes feel. Suddenly the teen rant, "nobody understands me," is disproved daily as they hear echoes of their stories and stresses and begin to see the patterns in how cultural stereotypes, and social narratives influence the shared content of their experiences. By listening to the adult women also share their roses and thorns and reveal similar stories of heartbreak, school stress, family love, and socializing with friends, the girls see the women as more than the grown-up staff, more than teachers or mentors, but as fellow humans with our own loves and scars. Everyone in the intergenerational circle, by expressing vulnerability and feeling the love and support from each other, recognizes that we often have similar struggles and similar joys.

We then create an "entering rehearsal" ritual that incorporates elements of everything we have agreed we need in order to be successful during each day's rehearsal. Girls might articulate: respect each other, listen, be creative, take constructive risks, try new things, be prepared, and have fun. The "entering rehearsal" ritual is created collectively by the girls and must include sound and movement, build and focus energy, and be able to be executed by any combination of girls. For example, one group of girls constructed a ritual that involved a brief physical and vocal warm-up, a quick massage circle where everyone rubbed the shoulders and back or the girl next to her, a moment when everyone had to try to make eye contact with everyone else and a "round-robin" when each girl spoke a word that represented the positive quality she was bringing to the room that day such as "trust," "fun," or "enthusiasm." Every viBe rehearsal ends by "viBing out," a ritual where all participants hold hands in a circle and one girl starts a "pulse" by squeezing the hand of the girl next to her, who then in turn squeezes the next hand as the pulse is passed around the circle. During the passing of the pulse, the goal is to also make eye contact with everyone in the circle. After the pulse has gone around the circle at least once or twice, someone screams, "Power viBe!" and everyone squeezes both hands and rushes into the center of the circle. Then everyone lets go and bursts into applause, signaling the end of rehearsal.

These opening and closing rituals, repeated at every rehearsal, build continuity, connect everyone physically, enable everyone to share personal experiences, and establish structure. They allow us to contain the space of rehearsal within their boundaries and to hold it as sacred, a space where we all feel a deeper connection to each other and a promise to maintain the loving vibe through the length of the process.

Recognizing Our Common Humanity through Self-Expression

Every rehearsal includes multidisciplinary opportunities for girls to express themselves and articulate how they are feeling—through poetry, dance, monologues, scene writing, and songs. We provide the girls with writing prompts to help them begin new pieces or initiate various activities and discussions to stimulate dialogue that inspires new material. For example, I might invite them to complete the phrase "I love you, but . . ." or "I knew you had my back when. . . ." When all girls respond personally to the same prompt or activity, they have the opportunity to both express themselves and also see how their experiences, stories, and feelings are similar. Sharing through performance amplifies the girls' voices when the audience sits silently in the darkness of the theater and listens to their rehearsed and uninterrupted words. Sixteen-year-old Xaria tells me:

> My poetry is how I feel and I write it for me. I don't write it for anybody else and when I speak it—it's not a bad thing but I'm forced to

speak my voice to everybody else and make them realize how I feel without actually trying to and it's not a bad thing that I'm being forced to do
that 'cause then other people get the point 'cause after the viBe show, everyone was like: "Is that how you really feel?" And I'm like, "Yeah, it's how
I really feel." And they'd say "I feel the same way." And it's funny 'cause I
thought keeping my poetry to myself was basically . . . like I thought it
was making my poetry more special by keeping it to myself. But I realize
that speaking about it, it made it more special because speaking about it
does not make it less mine but it makes it other people's own too and it
actually helps.

Xaria expresses the way that girls' original performances have an impact
on people beyond the girls in the program. Imagine teenage girls and
boys sitting in their velvet theater seats and hearing their peers expressing feelings of rage, fear, hope, and desire, feelings they have experienced
as well, though possibly never had the courage to articulate. Recognizing
the humanity in others, hearing one's own deepest secrets echoed by people who might look nothing like them on the surface, helps bridge the
ever-widening gaps between us.
Izzy shares:

Art kind of makes you explore parts of yourself and you're doing that with
other people especially other woman who you didn't think you'd meet. Because some of us are from uptown, some of us are of Caribbean descent.
It makes you connect on a deeper understanding of like, "we don't come
from the same background . . . but I get you," because we have a moment
that was shared in poetry, or in song or in dance. And I've had that with
multiple girls.

When girls are writing a play together, they have to agree upon one narrative, a story that they need to tell, that every girl feels connected to. We
make decisions by consensus. If any one person hates an idea or refuses
a storyline, we go back to the drawing board until we find a story everyone is passionate about and feels connected to. Inviting girls to co-write
a play demands that they recognize that they have similar stories to tell,
similar struggles to express, and similar dreams to chase. The process of
getting there, though, is never completely smooth.

Let's peek into the rehearsal room from Izzy's show: Nine hands scratch pens against paper with a frenzied melody. Some girls hum as they write, letting the rhythm of their words bounce out of their lips as they stab stories into paper. Izzy sits on the edge of her metal folding chair, foot bopping to a beat only she can hear as she scribbles words and phrases on the opened binder in her lap. Her broad shoulders and wiry arms flex muscles from the force of her writing. Naima, fourteen, reties her hijab, her large black eyes drifting upward in concentration as she sinks her body into the red velvet, dusty couch. She taps her purple pen against her thigh, her jeans tight as a drum for her body's percussion. The girls sit in a spiral around four primary-colored poster boards on the floor. "Content" is written in curly lettering at the top of one poster followed by a list of phrases scrawled in round, bubbly handwriting stating narrative loops such as "teen pregnancy," "boy who hits his girlfriend," and "parents putting too much pressure on kids." Saliesha, black hair stretched so tightly in a ponytail that her sea foam green eyes seem to bulge out of her face, moans, "I don't got *nothing* to write about." She flips through the posters illuminating the girls' ideas from the past three weeks of rehearsal.

Saliesha's single outburst breaks the rare tranquility of nine hushed teenage girls. Ever helpful Izzy interjects: "Why don't you write about your mom? You're always talking about how she makes you so mad. That could be a scene or something. She's been your 'thorn' like every day this week." Scowling Jennifer busts into the conversation: "I still don't get this whole idea. *Where* are we supposed to be? In a prison? I think it seems stupid. I thought we were gonna write about—." Naima cuts her off: "We've been talkin' this out for like five rehearsals a-ready. We need to get the script done! Just write!" "Don't yell at me." "I'm not yelling!" "Whoa, whoa, whoa. Hold up! Why you always gotta tell everybody what to do? I'm sick of yah gettin' up in mah business!" Words are shot like arrows across the space, as soon as one girl cocks her bow, another blade is shot, hitting and missing targets. Voices escalate. Curses fly, smashing into skin and hearts with abandon. Tears leak out eyes dragging smudges of mascara as they trickle down cheeks.

I stand in a rare gesture of authority. "Ladies. What is going on? Listen to each other. Listen to yourselves." I am ignored at first, muted by the crossfire. Then Izzy's voice slices through the hurricane and commands focus. "Guys. What are we doing? We're trying to make our play now. Why all the *drama*?" One at a time, the girls rest their cases. One at a time they speak their fears for the script, their building and unspoken horror of the imagined future moment when they will perform this collaboratively written play in front of their peers, parents, and community. The reality of the seeming impossibility of this endeavor haunts me again. Though I have directed more than seventy productions such as this one, each one at this moment of challenge feels like a potential miracle. How does a collective of teenage girls write a play together? The process, like any living thing, is never perfect. Yet it is within these moments of chaos and rock-bottom scuffling that I can begin to understand its function and potential for transformation. I do not want to paint a glossy picture that every minute of every rehearsal is hand-holding bliss of kumbaya. But like a true sisterhood, bickering can be the coat of armor that protects us from the vulnerability of exposing our hearts. These ruptures within the process help to dig beneath the surface and allow girls to authentically express their fears. Without explosions such as the one described here, the exhilaration on opening night would not taste so sweet. The performance, when the girls must get to the point where they trust each other enough to all work together onstage, is the antidote to the potential poisons unfurled within the process.

Delilah describes the necessity of collaboration within the process:

> In work with others, you have a team, you have a collective, so you have other people. They're a support system. They're a backbone. They can help you—you know run lines. It's just that, you know you have to rely on other people so the decisions that you make are not decisions that only you agree with. You have to run it by everybody else. You have to pretty much you know work with everyone else.

The teaching artists of viBe do not tell girls how to solve personal problems or those of the world they live in. Instead, our approach is to help girls define the issues themselves and think about them as a group. For example, we often begin rehearsals by asking the girls to think about what they would like to change in their community, or to describe something they feel is unfair in their lives. Their thoughts propel the rehearsal forward, and they are encouraged to come to their own conclusions about who or what is responsible for life's challenges and dilemmas and strategize what can be done to overcome them. The diversity of experiences that the girls possess contributes toward exploring multiple layers of one situation, and allows girls to help each other deal with personal struggles and to find solutions in unlikely places—from unexpected sources. Sometimes it is the shy and quiet girl who rarely speaks up who offers guidance on how to stand up to an abusive stepfather. Other times it's the outgoing jokester who reveals she has no friends in high school and skips lunch to avoid sitting alone and asks advice on how to make new friends.

Seventeen-year-old Saliesha describes how "therapeutic" it is for her to share personal experiences with her friends in viBe, and then translate these experiences into performances:

> I think it's good to have an experience like viBe um because it is like a therapy session for me. At least um we talk about things that, you know, we can't talk about with, like, other people or anywhere else and like everybody has an open mind so it's never um it's never really a bad thing or it's kinda like a therapy session. You know if it really stings and you know—you write about it, you act it out, you know you can sing it—you know it's a good experience.

And eighteen-year-old Sade tells me:

> You get to understand that we all want the same things in life: love and respect. And being in a theater group together—you get to know people like that because you are writing and talking about really personal things.

For example, Zahyria often came to rehearsal and spoke about tensions in her relationship with her best friend. She would describe how she felt that they had grown apart since Zahyria came out as a lesbian and started dating a girl. As she began to write text for the play that presented this issue, we asked her questions about her situation and challenged her to find a creative way to represent this story dramatically. We did not tell her what and how to write it. Organically, other girls chimed in with their own experiences and strategies for dealing with ruptures in their close friendships. With input, opinions, comments, and choreography from the other girls, Zahyria created and performed a poetic monologue in the play where she spoke directly to her friend. Onstage, other girls surrounded her supportively as she spoke her truth about missing her best friend and apologizing for allowing her new relationship to interfere. The other girls in the show helped her craft the poem and stage it in performance. Through this collective, creative problem solving, girls learn new ways to solve their problems and trust that their peers may offer powerful solutions. On opening night, Zahyria stood in her spotlight and spoke out into the darkness:

Subliminal messages have been sent through our silence
Trying to fight against the odds
Wanting more than air to be with her and only her
Wanting to feel like I'm hers and she's mine
That's all that matters, nothing else is relevant
Trying to find the solace in our peace of mind
Is a needle in a haystack
Yet she's got the golden ticket
And I love her. I love her and what more is there to say
I don't see regret in my future, I don't even see tomorrow
I see right here, and right now with her faint smile and dark hair
On her Batman sheets I see the first girl I've ever loved
And I see the person who gets me the most
Our silence is conversation all the time
Never have I felt so connected
But my situation has caused a complication
And I'm wanting a relationship
But time has got me facing shit
Wanting to be patient
But I need her
Never would that word come through my vocals if it wasn't true
But her and me and this friendship must be
Us coexisting with each other is what I need
Don't you see I said it again; the reality is crystal clear . . .
For me to be happy, slightly selfish and a lil indulgent
Inside I have emotions untold, unheard,
Can't seem to comprehend my actions, wondering how I got here

My intentions were not to hurt her . . .
I can't seem to grasp this hurt
My chest, my mind my heart my conscience aches
Realizing my apologies are of no use
My actions could do no good
"Sorry" does not change it or make it any better . . .
But that's all I am
Sorry. I'm sorry. I don't deserve.

And from that darkness, a deep voice trembling through tears, shouted back at her using her childhood nickname, "I love you, Pookie!" Two best friends needed the "fourth wall" of the theater to communicate their thick love for each other. And the hundred people in the audience were there to witness this emotionally charged reunion and perhaps consider the broken friendships in their own lives and see the hope for reconciliation.

In addition to written text, every production includes a group dance and a group song created by the girls and performed by everyone together. Choreographing a dance together is another technique for fostering connections. Often a couple of girls in each group emerge as super strong dancers and/or choreographers, which allows them a chance to step up as leaders and assess the skills and abilities of the rest of the group. Some girls express themselves best through words, others through movement or song. Not every girl is a poet or a comedian or feels confident belting ballads, so we aim to provide opportunities for each girl, no matter where her unique talent lies, to shine as an individual as well as part of the ensemble. In the group dance, everyone has a part, and following the music demands that the girls learn how to move in unison, as a unit, keeping up with the same beat. They need to trust each other and design and execute a dance that fits each individual's ability while also allowing space for more advanced moves.

Every dance has a theme or an intention. We never include a dance number in a show just to have a spontaneous dance. Our actions always have meaning, and every moment communicates something related to the narrative, themes, or characters in the play. Through dance, girls experience an embodied form of storytelling and connection where they use movement, gestures, and rhythm to advance their narrative. For example, in "UNFINISHED: Girls of Today, Wives of Tomorrow," a play written by our group of teenage girls set in a dystopian future where all girls are forced to attend boarding school where they are trained to be a "good wife," they created a bold and celebratory dance piece for the final scene. Set to Laura Mvula's song "That's Alright," the dance expressed the girls' feelings and connections with each other in the moments after they escape their oppressive boarding school/prison and break free. In creative ways that transcended speech and language, the dance communicated the energy, love, and passion that the girls possessed. It began with a synchronized series of movements expressing celebration and then evolved into a section where each girl freestyled on her own and showed her unique style and rhythms. It culminated with each girl laughing and collapsing on top of each other in a pile of exhaustion in the center of the stage. At times deep friendship and bonding looks like girls moving in unison, or maybe it is girls stepping to their own beat but alongside each other, or maybe it is a pile of giggles on the floor. And maybe, also, it is all of the above.

Conclusion

Applying theater to the crisis of connection can sometimes create a space drenched with potential for deeper connections through collaboration, trust, and creative expression. And sometimes not. This strategy is not failsafe, nor do I naïvely assume that any group of girls can spontaneously become best friends just by making a play together. As artists, activists, policymakers, and scholars, we need a massive, multipronged, multidisciplinary strategy to begin to retie the broken bonds that capitalism, patriarchy, poverty, racism, and other forms of oppression have wrought on our communities. But as organizations such as the US Department of Arts and Culture advocate, "Art and culture are powerful means of building empathy, creating a sense of belonging, and activating the social imagination and civic agency necessary to make real change."[15]

These processes are as imperfect as humans ourselves. But I can boldly state that though collaborative theater making might not be the end of our crisis of connection, it is most certainly a very promising beginning. I conclude with a scene written and performed by girls in our 2015 production, *This Is Not a Safe Space*:

GRACE, LAILA & MICHELLE
So here we are

LAILA
In this unsafe space
That every day we fight to survive in

MICHELLE
But I am not alone any more
Today I fight with a sisterhood

GRACE
We find strength in our experiences

LAILA
We lean on each other when the weight of these traumas grows too
    heavy

MICHELLE
And we are demanding more from this world, which feels entitled to
    our bodies and dismisses our words

GRACE, LAILA & MICHELLE
You cannot silence us any longer!

NOTES

1   Jennifer L. Pozner, *Reality Bites Back: The Troubling Truth about Guilty Pleasure TV* (Berkeley, CA: Seal Press, 2010).
2   Jessica Bennett, *Feminist Fight Club: An Office Survival Manual (For a Sexist Workplace)* (New York: HarperCollins, 2016).
3   Lyn Mikel Brown, *Girlfighting: Betrayal and Rejection among Girls* (New York: New York University Press, 2003).
4   Carol Gilligan, *Joining the Resistance* (Cambridge: Polity Press, 2011); Sarah Blaffer Hrdy, *Mothers and Others: The Evolutionary Origins of Mutual Understanding* (Cambridge, MA: Harvard University Press, 2009); Niobe Way, *Deep Secrets: Boys' Friendships and the Crisis of Connection* (Cambridge, MA: Harvard University Press, 2011).
5   See the viBe Theater website, www.viBeTheater.org.

6 Kathleen Gallagher, *The Theatre of Urban: Youth and Schooling in Dangerous Times* (Toronto: University of Toronto Press, 2007); Dorothy Heathcote and Gavin Bolton, *Drama for Learning: Dorothy Heathcote's Mantle of the Expert Approach to Education* (Portsmouth, NH: Heinemann, 1995); Anthony Jackson, *Theatre, Education and the Making of Meanings: Art or Instrument?* (Manchester: Manchester University Press, 2007); Anthony Jackson and Chris Vine, eds., *Learning through Theatre: The Changing Face of Theatre in Education* (London: Routledge, 2013); Robert J. Landy, *Handbook of Educational Drama and Theatre* (Westport, CT: Greenwood, 1982); Helen Nicholson, *Applied Drama: The Gift of Theatre* (Basingstoke: Palgrave Macmillan, 2005).

7 Jenny Hughes and Karen Wilson, "Playing a Part: The Impact of Youth Theatre on Young People's Personal and Social Development," *Research in Drama Education* 9, no. 1 (2004): 57–72.

8 James Catterall, Richard Chapleau, and John Iwanaga, "Involvement in the Arts and Human Development: General Involvement and Intensive Involvement in Music and Theatre Arts," in *Champions of Change: The Impact of the Arts on Learning*, ed. Edward B. Fiske (Washington, DC: Arts Education Partnership and the President's Committee on the Arts and the Humanities, 1999), 1–18.

9 All names have been changed to pseudonyms selected by the girls themselves.

10 Catherine Clement and Julia Kristeva, *The Feminine and the Sacred*, trans. J. M. Todd (1998; New York: Columbia University Press, 2001).

11 Lisa Schirch, *Ritual and Symbol in Peacebuilding* (Bloomfield, CT: Kumarian Press, 2004).

12 Sharon Lamb and Lyn Mikel Brown, *Packaging Girlhood: Rescuing Our Daughters from Marketers' Schemes* (New York: St. Martin's Press, 2006).

13 Bobby Chris Alexander, *Victor Turner Revisited: Ritual as Social Change* (Atlanta: Scholars Press, 1991), 139.

14 Marcel Proust, *Swann's Way*, trans. C. K. Scott Moncrieff (1913; Mineola, NY: Dover, 2002).

15 See the US Department of Arts and Culture website, www.usdac.us.

16

Letting Men Care

Supporting Engaged Fatherhood to Radically Disrupt the Gender Binary

GARY BARKER

The Problem

In modern society, we don't value men's caregiving. From the logo of the UN's agency for children (UNICEF, which features a mother and a child) to the maternity unit that doesn't really know what to do with fathers, the day care center that addresses its notes every day to "mom," and our household-focused marketing showing mothers cleaning the house while fathers tend cars, we remake the gender binary every day. The result is that we discourage men and boys from caregiving and from their human potential.

Just how big is the problem? Globally, women and girls carry out on average three times the amount of daily hands-on care work (meaning the work we do to maintain our homes and the care of others, whether young children or other family members).[1] The world's countries have signed a global plan for development (the Sustainable Development Goals) that calls for equality between men and women and calls attention to this unequal divide in the care work. But that plan doesn't state anywhere the simple but radical idea that the world needs men and boys doing half of that daily care work.

Women's rights activists have long called attention to what this disproportionate burden of care work means for women. First, it keeps them from being all they want to be in their professional, social, and community lives. Second, it devalues care by making it a secondary function, a lesser activity compared to men's prescribed role of provider. It makes caregiving banal, a task to be avoided or carried out by a lesser human being.

We know what the gender binary and the construction of care work as being a feminine role or function means for women's lives. But the part we too often miss is this: it also shapes boys' and men's lives. It channels us into being the designated achievers, breadwinners, and providers (and too often the designated carriers of weapons) and to be performance-oriented. As Carol Gilligan cogently puts it: "Patriarchy creates rifts in the psyche, dividing everyone from parts of themselves and undermining basic human capacities."[2] For men, the part that patriarchy too often takes from us is our capacity to care for and connect to others.

To be sure, routine tasks such as feeding, bathing, and clothing children are increasingly shared more equitably among heterosexual couples in the United States and in some other middle- and upper-income countries. But other realms of caregiving are still highly gender-divided. Many men continue to cede most responsibility for family health care practices (a form of caregiving), along with the care of elderly parents. Media messages, when they portray men as fathers, often visibly exclude them from routine caregiving practices. For example, parenting magazines are almost never directed at fathers, and when they are, they try to send a message about how fatherhood can be fun and "manly."[3] The necessity of affirming a traditional form of masculinity in these scenarios makes it explicit that "warm, loving, and involved parenting and primary caregiving are still considered feminine."[4]

Central to the gender binary in terms of caregiving is the workplace and the historical legacy of men's roles as breadwinner. A recent review of fatherhood research we presented in "State of America's Fathers" highlights study after study from the United States and abroad showing the challenges to men and women who seek to balance work and family life, and the very real barriers to men and women who seek to devote more time to caregiving.[5] These barriers involve the subtle and not-so-subtle norms in the workplace (which generally do not value men's or women's roles as caregivers), but also the reality that families depend on the historically higher wages of men. Add to these barriers the lack of paid leave in the United States and many other countries, and in particular the lack of paid leave for fathers in those workplaces that do offer some paid leave.

Other barriers include the fact that men have tended not to pursue careers that involve caring or caregiving. This trend emerges in part because many female-dominated professions are still paid less than traditionally male-dominated professions, even if these caregiving professions require a similar level of education. Between 1980 and 2014, women made great progress in pursuing traditionally male-dominated career fields, while men lagged far behind in pursuing traditionally female-dominated professions. To be sure, certain traditionally feminine fields like nursing and teaching are paid significantly less well than those professions considered to be more masculine. Thus, economic forces are partially to blame for keeping men from traditionally female professions. These forces also serve to reinforce inequalities: men's higher salaries on the whole, as well as the continued devaluation of care (and the women who take on the majority of it). One recent study found that even when women expand into less traditional careers, wages decrease as women become a majority in the field.[6]

There are other cultural barriers to men's participation in the caregiving professions. The media is at least partially responsible for perpetuating a fear of unmarried men's involvement with children as a signifier of "stranger danger." Overemphasis on stories about men as abusers and child molesters reinforces a public sentiment that men are likely to treat children badly.[7] This social construction of men as being dangerous to children dissuades men from getting involved in nurturing activities or work with children in caregiving professions. Additionally, pernicious—and false—linkages between homosexuality and pedophilia have also contributed to gay men being seen as threats to children, affecting their ability to adopt and even in extreme cases blocking them from certain professions and volunteer roles involving caring for children. These messages too reinforce the gender binary and drive the crisis of connection.

Social norms that devalue these fields for nonfinancial reasons are likely at play as well. While there has been a concerted effort to get more girls and women involved in the STEM fields, there has been no equal attempt to get more men into HEAL jobs (health, education, administration, literacy).[8] According to the US Bureau of Labor Statistics, 80 percent of jobs are performed by predominantly one gender.[9] Rigid, binary gender norms have no small part in reinforcing this dynamic. Elevating care as something that is both socially and financially valued *and* expected of all genders may help to increase men's roles in both paid and unpaid care work, so everyone in these professions will benefit, and so that boys and girls see adults of all genders doing hands-on care at home, and in other spaces.[10]

Change Is Happening, but Not Fast Enough

To be sure, there has been more attention to fatherhood in recent years. In the United States and other parts of the world, fatherhood has been in the media and is being studied more than ever before. After years of being seen as the second parent, the helper, or a distant, authoritarian caregiver, fathers are getting a fairer share of attention in the United States and globally. In US popular culture, online magazines such as *Fatherly* are finding growing readership and sponsorship. Websites, blogs, and a plethora of seminars and events for fathers and those who work with them are tapping into a reality: men around the world are doing more of the hands-on caregiving than in the past, even if not yet at equal levels as women, and are attaching more of their identity and source of life satisfaction to being hands-on, caregiving fathers.[11]

Much of this emerging research focuses on impediments to men and women trying to juggle the realities of caregiving with their work lives outside the home. It treats parents as co-administrators trying to solve the problem of not having enough time on their hands.

The questions that do not get asked frequently are the following: How does hands-on caregiving matter for men, and for shaping the social constructions of masculinities? How might men and boys doing more care work be part of responding to our crisis of connection? How does repressing men's caregiving cut them off from their ability to care? This chapter looks precisely at this issue. Getting to the heart of it, the problem and the solution are this: Might involved, hands-on, taking-on-that-sleepless-night-with-the-crying-baby kind of caregiving be a way to change emotionally restrictive versions of manhood into more caring and connected versions of manhood, and connected versions of humanity, and thus address the crisis of connection at its root?

This chapter starts first with why fatherhood and caregiving matter for men, their partners, and children, and then turns to what my organization, Promundo, does to attempt to create a (modest) revolution in how we think about men as inherently caring and as caregivers, and why it all matters for the crisis of connection.

Why Men's Caregiving Matters

Because the world largely ignores men's potential as caregivers, it is important to start with some of the emerging findings about men's caregiving and why it matters for the crisis of connection. A brief summary of that research affirms that (1) men are as biologically wired to care as women are, (2) men's caregiving matters for children as much as that of any caregiver, (3) men's caregiving is not some exotic or different kind of caregiving compared to that of mothers and women, and (4) we do real harm to men and boys and reinforce the crisis of connection when we cut men and boys off from their caregiving potential.

We Are All Biologically Wired for Care

One of the ways the gender binary works is by convincing us that socially constructed roles and ideas are real—that male and female differences are innate or biologically based. Thus it is important to affirm this: an emerging body of research finds that men are equally as biologically wired to care for infants as women are, apart, of course, from breastfeeding and giving birth. Fathers who are physically close to their babies and who are actively and directly involved in caring for them (even if they are not biological fathers) change biologically in ways that are nearly identical to mothers. Research finds that levels of "nurturing hormones" are similar in men and women exposed to "infant stimuli" before their babies are born (watching a video of a baby, listening to an audiotape of babies' cries, holding a doll wrapped in a blanket recently worn by a new born) and when interacting with them afterward.[12] Within fifteen minutes of holding a baby, men experience increases in the hormones that facilitate responsiveness to infants (vasopressin), closeness and care (prolactin), and affection and social bonds (oxytocin).

In short, men's bodies react to close connection with children similarly to how women's do. Our biochemistry as men changes to facilitate our bonding with young children. These physiological changes are likely part of our evolutionary legacy: hominid children with more caregivers and more attuned caregivers were more likely to survive and thrive than those with fewer.[13] And caregivers who focused their attention on their fragile hominid offspring were more likely to ensure that their genetic line continued.

Numerous authors have affirmed that our human evolutionary history means that as humans, both men and women, we are all wired to be cared for and loved. In fact, we survive and thrive only if we have those two things. The corollary is that all of us, male and female, are also *born to love and to care*. In other words, we all, male and female, possess the epigenetic traits (referring to those biological traits that are activated by our environment) that interact with our social environment to give us the innate human capacity to be connected, nurturing, crazy-about-children caregivers.

Why Fathers Matter for Children

That fathers matter for children is now widely accepted. And fathers matter for raising children, boys and girls, who care and connect deeply with others. There is ample evidence that fathers' increased engagement in caregiving activities boosts a variety of social, emotional, cognitive, and behavioral outcomes for children. Multiple studies report that fathers' taking 40 percent or more of the caregiving responsibility in the family is associated with positive outcomes in test scores and cognitive achievement.[14] A review of eighteen research studies on father involvement and child outcomes found that in seventeen of those studies fathers' greater involvement was associated with positive social, behavioral, psychological, and cognitive outcomes for children. Specifically, father involvement was associated with decreased behavioral problems in boys and psychological problems in girls.[15]

Furthermore, evidence shows that when men are engaged from the start of children's lives—whether by participating in prenatal care and education, being present during childbirth, or taking leave from work when a child is born—they establish a pattern of greater lifelong participation. In essence, they flex their nascent caregiving abilities and learn to use them. Fathers' ongoing positive involvement in the lives of their sons and daughters—listening to them and involving them in decision making—enhances children's physical, cognitive, emotional, and social development and can contribute to their happiness.[16]

When fathers engage in housework and child care and spend time with their sons and daughters, they contribute to boys' acceptance of gender equality and to girls' sense of autonomy.[17] In other words, involved fatherhood subverts the gendered binary. Engaged fatherhood can also help protect children from violence, abuse, exploitation, and neglect, and it can help ensure their access to health and education. When daughters and sons see their fathers in respectful, nonviolent, equitable relationships with their mothers and other women, and in the context of gay couple relationships, they internalize the idea that men and women are equal, that intimate partners treat each other with respect, and care for each other, and these children often grow up to pass these notions of respect and equality on to their own children.[18]

The overwhelming conclusion is that fathers matter for children, and they matter for helping to raise sons and daughters who are more likely to become involved, equitable, attuned caregivers themselves. Involved fatherhood, then, can bring men back from the crisis of connection and unleash their oft-repressed human potential for caring for others. And, together with involved mothering and support from other caregivers, it sets their children on a path to be more caring and connected.

Do Fathers Matter Differently Than Mothers?

Some fathers and some child development researchers want to find unique contributions of fathers to child development—that is, they want to affirm not only that fathers matter as co-parents in the context of heterosexual families but also that fathers contribute something inherently different than mothers do. Most of the time this "different" or unique contribution focuses on playing or helping children to acquire some trait that is considered traditionally male, like being tough. But here the framing of the question itself reinforces the gender binary.

To be sure, some studies find that fathers—at least in North America and Northern Europe, where most of the research has been carried out—contribute to children's development in ways that are different from mothers' contributions. But even if these differences are real, it is important to affirm that they are not biologically or genetically driven. They are a result of dividing our world into binary gendered patterns in which women continue to do a greater share of the hands-on caregiving and men continue to do more of the breadwinning. They are also a result of copying the gendered patterns of care many of us saw from our own parents, in which mothers are more likely to soothe and nurture while fathers are more likely to focus on play.

All of these functions, and many more, are necessary and part of caring for children; the issue is that they too often become gender-divided parenting styles that reinforce patterns that women and girls care, while boys and men are seen as careless. And herein, we reinforce the crisis of connection, which means that we must also disrupt this idea that men care for children in some special or different way. Instead, we must affirm that men quite simply provide care.

In affirming that fathers and other male caregivers matter for child development, the key point is that having *more* nurturing caregivers is better than one in terms of a child's development. The child development literature attests to the need for one caregiver (or more than one) who is *crazy about the child*, in the sense that the individual puts the child's needs above his or her own and is consistent and attentive, regardless of his or her sex. Seeking to affirm or identify a unique role for fathers or men—a role different from that of mothers and other caregivers— may at a practical level help us to engage some fathers by making fathers feel special. Certainly all of us who are fathers (or mothers or any caregivers) want to feel our contribution to our child is unique, and it is. But the reality is that as fathers we matter to children the same way that mothers and other caregivers do—meaning we matter to the extent that we nurture, support, connect, and provide consistent and developmentally appropriate care. Seeking a unique role for fathers too often reinforces the binary of gender differences rather than affirming the human capacity for nurturing of *all genders* and all of us who connect to children.

What Do We Get When We Keep Men from Caring?

Numerous authors—Niobe Way, Michael Kimmel, and other contributors to this book among them—have written about the way that gender norms suppress the emotional lives of men and boys and keep from them having the deep connections they desire with those around them.[19] The gendered socialization of boys in the use of physical violence is another result and a driver of men's limited propensity for self-care and care of others. Boys' higher rates of victimization from physical violence in their homes, schools, and communities is also related to the creation of socially valued versions of men and boys as tough, aggressive, and willing to defend their families, communities, peer groups, and individual reputations with force if necessary.

Another example of the harmful effects of the gendered socialization of men boys is suicide, one of the most dramatic global indicators of the gendered crisis of connection. Men represent two-thirds of the more than eight hundred thousand suicides that occur globally per year. Men's lower rate of seeking help for mental health needs and for dealing with sexual and other forms of violence is an additional example that has been well-documented and underlines how poorly men fare when it comes to caring for our own bodies and psyches. All of this is evidence of a crisis of connection in men that emerges from the gender binary. It is not merely that we repress the emotional skills of men and boys. It is that we create a gender binary that treats women and girls as lesser beings and makes men value achievement over connection.

As another example, a recent national survey in the United States indicated that one out of every three adults over the age of forty-five now reports feeling lonely, whereas only one out of every five adults reported feeling lonely ten years ago, with single men more likely than single women to report feeling lonely, and married women more likely than married men to report feeling lonely.[20] The conclusion we can take from this study is that men, by being emotionally cut off from themselves in a patriarchal and gender binary system, are not particularly good company or companions for their spouses or for themselves. This sense of isolation and loneliness is no doubt one of the factors associated with men's higher rates of suicide.

In sum, boys and men in the United States and elsewhere are often encouraged to repress their emotions and to see their primary roles and social identities as provider. If they cannot live up to this model, they are subject to ridicule and scorn and often internalize a sense of emasculation by not living according to the gender binary. Other men externalize their sense of failed masculinity when they are unemployed, for example, by becoming the "angry white men" that Kimmel calls them.[21] Again, we see how the gender binary, while it oppresses women, also hurts men.

Additional evidence of this association between rigid forms of masculinity and men's mental health and the crisis of connection comes from representative household surveys we have carried out in more than sixteen countries from Latin America, Europe, sub-Saharan Africa, and parts of Asia (with analogous data from the United States). The study was created by my organization and is called the International Men and Gender Equality Survey (IMAGES). It assessed men's agreement or adherence, or their disagreement with, a series of attitude and social norm questions. A consistent finding in country-level IMAGES results is that adult men who believe in inequitable and traditional norms related to manhood (toughness, superiority over women, rigid division of caregiving roles, among others) are more likely to report suicide ideation, depression, and binge drinking. They are also less likely to report life satisfaction and overall happiness.[22] The clear conclusion from this research is that rigid, inequitable views about manhood are associated with men's gendered crisis of connection. The other conclusion is that in many parts of the world, the United States included, the gender binary is alive and well and is a key driver of the crisis of connection.

How Promundo Disrupts the Binary and Unleashes Men's Caregiving Potential

Together with other researcher-activists, I founded Promundo in Brazil in 1997 to look at ways to engage men and boys in overcoming the gender binary. Through community-based programs, applied research, and national and international advocacy, we seek to reduce violence, achieve better health outcomes, promote men's caregiving, and engage men in promoting equality between men and women.

Our work generally starts with qualitative and quantitative research that seeks to identify ways that boys and men already subvert the binary (and women and girls who do the same), and tries to build on that. Sometimes we call these men and women "voices of resistance." Our belief is that by understanding these "subversives" who already break the binary, we can build on their narratives and pathways to promote change at the community level.

As an example of this kind of research, we carried out life history interviews with eighty-three men across five countries (India, South Africa, Mexico, Chile, and Brazil), working with local researchers to identify men who did atypical kinds or amounts of kinds of care work in their settings. Most of the men interviewed were primary caregivers, staying at home at least part of the time to care for their children; others were men in caregiving professions that were atypical for their countries. This research, called the Men Who Care Study, found in diverse cultural settings that providing daily, hands-on care enriched men's lives, and gave them new insights into women's and girls' gendered experiences and the experiences of people oppressed by homophobia.[23] These men also said it gave them new perceptions and opened up new avenues for connecting to others (male friends, other family members, female or male intimate partners) in relationships of greater emotional honesty and empathy. In other words hands-on caregiving for these involved men facilitated greater connection in numerous relationships.

Interestingly, most of the men did not report that they came to be more involved caregivers because of some "gender aware" epiphany that rigid norms about manhood were a problem that they needed to throw off. In interview after interview, the men described how life circumstances made them take on caregiving. These included having to migrate for family or work reasons, the illness of their spouse or partner, or being unemployed while their wives had work. In the course of having to do the hands-on care, these men from diverse countries and diverse socioeconomic backgrounds found that caregiving transformed them in multiple and positive ways.

But there was a dark lining and cost to the men for taking on caregiving: most of them said they were worried that their children saw them solely as caregivers. They felt less masculine by being un- or underemployed and worried about what their children thought of them. Those primary caregiving men who also worked outside the home in paid employment at least part of the time reported feeling more secure in their "male identities." What we take from this conclusion is that the world around men continues to reinforce the gender binary notion that stay-at-home fathers (and stay-at-home mothers in many parts of the world) and caregiving in general are less valued than the breadwinning we do outside the home. Indeed, one of the global challenges of encouraging men and boys to take on more caregiving is that we do not, as societies, value care and care work in general, no matter who does it. The narratives of the men we interviewed in the Men Who Care Study reminded several of us who did the research of things we had heard our mothers (nearly always our chief caregivers) say, namely that their work in the home was rarely appreciated.[24]

Building on this research, we started the MenCare campaign in 2011. The campaign aims to engage men as active, nonviolent partners and caregivers in order to empower women and girls, and to achieve health and well-being. MenCare is the first ever global fatherhood campaign. Since its start, MenCare has grown to be active in over forty countries. MenCare disseminates global research, evidence-based programming, and strategic advocacy goals. This includes the first-ever global State of the World's Fathers (SOWF) report, and the nine other country and regional reports it inspired.[25] This advocacy work enables partner organizations around the world to work in their communities and with their national governments to advocate for change. SOWF and other reports, for example, have inspired action and built on growing debates around paternity and paid, nontransferable parental leave globally as a key strategy for enabling and encouraging men's caregiving.

Promundo's initiatives also include developing and evaluating methodologies for parent training that engages fathers (called Program P), training for health providers and child care workers in how to engage men, and community-based actions for young men to question rigid notions of manhood, through an evaluated curriculum called Manhood 2.0. We also work in areas affected by high rates of urban violence in Brazil, and in conflict-affected areas in the Democratic Republic of Congo (DRC). In the eastern part of DRC we founded a local organization dedicated to engaging men to help communities and women overcome legacies of sexual violence from the conflict, in an initiative called Living Peace. That initiative brings together men who have used violence against their partners, men whose wives were raped during the conflict in DRC, and men who are seen as positive voices in their communities, to support each other in changing violent notions of manhood. A two-year follow-up evaluation of the initiative found that in more than 90 percent of households men's use of violence against their female partners had reduced, couple relationships had improved, and men had increased their participation in the daily care of children.

In some countries—including Brazil, Croatia, Chile, Nicaragua, and Rwanda—our approaches not only have changed the lives of individuals and communities but also have been taken up by the public sector. Specifically, ministries of health, education, and gender equality have seen the impact of our work and requested that we train their staff via official public health clinic protocols, public school curricula, or economic empowerment activities accompanying national programs for women's empowerment.

Building on Evidence of the Benefits of Men's Caregiving

At the heart of all of these programs is taking a positive approach that men and boys have the innate capacity to care and develop deep connections, to develop and live empathy and in the process to become allies of women and girls in subverting the gender binary. Rather than blaming individual men for violence (while we must hold them accountable), for example, we work to change the social norms that create and reinforce violence. We engage as allies those men and women who already see the gender binary for what it is: a creator of inequality.

In our advocacy, we both gather and review data showing the benefits of men's involvement in violence prevention and in caregiving. For example, our research and that of others have affirmed that involved caregiving is good for men themselves. Greater engagement in caregiving and fatherhood brings benefits to men's health, including reduced risk taking and improved physical, mental, and sexual health.[26] Men who are involved in meaningful ways with their children consistently report this relationship to be one of their most important sources of well-being and happiness.[27] Equally important, the research shows that the female partners of involved fathers are happier and report closer intimate relationships with their male partners.[28] Moreover, involved, nonviolent fatherhood can help break cycles of violence against women. Data from numerous studies, including our own, show that boys who saw their fathers use violence against their mothers are more likely than the sons of nonviolent fathers to grow up to use violence against their own partners.[29]

From Individuals and Communities to Countries

What might change look like at the country level in terms of achieving a massive increase in men's caregiving? What would happen if we promoted a full package of policies to encourage caregiving by men across a country? Research from Norway is illustrative. While far from perfect, Norway consistently ranks among the most gender equitable countries. In addition to other gender equality policies—and an extensive social welfare system—in 1993 Norway introduced paid and extensive paternity leave along with campaigns to promote the use of it. The impact of the policy change has been strong and lasting. Surveyed almost twenty years after the reform, parents with children born after the implementation of the reform reported 11 percent less conflict over household work than did those who became parents *before* the policy changed. These parents did not differ from pre-reform parents in their attitudes toward gender equality, which likely indicates the wide range of factors and social norms that shape those attitudes. Support for public child care was also higher among men involved in caregiving. In other words, when men did more of the caregiving they were also more likely to favor policies that support children.[30]

Another study in Norway found that the incidence of violence against women or children in father-dominated homes was three times higher than in more equitable homes, that is, where fathers shared caregiving tasks more equitably with women. This study concluded that paternity leave contributed to more involvement by men in the home and subsequently, at least indirectly, was a driver of lower rates of family violence. The study asserted that rates of men's use of violence in the home, against either children or women, declined over the period of 1986 to 2006 and that men's use of paternity leave, which was associated with higher rates of men's caregiving, was at least one of the drivers of this national decline.[31]

Conclusions: Disrupting the Binary

If, then, men's involvement in caregiving helps disrupt the gender binary, helps achieve the full equality that women and girls deserve, is positive for children, and is positive for men themselves, what do we need to do to encourage more of it? It is clear that to achieve full gender equality and maximum well-being for children, we need to move beyond rigid, limiting definitions of fatherhood and motherhood and move toward what children need most to thrive. This is not some minor question of encouraging men to be nice by doing more nurturing and caring. This is an issue of social and economic justice and of ending the crisis of connection. To that end, changes are needed in policies, in systems and institutions, among service providers, within programming, and within data collection and analysis efforts.

To achieve a radical transformation in how we view care work, we need parent training programs with men and boys, as well as with women and girls, that challenge social norms and promote their positive involvement in the lives of children. We need more programs like Roots of Empathy and Manhood 2.0 that help to prepare boys and girls from early ages to be future caregivers *and* future providers.[32] We also need to recognize the diversity of men's caregiving and support it in all of its forms and family configurations, including single parents, adoptive parents, nonresident fathers, gay fathers, adolescent fathers, and extended families.

To answer the question posed at the beginning of this chapter, engaging men and boys in caregiving *is* about helping men to have the deep, meaningful connections to others that are at the root of well-being and happiness. While affirming this, we must also introduce a major caveat: while increasing men's caregiving matters in and of itself, it matters *what* fathers, mothers, and other caregivers teach children. The content and the kind of moral justice we impart to our children in our caregiving is as important as men and women equally sharing the care work. There are, no doubt, many fathers and mothers who care deeply for their children and create lasting bonds and connections with them (and equally share in that care), but who, for example, are racist, classist, or homophobic or ignore the major realities of how our consumer and business practices are harming our planet. Passing on such toxic messages and examples to our children, even if men are doing half the hands-on care work in such households, hardly contributes to reducing the crisis of connection and creating a more socially just world.

Indeed, it is not enough merely to promote men's caregiving in our oft-isolated nuclear families in the face of systemic social injustices that make it impossible for too many other fathers and mothers to care for and connect with their children. When we think about men's caregiving in the United States, for example, we should also consider this stark reality: mass incarceration has resulted in 2.7 million children having an incarcerated parent, 92 percent of them fathers, and more than 60 percent of them low-income men of color.[33] To discuss caring and caregiving means promoting among men and women as policymakers and citizens an ethic of care for *all* of those around us.

The revolution in caregiving and connection requires that we come to see caring and caregiving not as a male or female attribute, but simply as a human attribute. It also means that we must value and support the ability of *all* families in *all* family configurations to have the means to care and be cared for. We must disrupt both the gender binary that pushes men away from caregiving and an overly competitive, materialist societal model that creates winners versus losers and leaves the so-called losers to fend for themselves.

This means that we must promote men's caregiving and connection in ways that go beyond simply *me and my own in the privacy of my nuclear family*. It means that promoting men's caregiving must be about the collective *us* and particularly about those families most affected by legacies of our lack of connection, solidarity, and social justice. We need men and women to care—for their own children, and families, and for *all* families and children. That's when we disrupt the binary and resolve the crisis of connection.

NOTES

1 Ruti Levtov, Nikki van der Gaag, Margaret Greene, Michael Kaufman, and Gary Barker, "State of the World's Fathers: A MenCare Advocacy Publication" (Washington, DC: Promundo, Rutgers, Save the Children, Sonke Gender Justice, and the MenEngage Alliance, 2015).

2 Carol Gilligan, "Moral Injury and the Ethic of Care" (lecture, Víctor Grífols Foundation for Bioethics, Barcelona, April 17, 2013).

3 Glenda Wall and Stephanie Arnold, "How Involved Is Involved Fathering? An Exploration of the Contemporary Culture of Fatherhood," *Gender & Society* 21, no. 4 (2007): 508–527.

4 Ibid., 521.

5 Brian Heilman, Geneva Cole, Kenneth Matos, Alexa Hassink, Ron Mincy, and Gary Barker, "State of America's Fathers: A MenCare Advocacy Publication" (Washington, DC: Promundo-US, 2016).

6   Claire Cain Miller, "As Women Take over a Male-Dominated Field, the Pay Drops," *New York Times*, March 18, 2016, www.nytimes.com.

7   William Marsiglio, *Men on a Mission: Valuing Youth Work in Our Communities* (Baltimore: Johns Hopkins University Press, 2008).

8   Richard V. Reeves and Isabel V. Sawhill, "Men's Lib!," *New York Times*, November 14, 2015, www.nytimes.com.

9   Bureau of Labor Statistics, "Employed Persons by Detailed Occupation, Sex, Race, and Hispanic or Latino Ethnicity" (2011), www.bls.gov.

10 Marsiglio, *Men on a Mission*.

11 The author led a review of the US data and new research on this as part of "State of America's Fathers," published in June 2016 (www.men-care.org), and an international review of the research as part of "State of the World's Fathers," released in June 2015 (www.men-care.org). Special thanks to my co-authors of those publications for allowing me to draw on them for this chapter.

12 Anne E. Storey, Carolyn J. Walsh, Roma L. Quinton, and Katherine E. Wynne-Edwards, "Hormonal Correlates of Paternal Responsiveness in New and Expectant Fathers," *Evolution and Human Behavior* 21, no. 2 (2000): 79–95.

13 Sarah Blaffer Hrdy, *Mothers and Others: The Evolutionary Origins of Mutual Understanding* (Cambridge, MA: Harvard University Press, 2009).

14 Tamara Halle, "Charting Parenthood: A Statistical Portrait of Fathers and Mothers in America" (Child Trends, 2002), www.childtrends.org; Jo Jones and William D. Mosher, "Fathers' Involvement with Their Children: United States, 2006–2010," *National Health Statistics Reports* 71 (2013): 1–22.

15 Anna Sarkadi, Robert Kristiansson, Frank Oberklaid, and Sven Bremberg, "Fathers' Involvement and Children's Developmental Outcomes: A Systematic Review of Longitudinal Studies," *Acta Pædiatrica* 97, no. 2 (2008): 153–158, doi:10.1111/j.1651-2227.2007.00572.x.

16 Catherine Panter-Brick, Adrienne Burgess, Mark Eggerman, Fiona McAllister, Kyle Pruett, and James F. Leckman, "Practitioner Review: Engaging Fathers—Recommendations for a Game Change in Parenting Interventions Based on a Systematic Review of the Global Evidence," *Journal of Child Psychology and Psychiatry* 55, no. 11 (2014): 1187–1212; Natasha J. Cabrera, Jacqueline D. Shannon, and Catherine Tamis-LeMonda, "Fathers' Influence on Their Children's Cognitive and Emotional Development: From Toddlers to Pre-K," *Applied Developmental Science* 11, no. 4 (2007): 208–213; Jessica Davis, Stanely Luchters, and Wendy Holmes, "Men and Maternal and Newborn Health: Benefits, Harms, Challenges and Potential Strategies for Engaging Men" (Melbourne: Compass: Women's and Children's Health Knowledge Hub, 2012); Adrienne Burgess, "The Costs and Benefits of Active Fatherhood: Evidence and Insights to Inform the Development of Policy and Practice" (London: Fathers Direct, 2006).

17 Ian DeGeer, Humberto Carolo, and Todd Minerson, "Give Love, Get Love: The Involved Fatherhood and Gender Equality Project" (Toronto: White Ribbon Campaign, 2014).

18 Burgess, "Costs and Benefits of Active Fatherhood"; Gary Barker, Juan M. Contreras, Brian Heilman, Ajay Singh, and Marcos Nascimento, "Evolving Men: Initial Results from the International Men and Gender Equality Survey (IMAGES)" (Washington, DC: International Center for Research on Women and Instituto Promundo, 2011); DeGeer, Carolo, and Minerson, "Give Love, Get Love."

19 Niobe Way, *Deep Secrets: Boys' Friendships and the Crisis of Connection* (Cambridge, MA: Harvard University Press, 2011); Niobe Way, "Boys' Friendships during Adolescence: Intimacy, Desire and Loss," Journal of Research on Adolescence 23, no. 2 (2013): 201–213; Michael Kimmel, *Guyland: The Perilous World Where Boys Become Men* (New York: HarperCollins, 2008).

20 Niobe Way, "Opening Comments" (lecture, Project for the Advancement of Our Common Humanity, New York, September 26, 2013).

21 Michael Kimmel, *Angry White Men: American Masculinity at the End of an Era* (New York: Nation Books, 2013).

22 Barker et al., "Evolving Men."

23 Gary Barker et al., "Men Who Care Study: A Multi-country Qualitative Study of Men in Non-traditional Caregiving Roles" (Washington, DC: Promundo and International Center for Research on Women, 2012).

24 Ibid.

25 Levtov et al., "State of the World's Fathers."

26 Christine Ricardo, "Men, Masculinities and Changing Power: A Discussion Paper on Engaging Men in Gender Equality from Beijing 1995 to 2015" (Washington, DC: MenEngage Alliance and UN Women, 2014).

27 DeGeer, Carolo, and Minerson, "Give Love, Get Love."

28 Burgess, "Costs and Benefits of Active Fatherhood."

29 Barker et al., "Evolving Men."

30 Andreas Kotsadam and Henning Finseraas, "The State Intervenes in the Battle of the Sexes: Causal Effects of Paternity Leave," *Social Science Research* 40, no. 6 (2011): 1611–1622.

31 Øystein Gullvåg Holter, Helge Svare, and Cathrine Egeland, "Gender Equality and Quality of Life: A Norwegian Perspective" (Oslo: Nordic Gender Institute, 2009).

32 See Gordon, this volume.

33 Pew Charitable Trusts, "Collateral Costs: Incarceration's Effect on Economic Mobility" (2010), www.pewtrusts.org; Sarah Schirmer, Ashley Nellis, and Marc Mauer, "Incarcerated Parents and Their Children: Trends 1991–2007" (Washington, DC: Sentencing Project, 2009); Thomas P. Bonczar, "Prevalence of Imprisonment in the U.S. Population, 1974–2001" (Washington, DC: Bureau of Justice Statistics, 2003).

17

Rehumanization through Communalized Narrative for Military Veterans

STEPHAN WOLFERT AND ALISHA ALI

Military veterans gather in front of a hot room stuffed full of friends, family, and strangers. The veterans range in age from their early twenties to mid-eighties. They served in different branches and had different experiences, during war and during eras of "peace." Few of the veterans, if any, long to be actors, and even fewer have any experience acting, especially Shakespeare. Yet that is exactly what they are here to do. They seek to share some of their most traumatic life and/or military experiences, through monologues from Shakespeare, to a group who've never heard them talk about this before. The group is witnessing a transformation, a journey of healing, a process of change forged through the power of human connection.

Of the many existing obstacles on the path to a common humanity, war is perhaps the most extreme. In the US military, the recruitment, systematic indoctrination, and intense training of young men and women is based on a process of dehumanization—a dehumanization not only of those deemed the enemy, but also of the young recruits themselves as they progressively learn to disconnect from the human capacities of compassion, empathy, and mutual understanding. This chapter describes the DE-CRUIT program, which was designed to foster returning veterans' reintegration into society by addressing conventionally recognized symptoms of posttraumatic stress and by rehumanizing veterans to themselves, to each other, and to the broader community. The program is a veteran-informed, strengths-based group intervention that integrates components of trauma therapy with key elements from classical actor training. Through our examination of this program, we will demonstrate that human connection is an essential element in any intervention aimed at helping veterans and in helping us as a society come to terms with the aftermath of trauma, violence, and destruction.

Themes of Common Humanity That Have Informed the Development of DE-CRUIT

The work of DE-CRUIT as a grassroots organization has been ongoing for many years. However, it wasn't until the integration of DE-CRUIT into the broader work of research in the area of trauma treatment for military veterans that the true possibilities of its impact became clear. Through partnership with a university-based research team, the DE-CRUIT program has been able to achieve two crucial goals that have aided its implementation and expansion. The first of these goals is the manualization of the DE-CRUIT treatment sessions, which now integrate empirically supported techniques from cognitive processing therapy and narrative therapy. The second goal is the formalized evaluation of the therapeutic effects of the program, which are now being measured through systematic pre/post assessment of psychological variables such as posttraumatic stress and depression, as well as physiological and neurological variables. Together, these advances have led to ongoing improvements and revisions to the DE-CRUIT framework that will allow us to better serve the needs of veterans.

These advances have also allowed us to see how the DE-CRUIT program can play a role in addressing the crisis of connection experienced by veterans and others who have had similar experiences. Military veterans are a population rife with crisis and with disconnection, largely because for years they operated at the most extreme opposite of humanity: war. Training for and conducting war—where the primary task is killing—require diminishing the humanity of the perceived adversary. To dehumanize the adversary, soldiers must first strip away any references to their humanity and instead call them "the enemy" or "targets." Throughout our military history we have deepened this dehumanization process by giving the enemy derogatory nicknames. For example, during the Vietnam War, American troops called the North Vietnamese soldiers and Viet Cong fighters "Charlie" and "Victor Charlie" (the phonetic translation of VC referring to Viet Cong), respectively. Even more insulting, racist, and therefore dehumanizing were terms such as "gook" and "slope," which were invoked for all Asians and Southeast Asians. During the wars in Iraq and Afghanistan too, we saw the exact same method of dehumanization. For example, the term "hadji," originally a term of respect for pilgrims who went to Mecca and completed the Hajj, was instead appropriated by US and UN forces and turned into a racist slur meant to both dehumanize Arabs and serve as a general term used by all comrades when referring to Arabs. In every component of training in the US military, the camaraderie-based model is fundamental. A sustained existence in this type of environment deepens the dehumanization for anyone who is not soldier, sailor, marine, or airman, ultimately resulting in a disconnection from the humanity of the "enemy" and their own. Moreover, after military service is complete, service members do not receive any training to reconnect to their humanity. In order to facilitate this reconnection, DE-CRUIT uses three central themes.

Resisting the Binaries That Misrepresent Reality

Within the work of DE-CRUIT, we have seen the binary of the expert versus the victim as a particularly damaging duality. This binary is evident in mainstream treatment models that posit a stance of the expert practitioner who is superior in knowledge and experience to the victim-survivor who is the flawed, defective recipient of treatment. In examining the DE-CRUIT program, we have learned that the victim is sometimes the best expert. The trained facilitators who deliver the program are themselves veterans who have experienced trauma and who have successfully gone through DE-CRUIT as participants. Their firsthand knowledge and deep-rooted understanding of the types of trauma encountered by veterans and of the pervasive effects of this trauma allow them to develop a highly effective therapeutic rapport with the participating veterans and to encourage openness and sharing within the therapeutic group process.

Subverting Differentials of Power That Undermine Our Practice

In our work, we have also engaged in discussions about the disempowerment of marginalized groups and about societal forces that subjugate the knowledge of members of these groups. Veterans themselves are marginalized within society, and the knowledge that exists within the veteran community about creative, effective ways of treating trauma and supporting returning veterans as they attempt to reintegrate into the civilian world are often discounted in favor of mainstream medical treatments. While we acknowledge that different treatments can work differently depending on the particular veteran who is seeking help, we are insistent in our work that alternatives to medical approaches must be presented to veterans. Medical models of care can often be alienating and dehumanizing;[1] for this reason, models like DE-CRUIT are essential as veteran-derived, arts-informed approaches may be able to reach veterans who would otherwise reject treatment.

Forging Connections across Difference

A third theme that has been important in the developing work of DE-CRUIT is the emphasis on the need to forge connections across seemingly disparate groups within society. In DE-CRUIT, these types of connections have been seen to be therapeutic on a number of levels. For example, from a therapeutic standpoint, we have seen the benefits of including as group participants veterans who differ from each other in terms of demographics (e.g., age, gender, ethnicity), military experiences (e.g., including veterans of current wars alongside those from the Vietnam and Korean wars), and ranks and jobs within the military. Seeing the commonalities in the effects of trauma across these different subgroups has allowed the veterans in DE-CRUIT to gain a broader perspective on their own personal trauma and also to share their personal narratives in a healing space that values diversity and diverse stories.

The Beginnings of the DE-CRUIT Program: One Veteran's Story

I (Stephan) spent more than two decades seeking to answer the question "what the hell is wrong with me?" through the plays of William Shakespeare, classical actor training, and embracing the First Nation's lessons of theater as medicine.[2] My quest allowed me to change my narrative from "what is wrong with me?" to "what *happened* to me?"

What happened to me is what happened to all veterans in this country. We were recruited, or drafted, at a psychologically malleable age, and then were wired for war, but at the end of our military services we were not unwired from war. We were not rewired for society. Further complicating matters, we were amputated from our community of comrades, our structure, our mission, our purpose, our support, and dumped back into the communities from which many of us fled. After all, at least 70 percent of draftees and enlistees since Vietnam have been from working-class or poor families.[3] And now we are back in communities that, generally speaking, lack the resources to reintegrate their veterans.

When I entered the military I had a recruiter. My recruiter prepared me for military service. He drove me where I needed to go, helped me with my paperwork, assisted with every aspect of preparing me for military service. But when my military service was over, where was my de-cruiter? Where was the person who could prepare me for life after the military? Where was the person to help me leave the training behind, to transition my skills to civilian jobs, to help me connect with the resources, to unwire me from war?

My quest to answer the simple question of "what is wrong with me?" led to the creation of DE-CRUIT. Through partnering with university-based researchers, DE-CRUIT was able to expand more in the past three years than in the entire decade prior. This partnership has helped me to realize that, ultimately, trauma and military training disconnected me from my own humanity and from the humanity of others. DE-CRUIT has thus been able to refine its techniques to create the current model designed to help military veterans literally rewire their brain to reconnect to our common humanity.

What I learned to be the most important mechanisms of DE-CRUIT that reconnect military veterans to their humanity are the following:

- The top priority is to provide the veteran-participants a safe space to
  a. Take up time and space to "speak what we feel and not what we ought to say" (Shakespeare, *King Lear*, act 5, scene 3).
  b. Make big, bold choices that mimic the life-and-death circumstances of the military, but unlike the military no one actually dies (because it's theater, not real life).

c. Dare to fail. Antithetical to the military binaries of "go or no go" and "friend or foe," DE-CRUIT uses theater because it lives and thrives in between binaries. Participants are encouraged to deliberately "fail" and discover that in the creative process there is no such thing as true failure. This frees the veteran-participants to become progressively bolder over time.

d. Do rather than "discuss." This means working on a scene or monologue by actually performing it rather than simply talking about it. Embodiment versus intellectualizing.

e. Embrace process over product and observation over judgment. This requires participants to practice rehearsing rather than focusing on the performance and to observe what is happening moment to moment rather than assessing what is happening as good or bad.

- Camaraderie is an essential component when training American military personnel. Broadly speaking, it is used to distance service members from their humanity in order to bypass empathy in combat situations. In fact, the US military studied the former Soviet Union's ideologically based military training and compared it to America's camaraderie-based model for effectiveness in both kill ratio and mission completion; the study found that camaraderie provides a far broader, greater, and longer term impact on service members when compared to ideologically based training: "In military writings on unit cohesion, one consistently finds the assertion that the bonds combat soldiers form with one another are stronger than the bonds most men have with their wives."[4] Grossman found that creating a feeling of accountability to one's comrades increased the number of soldiers who shoot to kill. It therefore seems logical to extend this practice post-service and to use camaraderie when reconnecting veterans to their humanity.[5] However, in particular contrast to the military's camaraderie for war, DE-CRUIT uses ancient practices of camaraderie for self-expression, performance, and creativity.[6]

- Ritual provides a routine on how to begin and how to end. For example, we perform a group ritual to begin and end each DE-CRUIT session. And individually we perform a ritual to begin working on a scene or a monologue and to end the work. Ritual makes something special and therefore repeatable, and when repeated becomes routine—and this discipline then morphs that routine into habit.[7] These rituals are applicable to everyday life as well. Rituals are invoked for everything from preparing to sleep to recovering more quickly from an anxious moment or being triggered into a full-blown traumatic episode.

- Shakespeare's verse provides the heightened language needed to adequately describe the complex feelings that the veterans have locked within them. This verse also unleashes emotions, memories, and trauma within the veterans—emotions that had long been locked away. For veterans who have been repeatedly retraumatized, the elevated verse offers a path through the veterans' trauma by allowing them to continue to work through language that is foreign to them while also elevating their experience though dramatic form.

The theater offers a safe space and a welcoming community in which to share my story without being judged or condemned. The theater kept me from being yet another veteran statistic. By examining and acting Shakespeare through a veteran lens, I was able to understand what happened to me, to better understand my experiences. By applying classical actor training to my everyday life, I have built new habits to replace my military conditioning.

Components of the DE-CRUIT Program

The DE-CRUIT framework has evolved over recent years into a formalized model that integrates not only elements of theater but also principles from trauma therapy. The model comprises three main components that function together to meet the psychological needs of veterans who are struggling with the effects of trauma and with the challenges of reintegrating into civilian society. The three components are as follows:

Unit Cohesion

The notion of unit cohesion is a military concept that reflects the psychological factors that bond soldiers together as they aim to achieve the desired goals of a military mission. This sense of cohesion is crucial in connecting soldiers to each other as they take life-endangering risks. However, in civilian life, veterans struggle when they don't have that daily bond to rely on, and alienation ensues. To address this alienation, the DE-CRUIT program brings veterans together and allows them to bond through a connection forged by their common humanity and by their continuing connection shared with all fellow veterans. This cohesion is an extension of the traditional group therapy model that aims to create mutual support among group members; the DE-CRUIT approach adds to this support by making use of the special bond that already exists between veterans.

Communalization of Trauma

In addition to the bond of unit cohesion, the DE-CRUIT program draws upon psychiatrist Jonathan Shay's notion of the communalization of trauma as an essential component in supporting veterans in their societal reintegration and in their psychological wellness.[8] The process of communalization begins with having the veterans write a personal *trauma monologue*, which is a first-person account of a specific military trauma they experienced. The monologue is structured upon the model of the Shakespearian monologue. After all veterans in the group writes their personal trauma monologue, they relinquish their monologue to a fellow group member who will memorize, rehearse, and ultimately perform that monologue for the group at the final DE-CRUIT session. Through this interconnected process, the DE-CRUIT method allows participating veterans to hear and see their own traumatic experience performed by a fellow veteran, for whom they may have more empathy and compassion than they have for themselves. This connection through compassion is a crucial step in self-acceptance and healing as veterans learn to forgive their own adaptive responses to trauma that may have precipitated many of the life struggles they are experiencing now.

Therapeutic Embodiment

The DE-CRUIT program integrates key elements of relaxation, breathing, and physical grounding in every session. The expectation is that all participating veterans will adopt a daily personal routine of various forms of physical relaxation that they will continue throughout their time in the program and beyond. Research on the therapeutic effects of relaxation and breathing techniques in psychotherapy for trauma has shown positive psychological and neurological outcomes.[9] In the

DE-CRUIT method, veterans are supported in their daily practice of these techniques by drawing on the routinized structure that parallels the routines that they followed in military life. Additionally, the veterans in the group use the various breathing and grounded techniques to help them to master the spoken verse they will use in performing their fellow veterans' monologues of trauma.

The DE-CRUIT Method in Action: Telling Human Stories through the Trauma Monologue and the Soliloquy Algorithm

The epitome of DE-CRUIT in action (demonstrating the process of camaraderie, Shakespeare, classical actor training, and psychology in the healing of trauma) is the point in the program in which the veterans write their trauma monologues and the facilitator uses the "Shakespeare Soliloquy Algorithm" to assign a Shakespeare soliloquy or monologue.

In keeping with our use of establishing routines, facilitators begin each class with a circle, complete the routinized grounding, conduct a "check-in," and participate in a brief warm-up. The facilitator then shares a personal story (e.g., "the incident that most affects me . . ."). While each of these steps is simple in appearance and easy to complete, together they are the culmination of extensive experience, hold crucial worth in the rewiring of veterans' trauma, and are at the antipodes of military training.

- *Rituals:* Facilitators establish routines through rituals because they are a way to rewire habits that we want to replace. Rituals are simply a way to begin or end something, whether a ritual to get into and out of "character," bowing upon entering and exiting the group space, or a ritual to ground and breathe to recover from a traumatic memory or moment. Making something a ritual makes it memorable and therefore repeatable. If one repeats a ritual it eventually will become routine, and "over time, as the daily routines become second nature, discipline morphs into habit."[10]
- *The circle:* At the beginning of each DE-CRUIT meeting, participants stand in a circle together. The circle creates equity and eliminates a hierarchy. In the circle, everyone can see each other and all are equal.[11] The circle, therefore, undoes the hierarchy of the traditional military structure.
- *Grounding:* To deepen their connection with each other in the circle and to ourselves, participants stand in a grounding rather than a military

position. A grounding position is basically the beginning position of any practice focused on mindfulness: yoga, meditation, singing, acting, and others. Feet are placed shoulder-width apart in parallel position, knees, hips, and shoulders relaxed, belly relaxed to allow breath to drop fully into the body, lips parted, jaw open, fully receiving the sights, sounds, and air of the surroundings. We use the image of a toddler as guidance for this position because, generally speaking, toddlers use their skeletons and bodies in exactly the way they were designed to function. Toddlers have not yet allowed societal pressures to alter the way in which they stand, walk, breath, or bend to pick something up off of the floor.

- *The "check-in"*: For the initial check-in of the session, participants may be standing or seated, as long as there is nothing blocking the front of each person or the space between participants. One at a time, around the circle, each person shares how he or she is feeling at that moment. It is important to focus on *truthful feelings in the moment*, since it is very easy to recap an upset from earlier. We guide participants toward being honest, focused on sharing feelings, and remaining in that moment. This is an exercise that requires practice. Early on, participants will say a great deal, but actually share very little. Therefore, early in practice participants may say anything, and eventually we ask them to go back and share again and invite them to trim the excess. The participants are always encouraged to strive toward being "brief but brilliant," but this comes only after participants are feeling comfortable enough to be truly honest and know they will not be judged or condemned.

In addition to striving toward sharing feelings in the moment, the practice of speaking in the first person is important. It is very common in contemporary vernacular to refer to oneself by saying "you," such as, "You know how when you're walking down the street, and you are always looking for the threat?" In this case, the speaker uses "you" three times, but two of them refer to the speaker. We guide participants to own the act of "looking for the threat." We invite them to find in their own words what they mean but now using "I" or "me." This results in a new sharing that looks like this example: "When I walk down the street, I am always looking for the threat."

By beginning every class in this way, participants are creating new habits, including self-expression, sharing of feelings, listening to others, speaking in the first person, owning their feelings, thoughts, and actions, trusting in and reducing judgment of others, and clarity and specificity of speech. All of these skills are developed by a simple "check-in."

After the opening rituals, facilitators begin each new DE-CRUIT session with a personal story. The benefits of self-disclosure from the facilitator's life include the following:

- Tie personal trauma into the theme for that particular class
- Demonstrate leading by example in self-disclosure
- Close the distance between facilitator and participant (this is counter to military training, since, in order to train service members to kill, the military must create a distance from both our own humanity and the humanity of others)
- Be viewed by veteran-participants as a peer who has suffered, which can help the facilitator reach participants therapeutically

Overwhelmingly, veterans have stated that they were not planning to share during the session but did so because, after the facilitator shared a personal story, the veterans felt safe enough to now tell their own truth. Countless veteran-participants have expressed that they had never shared these personal stories before.

After a personal story, facilitators switch to helping the veterans write their own "trauma narrative." By this point in the DE-CRUIT program, each veteran-participant has completed three prompts (one spoken and two written) and is therefore familiar with expressing himself or herself through writing prompts. The veterans are now given the writing prompt "The incident that most affects me . . ." and are sent off to write for fifteen minutes, then regroup for any volunteers who would like to share their writing with the group. After sharing, the group discusses a handout explaining trauma-related cognitive "stuck points." Veteran-participants are asked to draw the parallels of stuck points they may have from their prompted story. Building on the momentum of self-discovery and deepening self-examination, veteran-participants are asked to condense their story into a single sentence. This process not only personalizes their experience/story by writing in the first person but also embodies the experience by requiring them to specifically describe and place feelings in their body.

Volunteers who so desire may share their sentence with the group. Then they hear a list of symptoms and are asked to write down any that they are experiencing (they will not share this with the group). On the second read through of the list, they are instructed to circle the symptom that they feel affects them the most, at least lately. The final step is for each veteran to privately show or tell the facilitator his or her single selected symptom. Based on this symptom, on the facilitator's overall knowledge of the veteran, and on guidance written in the facilitator's manual, the facilitator selects a soliloquy from the DE-CRUIT packet for each veteran: in this packet are a set of Shakespeare's soliloquies that relate closely to symptoms of posttraumatic stress disorder and to common symptoms that veterans experience after separation from military service.

Very often the veteran-participants are unaware how this process will all come together, and they doubt whether they will even share their story. Invariably the process *does* come together and generally *all* veterans do share their stories because they are depending on each other in this disorienting but creative experiment. The driving force is camaraderie— whatever happens has been created by *them*, by their trust in one another to share and support each other in their personal traumas. One by one, all veteran-participants stand before the group and speak their Shakespeare soliloquy aloud. The *only* requirement/instruction is that they ground, take in a breath, and speak a single line of verse (ignoring punctuation for now; and for the very few soliloquies in prose, they may speak according to the punctuation). After they have spoken the entire monologue, one line of verse at a time, aloud before the group, they are asked "What do you think it means?" For our purposes, whatever they think it means is exactly what it means. We do not, as is common with most acting techniques, provide context for the soliloquy, scene, or play. The text is deliberately being taken out of context and being used for *our* context. Therefore, whatever it means *to them* is what it means. If they have no idea what it means, they are asked to "dare to be wrong" and blurt out their first guess.

Next we go through the soliloquy in the same manner, line by line, using the DE-CRUIT *text grid*. This grid is used to guide the veterans in speaking a line of verse and then saying immediately a second time but in their own words (describing what it means to them); they are also encouraged to describe a time in their experience when they have felt that way.

In the next step, the veteran-participants read aloud their completed writing from the prompt "the incident that affects me most . . ." and then transition directly into reading their Shakespeare monologue aloud (as always, practicing the technique of grounding and breathing in before each and every line).

This is the entirety of the work not only for the remaining classes but also for the culminating class performance. For the final class, the veteran-participants invite a few people who they feel may need to hear their voice. Their performance is a seamless interweaving of their narrative with the Shakespeare soliloquy that was selected for them. The focus of the public presentation is to provide them the opportunity of practicing in front of a live audience, giving them the chance to take up the time and space they need to breathe and express themselves— and to provide a safe space for them to "testify" and be "witnessed" or heard. The focus of the personal narrative is to externalize their story so that they may rewrite that story and recover more quickly from stuck points. The focus of the Shakespeare soliloquy is to provide a heightened language for their narrative while practicing the grounding and breathing that are ultimately the theater skills that we hope they will transfer into a life skill to aid in the recovery from anxiety and other symptoms when their stuck points begin to take over.

Therapeutic Self-Disclosure and the Healing Potential of Human Connection

As is evident in our description of the DE-CRUIT process, narrating one's experience of trauma is viewed as central to healing. Storytelling and self-disclosure have become increasingly significant elements of the DE-CRUIT program as it has evolved over the recent years. From these element have emerged a greater understanding of the therapeutic potential of human connection for those who have experienced trauma. In particular, we have seen that the combination of self-disclosure of traumatic experience on the part of the program facilitators and the use of Shakespeare's narratives has created a therapeutic space in the DE-CRUIT sessions wherein participating veterans feel connected to the facilitator, to each other, and to the overall story of the suffering of trauma shared by veterans and by the traumatized characters in Shakespeare's plays.

We use the term "mimetic induction" to describe the healing potential of Shakespeare's verse that uses vividly realized stories of trauma and its aftermath to invoke in us an understanding of the human experience of suffering and triumph over suffering.[12] Drawing upon Oatley's interpretation of Auerbach's notion of mimesis as the simulation of human encounters that mimic our own experiences and connect us to our potential for self-understanding and compassion,[13] we have seen the benefits of empathy among the veterans in the DE-CRUIT program as they become more forgiving to themselves through Shakespeare and through the stories shared by other veterans.

Part of this process of forgiveness also involves the stories shared by the group facilitators as they describe what they have learned from dealing with their own experiences of trauma and how they have learned to forgive themselves for what they had previously viewed as weaknesses (e.g., the expression of fear and other emotions typically seen as incompatible with military composure). The connection that this forges within the group is crucial to the healing process. This process also parallels the documented benefits of peer-to-peer therapeutic encounters that practitioners and trauma survivors have recounted as being central to ongoing support and recovery.[14] Specifically, the treatment of trauma through encounters with peers who are further along the path of healing is particularly helpful for trauma survivors because the process uses human connection as the key to therapeutic change.

Similarly, feminist therapists have outlined the benefits of self-disclosure in therapy as an alternative to the traditional "bank-slate" therapist who is all-knowing and who does not reveal any personal experiences.[15] Again, human connection is enhanced when therapists show themselves to be human and describe the ways that they have dealt with challenges in their own lives. In the DE-CRUIT program, this use of connection is further enhanced by the underlying camaraderie that already exists between veterans. We have thus seen that there are often compelling reasons for the DE-CRUIT facilitators to themselves be military veterans who have worked on the struggles of trauma and community reintegration.

Extending the DE-CRUIT Model: Expanding the Reach of Human Connection for Therapeutic and Social Change

Over the past several years, the Veterans Center for the Performing Arts has used the DE-CRUIT program to transform the lives of large numbers of veterans. We have now begun to use the results of the program to contribute to the scientific literature on trauma and to inform advances in clinical practice for veterans.[16] Through ongoing partnership with New York University, the DE-CRUIT program will continue to expand its evaluation of the immediate and long-term psychological and practical needs of veterans. Additionally, the program will expand in terms of its offerings (e.g., with extended programs, week-long intensives, and weekend-long retreats) and through outreach to particularly high-risk, marginalized groups of veterans (including older veterans, female veterans, college student veterans, and veterans who now work in ongoing life-endangering fields such as law enforcement and firefighting) and will forge veteran-civilian dialogue to encourage community integration of veterans. In all of these expansion efforts, the core DE-CRUIT focus on the transformational power of human connection continues in both the implementation of the program and our plans for delivery of the program nationally and within communities that can benefit from interventions founded on the principles of common humanity.

NOTES

1 Paula J. Caplan, *When Johnny and Jane Come Marching Home: How All of Us Can Help Veterans* (Cambridge, MA: MIT Press, 2011).

2 Yvette Nolan, *Medicine Shows: Indigenous Performance Culture* (Toronto: Playwrights Canada Press, 2015).

3 "Who Bears the Burden? Demographic Characteristics of U.S. Military Recruits Before and After 9/11" (Center for Data Analysis Report on National Security and Defense, November 7, 2005), www.heritage.org.

4 Richard A. Gabriel, "Combat Cohesion in Soviet and American Military Units," *Parameters* 8, no. 4 (1978): 16–27.

5 Dave Grossman, *On Killing: The Psychological Cost of Learning to Kill in War and Society* (New York: Back Bay Books, 2009).

6 Nolan, *Medicine Shows.*

7 Twyla Tharp, *The Creative Habit: Learn It and Use It for Life* (New York: Simon & Schuster, 2003).

8 Jonathan Shay, *Achilles in Vietnam* (New York: Simon & Schuster, 1995).

9 Gregg D. Jacobs and Richard Friedman, "EEG Spectral Analysis of Relaxation Techniques," *Applied Psychophysiology and Biofeedback* 29, no. 4 (2004): 245–254; Laura Pierce, "The Integrative Power of Dance/Movement Therapy: Implications for the Treatment of Dissociation and Developmental Trauma," *Arts in Psychotherapy* 41, no. 1 (2014): 7–15; Emma M. Seppala, Jack B. Nitschke, Dana L. Tudorascu, Andrea Hayes, Michael R. Goldstein, Dong T. H. Nguyen, David Perlman, and Richard J. Davidson, "Breathing-Based Meditation Decreases Posttraumatic Stress Disorder Symptoms on U.S. Military Veterans: A Randomized Controlled Longitudinal Study," *Journal of Traumatic Stress* 27, no. 4 (2014): 397–405.

10 Tharp, *Creative Habit*.

11 Nolan, *Medicine Shows*.

12 Alisha Ali and Stephan Wolfert, "Theatre as a Treatment for Posttraumatic Stress in Military Veterans: Exploring the Psychotherapeutic Potential of Mimetic Induction," *Arts in Psychotherapy* 50 (2016): 58–65.

13 Keith Oatley, "Shakespeare's Invention of Theatre as Simulation That Runs on Minds," *Empirical Studies of the Arts* 19 (2001): 27–45; Erich Auerbach, *Mimesis: The Representation of Reality in Western Literature* (Princeton, NJ: Princeton University Press, 1953).

14 Will Hall, *Outside Mental Health: Voices and Visions of Madness* (Portland, OR: Madness Radio Press, 2016).

15 Judith Worell and Pamela Remer, *Feminist Perspectives in Therapy: Empowering Diverse Women* (New York: John Wiley, 2003).

16 Ali and Wolfert, "Theatre as a Treatment."

18

A New World

Youth, Voice, and Connection

KHARY LAZARRE-WHITE

What are the connections between art and activism, between creativity and social change? How is it that stories can heal and transform both the storyteller and the listener? How do art and activism, when inter-connected and creatively woven together, inspire and transform the world? When art is inspired by action for social justice, when activism produces profound artistic commentary, connections are made, the "other" becomes understandable, a potentially foreign experience can be brought close, made real, even become your own. Often the experience is displayed through images: the photo of a boy pulled from the rubble in Syria; a migrant child drowned in the Mediterranean; a young girl run-ning from the burning effects of napalm in Vietnam; the face of Emmett Till; dogs and water hoses unleashed on children in the American South; the video of the last moments of Eric Garner's life—sometimes intensi-fied by words: "I Can't Breathe."

We live in a time when so many crave connection—even with the on-slaught of social media and access to communication around the world, too many of us feel unconnected, unmoored. For this reason, in part, an abundance of constructed or intentional communities are being created, formed around shared ideas, focused on exploration or solutions, music or art gatherings, social change efforts, politics, or commonly desired destinations. People are seeking affiliation with people who seek similar experiences in a world of alienation and separation. For many reasons people long to connect.

The word "radical" means to "to grab something at its root." I am the co-founder and Executive Director of the Brotherhood/Sister Sol (Bro/Sis), an organization where we are dedicated to providing comprehensive youth development, training educators on our model, and working to influence policies that affect our young people. We are a radical organization because we seek to bring a deep political analysis to our work, we organize for social justice, and we help our children grasp things at their root, and once they do, to develop their voices—voices for action and change.

A deep and profound disconnection is felt by many of our young people. They are disconnected, in many ways, isolated and dissociated, because they are still told, each and every day, with unnerving clarity, that they are not expected to fully participate in this nation, that this nation is not fully for them. The reminders and lessons are multiple—and repeated with numbing frequency. One often experiences exhaustion at the repetition, exhaustion at the cyclical nature of your mother's story and your father's story becoming your story, of having to continue a struggle as old as this nation.

To be born black in this country, to know the unique experience and reality associated with this identity, is often to feel disconnected and detached from the nation's narratives, the false stories of origination, the fallacy of a meritocracy. It is to be dulled and enraged. One knows not only that equal opportunities have not been afforded—but instead that one faces a much more difficult path in life due to no other reason than the color of one's skin, that we live not in a postracial time, but in a virulently racial time. It is to know that to be black and American is an inescapable conflict.

While the immigrant has been central to the development and expansion of this country, historically immigrants of all colors and nationalities, today's immigrant experience is framed as one of brown people, the "other"—"other faiths" and "other languages." To see the nation through the eyes of an immigrant, whether the immigrant is oneself or one's parents, and to live in a time when the national discourse is one of vitriol toward your people, your reality, your religion, your language, and your very journey to becoming an American—all of this leaves you feeling isolated and unmoored. The policies of deporting millions of people—hardworking and industrious people—and of building walls and banning faiths are attacks on you, for even if this is not your specific story, the policies will touch you and your community. Your people.

There is a national conversation around education—yet one that offers few solutions to the systemic issues that economically poor children, overwhelmingly black and brown, face in a failing public school system. If you are a child in such a school, if you know that you are not being prepared to compete in society, that you are not learning the necessary analytical and technological skills to participate fully, and that you have been sold a false map, one that depicts hard work as the inevitable path to success—what feeling could that provide but one of disconnection, a daily reminder of the educational caste system in which you are mired, that you are caught in an educational system of mediocrity? If your community is policed in a racially disparate manner, if you know jails are filled with people from your community, your family and friends, many of whom would not be incarcerated if they merely lived in a different zip code and had committed or been accused of the same crimes or misdemeanors, if they had not been born economically poor, black or brown, then you cannot help but feel disconnected from the platitudes of equality and equity.

For generations, such experiences have produced a simple question: Is this nation my nation? If you are an aware human being, this question is constant. And yet, paradoxically, the answer has always been, and must continue to be yes. It may be a conflicted, eyes wide open, steeled yes, but a yes all the same. For it is a reality of history that black and brown people, the immigrants, those cast aside, the workers, the poorly educated, the expendable—these people have built this nation.

Bro/Sis has been an intentional, formed community since it was founded in 1995. It was created to connect young people to one another, to their historical legacy of the African diaspora, and to a community of elders who would guide and support them. The themes our community was founded on have been a part of our very logo since our creation—Positivity, Knowledge, Future, and Community. These are aspirational goals—the connective tissue that binds us. To be a part of Bro/Sis's community, to find community with us—these too must be your guiding aspirations: to live positive lives, to always seek knowledge, to work toward a better future for all, to create community. The work to reach these aspirations may be hard; it involves self-exploration and discipline, self-awareness, and, at times, profound change—but we know we will travel with others along the way.

As important as the adult guides are to the young people on this journey, the young people's peers are equally essential—they form a community of children, young men and young women, who will walk together—often acting and believing differently from what society expects of our children in general, and especially of black and brown children from tough urban communities. The building of this community also takes work on the part of the adults—difficult, hard, steady work: to confront who we are—our natures and how we have been nurtured. During one of our many staff meetings, one filled with reflection and tough conversations, a longtime staff member said he had never been in a workplace before where he had been asked, as an adult, to grow so much, to work on his own issues and development so deeply. To guide our children to be more connected, more reflective, more moral and ethical in their behavior, more steadfast—we too, as the guiders, must do this difficult work.

Art has always been a central aspect of movements for social justice—art spurs creative thinking across disciplines, provides what has been named "imaginative identification" by Chinua Achebe. *Imaginative identification.* It is a depth of identification that has the liberating and mighty power to allow us to truly connect to another—not merely to empathize or intellectually understand someone else's experience, but the more expansive, deeper work of actually imagining the other's experience as your own. Achebe writes: "Things are not merely happening *before* us; they are happening, by the force and power of imaginative identification, *to* us. We not only see; we *suffer* alongside the hero and are branded with the same mark of 'punishment and poverty.'"[1] I know of no concept that can better respond to our current crisis of connection, the disparate and divided worlds that so many hide within. Rather, Achebe asks us to truly identify with the crisis, or pain or journey of someone else—someone different—younger, older, from an unfamiliar corner of the world or city, with a different skin color, gender or sexual identity, set of beliefs, or religion.

Richard Wright once said: "The blues were created on the pavements of the city, in saw mills, in lumber camps, in short, wherever the migrant Negro, fresh from the soil, wrestled with an alien reality."[2] These migrants, black folk from the South, left an old world, and entered a new world. Immigrants in experience if not in name, they used their experiences to create an artistic form that accomplished two things: they formed a common language that bound them to each other, an expression of their pain and lived reality that built community and belonging through music; and their voices expressed an experience that informed a wider world. Their creative expression made them less alien to others and created a sense of belonging for them. For decades—for a century—many of varied backgrounds heard this story, one that was new, even foreign, and yet somehow familiar, and it became their own.

Much of the work we do with young people is based on developing "voice." By voice we mean the external, the effort that hopefully leads toward Wright's concept of commenting on their world so that others might understand what they have experienced and seen; and also the internal process, an interior voice that allows them to heal from trauma and make sense of the world. At Bro/Sis we help young people to redefine manhood and womanhood, to confront outworn and sometimes destructive norms of masculinity and femininity, so they can imagine and act on being who they truly are, reclaiming personal identity, often in ways that counter the voices and images they hear and see, and are taught to obey. They learn the glorious and horrific history of their people in America, a history that helped to form them—and this knowledge is liberating as it connects them to a long shared struggle for freedom and equality: a place of belonging.

The educator Maxine Greene has written: "It is a conscious endeavor on the part of individuals to keep themselves awake, to think about their condition in the world, to inquire into the forces that appear to dominate them."[3] We are trying to help young people comprehend and question concepts that have dominated them, to discover their own powers and their ability to transform themselves. Our theory of personal change is connected to a broader understanding of social and political change. One sphere is intimately connected to the other. We provide comprehensive guidance, love, support, and education. We teach our young people, from early childhood to high school age and beyond, to value discipline and form order in their lives; then we create access and opportunities within which they can develop and experience agency. We teach our young people to question the origins of poverty and oppression, the poor schooling they receive, the violence and trauma many are faced with on a daily basis, and then to work to counter these forces. We want them to open their eyes, or as one of our founding youth members expresses it, our work is to help youth to open a third eye. We want them to awaken.

We practice and believe in a holistic approach to supporting young people. Our members experience month-long international study in Africa, the Caribbean, and Latin America. Through community organizing training they learn to become social change makers. They learn the skills and use our platform to speak out against the poor schooling that has been deemed acceptable, the unconstitutional policing that has become a part of their lives; they speak out for access and opportunity and justice. Part of our work involves exposing our youth members to the wonders and diversity of the arts, to the possibilities of college and a lifelong love of learning, and in our community garden we teach environmental sustainability. Through single gendered rites of passage programming we work to help them hone a moral and ethical code of conduct. Our young people travel on this journey of defining for themselves who they will be in society—and then speaking of it, out loud, in their own creative and deepened voices. Albert Camus, the French philosopher, wrote, "A world that can be explained even with bad reasons is a familiar world. But, on the other hand, in a universe suddenly divested of illusion and lights, a man feels an alien, a stranger."[4]

There are many times when, as a staff, we debate the best methods and approaches for revealing the illusions and façades our youth are confronted with—we know from our own experience that illusions removed too callously can result in pain. Our children are called "the poor." The word "poor" is defined as lacking in value or worth, without quality, inferior, deficient. Many of our children observing the conditions they were born into initially believe there is something wrong with them, that they are the ones who are deficient or lacking in worth, that they have limited value due to being born black or brown, or undocumented, or with a lack of access, without financial resources. But there is also profound strength to be found in this awareness. This unsettling of a previously familiar world can be the beginning of struggle, the birthplace of great art, the earth from which social justice grows. Once such awareness occurs, a central part of our work is to guide our young people from feelings of strangeness, from this initially *alien* reality, to an understanding of their connection to generations who pushed back against these realities, and to those currently struggling around the world.

A young member once came to me seeming distracted. Clearly much was on his mind. While he was doing well in school and usually had a comedic and vibrant personality, this day he seemed on edge, and it was obvious he needed to talk. As is common with so many young people who have been traumatized in urban America by what they have seen— his story was slow to come out of him. As youth grow and pass through their developmental stages, it is not what they want from you as a caring adult that changes, or the substance of the conversations they need that alters, but instead, it is your approach as the adult that must change and the tone and rhythms of your questions and advice. They want the same guidance—they need a new language.

As we talked his words flowed. Over the past week he'd been exposed to a level of trauma that would have left well-formed adults needing medication, therapy, even potentially hospitalization. He had experienced this level of trauma because he was born poor and lives in one of the toughest housing projects in New York City—a place society explains away with bad reasons, an explanation based on making those in power and with access and resources feel comfortable, a desire to create a familiar world and order.

In the span of a week, his next-door neighbor had been shot and killed, a woman had been burned and thrown off an adjoining building's roof, and one hot evening the police had raided the housing projects' collective courtyard and beaten up and arrested four of his friends—all on low-level charges of smoking marijuana, "carrying open containers," and "resisting arrest." He told me all this as if it were an ordinary occurrence. This had been his "familiar" world. Yet now, with growing consciousness, a part of him knew it was truly alien and needed processing. He had been a part of our organization for years, he had traveled with us to Ghana for a month, had seen college campuses and the art of New York City. The too often learned approach to manhood, to value dismissiveness and a tough shell, had morphed: he needed to express. This is one part of healing: understanding that this terror and such attacks on the spirit are not normal, but instead represent a crisis.

Still, part of him thought he should be able to process easily what he had experienced, to merely brush it off, to place the mask back on his face that enabled him to navigate this world, and then go about his daily activities. He came to us because he did not have support elsewhere that would help him through the process. His mother, while a loving and steady presence in his life, was also traumatized, and so when such incidents occurred, she simply prayed to God, turned up her music, and continued making dinner. His underfunded school did not have the necessary social workers on staff to help him confront these assaults on his life and find a way forward. He found his necessary support, guidance, and love with us—elders trained to help him, to explain that pain and rage and sadness and fear were healthy, that he should not hide these feelings away but do what had so often brought comfort in the past: write and talk. And so he did. He found words for his feelings, exploring what he had experienced in his life, describing the very trauma that had caused him to believe that this level of violence was his acceptable future and conditions. He was not burned and thrown off a roof; he was not brutalized by the police; he was not shot and killed—but part of him felt that this was to be his "ordinary" reality. If so, then such a world would make sense. It was simply what happened. But if not, such a world would need explaining, to be fought against and changed.

He found words to describe the poverty and violence of his world—his sense of deprivation. He said, "Why do I have to experience this? Why am I living in this kind of condition?" Those questions were a part of learning context, of transformation—a step toward an understanding of the world. He needed to hear and to express that it wasn't his fault that he faced this world as a mere boy, that there was nothing wrong with his family, that no child should be confronted with this kind of violence and that no child—none—should be expected to have the skills to navigate such a world. He had to know that in our society, grown and powerful adults allowed his current condition to continue and that he had been born into a world long established on premises of injustice and inequality.

Over 20 percent of New York residents are living in poverty. New York County has the greatest disparity of wealth of any county in America, with the top 5 percent earning $865,000 a year while the bottom 20 percent is allowed to live on less than $10,000.[5] Our school system of 1.1 million children graduates only 35 percent of its students college-ready and without need of remedial support. These are conditions that our society has allowed to continue. Such conditions speak not to this young man's lack of worth or quality or value—but to ours. We allow children like him to be born into a world where such horrific occurrences are familiar and known. This is allowed by our society because some children's lives are not deemed of sufficient value.

We often speak of the destruction that violence can reap—the murdered and injured, the families torn apart by gun violence in America. But what of the children born into those communities, neighborhoods rife with violence, where, even if they are never the victim of the bullet, even if they are never struck down, they live with a daily reality and awareness of the presence of violence, the danger that lurks around the corner, the specter that their lives are transient, lacking in security, can be snatched up at any moment? This too causes great violence to the human body, it is destructive of the psyche—it wounds terribly and causes so many children to become inured. They wrap themselves in protective layers, their faces so often become impassive—but the pain runs throughout them, and for some, the rage strikes out. In the end many cannot contain it—to do so would be to ask too much, to become inhuman. They seem to cry out with the poet Nizar Qabbani: "Love me . . . away from the lands of oppression and repression, away from our city which has had its fill of death."[6]

To be truly connected to the world it is often necessary to heal from our own trauma. But so many of our children born economically poor don't have the access to support systems that might allow them to heal, so they move through life not merely scarred, but actually carrying massive open wounds. What does it mean to be one of our undocumented young people? To be described in the news and popular culture as "illegal" or an "alien"? Imagine, for just one moment, being a child who is described with such words—to be told each and every day that you do not belong, are *the other*. Imagine being told that your very being, your existence is "illegal." Use your imagination to identify with this reality. We have members who arrived in New York City from the Dominican Republic or Jamaica or Ecuador when they were just three or four years old, brought by parents or aunts and uncles, and brought on a family member's passport. They had no idea they had arrived without the proper paperwork, that their names did not match their social security numbers—that is, until they had already become American in identity, had lived here for over a decade, had, like many other American high school students, done their expected work and had begun, with us, their college preparation process. Suddenly the family whispers made sense—the averted eyes when they needed some form of paperwork began to become coldly clear. When they confronted family members, some of them undocumented themselves and thus also living in the shadows, often the adults struck out, and refused to help the children, afraid for their own status, of being uncovered and found. The children of Bro/Sis slowly learned that America was having a "national conversation" about sending them "back" to a "home" of which they had no memory, that this America had deemed them "illegal." And they began to wonder: What is home? Can home be the only place you have ever known—if you are not wanted? A personal crisis, had begun, one that affected their entire worldview— for if a child cannot claim a home, she has no foundation. Who are her people? Where is her community? Again a poet's words, this time Audre Lorde's: "If I didn't define myself for myself, I would be crushed into other people's fantasies for me and eaten alive."[7]

Self-definition becomes the process and the goal. It is often clarified by talking, reading, and collective conversation—and by the outlet of the arts. Their language, in their poetry and prose, personal oaths of commitment, and collective definitions of who they are—all collected in Bro/Sis's anthologies and performed on our stages; in drawings and paintings that hang from our walls; in the videos and documentaries we make that tell their and our stories—these fill our rooms and atmosphere—an unquestioned home.

"My job is making windows where there were once walls."[8] Michel Foucault's words describe our work, the work of helping young people find grounding and community and opportunity. When society has told our children they do not belong, when laws are enforced to tear apart their families, we help them to form windows. We counsel and support them; we hold them and talk with them; we help them to advocate on their own behalf; and we secure legal representation so they can apply for documentation and come out of the shadows. One of our young women, having been supported in this way, was able to quit her job after five years as a nanny, and return to school. She now has a master's in social work—and has dedicated her life to helping others. She wants to make sure that no child experiences what she has experienced—the feeling of being eaten alive.

Nicholas Peart is a name known, now, to many who have followed the news in recent years of police misconduct, harassment, and violence. He has been stopped and frisked by the New York City Police six to eight times at gunpoint. He was stopped when going to the corner store to buy groceries for his siblings. He was put in the back of police cars for walking down his block. On his eighteenth birthday, while sitting on a bench on a New York City street, eating McDonald's with his cousin, he was thrown down onto the sidewalk, a gun to his head, and searched. When the officer saw from his identification that it was his birthday, he laughed, dropped the ID on his prone back and wished him a happy birthday.

Over ten million stops occurred in New York City over a twelve-year period beginning in 2002—84 percent of those stopped were black or Latino. Of those stopped, only 6 percent were arrested, less than 2 percent were in possession of some form of contraband, almost always drugs, and less than 0.1 percent had a gun—the stated policy for the massive stops and infringement on the rights of the citizens of New York City. Though the police are required to have "reasonable" suspicion before stopping and frisking an individual—90 percent were completely innocent.

This is a policy that is enforced only in some neighborhoods—and only on some citizens. Nicholas was one of many, but with our support he learned to process these experiences and the resulting rage and pain. He decided to struggle, to fight back, and to do this through the written word and then speaking out. He agreed to become a named witness in the lawsuit brought by the Center for Constitutional Rights that sought to end the unconstitutional policy of "stop and frisk." He wrote an op-ed, printed in the *New York Times*, titled "Why Is the NYPD After Me?"[9] It became the most definitive commentary on "stop and frisk," the first-person story of what it felt like to have this experience. Generously, Nicholas allowed other people to identify with his story. Many were able to move beyond the abstractions, however gruesome, of these staggering statistics of over ten million stops in twelve years, and to understand the personal impact of one story—one young man. He removed the illusions that comforted so many readers, exposing the alien reality New York City allowed its citizens to experience, only because they were black and brown and lived in economically bereft communities. This practice was allowed to continue for the "stranger," the other. Nicholas provided an undeniable service, a gracious and benevolent offering to those who had been blind, opening their eyes, as they became personally connected to a festering crisis. At the same time, through telling his story, that of one courageous young man, he was able to do work that benefited himself as well, to "inquire into the forces that (sought) to dominate" him and to name them.

His article was read by millions. He has told his story at press conferences and high schools, on college campuses and law schools, for international and national television. Others might have become fearful of taking such a public stand, but he was empowered. One day a New York City elected official contacted us. At the time he was the relatively little-known New York City public advocate. He came to Bro/Sis and met with our young organizers who were working to reform policing in New York City, and he told Nicholas that his own view of the issue had been transformed, he now understood the personal experience of what it felt like to be stopped and frisked, that Nicholas had moved the issue from a general policy to a powerful personal story. Nicholas had allowed him to connect. The little-known public advocate become the mayor of New York City, and when he became mayor, Bill de Blasio dropped the appeal of the previous administration to a federal court's ruling that New York City had violated the constitutional rights of millions of New Yorkers. When the mayor announced the dropping of the appeal, he stood on the stage with the police commissioner, New York City's chief lawyer, and Nicholas Peart.

"When the victim is able to articulate the situation of the victim, he or she has ceased to be a victim but, instead, has become a threat."[10] These are the words of James Baldwin—he too was born black and poor in Harlem, with only a high school education, wrote words that altered national conversations. We want our young people to become this kind of threat—a threat to injustice, to victimhood, racism, sexism, and homophobia, but also a threat to the destructive ideas that young people internalize into their own bodies and spirits, about who they should be, who they are, to question and change the future of their stories. There is a freedom that comes with imagining a different world. There's a freedom that comes with claiming one's own history.

When teaching history at Bro/Sis, working to remove the illusions in which so many wrap themselves, when helping young people to challenge and question the society in which they live—we often find inspiration from a West African proverb: "When lions have their own historians, hunters will cease being heroes." We all see through a particular personal lens. It takes hard work to see the world through the lens of another, but it can bring profound illumination. A great force is released when we empower young people to tell their own stories. It is destructive of our humanity as a people and as individuals when stories are told only through the lens of those in power, only from the oppressor's point of view. When we teach the true history of America many children come to understand this proverb.

Who tells the story?

In most of the world there is no such thing as a woman's name. Due to long-standing patriarchy and systems built on handing down property from man to man—original female names do not exist. A woman may choose not to take her husband's name upon marriage, but in doing so she keeps her own father's name. If she has her mother's maiden name, then she has the name of her mother's father. Even if two women marry each other, and want to share a name, they must imagine a new name, or choose between the names of their fathers. A woman's name must be created anew.

Who has told us our history? Who names us, literally and spiritually? Whose language do we use when navigating our lives?

The populations of Brazil and the Caribbean and the United States are filled with people of African descent due to the "transatlantic slave trade." More black people live in Brazil than in any nation in Africa other than Nigeria. Tens of millions were taken from the African continent and brought to the Americas, and millions died on the way over during the "Middle Passage," their bodies thrown into the Atlantic Ocean. The poet Amiri Baraka once said that one can walk back to Africa on the bones of Africans. And yet this most horrific atrocity—the very experience that allowed millions to claim Haitian, Jamaican, Cuban, Dominican, Brazilian, and American nationality, among so many others—is described in language from the perspective of the traders in human beings, not of the enslaved. For the "Middle Passage" refers to the second leg in the "triangular trade." Draw the lines on a map: number one, from Europe with goods to Africa; number two, from Africa with cargo of humans to the Americas, the middle one; and finally, the third one, from the Americas back to Europe with goods for trade. For the enslaved, for the Africans, the atrocity, the experience, was not the "Middle Passage"—it was simply the Passage—the only one.

A renaming of their world. This work of art and education with young people is the work of healing from trauma and achieving transformation: it is the work of forming connections that unite and liberate. It encompasses a journey that connects people to their own history, to understand their own realities, and allows them to retell their experiences to others, bringing the light of consciousness, and enabling them to rename their world. This is the work we should aspire to for our young people. This is the work we must aspire to for ourselves. This opening of doors, the effort to remove illusions and flawed stories, fighting back against incomplete or false narratives, this difficult but necessary inquiry allows for the creation of new connections and the space for new stories—stories that reject a world that tells its children that they are without worth, invisible, that their own language cannot be used, that they do not matter, are alien, and do not belong. All of us crave and require community and connection to each other. We can provide and create this reality if we have the courage and commitment to redefine, retell, and rename the world.

NOTES

1 Chinua Achebe, *Hopes and Impediments: Selected Essays* (New York: Penguin, 1990), 144.
2 "The Music of Migration" (Museum of Modern Art, 2015), www.press.moma.org.
3 Bruce Weber, "Maxine Greene, 96, Dies; Education Theorists Saw Arts as Essential," *New York Times*, June 4, 2014, www.nytimes.com.
4 Albert Camus, *The Myth of Sisyphus* (New York: Vintage, 1955), 5.
5 Sam Roberts, "Gap between Manhattan's Rich and Poor Is Greatest in US," *New York Times*, September 17, 2014, www.nytimes.com.
6 Anne Barnard and Hwaida Saad, "Frantic Message as Palmyra, Syria, Fell: We're Finished," *New York Times*, May 21, 2015, www.nytimes.com.
7 Audre Lorde, "Learning from the 60's" (1982), www.blackpast.org.
8 Lewis Hyde, *Trickster Makes This World: Mischief, Myth and Art* (New York: Farrar, Straus and Giroux, 1999).
9 Nicholas K. Peart, "Why Is the NYPD After Me?," *New York Times*, December 17, 2011, www.nytimes.com.
10 James Baldwin, *The Price of a Ticket* (New York: St. Martin's, 1985), 628.

19

Resisting "Us versus Them"

Immigrants and Our Common Humanity

HIROKAZU YOSHIKAWA

One time this mother came to give a ride to her daughter,
you know, for school in the morning and on the way back
she got stopped and deported. Now in jail. Yeah. From the
school to the house. And many, many cases like that. And
that affected our students.
—Arizona public school teacher cited by Carmen Valdez,
"Lives of Immigrant Families Study"

We are in the midst of a severe crisis of disconnection regarding immigration in US society. Despite the general successes in the integration of immigrants, as measured by progress in education and livelihoods, one large group of over eleven million immigrants in America—those with unauthorized status—is excluded from the majority of opportunities for human development and everyday life.[1] Recent policy developments have heightened this exclusion to a degree not seen since the most recent large wave of unauthorized migration to the United States began nearly thirty years ago.

The unauthorized in the United States face several kinds of policy, social, and institutional exclusion. This group, despite its very high poverty rates, is not eligible for federal health insurance, whether under Medicaid or other provisions of the Affordable Care Act, with the exception of emergency Medicaid (specifically, child birth services). The unauthorized do not have access to formal employment opportunities. They therefore generally have much lower access to labor law protections in practice, and experience high rates of wages below legal minimum wage thresholds.[2] In the majority of the fifty states, the unauthorized cannot obtain driver's licenses. They are ineligible for the major of the government's safety-net policies. For example, although they can pay taxes by obtaining taxpayer identification numbers, they are ineligible for federal tax credits such as the earned income tax credit. They are ineligible for housing subsidies or food stamps (the Supplemental Nutrition Assistance Program). In nine states, unauthorized students are not eligible for in-state tuition to public universities or colleges. In some in which they are eligible, in-state tuition assistance is not provided (e.g., as of this writing, New York State).[3] In others, implementation is uneven such that service providers or guidance counselors communicate to unauthorized youth that they are ineligible to attend college, when in fact they may be eligible. Unauthorized youth therefore experience blocks to normative transitions to adulthood such as driving, applying for college, and formal employment.

There is strong evidence that these forms of policy, social, and institutional exclusion result in relational exclusion. For example, sociologist Roberto Gonzales has shown in his research on unauthorized youth that a substantial proportion of adolescents in their transition to understanding that they have illegal status ("learning to be illegal") withdraw from friendships. He finds that this occurs out of shame in revealing why they cannot get a driver's license, apply to college, or work.[4]

In addition, these policies can lead to or be the consequence of disconnection on the part of the public. Dehumanizing and criminalizing frames and opinions contrast with strong opinions toward inclusion and empathy. Experiences of discrimination since 2017 have increased substantially—suggesting that the relationships of everyday life in communities have been strained and in some cases become violent due to perceptions of immigrant, newcomer, and especially the combination of perceived Muslim and immigrant status. For example, anti-Arab, anti-Muslim, and anti-Hispanic bias crimes doubled in incidence in the city of Chicago in 2016, relative to the previous year and prior averages.[5]

More broadly, a climate of fear among the unauthorized intensified with the election of Donald Trump. Executive orders first banned all legal immigrants from seven largely Muslim countries, and then extended federal and local law enforcement emphasis in initiating removal and deportation proceedings from those convicted of serious felonies and crimes to those with misdemeanors such as traffic tickets or applying for formal employment. Widely publicized deportation of parents with decades of residence in the United States and without serious criminal charges coincided with the surge in bias crimes against immigrants, suggesting a new nationwide crisis of connection affecting immigrants.

This chapter chronicles the crisis of connection at both the policy and public perception levels as it affects the unauthorized and their families in the United States. It then outlines the sources of connection that have historically strengthened ties between immigrants and nonimmigrants in American society, drawing from the science of human connection, data on public attitudes, and the history of the United States as a country of immigrants. Finally, the chapter concludes with a discussion of potential solutions to the crisis of connection, with an emphasis on community, local, and state action.

How Did We Get Here? A Brief History of the Crisis of Connection Regarding Unauthorized Immigration to the United States

Prior to the late nineteenth century, the category of "illegal immigrant" did not exist in the United States. However, waves of European migration (from Germany and Ireland) in the 1940s brought about a political movement in the 1850s—the Know Nothing movement—that was anti-immigrant and anti-slavery, on the grounds that immigrants and slaves were taking jobs away from White Americans. In 1875, the first restrictive federal immigration law (the Page Act) was signed—identifying for the first time certain groups (Asian immigrants in particular) as "undesirable." This law came on the heels of efforts to bring large numbers of Asian workers into the United States to build the transcontinental railroad. As has been documented extensively, Asian workers' roles in this massive construction effort were often obliterated in visual and other representations.[6] At the same time, the visibility of this workforce stirred up xenophobic attitudes and ultimately legislation like the Page Act and the 1882 Chinese Exclusion Act. In 1924, major federal immigration legislation (the Johnson-Reed Act) further expanded many of these restrictions through a set of country-specific quotas. Asian, Latin

American, and Eastern and Southern European countries' quotas were severely restricted compared to those of Western European countries.

Country-specific and racially determined quotas on immigration persisted until the landmark Hart-Celler Act of 1965, which replaced the country-specific approach with a hemispheric approach. Mexico, however, continued to have special provisions in the law to restrict immigration across the southern border of the United States, as the continued "special case" that represented the single largest country-level source of low-wage labor in the United States, but also a threat as the potential largest source of immigration without papers.[7]

As concern over increases in immigration grew in the 1990s, particularly due to flows of unauthorized immigrants following economic recession in Mexico, pressures grew to restrict migration. In 1996, the Illegal Immigration Reform and Immigrant Responsibility Act greatly increased the categories of crimes that were grounds for deportation. In addition, and even more significantly, the authority of states and localities to enforce federal immigration policies was strengthened substantially. Subsequently, the Secure Communities program established mechanisms for state and local law enforcement to access federal immigration databases and begin removal proceedings for all who were in custody in local jails. Although some states and localities refused to implement Secure Communities and declared themselves "sanctuary" cities or states (e.g., the states of Illinois, Massachusetts, and New York; the cities of Los Angeles and New York City), many did.

By the early 2000s a debate in Washington and in the states arose concerning a solution to the widely perceived broken immigration system. Proposals for harsher enforcement and deportation contrasted with those for a pathway to citizenship. One example of a proposal for a pathway to citizenship was the one put forward by President George W. Bush in 2006, which would have allowed a pathway but only for those who could prove residency in the United States for a minimum number of years (at least eight years), lack a criminal record, pay a fine, and wait "in line" behind permanent legal residents and other temporary status holders waiting for citizenship. Bush worked closely with leaders in both parties of Congress to attempt to pass bills reflecting these principles (most notably the Comprehensive Immigration Reform Act of 2007, S.1348 of the 110th Congress). Such bills ultimately were not passed by Congress.

A separate set of bills focused on the population of unauthorized youth was proposed beginning in 2001 by a variety of congressional leaders (e.g., Luis Gutiérrez, Dick Durbin, and Orrin Hatch). The central bill that ensued, known as the DREAM Act, would have provided protected status for youth brought to the country before a certain age in order to ensure access to higher education, employment, and other forms of integration into society. These bills were the result of sustained community activism by youth—"DREAMers." These also failed repeatedly to be approved by Congress.

In response to the failure of both comprehensive immigration reform and DREAM Act bills to pass congressional votes, massive protests organized by the immigration activist community were held in 2006 and 2007—these protests incurred responses from those opposed to any form of "amnesty" and instead in favor of expanded removal and deportation.

Enforcement actions by the federal government became widespread in the mid- to late 2000s as well. Large workplace raids were widely publicized. The Postville, Iowa, raid on the Agriprocessors slaughterhouse was the largest on record, with four hundred arrests.[8] The group was handcuffed and also shackled in torso-to-leg chains in groups of ten as they were brought to a local fairground prior to being taken to prison. The Obama administration placed a moratorium on such large workplace raids, but went on to increase the numbers deported from the United States, up to 400,000 annually each year between 2008 and 2012, with gradually decreasing numbers thereafter (in FY 2015, 235,413, of which 165,935 were removals within a hundred miles of the southern border and 69,478 were interior removals).

Physical, verbal, and economic discrimination against immigrants perceived to be unauthorized—particularly those perceived to be of Mexican origin—rose during the 2000s. Violence against those who look "Mexican" increased, particularly in areas of the United States that had until recently had very low proportions of low-income immigrants. Marcelo Lucero, an Ecuadorean immigrant, was stabbed to death by a group of high school students in suburban Long Island, New York, who set out that morning to "kill a Mexican." They received prison sentences of six to seven years. Verbal discrimination in these years also became commonplace. For example, in the 2016 presidential election campaign, the Republican candidate Donald Trump questioned the competence of a judge due to his Mexican background. Wages among Mexican-origin immigrants in particular declined above and beyond what would be expected were it not for their unauthorized status.[9] In 2016, the Trump administration's entry ban on several countries with majority-Muslim populations coincided with a surge in violence against those perceived to come from the Middle East and South Asia.

These data suggest that increasing policy-based criminalization of unauthorized status in the 1990s and 2000s was accompanied by increasing dehumanization of the unauthorized and of immigrants from certain regions and perceived religions, as evident in racial profiling and violent discrimination. The increasing variation at the state and local levels in enforcement policies led to some unprecedented state legislation. In some cases, state rulings were found to be unconstitutional. For example, Alabama attempted to institute as a requirement checking of children's citizenship in public schools, an act counter to the 1982 *Plyler v. Doe* Supreme Court case, which ensured access to public education for all children in the United States regardless of citizenship status. This attempt was blocked by the court system.[10] The Trump administration's entry bans for legal immigrants from seven and then six majority-Muslim countries were each blocked by courts across the nation.

The Trump administration in early 2017 also implemented executive orders to bring policies on removal and deportation proceedings more in line with how they were in the 2000s. Federal law enforcement began to much more aggressively deport individuals who were exempted under Obama administration regulations—those with long-standing community or family ties to the United States, those with only minor offenses such as misdemeanors (a first-time crossing of the border or overstaying a visa just by itself became sufficient grounds for initiating removal proceedings, rendering all eleven million unauthorized immigrants at immediate risk of deportation).[11] Anecdotal evidence suggests widespread fear and anxiety as well as avoidance of public spaces on the part of the unauthorized.[12] The disconnection from American society and increased exclusion of the unauthorized from everyday life and relationships appear to have markedly worsened in the first months of the Trump administration.

Connection and Welcoming of Immigrants in American Society: A Counter-history

The science of human connection, across the evolutionary, psychological, educational, and biological sciences, suggests that humans are first and foremost social and emotional beings who need each other to thrive (Way, Gilligan, Noguera, and Ali, this volume). At a population level this need is reflected in tendencies of US society to foster inclusion and positive relations among the diverse groups that have made up the nation. Immigrant integration is part of the mythmaking of the United States. The reality of integration—as reflected in social, educational, and economic mobility across the first and second generations—held true for virtually all of the major immigrant waves of the twentieth century, including the Western European, Scandinavian, and Southern and Eastern European waves before World War II, and then the large Asian and Latino waves of immigration after the Hart-Celler Act. That is, the second generation in each of these cases largely advanced beyond their parents in levels of education, economic advancement, and social inclusion, as reflected in most cases in the "dissolution" of ethnic and immigrant identities in favor of "American" identity by the third generation.[13]

The widespread acceptance of these patterns of migration as contributions to American society is reflected in the phrase "a nation of immigrants."[14] The United States is often viewed and termed a nation of immigrants, despite the fact that the proportion of foreign-born in the country is not near the proportions in other nations (e.g., 85 percent in the United Arab Emirates). Yet the phrase is powerful in the United States precisely because it is a matter of identity for the development of the nation. The Catholic and Jewish faiths were associated with foreigners and the targets of discrimination for much of the twentieth century; as of this writing, all Supreme Court justices are either Catholic or Jewish. This remarkable "mainstreaming" of the immigrant groups of the twentieth century, while countered by increasing anti-Semitism in the Trump era, is a remarkable and widespread demographic phenomenon.[15]

Solutions

Despite the long-standing tendencies of the United States to welcome immigrants and view itself as a nation of immigrants, the current crisis of connection is harshly targeted toward the unauthorized. This group is considered "undeserving" in ways that have long been reflected in racial stereotypes of the undeserving poor (African American, lazy, underperforming).[16] The dehumanization of the unauthorized and the equating of "illegal immigrant" with violence, radical terrorism, and general threat to society aligns, moreover, with global nationalist movements that have targeted a variety of immigrant populations, most notably Syrian and other refugees from the Middle East. Despite the fact that refugees from Middle Eastern countries, like other immigrants, tend to commit fewer crimes than the native-born, these groups were targeted for entry bans by the Trump administration.[17]

What solutions are possible with what seems like an inexorable and continued movement toward disconnection and dehumanization on issues facing the unauthorized in the United States? Three types of interventions may be useful in strengthening the common humanity that can bring all Americans together regardless of citizenship status—focusing on network-level relations, reframing the immigration-policy discourse, and building welcome programs and policies at the community and city levels.

Network-Level Relational Interventions

Relational interventions have not been tested for their impact on attitudes toward unauthorized immigrants. However, contact theory would suggest that as more people "come out" with this identity or status and those who know and love them acknowledge and integrate this identity into their relationship, support for the population may increase in public opinion and policy. For example, Becker and Scheufele found in their nationwide study that among a set of demographic, value, and social contact predictors of attitudes toward same-sex marriage, the variable of closeness of social contact (with close friend and relative being higher than co-worker or acquaintance or not knowing anyone) was most powerfully positively related to support for same-sex marriage, across age cohorts.[18] The association was even stronger for the younger than twenty-six age cohort than for older cohorts, indicating generational shifts that have occurred in US society on this particular social issue. The only other consistent predictor among demographic and value variables was religiosity and evangelical beliefs (which predicted lower support for same-sex marriage). This suggests that the decades of coming out of hundreds of thousands and ultimately millions of Americans, in the context of friendships and family, made a difference in the shift toward support of same-sex marriage, a shift that resulted in a wave of state-level legislation, federal executive branch changes, and ultimately Supreme Court legalization in 2015.

One policy change that encouraged much greater contact and "mainstream" integration of the unauthorized into American society was Deferred Action for Childhood Arrivals or DACA. This 2012 executive order of the Obama administration, aiming for greater integration of DREAMer youth, resulted in nearly half of the unauthorized youth in the United States receiving a temporary reprieve from deportation and access to health care, formal employment, and markers of integration such as driver's licenses. Research studies show immediate integration effects—new jobs, increases in wages, higher expectations, and aspirations for the future.[19] The integration in workplaces, higher education institutions, and community settings that DACA wrought was powerful and immediate, even though the reprieve was temporary (and at this point uncertain under the Trump administration).

If such a sequence of relationships and social integration were to occur in support of a pathway to citizenship, those with this status might be urged to come out to their friends and relatives. The barriers to this coming out are quite challenging, in that revealing one's identity as unauthorized may risk knowledge by law enforcement authorities, who as we have seen have power in many localities to initiate federal removal investigation and proceedings. DREAMer activists have done much to bring the unauthorized themselves into leadership positions. However, it has been a challenge for the larger number of unauthorized parents of US citizen children to come out with this status, as they fear the consequences of deportation not just for themselves, but for the trauma and separation it may cause for their children and family members. However, coming out to networks and acquaintances may feel somewhat safer than doing so in public. If relational factors are powerful in the changing of social attitudes on this topic, it may be useful to encourage conversations across status lines in the many contexts where the unauthorized meet those with authorized status—in schools, workplaces, community-based organizations, faith-based organizations, and other community settings.

There is a second arena of coming out that involves friends and relatives themselves speaking out on the issue of unauthorized status and a pathway to citizenship. If eleven million unauthorized individuals are currently residing in the United States, many millions more represent their social networks, co-workers, friends, and relatives. Speaking out on the issue might not require identifying specific individuals. Media campaigns could urge Americans to speak out on the issue, based on their experience of knowing and loving someone in their networks who may be unauthorized.

Framing Interventions

The framing of policy options can matter for the task of shifting public opinion and support. Haynes and colleagues found that an "opportunity to become citizens" frame was more effective than an amnesty frame in shifting support toward legalization of the unauthorized.[20] This suggests that pushing toward "we" is more effective than starting with a "them" frame.[21] Building a common identity as Americans in messaging, rather than simply framing issues facing immigrants as limited to one segment of US society, is an implication of this finding from communications science.

Another implication is to consider both emotional and cognitive approaches to perceiving "other" groups. Haynes recently contrasted a perspective-taking frame and a pure-affective-empathy frame in their potential power (relative to a control group) in increasing endorsement of comprehensive immigration reform and pro-immigration policies.[22] In both the perspective-taking and pure-affect conditions, individuals read a story about an undocumented immigrant mother separated from her newborn child by immigration authorities. In the perspective-taking frame, reading the article was preceded by the message, "Free yourself to empathize with the woman in the article. Try to feel the full emotional impact of what this woman has been through. Additionally, please put yourself in her position. Try to imagine what she is going through and how it has affected her life as if it were your own." In the pure-affect frame, reading the article was preceded by, "Free yourself to empathize with the woman in the article. Try to feel the full emotional impact of what this woman has been through."[23] The perspective-taking frame was significantly related to increases in endorsing pro-immigration policies (e.g., the DREAM Act; comprehensive immigration reform with a pathway to citizenship), while the emotion-giving frame was not. Specifically, 62 percent of the participants in the perspective-taking condition subsequently reported endorsing a pathway to citizenship, compared to 37 percent of the control group and 44 percent of the pure-affective empathy group.[24]

And even more strikingly, the impact of the perspective-taking frame was substantially more positive among those who reported not knowing any people with unauthorized status than among those who did. This finding suggests a way forward for efforts to convince those not living in proximity to the unauthorized (the bulk of policymakers who oppose a pathway to citizenship live in areas with very low proportions of unauthorized immigrants). Efforts to increase empathy alone may not be sufficient in changing policymakers' or the public's attitudes—it seems necessary to also explicitly place oneself in the position of the unauthorized. This could be done even if the target population does not know any unauthorized individuals themselves.

Putting It All Together: Welcome Policies and Programs at the Community, City, and State Levels

Finally, the integration of framing and relational interventions could occur in the broader context of a movement in the United States toward "welcome" programs and policies. Powerful examples of national welcome policies have occurred in the recent Syrian refugee crisis (e.g., in Germany and Canada). In these instances, public leadership has been at pains to frame the policies as those emphasizing common humanity.

In the United States, some cities and localities have instituted both city-level identity and programs and policies as explicitly welcoming of newcomer Americans. For example, for over fifteen years New York City has had a Mayor's Office for Immigrant Affairs, tasked with working across city agencies to foster the inclusion of immigrant populations. Officials work to ensure that the educational, legal, health, and other social service supports for New York City residents are inclusive of the vast range of immigrant groups in the city, including the unauthorized.

Some New York City efforts to create inclusion and a common identity as New Yorkers across legal statuses include municipal NYC identification, or IDNYC. This identity card addresses a key barrier to inclusion of the unauthorized—their inability to get driver's licenses in many states. Without a driver's license or other US-issued photo ID, it can be difficult for the unauthorized to pick up their child at a public school, open a bank account, or apply for services or benefits, even for their citizen relatives or child. IDNYC solves these issues, with the city working with banks, the school system, and other systems to ensure that the IDNYC card can facilitate access and inclusion regardless of citizenship status. To build the "we" in this case and ensure that the card does not become associated with the unauthorized, the city added benefits such as free admission to multiple local museums, zoos, and other cultural organizations. The card was an immediate success, with enrollment greatly exceeding the city's expectations. In the first sixteen months, over eight hundred thousand city residents obtained an IDNYC card. Recipients of the card cited the free museum and zoo benefits as a primary reason for getting the card, indicating the success of this approach to inclusion. In all, 52 percent of cardholders surveyed in a process evaluation and 67 percent of immigrant cardholders indicated that they used it as their primary source of identification.[25]

Identity, as important as it can be for social inclusion, is but one piece of a more comprehensive potential approach to building social connection and a common shared sense of humanity between unauthorized immigrants and newcomer immigrants, on the one hand, and the US-born and longtime residents, on the other. Welcoming America is a national network of communities, cities, and counties that have explicitly built the welcoming of immigrants into the implementation of their policies, local media campaigns, and organizational work (see Table 19.1). Over seventy cities and counties have joined this movement, including a mix of cities across different policy contexts and immigration concentrations—for example, Akron, Memphis, New York City, and Raleigh.

TABLE 19.1. What Welcoming Cities and Counties Do

Plans: All relevant sectors, such as government, businesses, nonprofits, and others, work together to create a welcoming community climate that supports long-term integration.

Commits: Municipalities commit to institutionalize strategies ensuring the ongoing inclusion and long-term economic and social integration of newcomers.

Builds community: Newcomers and longtime residents find common ground and shared leadership.

Communicates: Messages of unity and shared values permeate the community through the media, through the voices of leaders, and among residents.

Sustains: Policies and practices are considered to ensure interactions between new and longtime residents remain positive and the community's economic vitality remains strong.

Source: http://welcomingamerica.org.

Importantly, these efforts do not limit themselves to media campaigns, but aim to share leadership in the community between new immigrants and longtime residents. Interactions between these two groups are encouraged to build the social ties and friendships that both strengthen the community and reduce dehumanization of immigrants. In the process, attitudes toward the unauthorized are likely to shift (although there is currently no evaluation evidence yet to support such shifts in these cities and counties).

The Welcoming America movement represents an important community- and city-level framework grounded in actual city experiences. It builds on the sense of community, rather than individual merit and accompanying blame, which is just as powerful an underlying discourse in US policy and history.[26] As this campaign grows, it could incorporate the lessons from relational and reframing interventions discussed above.

Conclusion

The dehumanization of unauthorized immigrants in the United States has been an increasingly powerful force in communities, states, and the nation. The enforced disconnection directly affects not just the estimated eleven million residents of our country who are unauthorized, but more broadly the sense of unity and common humanity of all Americans. Federal policy toward the unauthorized has moved toward greater criminalization, removal, and deportation in the past twenty years, with a sharp increase since the beginning of the Trump administration.

With exceptions that are temporary and limited, such as Deferred Action for Childhood Arrivals, our nation has been unable to move toward a pathway to citizenship and inclusion. Historically we have been here before—outright exclusion of specific racial groups among immigrants was a central focus of immigration policy in the United States in the late nineteenth century. Over time, as the children of European and Asian immigrants grew to adulthood, their integration into peer, school, community, and other contexts of US life occurred at a generation-to-generation pace, but was generally in the direction of social, education, and economic mobility as well as inclusion in the institutions of everyday life. We are seeing recent targeted increases in discrimination and violence toward specific groups (as noted, those perceived as Muslim or from the Middle East and South Asia, for example); however, such shifts in perceptions, discrimination, and violence have "swung back" over time as they did over the course of the twentieth century.

The disconnection and increasing discrimination faced by the unauthorized could however, be countered powerfully through interventions and policy that build connections, inclusion, and welcome into the work of organizations and government. In addition, public communications and messages on the issue of unauthorized immigration could be much more intentionally framed, based on recent evidence, to emphasize the combination of perspective taking and empathy and opportunity, rather than amnesty. Ultimately the cumulative impact of millions of human relationships across the divides of citizenship status could build a more inclusive future for this nation of immigrants.

NOTES

1 Mary C. Waters and Marisa G. Pineau, eds., *The Integration of Immigrants into American Society* (Washington, DC: National Academies Press, 2015).

2 Matthew Hall, Emily Greenman, and Geroge Farkas, "Legal Status and Wage Disparities for Mexican Immigrants," *Social Forces* 89 (2010): 491–514, doi:10.1353/sof.2010.0082; Hirokazu Yoshikawa, *Immigrants Raising Citizens: Undocumented Parents and Their Young Children* (New York: Russell Sage Foundation, 2011).

3 H. Kenny Nienhusser, "Undocumented Immigrants and Higher Education Policy: The Policymaking Environment of New York State," *Review of Higher Education* 38, no. 2 (2015): 271–303.

4   Roberto Gonzales, *Lives in Limbo: Undocumented and Coming of Age in America* (Berkeley: University of California Press, 2016).

5   Zak Koeske, "Hate Crimes Rose 20 Percent in 2016, Marking 5-Year High, Police Data Show," *Chicago Tribune*, March 3, 2017, www.chicagotribune.com.

6   David L. Eng, *Racial Castration: Managing Masculinity in Asian America* (Durham, NC: Duke University Press, 2001).

7   Nae M. Ngai, *Impossible Subjects: Illegal Aliens and the Making of Modern America* (Princeton, NJ: Princeton University Press, 2004).

8   Ajay Chaudry, Randolph Capps, Juan Pedroza, Rosa Maria Castaneda, Robert Santos, and Molly M. Scott, "Facing Our Future: Children in the Aftermath of Immigration Enforcement" (Washington, DC: Urban Institute, 2010).

9   Douglas S. Massey and Kerstin Gentsch, "Undocumented Migration to the United States and the Wages of Mexican Immigrants," *International Migration Review* 48, no. 2 (2014): 482–499.

10 Campbell Robertson and Julia Preston, "Appeals Court Draws Boundaries on Alabama's Immigration Law," *New York Times*, August 21, 2012, www.nytimes.com.

11 Jennifer Medina, "Trump's Immigration Order Expands the Definition of 'Criminal,'" *New York Times*, January 26, 2017, www.nytimes.com.

12 Max Fisher and Amanda Taub, "What Can Happen When Migrants Are Pushed into the Shadows," *New York Times*, February 23, 2017, www.nytimes.com.

13 Richard Alba and Victor Nee, *Remaking the American Mainstream: Assimilation and Contemporary Immigration* (Cambridge, MA: Harvard University Press, 2009).

14 Donna R. Gabaccia, "Nations of Immigrants: Do Words Matter?," *Pluralist* 5, no. 3 (2010): 5–31.

15 Waters and Pineau, *Integration of Immigrants into American Society.*

16 Martin Gilens, *Why Americans Hate Welfare: Race, Media, and the Politics of Antipoverty Policy* (Chicago: University of Chicago Press, 2009).

17 Waters and Pineau, *Integration of Immigrants into American Society.*

18 Amy B. Becker and Dietram A. Scheufele, "New Voters, New Outlook? Predispositions, Social Networks, and the Changing Politics of Gay Civil Rights," *Social Science Quarterly* 92, no. 2 (2011): 324–345.

19 Roberto G. Gonzales, Veronica Terriquez, and Stephen P. Ruszczyk, "Becoming Dacamented: Assessing the Short-Term Benefits of Deferred Action for Childhood Arrivals (DACA)," *American Behavioral Scientist* 58, no. 14 (2014): 1852–1872; Marcelo Suarez-Orozco, Robert Teranishi, and Carola Suarez-Orozco, "In the Shadows of the Ivory Tower: Undocumented Undergraduates and the Liminal State of Immigration Reform" (UndocuScholar Project, Institute for Immigration, Globalization & Education, UCLA, 2015); Hirokazu Yoshikawa, Carola Suarez-Orozco, and Roberto G. Gonzales, "Unauthorized Status and Youth Development in the United States: Consensus Statement of the Society for Research on Adolescence," *Journal of Research on Adolescence* 27, no. 1 (2017): 4–19.

20 Chris Haynes, Jennifer Merolla, and S. Karthick Ramakrishnan, *Framing Immigrants: News Coverage, Public Opinion, and Policy* (New York: Russell Sage Foundation, 2016).

21 Moira O'Neil, Nathaniel Kendall-Taylor, and Susan N. Bales, "Finish the Story on Immigration: A FrameWorks MessageMemo" (Washington, DC: FrameWorks Institute, 2014).

22 Chris Haynes, "A Study of the Effect of Empathy on Public Opinion on Immigration" (PhD diss., University of California, Riverside, 2013); Haynes, Merolla, and Ramakrishnan, *Framing Immigrants*.

23 Haynes, "Study of the Effect of Empathy"; Haynes, Merolla, and Ramakrishnan, *Framing Immigrants*.

24 Haynes, "Study of the Effect of Empathy."

25 Tamara C. Daley, Laurel Lunn, Jennifer Hamilton, Artis Bergman, and Donna Tapper, "IDNYC: A Tool of Empowerment (A Mixed-Methods Evaluation of the New York Municipal ID Program)" (Washington, DC: Westat, 2016).

26 David T. Ellwood, *Poor Support: Poverty in the American Family* (New York: Basic Books, 1988).

20

Love, Actually

Reflections from Three Religions

RABBI BURTON L. VISOTZKY, REVEREND CHLOE BREYER,
AND DR. HUSSEIN RASHID

We three, a Conservative rabbi, an Episcopal priest, and a Shi'ah Ismaili leader, are longtime colleagues who have worked together on dialogue and beyond. We have studied together, broken bread together, and traveled the globe together discussing and acting on pressing issues: locally, nationally, and internationally. The immersion of each of us in our own particular religious communities sustains us to work together across religious borders. As religious leaders, we three share a concern about the crisis of connection or perhaps worse, the pattern of disconnection from our own humanity and the humanity of others that lies at the root of many of our current global problems.

In the conversation that follows we explore how within each of our religious traditions there is recognition of our common humanity, in that we each are the offspring of the first human who was created in God's image. This profound reality in our lives leads us to expressions of love: love for God, in Whose image we were created, love for our-selves, love for those of our own religious traditions, and love for the Other, the one who does not share our religion.

Given our positions in "Religions of the Book," we engage one an-other around our classical texts: celebrating their similarities, probing their weaknesses and problematic traditions, and acknowledging dif-ferences and disagreements. We each emphatically speak the language of our individual tradition, so much so that it may appear on occasion that we are speaking past each other. In the end, however, we all agree that the best prescription from each of our respective religions to the crisis of connection may be summarized in one word: love.

Burt Visotzky

I begin our conversation by paying attention to the Hebrew Bible's book of Leviticus, which sits at the center of the Five Books of Moses. Chapter 19 of Leviticus is read annually in synagogues and referred to in Hebrew by its opening command: *kedoshim tiyu* "Be holy, (*kedoshim*), as I the Lord your God am holy" (Lev. 19:3). God commands the Israelites, among whom I include myself, to a life of holiness. What exactly this means is spelled out in part in the rest of the chapter, as well as in the rest of the book of Leviticus. In fact, how to be holy is spelled out in just about every Jewish book ever written. But the chapter in Leviticus 19 may give a contextual clue when a corollary command is given just a few verses later, "Love your neighbor as yourself, I am the Lord" (Lev. 19:18). Here we see love actually.

Yet the command to love and the command to be holy may have a soft underbelly of narrow particularism. Leviticus as a book famously distinguishes between Us and Them: Priest versus Israelite, Jew versus Gentile, Men versus Women, Straight versus Gay (cf. Lev. 18), Clean versus Unclean. At best this is tough love. At worst, we are looking at bald prejudice and ugly Jewish chauvinism. The earliest rabbinic commentary (Sifra) on the passage starkly states "'be holy' means be separate."

Alas, we could fairly characterize the command to "love your neighbor" within its context as teaching particularism: "Love your *Jewish* neighbor as yourself." Indeed, some say "your neighbor as yourself" literally means the neighbor who is most like yourself: the Jew. Maybe worse, it has been taken to mean: love him until he becomes a member of the covenant just like you (the view of Rabbi Tzvi Elimelekh of Dinov [1783–1841] in his commentary, *Maayan Ganim*). Part of me is deeply offended and put off by this kind of excruciating exclusivism. But another part of me confesses that if we read the biblical command in its entirety, it says, "You shall not take vengeance or bear a grudge against *your kinsfolk*, love your neighbor as yourself,

I am the Lord" (Lev. 19:18). Yikes, maybe all this loving your neighbor extends no further than to one's kinsfolk, clan, tribe, or gang!

Chloe Breyer

I see the problem you are getting at. One of the most popular readings for Christian weddings comes from the Apostle Paul's First Letter to the Corinthians:

> Love is patient; love is kind; love is not envious or boastful or arrogant or rude. It does not insist on its own way; it is not irritable or resentful; it does not rejoice in wrongdoing, but rejoices in the truth. It bears all things, believes all things, hopes all things, endures all things. (1 Cor. 13:4)

When Paul first wrote these words they weren't directed at a bride and groom, however. In fact, they came toward the end of a letter in which Paul gave the entire institution of marriage a very mixed review (1 Cor. 7:28). Marriage, he tells his early Christian readers, is more often than not a distraction from preparing for the second coming (1 Cor. 7:29–35).

Instead, in his First Letter to the Corinthians, Paul sent his advice about love to an intentional community—a diverse community of Jews and gentiles, rich and poor, slaves and free citizens—followers of the Way, as they knew themselves to be at that time before the term "Christian" widely used. It was a community reflecting the ethnic and religious diversity of an outpost of the Roman Empire. It was a community striving to do and be something quite different in the world— defying taboos around table fellowship, sharing money and resources, worshiping together, and seeking to model a kind of self-emptying love as revealed by God in the life, death, and resurrection of Jesus.

The reality of life on the ground in this early Christian community did not match the aspirations of the apostle. The Christians of Corinth were experiencing troubles. It appears that they understood about half of Paul's message—the part about being the first fruits of the Kingdom of God and living in the end time (2 Thess. 2:13). The other half of the good news—that they were to love one another despite caste or income or gender; and that this new dispensation wasn't supposed to relieve people of the moral obligations the prophets of old had taught—that part the Corinthians seemed to have missed.

Far from being the countercultural alternative intentional community, a sign of hope in a broken world, the Corinthian followers of the Way were looking a lot like the world around them—letting difference divide them rather than reflecting God's glory, suing one another (1 Cor. 6:1–8), engaging in sexual immorality (1 Cor. 5:1–5), and partaking in the Lord's Supper unworthily (1 Cor. 11:27–33). Paul's words from First Corinthians 13 were intended to remind this early community that being faithful means serving the other, modeling God's self-giving love and passion for justice—reminding them not to let the freedom of one become the stumbling block of another. This is one important understanding of love from a Pauline perspective. Paul reminded the early Christians at Corinth that loving one another, they became one body—diverse, connected, and interdependent.

Hussein Rashid

I must confess to an uneasiness with the emphasis on love. It seems like such a Christian concept, where love is the overriding principle. It is so dominant and expected that it makes it hard to express my own authentic religious values.

Love is not absent from Muslim traditions, but it is manifest in a completely different way. The love of humans and the love for God are in a dialogic relationship. The love of humanity opens us to understanding the love of and for God, and the love for God humbles us enough to love humanity. We speak of an ephemeral love, the love of humanity, and a True Love, that of God. It is the Love of God that is paramount.

Because God is definitionally indescribable, we may find it hard to love God with all our being because the Divine is transcendent. As a result, God blessed us with the Prophet Muhammad (SAWS) and his family (AS). It is by loving the people that God loved that we can approach the love of God more easily.

It is through the love of God and God's beloveds that we are called to the action of justice. To paraphrase Rev. Dr. Cornel West, justice is what love looks like in practice.

Chloe Breyer

Hussein, I am reminded of the words of the revered theologian Linus in Charles Schultz's comic strip *Peanuts*. Linus says, one day, after an argument with Lucy, "I love mankind. It's people I can't stand." In other words, it's one thing to love an abstract concept like "humanity," but it's another thing to love actual living, breathing, imperfect human beings. In some ways you addressed this distinction by saying that the Prophet Muhammad reflected God's likeness in human form. But what about the vast number of human beings who fall short of this high standard? I'd like to hear more about how, from a Muslim perspective, a transcendent and unknowable God helps us in the gritty work of loving difficult, imperfect people—people, I suppose, who look a lot like most of us.

Also, regarding the centrality of love in the Christian faith, Dr. Cornel West owes a debt to the twentieth-century ethicist and theologian Reinhold Niebuhr. Niebuhr, throughout his writings in the first part of the twentieth century, assumes a difference between the private and public sphere and concludes that justice is the best expression of God's love in the *public* square. In small groups or in the private sphere, God's love is expressed in charity and mercy, values that we see in the many words of Jesus. In Matthew 25:34–36, for example, Jesus tells his disciples that at the Judgment the sheep and goats will be separated on the basis of charitable and merciful behavior.

> Then the king will say to those at his right hand, "Come, you that are blessed by my Father, inherit the kingdom prepared for you from the foundation of the world; for I was hungry and you gave me food, I was thirsty and you gave me something to drink, I was a stranger and you welcomed me, I was naked and you gave me clothing, I was sick and you took care of me, I was in prison and you visited me."

It is true that too often, Christians will deny the important political implications in direct service to the poor, hospitality to the stranger, and visitation to the sick and imprisoned. We can be too quick to divorce these acts of mercy from the systemic injustice that so often seems to require them. (Jesus, steeped as he was in the prophetic tradition, would doubtless have understood this.) Yet—and perhaps this *is* in contrast to Islam and Judaism—love in Christianity appears to find full expressions in mercy and charity as well as in justice. (On a personal note, many years ago I had the great honor of working with the late Rabbi Arthur Hertzberg who, upon hearing that I was the product of a Jewish-Christian marriage, wryly warned me of the dangers of inheriting "Jewish guilt and Christian charity, which are often a dangerous combination.")

Hussein Rashid

Chloe, thanks for pointing out that the original quote is from Reinhold Niebuhr, not Cornel West. You raise two incredibly important points for me. The first is about the distinction between collective humanity and individual humans. I think the idea of realizing our own insignificance before the Glory and Majesty of the Divine is what allows us to see the humanity in each other. It is not just about seeing the log in our own eye first, but that we are created to know God. There are the Divinely appointed leaders, like the Prophets and the Imams, but we can also recognize God in each other. The human is not separate from humanity, and there is no humanity without humans. Each approach offers an entryway into expressing one's faith and piety, but they are connected and self-reinforcing.

The second point your raise is about mercy and charity. From my perspective, these are manifestations of justice. The Qur'an repeatedly describes God as the Merciful and the Compassionate. These are qualities that Muslims strive to manifest. The distinction I would make is between just acts, such as offering food to the hungry, and justice, which would entail making sure there were no hungry. It is, as Dorothy Day once said, the need to free the slave *and* to end slavery.

Imam Ali (AS) teaches us that faith leads to action. As a result, belief results in a *practice* of faith. While the focus is often on ritual practice, the Qur'an tells us that this is a mistaken understanding of the relationship between faith and action. Rather, it is about thinking about our obligations to each other (2:177). In that same verse, there is a strong sense that charity is the purpose of material wealth. I would argue that Muslim economics, like the other Abrahamic traditions, is about how to equitably distribute wealth, and prevent the consolidation of capital in the hands of a limited few. It is justice, but also implicitly based on the premise that wealth is an idol that keeps us from acknowledging the value of other people, and from recognizing God.

Burt Visotzky

I jump in here to point out that this dialogue makes it seem as though there is a disagreement about the fundamentals of the relationship(s) among love, justice, faith, mercy, and action. But I think if there is any disagreement it is only semantic: all three religions of the Book (viz. Judaism, Christianity, and Islam) believe that our practice demonstrates our faith, and that our mercy and charity is our way of *Imitatio Dei*—indeed, one of the earliest rabbinic commentaries on the verse from Leviticus I quoted above, "Be holy (*kedoshim*), as I the Lord your God am holy" (Lev. 19:3), reads: "just as God is merciful and compassionate, so we must strive to act with mercy and compassion." I'll come back to this text again, for it is foundational in Jewish teachings about our connection to both the humanity of others and their holiness.

Hussein Rashid

Yes, but we also must avoid being reductionist when speaking of God. Allow me to embrace complexity and nuance here.

The Qur'an is the foundational text for Muslims, but it is not a linear narrative. As a result there is a layering of moral messaging. It describes the complexity of how we think of God.

The Qur'an tells us about the nature of God, and God is ultimately indescribable. The Qur'an says that God is the Light (24:35). There is nothing more difficult to describe than light. It is intangible and we always strive for it. It makes all things possible and is the source of our existence. Even in shadow, we know there must be light out there to make the shadow.

At the same time, we can still know God in an intimate way. The Qur'an also tells that God is closer to us than our jugular vein (50:16).

The vein that connects our head and heart, the circuit of life, God is nearer and dearer to us than that vein. Our very heartbeat is our own best reminder of God's existence. It is a visceral and familiar connection to God.

Yet, as much as our own body reminds us of God, the Qur'an is still needed to be revealed to the Prophet Muhammad (SAWS). The text constantly tells us to remember God, to not forget God, and recognize that God reminds us every moment of the Divine around us. We are forgetful creatures. When we forget God, we elevate our own selves to be the center of our personal worldviews. That perspective is inherently exclusionary. We affirm ourselves through external markers: wealth, goods, "likes," and retweets. If anyone else has something similar, we are in opposition to that person.

Imam Jafar as-Sadiq (AS), part of the line of Divinely appointed successors to Prophet Muhammad, says in *Lantern on the Path* that true faith has four areas of conduct: with God, with the self, with others, and with creation. The struggle of faith is maintaining the balance of these areas of conduct. In forgetting God, we are already out of balance, and our relationships with anyone or anything not the Self is damaged.

We must think first about our relationship with God, before we can think about our relationship to each other. In Arabic, the word for prayer is *ibadat*, which is related to *abd*, or to be a servant of God. By accepting the role of a slave, we willingly give up our agency and freedom. However, it is not something that we can simply say or do. It is a transformation that must take place. One offers prayer, *ibadat*, because one is a servant of God, *abd Allah*, but one cannot become a servant of God until one offers prayer. It is a cycle of commitment and transformation. It is a process, not a state. Because God is our true Master, everything we do is for the sake of God. This process and this realization are the first step in understanding our relationship to the world.

If all of creation is God's reminder to us, then we have an obligation to pay heed. It is a trust that we have been given, one that has to be nurtured and cared for, so that we are constantly thinking of God. We are uncomfortable with idea of *ibadat*, because this means servitude to God, and we are unfamiliar with the idea of a subservience that works to negate who we are, to absorb us in Light. Instead, we will erase ourselves in consumerism, because we understand material goods.

While you focus on how to expand the reading of your scripture, I approach my scripture as guidance on how to avoid forgetting God and God's creations, including other people. Our natural instinct is to erase ourselves in consumerism, because it is easier for us to understand material goods, than to engage with spiritual reward. To give up that consumerism is an opportunity to return to awe. To tremble when the Qur'an says God is the light of the heavens and the earth. To open ourselves to the idea that there is something we cannot describe or comprehend, because there is nothing more indescribable than light.

It is in prayer that we are reminded of our place in creation. No matter what we do, *taqwa* (God-consciousness) makes us realize that there is always something greater. *Allahu Akbar*. God is greater. Greater than anything we can conceive of. It is because of our servitude that we can achieve greatness, but still God is greater. We will always have more to strive for. More good; more compassion; more service.

When we pray, we remember that we are not the purpose of creation. The Qur'an says that when all else perishes, the Face of God will remain (55:26–27). Creation is temporary, and only God is eternal.

It is in entering prayer that we enter into conversation with God. In the Qur'an, God repeatedly says *kun fa-yakuna*, "Be and it will be." That first *kun*, that first "Be!," is the beginning of the conversation with God. We do not expect an answer, we are not due an answer. But to think that God is not always conversing with us is to ignore the signs of creation that surround us. In the Qur'an, God keeps telling us that in creation are signs for those who pay heed.

It is in the sign of light, we see other people as part of creation as well. God says in the Qur'an that God will make the way easy for us, so that *ibadat* is linked to *mu'amalat*, obligations to humanity. We are called to service. To say that we serve because of our faith tells only part of the story. It sounds as though faith is the cause of our service, which it is. However, like prayer, it is a process, so that service should also be seen as a chance to deepen our faith. Service is *ibadat*. It should be a time to reflect, to be intentional, and to be mindful.

Burt Visotzky

I would say "Amin!" but want to note that LOVE is a concept found already with strong emphasis in the Hebrew Bible and it continues to have a central role in rabbinic literature and in our Jewish liturgy, even today. Further, we have seen love manifested in the push/pull of imperfect humans in service, or better perhaps, in servitude to a perfect God. We each speak through the lens of our faith tradition and its core teachings. For me, resisting the narrow reading of particularism I have uncovered, I must ask myself whether there is a universalist, outward-looking reading of "love your neighbor as yourself" in Jewish tradition. I am happy to say there is. In a medieval compilation often referred to as a "minor" tractate of the Talmud (Kallah Rabbati chap. 4) we find the interpretation of the command as follows: "by loving your neighbor you come to see the ways he is like you." This is most welcome, for it emphasizes exactly the recognition of our common humanity that we are seeking. But still, given my earlier exploration of the narrower reading of Jewish tradition, I yet ask why one would read so generously, especially given the fuller context of the verse and the fact that many read the command as only referring to Jews? Here, the broader context of Leviticus 19 comes to the rescue. Toward the end of Leviticus chapter 19 we read, "When a stranger resides with you in your land, you shall not wrong him. The stranger who resides with you shall be to you as one of your citizens; you shall love him as yourself, for you were strangers in the land of Egypt: I God am your Lord" (Lev. 19:33–34).

And universalist love of the Other is not limited to Leviticus 19:34. In Exodus the Israelites are commanded in an even stronger fashion: "If you meet your enemy's ox or his donkey going astray, you shall bring it back to him. If you see the donkey of one who hates you lying under its burden, you shall refrain from leaving him with it; you shall help him to lift it up" (Exod. 23:4–5). This is more than just loving the stranger or recognizing common humanity. The Exodus commandment requires compassion for your enemy, the one who hates you—or at least for such a one's animal. But surely this commandment applies to the human being as well as the animal, doesn't it? Let us be reassured by the biblical book of Proverbs, which makes it clear that it's not just the donkey, it's the enemy for whom we are commanded to show compassion: "If your enemy is hungry, give him bread to eat; and if he is thirsty, give him water to drink" (Prov. 25:21).

Chloe Breyer

This is true in Christianity as well. Turning from Paul to the Gospels, what does it mean to love one's neighbor in a Christian context? Jesus, steeped as he was in the scriptures of the Hebrew Bible, makes it clear,

> Do not think that I came to abolish the Law or the Prophets; I did not come to abolish but to fulfill. For truly I say to you, until heaven and earth pass away, not the smallest letter or stroke shall pass from the Law until all is accomplished. (Matt. 5:17)

Loving God and loving neighbor are central to Jesus's teaching. In Matthew's Gospel, when the Pharisees test Jesus and ask him which commandment is the greatest, Jesus replies,

> You shall love the lord your God with all of your heart and with all your soul and with all your mind. This is the greatest and first commandment. And a second one is like it. You shall love your neighbor as yourself. On these two commandments hang all of the law and the prophet. (Matt. 22:37–40)

But who is my neighbor? Who is it I am called to love? Burt Visotzky just asked a similar question about whether the neighbor love was intended to apply to the Jewish community or to the world outside of it as well. He pointed out two schools of interpretation. One supported the idea that the commandment to "Love thy neighbor" was meant only for those inside the community. The other suggested that it was a universal commandment applied to Jew and non-Jew alike.

The same ambiguity exists within Christianity over the commandment to love the other. All are one, Paul instructs the Galatians:

For all of you who were baptized into Christ have clothed yourselves with Christ. There is neither Jew nor Greek, there is neither slave nor free man, there is neither male nor female; for you are all one in Christ Jesus. (Gal. 3:27–28)

Such a passage might sound as if it employed a universalist approach, but in actuality the unity he speaks of exists only within Baptism, "the sacramental complement of faith the rite whereby a person achieves union with Christ" (*New Jerome Commentary*, 786). In other words, those who are baptized into Christ are united with one another.

The question "Who is my neighbor?" is a fraught one in the New Testament. It is repeated in the Gospel of Luke when a skeptical young lawyer asked what he must do to inherit eternal life. Jesus replies, sounding similar to his rejoinder to the Pharisees in Matthew, "Love the Lord your God with all of your heart and with all your soul and with all your mind. This is the greatest and first commandment. And a second one is like it. You shall love your neighbor as yourself" (Luke 10:28).

Apparently Jesus's reply wasn't enough for the young lawyer, and he sought, as Luke said, "to justify himself" (Luke 10:29) by asking who is his neighbor. Jesus answered with the story of the Good Samaritan: a man went down on the road to Jericho and was robbed and beaten by bandits. Three men come down after him. The first was a Priest, who passed the man by. The second was a Levite, who also passed the man by. And the third was the Good Samaritan, who stopped and cared for the man and took him to a nearby inn. Jesus then asked the young lawyer, "Which of these three, do you think, was a neighbor to the man who fell into the hands of the robbers?" He said, "The one who showed him mercy." Jesus said to him, "Go and do likewise" (Luke 10:25–37).

Hussein Rashid

Bringing what Burt and Chloe have just said into a Muslim perspective, we need to open ourselves to the possibility of a selfless, all-encompassing love, one that cannot be generated by human constraints. We have to recenter ourselves, so that we are not the center of our lives, but so that we are the nexus of a relationship with God. We start by being humble in God's presence, which leads us to care for that which God cares for, so that we discover our true selves. Then, we turn our true selves into agents of positive transformation that creates genuine empathy and love for others, ultimately allowing us to be grateful and close to God. We travel from the God that is Light which blinds us to submission to the God in our pulse, who is our boon companion. In the middle is where we form the relationship to each other.

With *iman* (faith), we have a love for God that is intrinsic to our being and that is realized in our deeds. Our service to others is not because of servitude to God, but for love of God. That means we love all of God's creation. We could not be open to that love until we had broken ourselves of our love of our own selves. And the first people to receive and accept this new love are the Prophet and his family, whom God sent for us to love.

We make webs of connections, and then communities. We have mastered making good neighbors, and then good neighborhoods, but the cost has been building good communities. We need to go back to valuing each other as people, and value ourselves in relation to other people.

We have no problem thinking of community. We do community work. To think *like* a community means a deeper sort of connection to our neighbor and a better awareness of her needs and desires.

What happens when we are faced with deeply divisive issues that are made by humans and speak to a group identity? We could be speaking of Kashmir, Syria, Iraq, or Palestine; abortion or same-sex marriage.

Some of these issues have religious overtones that undercut the goals of community building for the sake of justice, by having competing claims as to what justice is. The quest for justice demands that we still cultivate a human contact that emerges from a love of God and an understanding of our limited ability to understand God. We must remain humble.

The response is to constantly be in a state of redefining and re-creating community. When the community is static, we have a tribe that must be defended. Our circles of belonging must remain diverse and expanding. The move to justice requires us to constantly engage, but always as equals and partners.

There will always be those with whom we cannot come to an agreement. The first death threat I got was from the Jewish Defense League, for organizing a peace rally after the Hebron massacre in 1994; after that it was by a Christian who was offended that I was speaking in a church. I believe the Wahhabi ideologues of Saudi Arabia would be glad to see me dead, because I am a Muslim, not a Wahhabi. There is no community there. To deal with this gulf, we have to make informed, intentional choices as to who we will engage and how. We are known not just by the company we keep, but by those who avoid us. The call to justice demands work and empathy. This need to understand what motivates others should animate our service. The point of service is not the action, but the transformation. This is the call to justice: to love God, to accept that we are all in need, and to realize the best potential of all of us.

Burt Visotzky

Hussein speaks of an awareness of our neighbor's needs and desires. Part of loving another is precisely that ability to show compassion. With compassion one sees another and feels along with him or her. This ability to try to see the world from the place of the other is an act of love, as it requires us to truly stand outside of our own biases and prejudices, to see another whether they are of our family, tribe, or completely alien. It is a way of taking on a divine perspective, if you will. Just as God can see each human and know that creature compassionately, so must we try to do so. To that end, I stand in support of you Hussein and Chloe, when you are threatened and know that you have my back, too!

The biblical book of Deuteronomy ups the stakes in commanding not only love of God's other creatures, but love of God as well. The second-century sage Rabbi Aqiba is reported to have commented on the command "love your neighbor as yourself" by noting it was the great principle of the Torah. This is the same Rabbi Aqiba who is also reported as accepting his own martyrdom as the opportunity to "Love the Lord your God with all your heart, with all your soul, and with all your might" (Deut. 6:2).

It is not surprising then to see that the earliest commentary on Deuteronomy, attributed to the school of Rabbi Aqiba, equates the love of God with the love of humanity. It is written, "*Love the Lord* your God and walk in all God's ways, cling to God" (Deut. 11:22). The commentary I quoted above about Leviticus is relevant to the Deuteronomy verse commanding us to "walk in God's ways." The rabbis teach (Sifre to Deuteronomy): "Just as God is merciful (*rahum*) and compassionate (*hanun*), so you be merciful and compassionate . . . just as God is righteous (*tzadiq*) and loving (*hesed*), so you be righteous and loving." In another early commentary (Mekilta Beshalah 3) this move toward identification with radical, divine compassion is reiterated: "Abba Shaul said, Resemble God. As God is Merciful and compassionate, so you be merciful and compassionate."

Chloe Breyer

More guidance on a Christian view of loving one's neighbor comes from the words of Dr. Martin Luther King Jr. King describes neighborly love in the parable of the Good Samaritan in his final sermon in Memphis. On April 3, 1968, speaking to striking sanitation workers, King described the story of the Good Samaritan. King said he was convinced that it wasn't so much hurriedness or lack of empathy that stopped the Levite or the priest from caring for the man laying hurt on the side of the road as it was fear.

"It's possible," King preached in Memphis,

> that the priest and the Levite looked over the man on the ground and wondered if the robbers were still around. Or it is possible that they felt that the man on the ground was merely faking. And he was acting like he had been robbed and hurt in order to seize them over there, lure them there for a quick and easy seizure. And so the first question that the Levite asked was, "If I stop to help this man, what will happen to me?" But then, the Good Samaritan came by. And he reversed the question: "If I do *not* stop to help this man, what will happen to him?"

Exhibiting neighbor love in his own life and ministry, King, for example, shifts the line of inquiry from "If I stop to help the sanitation workers, what will happen to my job?" to "If I do not stop to help the sanitation workers, what will happen to them?"

Hussein Rashid

And let us complement the individual moment of holy action. To be aware of the Holy is to see the Divine in the everyday, which brings back our sense of awe and wonder. Awe is when we stand dumbstruck before the greatness of what we see and understand.

The demands of the world take us away from awe and wonder, and move us to the needs of now, with no time to witness the mysteries and blessings around us. And that means we do not see it in other people, which means we do not see it in ourselves. When we are humbled before the majesty of God, we are constantly grateful, and appreciate all that we have been given.

This is one of the easiest ways to remember God, to be grateful.

Gratitude requires a level of commitment to claim our humanity and is a spiritual practice. The Qur'an says that to be grateful is to receive blessings (14:7). When we are not grateful, we lose the ability to be captured by wonder, the wonder that surrounds us every day in creation.

In that humbling of our own selves in the majesty of creation, we are grateful. The cycle repeats. We are grateful, open to wonder, humbled, and made grateful. If we cannot be in awe, if we cannot be grateful, then all we have left is the mundane and all we focus on is problems. All we have is our own selves.

To be grateful is to acknowledge that we are blessed, and that we have an obligation to be generous in our blessing.

Imam Ali (AS), whom Prophet Muhammad named as his successor, states in *Treasury of Virtues* (135) that faith leads to deeds, and deeds lead piety. To get to faith, we need to begin by submitting ourselves to God. It is how we remove ourselves from the illusion of material validation. We must begin with the first promise we made to God: that God is our Lord; we come from God and we will return to God. Our commitment is to serve God. When we have broken ourselves of our own sense of superiority, we can see the wonders around us.

It is, ironically, extreme individualism that keeps us from reaching our true potential. We can only be what we imagine ourselves. We also view the world as a zero-sum game: the one with the most toys wins. This model depletes the world, and assumes that we are against each other. Starting with submission to God, we enter a realm of unbounded imagination, where anything is possible. It is possible because the Divine presence is all around us, in creation, including other people.

When we start delving into selfless motivation, we experience the difference between compassion and empathy. The latter, empathy, allows us to see beyond surface needs and get to core issues. It is a skill that needs to be cultivated and nurtured, but individualism precludes it. When we value ourselves with and through others, it is humanity.

A community of humanity allows us to achieve something that we cannot alone: the possibility of change. We are not alone. For every difficulty we face as individuals, there are many more individuals who have or are walking similar paths. For the change for the good that we seek to make in the world, there are so many more who wish to walk with us on the path of change.

This gathering of people for a greater good is justice. It is the manifestation of mercy and compassion. We know how another person wants to be treated, because we can truly, deeply empathize with her. We have lost ourselves to serve God, and have recovered ourselves by engaging with God's creation. That other person is intimately tied to who we are. We have seen the Divine through her, but have also built ourselves with the mortar of her presence.

Burt Visotzky

In reply to this beautiful image, I want to return to the section of Leviticus 19 on holiness. That passage famously, gloriously spells out the requirements of loving compassion for our fellow humans. In particular, Jews are commanded to care for others less well off in the Jewish community. The assumption is that God is the Creator of the world, so everything belongs to God. As the Psalmist puts it: "The earth is the Lord's, all that is in it" (Ps. 24:1). This helps us understand the sweeping redistribution of wealth commanded in Leviticus 19. The Torah requires Jews at harvest time to leave the corners of the field (Lev. 19:9–10), any dropped or fallen produce, and even the forgotten harvest for the Jewish poor to glean. It belongs to God and not the farmer; so God can command the farmer to give what is God's to another of God's creatures. The rabbis radically qualified this commandment by also requiring, "if the gentile poor wish to partake of that boon, we do not withhold it, in the interests of peace with the broader community" (M. Gittin 5).

This is a fabulous recognition that we do not live in isolation. We are all dependent upon one another. As such, the rabbis insist on sharing this boon with all poor. "In the interests of peace" with our neighbors the rabbis go so far as to say that in a city that had both Jewish and Gentile populations, which is to say, most cities, "the rabbinic charity officers would collect from and distribute to their gentile neighbors alongside the Jews, in the interests of peace" (T. Gittin 3). The command to compassion went beyond the alimentary or monetary. The rabbis note, "One would bury gentile dead and mourn them and offer condolence to their families, in the interests of peace. So too, one must visit the sick among the gentiles and dower their brides" (M. Gittin 5). Even the simplest of exchanges was regulated by this loving sensibility, as Jews are enjoined to acknowledge their gentile neighbors with the common Jewish greeting "Shalom," in the interests of peace, even extending those greetings for the gentiles' religious holidays (M. Avodah Zarah).

Chloe Breyer

Now, let me also refocus our vision on our dual relationships: both toward our fellow humans and toward God. Paul described the dynamic nature of God's love in this way in his letter to the early Christian community in Philippi:

> Let the same mind be in you that was in Christ Jesus who though he was in the form of God, did not regard equality with God as something to be exploited, but emptied himself taking the form of a slave, being born in human likeness. And being found in human form he humbled himself and became obedient to the point of death even death on a cross. Therefore God also highly exalted him and gave him the name that is above every name. (Phil. 2:5–10)

In this passage of scripture, Paul is describing God's dynamic movement from a position of privilege (i.e., heaven) to a position of non-privilege (i.e., earth) and back again. The exalted position of things unseen and untouched—the "metaphysical"—is suddenly unseated by those things that can be seen and touched. The Christ Hymn in Philippians describes this outpouring and nonstatic nature of God's love.

The Gospel of Luke's Resurrection account contains a hypothetical "redirect" sign helping our understanding of Christian love. Luke's account describes women being present at the tomb bringing spices to anoint the body of Jesus. They are surprised to find the stone rolled away and then even more shocked to find two men in dazzling clothes. "Why do you look for the living among the dead?" the two men ask. "He is not here, but has risen" (Luke 24:5).

Those women at the tomb could have hung around and debated with the Angel. They could have turned to each other and asked, very reasonably, what does this mean for us? But for some reason, not because these women were incurious or unintellectual, for some reason these women were redirected. Love pointed them in a different direction—back out into the world to proclaim good news, the love of God to the World.

Mary Magdalen, Mary the Mother of James, and the other women were propelled out of the tomb and into personal encounters with others. They followed the Angel's advice and got out of the house: "Why do you look for the living among the dead? He is not here, but has risen" (Luke 24:5). Love is the nonstatic nature of God.

Love is dynamic. It is the great redirection through the Resurrection that unseats our questions and propels us into encounter with the other. Love is on the move, and the promise and good news of Easter is that nothing will separate us from that love.

Hussein Rashid

I also want to echo the dual nature of Divine love. It is in empathetic service that I see myself in the other person. I not only see her humanity, but my own as well. The Divinity that is breathed into her is breathed into me too.

It is only in the other person that we can find ourselves. The Qur'an tells us that we are created nations that we may know one another (49:13), and that God could have easily created us as one community (16:93). That we are different tells us that we need to engage that difference. If God cannot be captured in simple descriptions, then any engagement with someone else is a revelation of the Divine in the world. The relationship with others teaches us more about ourselves as people, and thus more about our understandings and relationships with God.

Now that we have this awareness, we move from *islam* (submission) to *iman* (faith). We possess the belief of God's existence and God's presence in the world. We see it everywhere we turn, and we cannot help but remember the Divine with us too. We manifest a *taqwa* (God-consciousness) that is reflexive, rather than one we need to invoke. The result is that we see prayer in a new way. It is a conversation between ourselves and God. In that moment of prayer, we are at peace. However, once we leave the space of prayer we are agitated, because we recognize that the world is not at peace. We see the injustice of the world and know that God's Will is not being realized. God is the Most Compassionate and the Most Merciful, and suffering means that at least one of those qualities is not manifest in the world. The idyllic world of prayer is broken, and we need to manifest those Divine characteristics in the world to repair it.

We start with prayer, seeking to submit to God. We enter into service, and engage with other people. It is in meeting others with *taqwa* (God-consciousness) that we begin to understand who we are as individuals. That awakening to faith calls us to action that is grounded in love: love of God, love of self, and love of creation. We are then grateful to God, and enter into prayer, continuing the process of refining the soul, and always making a little more room for love.

Imam Zayn al-Abidin (AS) wrote one of the beautiful Muslim prayer books, *As-Sahifa As-Sajjadiyya*. In one of my favorite prayers, his devotion is that God is too exalted for us to remember properly, but it is the Divine command that we do so, so we will. And that is God's greatest gift to us, to remember God. It is in that remembrance that we do good deeds, are brought together, find serenity, and experience true love. To know another is to know God, and to know God is to know one another.

Burt Visotzky

Our religious sensibility constantly requires us to reflect on God and our relationship to the Creator. Our relationship with our fellow humans is mediated through our relationship with God. In Judaism, indeed, our relationship with our fellow humans is dictated by our covenantal relationship with God, Who commands the very details of those relationships. Primary in this mind-set is the notion that our fellow humans, each and every one of them, are created in God's image and likeness (Gen. 1:26). This demands that we recognize the divine reflection of our fellow and honor and love it. One of the earliest rabbinic texts (Pirke

Avot) sweetly dilates on this notion when it teaches: "It was an act of love that God created humanity in God's image and likeness. It was an act of even greater love that God revealed to humanity that we were created in God's image and likeness."

How good it is that we know we are God's creatures, who are created in God's very image and likeness. How essential that we recognize this in ourselves, and in every other, as well. In the story of creation God began by creating but one person alone. The rabbis reflect on the meaning of this narrative and conclude, "Humanity was created as a single individual for the sake of peace among humanity; that none might say to his or her fellow, 'my ancestor was greater than your ancestor'" (M. Sanhedrin 4). Knowing that one is created with a noble ancestor who had God's very breath/spirit vivify him allows the rabbis to further conclude, "Therefore every individual must say, 'For my sake the world was created'" (M. Sanhedrin 4).

That the rabbis were keen readers of Scripture after the fact is hardly a surprise. Their enterprise of interpretive reading, called Midrash, is chock-full of such theological-anthropological insights. But the biblical narrative itself has, as it were, an inner-biblical Midrash that celebrates the divinity in humanity. When Jacob, the eponymous ancestor of the people Israel, returns home after twenty years in exile, he is fearful of seeing his brother, whom he still regards as his enemy. He had treated Esau badly as a youth, cheating him out of his birthright. Yet while Jacob was in fearful exile, Esau waxed mighty and grew emotionally as well.

Jacob sought to propitiate his brother by bringing him gifts, gifts that were meant, perhaps, to atone for Jacob's feelings of guilt at how he had treated his brother. Or perhaps the wagon train of gifts was a form of bribery for Esau's affection. Yet when Esau finally once again beheld his long lost brother he "ran to greet him. He embraced him and hugged him. He kissed him and they wept" (Gen. 33:4). Jacob still implored him to take the gift, but Esau demurred, saying, "I have plenty" (Gen. 33:9) Jacob's response to his brother is an insightful commentary on the creation story so much earlier in Genesis. He tells the man he thought to be his enemy, "Accept from me this gift; for to see your face is like seeing the face of God" (Gen. 33:10).

This is the moment in which the father of the Jewish people's relationship to God is reflected in his relationship to his alienated brother. I is for me a guiding star of how one must behave toward others, toward Others. Would that we each could overcome our guilty feelings and our fears and see the face of God as we behold someone else. If we could do so, would it not shape our recognition of our common humanity and so our connection to one another? How, then, shall I behave?

Chloe, Hussein, Burt

Chloe: "And now faith, hope, and love abide, these three; and the greatest of these is love." Love actually.

Hussein: "O you who have faith! Be maintainers of justice and witnesses for the sake of Allah, even if it should be against yourselves" (4:135). Justice actually.

Burt: "Love your neighbor as yourself, I am the Lord" (Lev. 19:18). Love actually.

AFTERWORD

DAVID E. KIRKLAND

Certain books shed light on the soul, daring to make legible concepts like love—concepts that feel so enormous and so utterly difficult to fully grasp that we simply refuse them. In fact, my favorite reads have been books on such concepts, particularly on what cultural theorists call "the search for decolonial love."[1] What they were alluding to in this particular construction of love—love as decolonial, as quest to transform oppression—was a specific moment in the movement for racial justice in which weird gender wars flared up between writers of color, where the brothers were criticizing the sisters for being inauthentic, for being anti-male, for airing the community's dirty laundry.[2] For me, these criticisms were, of course, unfounded, but rereading Stanley Crouch's critique of Alice Walker, for example, made me feel the weight of *disconnection* on me—a rift in my soul expressed in my physical body.

The lessons of disconnection are not new. However, what I find fascinating in texts such as *Beloved* or *The Color Purple*, which explore the deep disconnections that plague our humanity, are the women—in this case women of color—who were creating maps in their fictions—the social, critical, cognitive maps, plotting matrixes for human connection far more dangerous to the structures that divide humanity than any of the criticism of Vygotsky or Marx.[3] For me, theirs has been a spiritual genius that offers a theory of transformation based on the strength each of us must find in love. What is becoming clear as I read these women of color is an art powerfully interwoven to the fabrics of community, for subaltern folk, for people who love each other in spite of systems of disconnection that have always worked to tug people apart. Through love and in love, these women were heeding Audre Lorde's exhortation by forging the tools that could not only take down the master's house, but also erect a new space in its place where people could authentically connect.[4]

Thus, every so often I get the pleasure of reading a courageous book. Though it seems odd that bravery could be defined as the audacity to speak of love in science, this is exactly what this book and its authors have done and, perhaps, much more. They have bravely sought to understand how our humanity is shaped in the transcendence of delicate love. In so doing, they speak to the manifold consequences related to misconfigurations and resistances to this love—the deep disconnections that create and compound human suffering on scales that leave us somehow unnaturally bound and wretchedly reimagined as lesser version of our best possible selves. Thus, the bravery of this book cannot be lost in the consequence that we have unfortunately perched *science* up in a place where topics of love seem out of place. Though love exists in the extremes—as fundamental and prodigious, guiding all aspects of human existence—in the social sciences, in particular, we suffer love to abstraction, as a subject too "soft" for serious investigation, an area of focus that somehow does not merit rigorous scientific study.

Of course, we dismiss the study of love to our collective peril. As the editors of this book and its authors suggest, it is in the study of love—i.e., "the science of human connection"—that we find the most compelling evidence of the root causes of human suffering, as well as powerful solutions to them. How lucky, then, are we to have a book courageous enough to break the silence, to explore people expressing their deep needs to strengthen fragile bonds? In this book, we glimpse into the lives of people fostering connections against the stubborn backdrop of a world that seems to be falling apart around them. Thus, as the crisis of connection lingers, unwavering in the shadows of human despair, this book has sought, at once, to understand and interrupt it.

It is here that we see, and clearly, the silhouettes and aesthetic identities of real people marked by what Way, Ali, Gilligan, Noguera, and their colleagues see as "decreasing levels of empathy and trust, and the rising indices of depression, anxiety, loneliness, and social isolation."[5] It is against the silhouette of a humanity that has become difficult to recognize that we feel our mortal ambiguities and witness the complexities of human narratives—or as Gilligan, Rogers, and Noel put it, the "cartography of a lost time." In this dance of light outlining darkness, this book has dared to stretch beyond just love and toward a science of human understanding through a rare and unique meditation on love—the stories and basics of beauty encased in all things human, such as four- and five-year-old boys resisting disconnection by embracing friendships that queer hegemonic nostrums of masculinity, or adolescent girls renegotiating the incipient terms of their existences as they move from girlhood to womanhood. In each chapter of this monumental book, we as readers and thinkers have been invited to explore how the world looks through the eyes of the disconnected fighting to preserve their links to themselves and others. As we *stay woke*—as Janie Ward invites us to do—we see Black girls rising to resist disconnection; we eavesdrop on the debate between "real" men versus good men as we learn to "let men care." This world feels familiar, the same as our world, but somehow the book has made it more legible.

In its light, this book raises an important set of questions about the world, about power, about philosophy, about politics, about history, about supremacy, and about love. In particular, it leaves us with questions tied to raced, gendered, sexualized bodies, of people as young as small children wielding a genius that has been curried, cultivated out of their own raced, gendered, sexualized subjectivities. All of this has everything to do with how we must understand the world, bearing witness to a love unshackled—to what Arrastia calls "love pedagogy," which teaches us to disrupt. It is at this point in the book where the science of human connection becomes, itself, the art of connecting, understood through both empathy and a world split open.

Unfortunately, many of us cannot see beyond the day-to-day divisions that parcel our lives. The social fissures that animate the everyday have become so normal that we find little space to question them. Indeed, the clarity achieved in this book, for so many of us social scientists and critics of culture, has been difficult to achieve. One does not have to read many books or articles to get a sense of how modern thinkers are trapped in the divide, retreating to regressive logics that resuscitate arguments that could have emerged from the 1970s embrace of "the culture of poverty."[6] These arguments concern me, as a critical intellectual and urban education researcher. I see in my own work the consequence of rupture— *the crisis of connection*—which plays out in enduring inequities that fuel systems of disparity, ultimately redesigning oppression and maintaining human suffering.

As the editors remind us in the introduction, "We are indeed in the midst of a crisis because as the bonds of solidarity and cohesion weaken our ability to address our societal problems and pursue our common interests is severely damaged." It is this damage that causes us to see some people as distorted, less innocent than they actually are, less human than they deserve to be seen. The artifacts of this damage are, in fact, the disconnections that define some people as disconnected, including our most vulnerable children—those marked as poor, Black, Brown, queer, trans, and so forth.[7] These artifacts persist on individual levels (e.g., intolerance, discrimination, stereotypes, mistrust) and endure as structural consequences (e.g., poverty, premature death, disparities in education, and so on). While the emphasis of analysis has too often privileged a focus on the disconnected, this book does well in arguing that we need to redirect our focus on the individual and structural disconnects—systems of suffering that are the root causes of our social rifts.

To blame the disconnected for the social condition of disconnection is a bogus explanation for the social inequity that this book questions. The logics of the culture of poverty, be them as they may, deterministically and too comfortably imagine how people have been shaped in situations that promote behaviors necessary to police in order to deter chaos and maintain order. It is this endeavor of law and order—the hypergovernance and policing of the otherwise unruly vulnerable body— that masks a deep set of dilemmas out of which the crisis of connection grows.[8] Perhaps most astounding is the idea, steeped in the logics of disconnection, that things such as quality education mean the eviction of vulnerable people from the educational enterprise.[9] Thus, the crisis of connection foments a war on poverty while simultaneously redesigning an unyielding war on the poor and the vulnerable.

This conclusion is disturbing—that we cannot and should not seek to educate, or better yet love, all people—that children who come from conditions inspired by gross inequities are expendable. Perhaps sadder is the idea that individuals who have so been labeled as expendable— the children we disproportionately suspend who are overwhelmingly Black, Brown, and poor; the women whom we fail at the cusp of adolescence and continue to fail throughout their lives by blaming them for assaults on their beings; the men we crucify for loving each other—bear the scars of our crimes against connection. These are people who face more trauma as opposed to less in and out of our schools, our courts, our hospitals, and all other facets of our social lives.[10] Data on pre-school, for example, reveal that these patterns emerge early and endure throughout the lives of children, shaping pathologies and phobias endemic of *the crisis*.[11] We now have convincing evidence that teachers and other school personnel view youth of color as older, more threatening, and less innocent than their White peers the same age.[12] These findings exemplify how, even as early as pre-K, biases get baked into our collective consciousness.

There are consequences to the consequences. Students who experience suspensions chronically perform less well in school, experience debilitating gaps in their learning, and are more likely to drop out than students never suspended at all.[13] These same students are more likely to have health issues, be un- or underemployed, and be incarcerated.[14] The chain of consequences continues through marriage and marriage-ability, the ability to parent and raise a family, and so on.[15] There also may be consequences not yet unearthed such as radical correlations of suicide rates by suspensions, and the consequences of retraumatization on mental health and learning.[16] The point is, however, clear: resolving the crisis of connection is precisely what is needed to fix our broken society.

We must start when people are young by perfecting ways to keep our children as connected as possible for as long as possible. This is not just a civil rights issue or an educational one. It is deeply a moral issue tied to dignity and a greater campaign to take care of people and invest in our common humanity. In this way, so much about this book is a promise to our children enveloped with actionable love, or as Cornel West put it, justice—"what love looks like in public."[17] It follows that injustice must be the public face of hatred. Thus, the crisis of connection raises moral questions: Do we hate our children? Do we hate ourselves?

This book has taken us beyond these questions (and others like it) because hate is not accurate enough a word to explain the public consequences of social injustice. The humiliation, the brutality, the coarse indignation of people whom we evict from our society go beyond just hate. In the space of publics, there are growing divides between the vulnerable and the safe, between those clothed in the bloody sheets of trauma and those armored by close-fitting systems of privilege. We know that some roam the earth more freely than do others. Thus, hatred doesn't maintain the disconnection of the vulnerable. Oppressive systems do.

Then justice recedes from Cornel West's definition of love in the prose of reality and in the backdrop of stubborn systems of disparity, where the poetry of soundbites offends moral sensibilities to achieve a truth beyond just us. In this space, there is only freedom. Thus, if this book leaves a single impression, I hope it is this: No longer can we have overly poetic conversations that define the science of human connection based on a system of obligations, based on the philosophical instrumentalities that sanction apparatuses of oppression. For justice systems have destroyed more vulnerable bodies, more Black and Brown bodies, than the injustice systems they mirror. Before courts, there were the auction blocks, and before juries, there were the hideous galleries. Then we must append Cornel West's axiom on love based solely on the new perspectives shared in this book. It is here that we understand that freedom is what love looks like, period. And for the many millions of bodies that we offend with our chains, either through justice systems or education apparatuses that redesign and maintain human oppression, justice can never be enough. Our work must strive for freedom for a people broken into a million shards. This requires restoration, the type of restoration that not only puts back together broken pieces but also heals broken souls.

Each of the authors in this book shares notes to help readers understand that restoration is indeed possible, that connection is a human science worth advancing. What the authors have produced in knowledge is something that the world needs to hear in order to understand itself—the transcendence of love gripped by sincerity. Having read this book, I now know that I needed this knowledge in order to understand myself in a world "beset by a crisis of connection." To me, these notes are not only forging our radical-emancipatory epistemologies—the source code for our healing—but also fundamentally rewriting the social sciences through questions that delve into places once viewed as soft, places that desires hearings—places of the soul and of the body (its oppressions and interpellations and possibilities).

In their book *Between Voice and Silence*, Taylor, Gilligan, and Sullivan present a "voice-centered methodology of knowing" that makes it possible to unchain ourselves and others by "listening." Listening to "the unspoken," they write, to "places where there is no voice," where people have silenced their experiences or have simply not been heard," is a profound quest into the soul of the speaker as well as the listener.[18] I believe that the most significant contribution of this masterful collection deals with reframing how we listen—particularly to young people and to families we too often disregard. The greater lesson that the authors share is found in their own listenings, which are not found in the typical systems of thought that guide our views of the world. Thus, their work is found not in conquest or purchasing, but in respect, a profound respect and patience. In this respect and patience, we are shown the radiant truth of how profoundly constituted we are of our situations. Or, said differently, how indissolubly our identities are bound to the regimes that imprison us. This isn't it, though. Although we exist in the limiting labyrinth of our situations, we exist also in the possibility that we play both Theseus and the Minotaur on life's stage, where our stubborn wills alone offer strategies of hope, spinning the threads that will make escape from the labyrinth possible.

In the end, the authors teach us that authentic connection must have vulnerability, forgiveness, and acceptance as its prerequisites.

NOTES

1 Quoted in Y. C. Figueroa, "Reparation as Transformation: Radical Literary (Re)imaginings of Futurities through Decolonial Love," *Decolonization: Indigeneity, Education & Society* 4, no. 1 (2015): 41–58.
2 Stanley Crouch, "Aunt Medea," *New Republic* 19 (1987): 38–43.
3 Toni Morrison, *Beloved* (New York: Knopf, 1987); Alice Walker, *The Color Purple* (New York: Harcourt Brace Jovanovich, 1982).
4 Audre Lorde, "The Master's Tools Will Never Dismantle the Master's House" (1979), in *Sister Outsider: Essays and Speeches* (Trumansburg, NY: Crossing Press, 1984), 110–113.
5 See the introduction, this volume.
6 Oscar Lewis, "Culture of Poverty," in *On Understanding Poverty: Perspectives from the Social Sciences*, ed. Daniel P. Moynihan (New York: Basic Books, 1969), 187–220.
7 See Marc Lamont Hill, *Nobody: Casualties of America's War on the Vulnerable, from Ferguson to Flint and Beyond* (New York: Simon & Schuster, 2017).
8 Bernard E. Harcourt, *Illusion of Order: The False Promise of Broken Windows Policing* (Cambridge, MA: Harvard University Press, 2009).
9 Russell J. Skiba, Robert S. Michael, Abra Carroll Nardo, and Reece L. Peterson, "The Color of Discipline: Sources of Racial and Gender Disproportionality in School Punishment," *Urban Review* 34, no. 4 (2002): 317–342.

10 Pamela Fenning and Jennifer Rose, "Overrepresentation of African American Students in Exclusionary Discipline the Role of School Policy," *Urban Education* 42, no. 6 (2007): 536–559.

11 Walter S. Gilliam, Angela N. Maupin, Chin R. Reyes, Maria Accavitti, and Frederick Shic, "Do Early Educators' Implicit Biases Regarding Sex and Race Relate to Behavior Expectations and Recommendations of Preschool Expulsions and Suspensions?" (Research Study Brief, Yale University, Yale Child Study Center, 2016).

12 Phillip Atiba Goff, Matthew Christian Jackson, Brooke Allison Lewis Di Leone, Carmen Marie Culotta, and Natalie Ann DiTomasso, "The Essence of Innocence: Consequences of Dehumanizing Black Children," *Journal of Personality and Social Psychology* 106, no. 4 (2014): 526–545.

13 Sean Nicholson-Crotty, Zachary Birchmeier, and David Valentine, "Exploring the Impact of School Discipline on Racial Disproportion in the Juvenile Justice System," *Social Science Quarterly* 90, no. 4 (2009): 1003–1018.

14 Pedro Noguera, *The Trouble with Black Boys: And Other Reflections on Race, Equity, and the Future of Public Education* (San Francisco: Jossey-Bass, 2008).

15 William Julius Wilson, *The Truly Disadvantaged: The Inner City, the Underclass, and Public Policy* (Chicago: University of Chicago Press, 2012).

16 Christopher M. Layne, Jared S. Warren, William R. Saltzman, John B. Fulton, Alan M. Steinberg, and Robert S. Pynoos, "Contextual Influences on Posttraumatic Adjustment: Retraumatization and the Roles of Revictimization, Posttraumatic Adversities, and Distressing Reminders," in *Psychological Effects of Catastrophic Disasters: Group Approaches to Treatment*, ed. Leon A. Schein, Henry I. Spitz, Gary M. Burlingame, and Philip R. Muskin (New York: Haworth, 2006), 235–286.

17 Cornel West, *Race Matters* (Boston: Beacon, 2000).

18 Jill McLean Taylor, Carol Gilligan, and Amy M. Sullivan, *Between Voice and Silence: Women and Girls, Race and Relationship* (Cambridge, MA: Harvard University Press, 1997).

ACKNOWLEDGMENTS

We first want to thank the contributors to this volume for sharing their work and working closely with us to write chapters that fit together into a coherent whole and tell the five-part story from the science and practice of human connection. All of the authors in this volume are members of a think and do tank at New York University that we (Niobe Way, Carol Gilligan, Pedro Noguera) developed in 2013 called the Project for the Advancement of Our Common Humanity (PACH; pach.org). Thank you as well to Margaret Suh, who, almost single-handedly, made this book happen. She dealt with over twenty contributors, reminding them of forms they had yet to submit, the edits they had yet to address, and the emails to which they had yet to respond. Nevertheless, she persisted. We are deeply grateful for her efforts. We also want to thank Katie DeAngelis, who also, almost single-handedly, completed the book by entering in all the edits during the copyediting and proofing stages and writing the two hundred endnotes in the first chapter. She too persisted despite the middle-of-the-night panic attacks by the senior editor (aka Niobe). Much gratitude also goes out to Jennifer Hammer, the editor at New York University Press, who immediately understood the importance of the book and provided feedback every step of the way. She even provided the old-fashioned type in the form of line editing. Thank you Jennifer! The Einhorn Family Charitable Trust Foundation graciously provided the financial support for the work involved in pulling together this volume. We thank them deeply. Finally, kisses and hugs to our families for providing critical insights, encouragement, and support for the work that we do.

Niobe Way is Professor of Developmental Psychology in the Department of Applied Psychology at New York University. She is the Founder and Executive Director of the Project for the Advancement of Our Common Humanity (PACH; pach.org). She is also the past President for the Society for Research on Adolescence. Her research focuses on the intersections of culture, context, and human development, with a particular focus on the social and emotional development of adolescents. She is interested in how schools, families, and peers as well as larger political, social, and economic contexts influence the socialization of gender and race as well as the processes of child development. In addition, she focuses on social identities, the effects of gender and racial/ethnic stereotypes on adjustment, and friendships. In addition to her numerous journal articles and blogs, her books include *Deep Secrets: Boys' Friendships and the Crisis of Connection*, *Everyday Courage: The Lives and Stories of Urban Adolescents*, and *Urban Girls: Resisting Stereotypes, Creating Identities*. She has been studying the social and emotional development of girls and boys in context and culture for almost three decades. She currently leads The Listening Project, funded by the Spencer Foundation, in middle schools across New York City.

Alisha Ali is Associate Professor in the Department of Applied Psychology at New York University. Her research examines the ways that trauma, oppression, and violence cause mental health problems, particularly in disadvantaged groups. She also studies community-based interventions that address these problems, including arts-based programs for military veterans and domestic survivors, and empowerment-based programs for low-income high school students. She is co-editor with Dr. Dana Crowley Jack of the book *Silencing the Self across Cultures: Depression and Gender in the Social World*, which received the American Psychological Association Division 52 book award. Her research is funded by a range of federal agencies and private foundations, including the National Institutes of Health, the National Endowment for the Arts, the American Psychological Foundation, the Allstate Foundation, the Loeb-Thirdpoint Foundation, the Robin Hood Foundation, and the Jack Kent Cooke Foundation.

Carol Gilligan is best known as the author of *In a Different Voice*, "the little book that started a revolution." Following *In a Different Voice*, she initiated the Harvard Project on Women's Psychology and Girls' Development and published five books with her students, including *Meeting at the Crossroads* (with Lyn Mikel Brown), a New York Times notable book of the year. She was the Patricia Albjerg Graham Professor of Gender Studies at Harvard, the Visiting Pitt Professor of American History and Institutions at the University of Cambridge, and is currently University Professor of Applied Psychology and the Humanities at NYU and a visiting professor of gender studies at Cambridge. Her books include *The Birth of Pleasure: A New Map of Love*; *Kyra: A Novel*; *Joining the Resistance*; and, most recently, *Why Does Patriarchy Persist?* (with Naomi Snider) and *Darkness Now Visible: Patriarchy's Resurgence and Feminist Resistance* (with David A. J. Richards). A recipient of the Heinz Award for her contribution to understanding the human condition and a Grawemeyer Award for her contribution to education, she was named by *Time* magazine in 1996 as one of the twenty-five most influential Americans. In 2017, she initiated the Radical Listening Project at NYU.

Pedro Noguera is Distinguished Professor of Education at the Graduate School of Education and Information Studies at UCLA. His most recent books are *Excellence through Equity* (2015) and *Race, Equity and Education* (2015). Prior to joining the faculty at UCLA he served as Professor and holder of endowed chairs at New York University (2003–2015), Harvard University (2000–2003), and the University of California, Berkeley (1990–2000). From 2009 to 2012 he served as Trustee for the State University of New York (SUNY) as an appointee of the governor. In 2014 he was elected to the National Academy of Education.

ABOUT THE CONTRIBUTORS

Lisa Arrastia is Head of the Upper School at Brooklyn Friends School in New York, and she is the founding director of the Ed Factory. Originally from New York City, she is the editor with Marvin Hoffman of *Starting Up: Critical Lessons from 10 New Schools* (2012), and her articles have appeared in *Journal for Critical Education Policy Studies, Antipode, Exposure,* and the *Huffington Post.*

Gary Barker is CEO and founder of Promundo-US, an international NGO that carries out research and advocacy and implements programs to engage men and boys in gender equality and transform toxic masculinities. He is co-founder of the MenCare campaign, a global campaign to promote men's involvement in caregiving and is co-Principal Investigator for the International Men and Gender Equality Survey (IMAGES), which has been carried in out in more than thirty countries.

Reverend Chloe Breyer directs the Interfaith Center of New York, an organization that works with hundreds of grassroots religious leaders and civic officials to address the city's most pressing social problems. An Episcopal Priest in the Diocese of New York, she also serves as Associate at St. Philip's Church in Harlem. She recently received her doctorate from Union Theological Seminary in Christian ethics.

Judy Y. Chu is Affiliated Faculty in the Program in Human Biology at Stanford University. She is author of *When Boys Become Boys: Development, Relationships, and Masculinity,* and co-editor with Niobe Way of *Adolescent Boys: Exploring Diverse Cultures of Boyhood.* Her research highlights boys' relational strengths and how boys' alignment with conventions of masculinity can hinder their relationships and wellbeing. She is Editor of the *Mask You Live In* Curriculum by The Representation

Project, and serves on the Global Men's Health Advisory Committee at Movember Foundation.

Judith A. Dorney is Associate Professor Emerita of Educational Studies and the Women, Gender, and Sexuality Program at SUNY New Paltz. Her research interests focus on the construction of gender and race for women educators in schools. She is Executive Director of the newly developing SAGE Center (Shakespeare, the Arts, Gender and Education) in Pittsburgh, Pennsylvania.

Dana Edell, MFA, PhD, is an activist-scholar-artist-educator and Executive Director of SPARK Movement (www.SPARKmovement. org), an intergenerational girls' activist organization working toward anti-racist gender justice through training and supporting girls and their allies to take action, produce theater, create videos, write blogs, and launch global action campaigns. She has directed and produced more than seventy original theater productions written and performed by girls about social justice issues and consults with organizations to create feminist curricula for youth programs. She was co-chair of the Girls' Participation Task Force at the United Nations and teaches Theater and Activism at NYU and CUNY.

Mary Gordon is an award-winning international social entrepreneur, educator, author, and child advocate. She is Founder and President of Roots of Empathy, which has offered evidence-based classroom programs informed by the power of empathy since 1996 to almost one million children. She is a recipient of the 2018 Governor General's Innovation Award, a member of the Order of Canada, and a winner of The Manning Innovation Award for the top social enterprise in Canada. She speaks internationally on well-being in childhood, building inclusive societies through the development of empathy, and breaking generational cycles of violence.

Michael Kimmel is one of the world's leading experts on men and masculinities. He is SUNY Distinguished Professor of Sociology and Gender Studies at Stony Brook University. Among his many books are *Manhood in America*, *Angry White Men*, *The Politics of Manhood*, *The*

Gendered Society, and the best seller *Guyland: The Perilous World Where Boys Become Men*. With funding from the MacArthur Foundation, he founded the Center for the Study of Men and Masculinities at Stony Brook in 2013.

David E. Kirkland is Executive Director at the NYU Metropolitan Center for Research on Equity and the Transformation of Schools and Associate Professor of English and Urban Education at New York University. A leading national scholar and advocate for educational justice, Dr. Kirkland holds a PhD from Michigan State University. His most recent book is *A Search Past Silence: The Literacy of Young Black Men*. He is also co-editor of *Students' Right to Their Own Language*.

Khary Lazarre-White is a social entrepreneur, writer, organizer, and attorney. In 1995 he co-founded the Brotherhood/Sister Sol, a nationally renowned, comprehensive youth development and educational organization. The organization provides direct service, trains educators across the nation on its model, and organizes to advance policy and social change. He received his bachelor's of arts with honors in Africana studies from Brown University and his juris doctorate from the Yale Law School, where his focus was international human rights law and constitutional law. He writes regular opinion pieces and essays. In 2017 his first novel, *Passage*, was published.

Joseph D. Nelson, PhD, is Assistant Professor of Educational Studies at Swarthmore College, and Senior Research Fellow with the Center for the Study of Boys' and Girls' Lives at the University of Pennsylvania. He is a sociologist of education and a school ethnographer who employs interdisciplinary frameworks to examine identity, culture, and urban schooling from a qualitative inquiry stance. His scholarship to date has explored how school culture influences Black boys' engagement and identities during childhood and early adolescence. These empirical projects have led to publications with *Harvard Educational Review*, *Teachers College Record*, and *Psychology of Men and Masculinity* and the guest co-editorship of a special issue on boys' education in *Journal of Boyhood Studies*. His research has been supported by the National Academy of Education/Spencer Foundation, the Ford Foundation, and the International Boys' School Coalition. In his hometown of Milwaukee, he taught first grade in a single-sex classroom of Black and Latino boys.

Normi Noel is Theatre Director and longtime member of Shakespeare & Company, Lenox, Massachusetts. She is a designated Linklater Voice Teacher, and has taught at NYU, Boston University, MIT, and currently at Smith College. She has worked with army nurses, creating plays from their experiences in combat. *No Background Music* won a Sony Award, performed by Sigourney Weaver for the BBC.

Hussein Rashid is an adjunct faculty member at Barnard College as well as a writer and consultant. He received his PhD from Harvard University. An advocate of religious literacy, he publishes in both specialized journals and general audience forums on Islam and Muslims in the United States.

Michael C. Reichert is an applied and research psychologist who currently serves as Executive Director of the Center for the Study of Boys' and Girls' Lives, a research collaborative at the University of Pennsylvania practicing a unique model for youth participatory action research. He has served as supervising psychologist at an independent all-boys school in Pennsylvania since 1987, been principal investigator on several global studies of boys' education, and founded and directed a youth violence prevention program in the tri-state region around Philadelphia.

Victoria Rhoades, PhD, is Educator and Theatre Artist specializing in Shakespeare and Gender, Culture, and Human Development. A graduate of NYU and Northwestern, she creates spaces for girls, boys, women, and men to resist cultural expectations of gender by engaging the imagination, intellect, body, and voice through theatrical tools like Shakespeare.

Annie G. Rogers, PhD, Professor of Psychoanalysis and Clinical Psychology at Hampshire College, co-directs its Psychoanalytic Studies Program. She is a practicing psychoanalyst, Analyst of the Lacanian School of San Francisco, and Member of the Association for Psychoanalysis & Psychotherapy, Ireland. A recipient of a Fulbright Fellowship at Trinity College, Dublin, Ireland, Radcliffe Fellowship at Harvard University, Whiting Fellowship at Hampshire College, and Erikson Scholar at Austen Riggs, she is the author of *A Shining Affliction* (1995), *The Unsayable* (2006), and *Incandescent Alphabets: Psychosis and the Enigma of Language* (2016).

Leoandra Onnie Rogers is Assistant Professor of Psychology and Faculty Fellow for the Institute for Policy Research at Northwestern University. A developmental psychologist, she examines the ways in which racial and gender stereotypes shape the identity development of children and adolescents.

Corianna E. Sichel is a doctoral candidate in counseling psychology in the Department of Applied Psychology, Steinhardt School of Culture, Education and Human Development, New York University. Her research interests center around the broader social contexts, health, and mental health outcomes associated with oppression.

Deborah L. Tolman, Professor of Women and Gender Studies at Hunter College and Critical Social Psychology at the Graduate Center at CUNY, is a researcher, teacher, writer, mentor, and activist. She has studied adolescent sexuality and gender for twenty-five years. She has bridged academia and activism through the SPARK Movement, a feminist intergenerational initiative to engage girls as feminist activists and researchers, and directs sexgenlab.org to translate critical research on gender and sexuality for dissemination beyond the academy.

Rabbi Burton L. Visotzky serves as Appleman Professor of Midrash and Interreligious Studies and Director of the Milstein Center for Interreligious Dialogue at the Jewish Theological Seminary, New York.

Janie Victoria Ward is Professor and Chair in the Department of Education and Chair of the Africana Studies Department at Simmons College. For over thirty years her professional work and research interests have centered on the developmental issues of African American adolescents, focusing on identity and moral development in African American girls and boys. Along with her teaching responsibilities she continues to work with youth counselors, secondary school educators, and other practitioners in a variety of settings.

Stephan Wolfert is Founding Director of DE-CRUIT as well as company member and Director of Veterans Outreach for Bedlam. He left a career in the military for a life in Theater.

Hirokazu Yoshikawa is Courtney Sale Ross Professor of Globalization and Education at New York University. He studies the effects on children and youth of programs and policies related to immigration, early childhood development, and adolescent sexuality.

INDEX

Page numbers in italic indicate illustrations.